THE CHILDHOOD EMOTIONAL PATTERN AND COREY JONES

A Psychoanalytical Biography

THE CHILDHOOD EMOTIONAL PATTERN AND COREY JONES

A Psychoanalytical Biography

Leon J. Saul, M.D.

Emeritus Professor of Psychiatry, Medical School of the University of Pennsylvania

Honorary Staff, Institute of the Pennsylvania Hospital

Emeritus Training Analyst, Philadelphia Psychoanalytic Institute

VNR VAN NOSTRAND REINHOLD COMPANY

NEW YORK   CINCINNATI   ATLANTA   DALLAS   SAN FRANCISCO
LONDON   TORONTO   MELBOURNE

Van Nostrand Reinhold Company Regional Offices:
New York   Cincinnati   Atlanta   Dallas   San Francisco

Van Nostrand Reinhold Company International Offices:
London   Toronto   Melbourne

Library of Congress Catalog Card Number: 77-11652
ISBN: 0-442-27361-4
         0-442-27362-2 pbk.

Manufactured in the United States of America

Published by Van Nostrand Reinhold Company
450 West 33rd Street, New York, N.Y. 10001

Published simultaneously in Canada by Van Nostrand Reinhold Ltd.

15 14 13 12 11 10 9 8 7 6 5 4 3 2 1

Library of Congress Cataloging in Publication Data

Saul, Leon Joseph, 1901–
   The childhood emotional pattern and Corey Jones.

   Includes index.
   1. Psychoanalysis—Cases, clinical reports,
statistics.   I. Title.
RC506.S28   616.8'917'0926   77-11652
ISBN 0-442-27361-4
ISBN 0-442-27362-2 pbk.

Science! true daughter of Old Time thou art!
Who alterest all things with thy peering eyes.
Why preyest thou thus upon the poet's heart . . . ?

Edgar Allan Poe, "To Science"

Our lives are lived for us by forces of which we are but dimly if at all aware.

Georg Groddeck

I cannot accept any denial of personal responsibility.

John Nason

Everything in the emotional life is a quantitative balance of forces.

L. J. S.

The heart that has truly loved never forgets.

Thomas Moore

OTHER BOOKS BY LEON J. SAUL

Emotional Maturity

Bases of Human Behavior

The Hostile Mind

Technic and Practice of Psychoanalysis

Fidelity and Infidelity

Dependence in Man (with H. Parens)

Psychodynamically Based Psychotherapy

Psychodynamics of Hostility

The Childhood Emotional Pattern

PREFACE

In my early days as an analyst, after I learned to elicit a patient's childhood emotional pattern in the first one or two interviews, the patient would occasionally exclaim, "Why, I can see my whole life laid out!" And sometimes, under the impact of this insight, he would also say, "Why don't you write a novel about me?" I too felt the drama, but could only reply, "How I wish I had the ability to do so!"

One of my early patients was a lovely young matron, born and raised in Norway, seeking help in making a go of her marriage and the raising of her children here in a different country, while facing both her very real fears and her neurotic anxieties. As our insights expanded and deepened and her life improved, the pattern of her life emerged; and one day under the impact of this insight she exclaimed, "Why don't you write a novel about me?" I had to answer, "I've thought of it and have even read a little about your native land for background, but I lack the talent. Why don't *you* do it?" I had not completely forgotten this conversation when a young physician a few years junior to me came for help because of simple anxiety. The analysis was successful, and eventually, after much probing of reasons, he decided to become an analyst. After a judicious consultation with my own analyst, Dr. F., and an interruption to be sure his decision was not too neurotic, he continued with me in training analysis. He was open and honest emotionally, and we both felt that we understood his emotions well. Again the idea arose of a psychoanalytic autobiography, but he had never written; he suggested instead that I try it with all the help and cooperation that he could offer. Thinking this over, it seemed to me a fine opportunity to study in detail one single person—an individual of relatively good mental and emotional health—an ongoing life instead of a series of vignettes. My previous doubts about doing the biography of a woman (feeling sure I did not understand the subleties of the feminine mind, no matter how well I might comprehend the dynamics) were resolved by my decision to attempt the biography of a man so near my own age. So I agreed to try it, provided he would actually keep in close touch with me, after his analysis, and would give me what help I needed with the myriad details that would be required. His name was Corey Jones (a pseudonym). That is how I came to accumulate the detailed notes for this book, which is a biography and not a novel.

I have tried to put these notes together in chronological sequence, including such insights as I have felt sure of during their accumulation, which took a professional lifetime. Little did I foresee when we agreed to do this that life would be so busy that my seventy-third birthday would pass before time could be taken even to begin writing Corey's story. Biography should be written with as much insight as one finds available into the subject's motivations and reactions, including the influence of his earliest years, from conception to age six (for these are the most formative years), and the sex life should also be examined in detail, not presented only as innuendo. Biography is needed about common men in our century, not just outstanding figures of the past such as Washington, Jefferson or Lincoln. It is ironic that today, two hundred years after the fact, at the time of our Bicentennial, biographers are searching out the sex lives of our Founding Fathers. No doubt I am a post-Freudian man; why shouldn't we be honest about all matters human, and learn from them?

I hope this book will prove useful to others who are striving to mature and may learn from the struggles of Corey Jones; to parents in understanding what their children may be going through; to students of psychodynamics, who may gain some further insights from one life related in detail to complement the usual vignettes of a series of patients.

One difficulty in this writing has been in selecting only the significant and most salient details; they are so numerous that only a small fraction of them can be included in a volume of reasonable length. I have tried to keep exclusively to what seemed most significant and revealing psychodynamically. In so doing, it may appear that Corey Jones' relations with women have received disproportionate weight and space. This is mostly because it was a problem area for him, for excessive love needs continued with some hostility to his mother and sister in his childhood pattern. It seems to be the nature of the mind to dwell on problems. If one is solved, it concentrates on another. But how does Corey's sex life compare with that of other men?

Perhaps it is not disproportionate in the comparison. The many rich, close and lifelong friendships that Corey Jones had with men have not received sufficient attention. Whole important areas—such as his professional life—have received scant notice, while the problem area emerges too prominently from my notes. Even so, a reasonably full biographical statement would be ten or twenty times as long as this because so much transpired in a lifetime that was uneventful, although it included Corey's minor involvement in World War I and the interruption of four years' active duty in World War II.

In this attempt to show how Corey Jones' childhood emotional pattern shaped his life, what may have been undervalued is his identification with his mother. Adequately noted are the object relationship, the dependence, the love needs and sense of over-restrictiveness and control, but possibly the identification has been underemphasized—the large extent to which Corey unconsciously took over many of his mother's attitudes. This worked mostly for his good (for example, his habit of getting his work done before playing and his loving interest in others, which contributed to his make-up as a physician and his choice of medicine as a career).

Every person has in his mind a pattern of feelings and motivations that derives from the main potentials he is born with interacting with those who reared him and were close to him, especially before the age of about seven. Most of this balance of emotional forces, this dynamic core of the personality, is remote from consciousness in most people. Therefore, in a way, the analyst can usually understand each of his patients better than the patient can understand himself. But there is one person in whom the analyst can see the effects of this childhood pattern upon consciousness, feeling and behavior in greater detail than he can see it in any other human in the world; that person is himself. And if he has the psychological capacity, the sustained interest and perseverence—and especially if he has had some analysis by a psychodynamically well-trained analyst—then through his own vigilance and alertness he can gain increasing insights into his own childhood emotional patterns, and their effects upon how he lives his life. This is not a purely narcissistic, egoistic interest in himself; because especially if he is an analyst or dynamic psychiatrist, these insights into himself will increase his sympathetic understanding of his patients, his family and friends, and of all suffering humanity. It is in this spirit and with this goal that this book is written.

It is usually possible to reduce the dynamic patterns of each patient to a few sentences. Here in advance is what seems to me to be a rough approximation of the essentials of the pattern of Corey Jones, which we shall develop in detail in the text:

> Some seductiveness by his mother and a beautiful aunt who was young and childless, with much love given him and sustained despite birth of a sister at age five; adulation from mother and aunt and also from the sister, some overcontrol and overprotectiveness by mother and sympathetic understanding from father. These lead to some exaggeration of dependent-love needs, especially from women, with increased sexual attraction to them; self-confidence with some increased narcissism and competitiveness; and some rebellion against the overcontrol with anger and increased drive to independence; identification with mother and identification and inferiority feelings toward father, with envy and competition toward him. Hostilities repressed cause some anxiety; flight mostly into work.

The childhood pattern, then, is the basis in each of us of what is briefly called our "dynamics."

Some novelists, including so outstandingly insightful and intelligent a writer as Somerset Maugham, tell us that their tales represent an order, a pattern, upon the surface of chaos: "When he succeeds [in his story] . . . he has given you the pleasure of following out the pattern he has drawn on the surface of chaos."* I hesitate to disagree with great observers, but I think life is not chaos. It is true that human life in general, as we see it, moving among individuals, looks chaotic because it is so complex. But each individual's life has a very distinct pattern; this design is the unfolding of an emotional pattern of motivations and reactions formed in his infancy and earliest childhood by his genetic endowment interacting with the emotional and physical environment of these earliest days, weeks, months and years. Therefore every human life meets the ideal of fiction, in having a beginning, a middle and an end. Its trajectory traces a definite form laid down in earliest childhood. Every biography exemplifies this if the biographer has the material and the insight to discern and portray it. This I have tried to demonstrate in describing the life of one individual, Corey Jones.

*Maugham, S. (1953): *East and West*, p. xx.

I found early on that I could best feel my way into the emotional life of a patient by writing about him in the first person, and have adopted this as the technique of choice, as is evident in *The Childhood Pattern* and other books. This advantage outweighs the drawbacks, at least for me. Thus, in all but the final chapter, Corey Jones will appear as narrator.

LEON J. SAUL

ACKNOWLEDGMENTS

Those who helped me with this book and whom I hereby thank publicly are my super-secretary and personal bosun, Susan (Mrs. Vernon) Bender, who did all the typing and checked many details of the manuscript, drove me when needed and ran numerous errands; my daughters, Sue (Mrs. Richard) Spencer, Meg (Mrs. Carl) Sweatman and Cathy (Mrs. Blair) McNeill, who read the manuscript and offered helpful suggestions; my wife, who put up with my distraction and interruptions and evening monopoly of the dining room table; and June (Mrs. Walter) Strickland, librarian of the Institute of the Pennsylvania Hospital, who was always willingly available to provide books, articles and references.

PREAMBLE

"I have concluded," Corey Jones said to me, "that there are about eight or ten motivations for about everything we do. Into all our major decisions and actions and many minor ones flow all or most of these motivations in a final common path. One conscious reason for this biography is to put down, toward the end of my life, the main motivations and reactions which have directed its course, so that others may possibly learn something from it for the living of their own lives. But I well know that not many will be free enough from their childhood patterns to learn from my particular experience; we are all the products of our inherited potentials interacting with the physical and emotional situations into which we are born, as developed especially during those most formative days, weeks, months and years before the age of seven or eight. The childhood emotional patterns so formed shape our personalities and therefore the course of our lives.

"Writing this biography is also motivated by wishes to continue living, coming out in the reliving of my life through the memories related here, and thus regaining by recollection my still living youth and the adventures of maturity, and by wishes to leave for my children and grandchildren such a record as I wish my parents and grandparents had left for me; and I still hope others may possibly learn something from my own experiences. Of course there must be exhibitionism in my motives, as there must be in anyone who considers publishing anything, a desire to be admired; and of course, too, there is the hope for some income so that I can cut down a little on my work in these days of economic inflation. Perhaps too there is the element that is present in most writers to 'unburden one's soul,' perhaps it is something like relieving one's feelings—'abreacting'—for when it is finished, there is usually a diminution in feelings and in these memories themselves, as though such thoughts are now more off one's mind, and one is more free to turn his attention and energies elsewhere. As a physician I know that there is no protection against sudden death, and therefore writing a biography at my age may be motivated by an instinct toward self-preservation and an accompanying fear of death, appearing as a wish for immortality by leaving behind in writing the story of my life.

"This biography will tell a little of the struggles of one person to achieve maturity and inner peace. I was one of the very lucky ones, for in time my dynamics and the socioeconomic conditions joined together to help me. Even so, the process was a long and difficult one.

"Part of the satisfaction in my life lies in its devotion to the cause of science. But this is no place for learned exposition; rather it is appropriate only to the story of that one life I know best—my own— a life which may be of interest not because it is markedly different, distinguished or accomplished, but because of its being an everyday life of this century.

"Hunger and Love and Fear—all of us, motivated to survive, must choose or drift into a career or way of providing ourselves with the essentials of bare existence. And then, driven beyond the self-preservative by race-preservative instincts, we must manage the drives to sex and mating and parenthood. Beyond these forces of hunger, love and fear lies a fourth force more subtle and difficult to define that has been called 'finding oneself' or 'identity.' A degree of peace with oneself and with others is determined by one's success in achieving these four states of security and maturity; that in turn requires 'a deal of living.' I consider myself most fortunate in struggling through to a choice of career by the age of twenty-three and growing into it over succeeding decades; in finding a compatible mate some years after choosing my career and growing into marriage and parenthood; in finding my identity and benefiting from the diminution of turmoil plus the increased tranquility of these last twenty-five years. I do not believe there are faster ways. The only sound catalyst is insight into the psychological reality of oneself and of others. This facilitates the processes of growth, motivation and solving of the problems of life; it saves much time, but is never an instant panacea. Maturing is slow and requires much experience in living and much hard work. It does come down to the ability to work and to love (and to play)—to loving and being loved. How it was for me will become plain in the following chapters, with the hope that it may yield insights of use for others."

CONTENTS

CYCLE I

1
CROSSROADS

*Choose; you stand where the road divides . . . choose between storm and calm . . .
between joy and sorrow, between night and morning, between death and life . . . behind dawns the glow of morning.*

Henrik Ibsen,
"Brand"

I was alone in a strange city in a foreign land, said Corey Jones; I
had one friend but knew no one else. Looking back, I can feel the
sharp ache of my loneliness then. But at the time I did not realize it,
for impelled by the thrust of youth I saw myself as independent and
did not recognize that I was only striving for an independence I was
still far from achieving.

I was under such force of the sex drive as one can only be at the age
of twenty-one, and never having had intercourse. I felt as though I
lived on the edge of the ocean, never having been in the water, although
all around me were lovers, married couples, figures in plays and
advertisements and others disporting themselves. Now here I was, in
London. No one knew me, and all restraints were off!

It was near ten o'clock in the evening. The broad thoroughfare
was almost deserted, but the window lights were still on in some shops
and restaurants. How hungry I was for a woman! And there before me
was a girl looking into the window of a store. She was young, maybe
eighteen. She was slight, almost frail, but very pretty. She wore
little or no makeup. She was dressed in shades of brown in good taste,
possibly a trifle frilly. That is all I noticed at the time, for I was struggling so with the forces in my own mind that I was not free to observe
others carefully. I never had the ease some boys have with girls. I
feared I might insult a girl by trying to pick her up, and I feared rejection far more than I had any idea of at the time. But, very shyly,
I stood next to her and forced out a "hello." She looked at me in
silence.

"That's a pretty dress," I said of one in the window. It was an asinine remark, other-worldly. I looked at her and she stared at me, unsmiling and serious. We exchanged some inanities. She spoke Oxford English with no trace of Cockney.

"Do you have a place to go?" she asked.

I thought of the room where I was staying and the ultraproper landlady, and said, "No."

"I do," she replied quickly. "Have you a rubber?"

"No," I said, which was true.

"I won't do it unless you use one," she said.

This was not as I always had planned and wanted it. Maybe I was an idealist—and now I have some idea of what this is. I always wanted my first experience of sexual intercourse to be perfect, wonderful. That side of me pushed out the raw physical desire, and I heard myself say, "Then we won't."

But I did not walk on, nor did she. I gently took her arm and guided her by my side along the street. We walked together for a few blocks in silence. I asked her into a restaurant for coffee and cake and she accepted. We chatted a little about other inanities—the weather and how surprisingly good the cake was. Then we rose, I paid the check, and gave her a pound note. That was a lot of money for me in those days. She went off into the night and I turned toward my room. Later I could see that my own fear was partly active in this negative outcome, for I wondered what kind of place she had—and even if I might be slugged and robbed there. Behind this fear may have been a fear of sex because of the inhibitions of my upbringing, in which sex was never mentioned. I never considered the possibility of my having any sexual inhibition—the drive was too strong for that, with the wet dreams two or three times a week, and the masturbation for which I had great distaste but often could not resist.

Some people are so smart that they seem to know at given times what is happening in their minds and in the minds of others. I was very sheltered and knew very little about feelings and motives. As I said, I was too preoccupied dealing with my own violent feelings to have free attention to observe others. I think some fine writers have a clinical detachment which enables them to be so perceptive of others. Art, as Wordsworth has said, is emotion recollected in tranquillity. Now, years later, as I remember this brief encounter, I think of her slight frilliness. At the time it meant nothing, but now I can hardly bear to think of it for I have seen it in many girls since and it is a heartrending thing. It is the cry for love which is in all of us; but the frills make it sound like a hopeless cry, often the cry of a lost soul, as though a bit of lace and ribbon will attract the understanding, the support and the love. And this girl was so very young and so inexperienced! Or at least so I thought, in my own inexperience. Perhaps it was her first attempt. I think her silence was because of fear. What could have forced her to this, so against her makeup, against her feelings, in the face of fear? Was it financial poverty? As for myself, only in an occasional wild fantasy have I been able to separate the raw physiology of physical sex from personality. With the frail, pretty young girl, apart from my own idealistic and no doubt inhibited feelings, my common humanity went out to her. It sidetracked the lust. I gave her the money impulsively, with the sudden thought that she could have it without demeaning herself. Now I have learned how many such girls come to hate their bodies and themselves—not only prostitutes, but many girls who never take money but are of their own desires promiscuous. A few years after, a girl wanted me to go to bed with her, but I was not attracted and declined. She took it in good part and we remained friendly. Once we discussed dreams and she told me she had a repetitive one of being covered with feces. That made her think of a small child whose diapers needed changing— but she added, "At my age, sex is no more than a kiss goodnight." Although I said nothing, I knew sex meant a very great deal more to me and that she was quite unaware of how dirty her conscience made her feel for her promiscuity. I have since seen this in my practice in persons who go strongly against their early training.

From this experience I might have learned that my simple physical sexual drive was too intimately intertwined with intimate tender feelings toward women for me to satisfy it impersonally. But I was incapable of thinking in these terms because such ideas and such knowledge of psycho-physical reality were totally unknown to me. Nowhere in school, nowhere on the street, nowhere in any book had such understanding come to me. It should have; it should be known to every young person.

In later years, I learned that "As the twig is bent the tree is inclined" is far more than just an old adage. It is the most profound and fateful truth for mankind. I wonder if any country which so treats its children as to make them prostitutes can long survive? If you say all countries treat their children like this, then we must question whether humanity itself can survive, and if so, how well? For the child is in very fact the father to the man. How we treat our children determines what kind of adults we have, what kind of country, what kind of world.

I wondered about England after walking in Piccadilly once—even I, naive as could be, recognized that perhaps a fifth of the people out on the streets that evening were prostitutes. Not young, fresh, pretty, well-spoken like the slim young girl in brown, but brazen and old and smeared with makeup—bedraggled, like a caricature in a Dickens novel. Here I was, a fresh twenty-one, and one of these women who seemed to me to be about fifty, big and fat and repulsive, took my arm and tried to persuade me to come with her. Reflexly I said, "No, thank you," and the woman said, "Oh, you don't feel like it now? Just come along to my place and we'll have a cozy fire and a glass of wine first and you will!" I only felt revulsion, though in retrospect it is tragic—all those women, utterly devoid of femininity and sex appeal, and probably of hope, but the latter I didn't realize then. And what kind of men would agree to go with them? Even then there flashed through my mind fear for the future of England. From this first brief visit to that great island I traveled to France.

My friend Charles was in Paris when I arrived. He used to say, "Every man has two countries—his own and France." What a lift it was! France, I'd heard, was culture—but even then, to me, it was beauty and style: the little towns of the Midi, with the roads through them unpaved earth—but the girls dressed in taste and moving with style; the little three-franc dinners, served simply but with style.

Once back in Paris, Charles and I sat one day at lunch in a small cafe. It had sidewalk tables but was not one of the famous, crowded ones like the de la Paix, the Dome or the Rotonde. It was on a boulevard out toward the Bois. We finished our lunch in fine spirits, when I noticed two girls at a nearby table. They were no frail things, but healthy, wholesome, buxom. They looked to me like any normal American girls would—pink, strong, full-blown, attractive, wearing simple summer dresses. Both were goodlooking, one dark and the other blonde. I think of them as Nicolette and Antoinette.

I gaped. But as I did so, Charles must have given them a sign, for they smiled. He was fluent in French, for his mother had been born in France and came to America when she married Charles' father. So soon the girls were at our table, chatting, with me struggling to understand and with them highly amused at my schoolboy French. Could it be that Charles was on his way to bed with Nicolette, just like that? It could be—and it was. They asked me to come, to take Antoinette. She was above average in beauty and appeal, and so was Nicolette. Through my mind raced the ideal—my first sexual intercourse was to be on the highest level, not something paid for. Smiling, I blurted out a "Non, merci." It must have been inoffensive and friendly, because Charles said, "What is it? Do you want Nicolette, not Antoinette? Then why don't we switch?" But the machinery of my mind, automatically, produced another "No, thank you." I think it would do the same today, so little do we change in a lifetime. So I turned up the boulevard alone toward the Place de l'Opera. The sun shone, the sky was blue. Men and women walked by. I was still on the edge of the ocean that I longed to swim in. But my makeup left no regrets for this decision it had made for me. It had dawned on me that I did not want my first sexual intercourse to be with a prostitute.

Is this beginning to sound like a boast of moral superiority? It isn't that simple: my egotism is such that had there been clear black and white superiority and inferiority, I would have chosen the superiority. But how much more complex it is! Perhaps it is because of being the first child and having my mother as her only child for five years I have been limited to wanting a woman who is mine alone. In return, however, if I once found her, I felt sure it would never occur to me not to offer her complete faithfulness. In fact, I was aware of wanting to be married and seeking a wife almost since feeling any interest in girls, at age thirteen, and certainly since age fifteen when I dreamed of a gray-eyed (yes, like my mother!) girl in a tan suit whom I once saw but never met. Nor is that the whole story, for when I was perhaps seven or eight I startled the family one evening with the direct assertion that when I grew up I was going to marry my sister. My urge for superiority, moral and otherwise, was partly a childish way of trying to win the love of my mother and father, and later of everyone. Perhaps it was a conflict in egotism, in how to be superior. But the more superior I was morally, the more inferior in experience with women. The only solution I could see was marriage, which I longed for anyway, but meanwhile I wanted to experience sex. Thus far I had achieved neither.

That day in Paris, although I had heard of Freud and was intrigued by his idea of an "unconscious," I had no idea of the profundity of his discovery of how very little we know of what goes on in our own minds, motivations and feelings.

Charles was at my room less than two hours later.

"It was good," he said. "There was a mirror on the ceiling. And she had an orgasm, which is unusual." He too was only twenty-one. Had I felt less inferior and therefore had less need to bolster my self-esteem, I would have asked Charles what made him know his way around, what was wrong with me, such a combination of opposites, so insecure, yet in a way down deep so secure. Could he have told me? He was my mentor in France and I have been grateful to him for all these years since—my mentor in the ways of the world, but not in personality. Somehow, immature as I was, I felt stronger than he in character. But that was Paris in late spring, and joy was far more than character! And so was experience.

Charles wanted to show me Paris, and I was eager to see it all. On almost no money we somehow got everywhere. He suggested a peepshow, and about that I had no scruples. A man who even then struck me as shady and strange was our guide. We went to a small house and into a dark room. We were eased into chairs facing a wall which turned out to be a one-way screen. We could see into the next room, which was lighted and in which was a double bed. Without delay a man and woman entered, both completely nude. They got onto the bed and he started pumping her, front, sidewise, back, with rapid movements. He advertised his climax by pumping even faster. Then he left and a dog appeared. She took a position on her knees with her chest on the bed and the dog went ahead as though she were another dog. Then the lights in our room went on. It was a cubicle and there must have been a lot of them around the room with the bed in it. The shady greasy guide told us how wonderful it had been—come look at the spot on the bed showing that the dog had in fact ejaculated, and what an accomplishment for the man, he said, for who could be potent in intercourse knowing he was being watched? Then the man and woman—still nude—came into our cubicle. I was aware of little in my own feelings except curiosity, for I had never seen a completely naked woman. It was not much of a sight—she was dumpy, shapeless and, for me, totally sexless. I guessed she was "ancient," about forty. I thought of Mencken's simile: "Like a dumbbell run over by an express train." What my expression revealed I do not know, but Charles and the guide looked at me and said, "What's the matter?"

"Nothing," I replied. Charles gave the man and woman a tip, and I admired his poise and worldliness in doing so. Then the guide told us of the wonderful women upstairs and urged us to stay and find out for ourselves. But the peepshow had damped, not stimulated, my desire. If this revolting woman were a sample, I did not care to see the others. Later I learned that I was, if anything, hypersexed. And to my astonishment, with my feelings of inferiority, a woman not too many years after this experience would say to me, "What makes you have such intense sex appeal?" But at that time in Paris, my vague resolve not to initiate my sex experience with a prostitute was pretty well confirmed.

Later, I realized that England and France are relatively fixed societies. In the United States, being born in a cabin may help a boy become president, a poor immigrant can become a philanthropist, and a little girl might become a businesswoman or a senator. But in fixed societies, a girl has little choice but to remain a peasant and marry a peasant and scrape along on nearly nothing for her whole life—or else use her beauty to hazard a career as a courtesan, which just might carry her up the scale to people with charm, intellect, success and wealth. But Charles and I knew no sociology then. We knew nothing of the Grand Ecoles. We had never even read *Madame Bovary*. We had just graduated from college, but we knew nothing, at least nothing whatever of practical use for living.

We were young and in Paris in early summer. We lived on very little—breakfast of brioche and cocoa; getting about by walking, usually five or ten miles a day, occasionally by Metro. One inexpensive meal a day satisfied us, and we had no liquor except the *vin ordinaire*, and an occasional splurge in an excellent but inexpensive out-of-the-way restaurant that Charles always came up with—like the Auberge du Clou, where for dessert the great treat was strawberries and thick cream. We explored Montmartre, Montparnasse, Parc Monceau, St. Cloud, the Louvre, the Sorbonne. There was little we did not cover—on foot, which is by far the best way if one is young, healthy, well-rested and adequately fed.

When Charles left I was pretty lost. My French was improved but still the schoolboy variety. We had met an American artist, Ernest, and his mistress. This I had never seen before: Sharon was not my image of a mistress. She was not slinky and sophisticated but was from the United States, the Midwest, clear of eye, clear of brow,

frank, open, simple, beautiful, with no makeup, womanly, maternal—
a wholesome American young woman. Ernest seemed to me to be
ancient, face lined and careworn. He must have been thirty-five; he
had a certain strength, masculinity, knowledge of life. His paintings
were ugly but strong. There was one I remember of a waiter, big hands
on a little table, staring at you—blankly, but directly staring.

"What is this one?" I asked, and he replied, "That is what life has
done to him." I understood: it was not beautiful but it was true, it
was real. But why would anyone want it? Is the ugliness and tragedy
of life, realistically depicted, art? Only years later did I realize that
the picture reflected not only what life had done to the waiter, but to
the artist, to Ernest himself. In youth he had been utterly in love with
a rare lissome, highly gifted girl. All who knew her utterly adored
her. I still have a beautiful book of hers, which Ernest gave me, on
Indian folklore—sagas, songs, poems, and art. They married and
were supremely happy—perhaps too happy. Suddenly she was dead,
killed in an automobile accident. Ernest barely sustained his loss.
He survived but with what scars? His inner strength carried him
through to success as an artist and to his winning of this wonderful
Sharon (two such girls in one lifetime!), but still he sought to unburden himself of his suffering through his paintings. He had still
not recovered from what life had done to him years before.

And here was Sharon, living with him in his studio. I was too en-
vious of him for having such maturity and such a woman to question
how he did it; it never occurred to me to speak with him about it.
When they left for a vacation I was alone, yet this was not too bother-
some. I was supposed to be independent, and I was determined to
be just that. If you do not have a virtue, assume it—as someone told
me years later.

There was a girl at home whom I had been seeing—Nelda—we
were close. She hardly saw any other fellows nor did I date other
girls. We could have had sex, but we didn't. Today's youth would say
we were silly, I guess, to have missed sex then, but even now, fifty-
five years later, I think it was for the best, for her and for me. Now I
was alone in Paris, alone in my room. Charles was gone. Ernest and
Sharon were away. I began to think of Nelda. I was sorting out some
socks to wash when suddenly I felt her presence. I looked up and could
almost see her come in the door. It was the nearest I've ever come to
a hallucination. The longing for Nelda surged up, and I recalled bits

of conversation we had before I left for Europe. Dimly I sensed that she took my leaving as a desertion and that she envied me for being a man and able to go to the docks and wait for a job on a ship to work my passage. Would she follow? She had an aunt who was footloose. I went to the American Express office and checked sailings. Here was a possibility; a liner was due to dock at Cherbourg the next morning, so I met that boat-train and there, amazingly, was Nelda! I never believed in telepathy—it was simply heightened insight into what Nelda might do that led me to the boat-train, an insight born of my intense feelings and closeness to her. She was indeed with her young aunt. She smiled in her quiet reserved way, with pleasure and surprise. That week I took them to the best of what Charles had shown me. Then they left for Italy, and I left for Vienna with hopes of our meeting again in Innsbruck.

Later I will tell more about Nelda. She was everything—and yet, in some ways she was a little withdrawn, not fully or sturdily extroverted and healthy. I felt that sex was something I should not think of in relation to her—was it all my inhibition, or was it some little voice of warning for her or for me? She was everything—beauty, intelligence, sensitivity and a characteristic utter honesty. Also, in retrospect, I think she was of superior intelligence. It was many years before I came to recognize the great importance of intelligence in human relations, for the emotions always seem so much more determining than the intellect. The world suffers from too much hate and too little love, not from deficiencies of intellect. I had never known such a person. We had a fine week—but where would it all lead?

They had told me that the farther east one goes the better Europe gets. If one likes Paris, how much more so Vienna, and then even more Prague and Budapest! Maybe this is true for others, but not for me, or perhaps I only saw the externals of Vienna. I sat in a little *garten* and had supper. A quiet girl in an outfit a bit like Robin Hood's was at a nearby table. Feeling very worldly, I wrote a note asking her to join me and was about to call the waiter to take it to her when a man behind me intervened with, "She is a street girl, my friend. If you want a woman, you must go to a regular house for such women. They are licensed by the government, and have periodic physical examinations. It is not entirely safe there, of course, but much better than a street girl (strassenmädel)."

That dash of reality from a stranger finished forever all thought of prostitutes, on streets or in houses or any other place! In my mind, the subtle spell of Robin Hood's youthful femininity had evoked images of closeness with her, the meal together, Viennese music and a night in each other's arms. It had never occurred to me that she was a prostitute; my mind dictated a very different fantasy. All my fantasy was smashed by reality—a streetwalker, probably syphilitic, having a dozen men in an evening. I thought of Charles. "She had an orgasm; it was unusual." Shabby. How could I think of it, especially having Nelda, even though our romance was perhaps going nowhere? Fantasy, fantasy. It blinds us, it distorts reality. I was not the man-of-the-world, passing a note to a beautiful damsel; I was an ignorant näive child. Nobody at home—or on the street—or in college—had told me that at twenty-one you have about three orgasms a week no matter what; that if you don't masturbate you have them as wet dreams; that you are not shameful or inferior for this, masturbating only with a fantasy in your mind while other men know their way around in the world and know how to deal with women and have their sex with real women. I had read James Branch Cabell's *Jurgen*. Suddenly, magically, his body was twenty-one again and so he had the key to every bed chamber in the world. Well, I *was* twenty-one (nearly) and had no such key. What was wrong with me? It seemed so easy for Charles! And Nelda was there—but it was just not right to take her sexually. Now perhaps I have some hints of the answers. But not then. Yet, paradoxically, I had faith in myself, born as I know now of my parents' faith in me. I slept the beautiful deep sleep of youth and next morning packed my rucksack, purchased (with some trepidation but no difficulty) a tiny .22 calibre automatic, and set out on foot from Vienna to Mariazell on my way to Innsbruck.

That kind of independence I had. A lot of it, though, was a denial of dependence, part of a drive for a real independence which I had not yet achieved. But it was enough to deeply enjoy those glorious days in the mountains—a lover of walking, traveling light, drinking in the sun on the peaks, the rich woods, often sleeping under the stars, bathing in rolling streams, getting meals wherever and whenever obtainable and convenient. As I recall, for breakfast omelettes were usually offered as three-egg or five-egg. They were not like American omelettes. They were apt to resemble a large fluffy Boston cream pie without the chocolate. It was all soul-saturatingly beautiful. It was before the Nazis and the extermination camps—and North

Africa, and Stalingrad—and Japanese bayonet practice on Chinese—
and a quarter of a million German women raped by the Russians and
denied abortions by the East German government. (What have such
babies grown up to be? And the millions of Chinese children trained
to hate the United States, trained in a world of hate and brutal cruelty?)
How often I have thought of Pope's couplet: "Every prospect pleases
and only man is vile." On that walk to Innsbruck every prospect
pleased and vile men were remote. The Tyrol was huge yet intimate—
not the incomprehensibly distant vastness of the glacial Alps—and
of course best enjoyed while walking alone.

Swinging along I came up with two English girls, sisters. The older
was a trifle anxious, rather cautious. The younger one, though, was
bright-eyed, extroverted, full of humor and good spirits. I was still
too distracted by my own feelings to observe them closely, except
as sexually attractive girls. Whatever I say about them was simply
how I felt about them then, based however upon a degree of identification with each one; when used maturely, this is indeed a good way to
understand another person—perhaps the best, perhaps the *only* way.
We stopped a bit and rested. Liz, the younger, asked me a little about
myself, how I came to be there. She was admiring, contrasted me with
a "sissy," as she called him, whom they had met the previous week.
But she was not, I thought, artificially flattering. I was pleased, of
course, but felt no less inadequate underneath.

At one point we rested, sitting on a rock, and I hit a few twigs with
the little .22 automatic. Liz thought that was great! Although underage, I'd gotten some training in World War I but had never gone
overseas. I hoped to be in the artillery because I could not have taken
the close-up fear and the killing of the infantry; besides I was too
slender and light to cope with large athletic men. Maybe one gets used
to killing. But I felt awful the one time I shot a rabbit, and saw him
flip up, convulse and then lie dead—when a few seconds before he
was so full of life, bounding about at breathless speed, and I had shot
him not for sport but for the pot, for food while on a ranch.

It began to rain heavily. We three huddled under an overhanging
rock. It was twilight, and I offered to seek shelter; they agreed, so
I donned my poncho and set out to seek a cottage where we could
stay. My German was no better than my French, and the cottage I
found had only one room. But yes, they could give it to the girls and
put me up somewhere also. I returned to report to the girls, and told

them they could put us up but had only one room. Older sister looked frightened, but Liz smiled and her eyes danced. Then I said they were putting me somewhere else. Older sister looked relieved and Liz's eyes stopped their dancing. What a fool I felt myself! Instead of taking an interest in the sisters and their feelings, I was showing off. The hero had gone forth through the rain and found shelter; he was superior to erotic adventure, even the mildest. He was a spotless knight who would never let it be said that they (the girls) had slept in the same room with a man. I had denied Liz a harmless adventure, and what had I denied myself? Liz was so fresh and vital and healthy. In my embarrassment, I never even got their names or said that I'd be stopping in England—and could I see them? Perhaps Liz would have made a fine and happy wife and saved me all the years of search and struggle. But my marriage resulted from love at first sight and has been so good that there must have been a special emotional meshing, absent from all the other girls I'd met during those years of seeking and struggle.

I thought of Liz, and still think of her, as a possible wife and not as someone only for that first great experience with sex. Actually I was not ready for marriage, although I think I did have spirit and determination. I was too absorbed in myself and my own problems. I had not even a direction for a career, except that very broadly it would be in science. For business I had a strong distaste, even a revulsion, and although I loved the arts I knew I had no talent for music or painting; and they seemed poor ways to find financial security. That I would ever write a book never entered my thoughts. I did not think enough in terms of the needs of other people, for I was too insecure in myself, struggling too much for goals and directions, trying too much to make a good impression, to be admired, as I had been by my parents. I felt that I was somehow good, able, but also somehow inferior, inadequate (today I would say immature)—still too much like the child trying to impress others, too little like the parent; too interested in impressing Liz to have a balanced relationship with her. And so in the morning, covering loss with humor, we gaily said goodbye—and we never even exchanged addresses.

Those golden days glided by. It would take too long to reach Innsbruck on foot. I took a train. It went, I think, from Vienna through Innsbruck to Paris. I rode fourth class—or was third class the lowest? It was jammed. That meant most of us stood; I was crowded against an Englishwoman and, in my fashion, started chatting. She was about twenty-six, very pleasant but a little peculiar and, for me, devoid of sex appeal. Her name was Ardy. I forget how long we stood; I think about five hours. I don't remember how the arrangement was for tickets; but being plagued with indecision in many matters, especially those big ones concerning career and marriage, I gave no thought to decisions in other matters, just made them without thinking. I told Ardy I was getting off in time for dinner, would stay overnight and go on in the morning—either by train or possibly by foot. She said she'd had enough of this too, and would join me. Maybe I was unconsciously seductive. Not sexually, though. I wanted companionship, and perhaps she felt this. Perhaps she wanted to sleep with me. Ultra-näive as I was, yet I knew she would do so if I wished. But she was not my ideal for initiation into sex as Liz was, nor did she tempt me.

We got off at a small town and found the inn. Then followed a comedy in my German (as she spoke none at all), requests for "ein-bettiger" not "zwei-bettiger zimmers." I'd made clear to Ardy we would have separate rooms. Now I tried to explain it to the innkeeper. It seemed that they mostly had two-bedded rooms, few one-bedded. Finally it penetrated to my comprehension that he was not saying that we had to share a room, but only that one of us would get a room with one bed, the other a room with two beds but at no extra charge. We had a pleasant dinner, a companionable but totally unromantic stroll in the moonlight, and retired. The rooms were adjacent, and connected by a door. Ardy thought I was peculiar, and said so. But I didn't think so—and still don't. The situation was perfect but for me she had not the least sex appeal. She was just not for me at all. But for Liz, regrets—there I was indeed somehow inhibited. Liz was fresh, attractive, sexy youth. I guess Liz was like a part of me; I identified with her and her forthrightness, good humor, her down-to-earth quality. But Ardy was too unlike, too old, too heavy in body and spirit to arouse any sexual interest. We parted amicably and, for me, with no regrets.

Nelda was at Innsbruck, and in that small, picturesque town with its awesome backdrop of towering mountains I easily located her. She was out of the hotel temporarily but it was just before lunch, so I waited. She had gone out with Will, a tall handsome boy she had known back home. Competition was hard on me. On the one hand, I felt I could almost always win out. I felt so loved in my own family that it never occurred to me that life could be different. The women I had grown up with—Mother, Aunt and Sister—adored me. I guess we all expect the future to be like the past, which is one reason why people have so little imagination and are so fatally short-sighted. But I felt somehow inferior. I could not define it then. As time passed, it made me frantic for I could not understand it or cope with it. The unknown is what is invincible. All I sensed was that other men somehow knew the world better. I think I was groping for the words "mature" and "immature," although I could not have defined them. I've learned that most people cannot. Will, I assumed in advance, must have what I lacked. . . .

At noon Nelda came in. She was willowy, and now here she was in a dirndl blouse and skirt, moving fast, a little breathless, cheeks pink, eyes glistening. We greeted each other. As always, she was pleased to see me. In all ways but sexually we had been one for half a year. But I was in turmoil. "He kissed you," I accused, intuitively guessing. She nodded assent.

I was in a fever of jealousy. Amazingly, Will withdrew on my arrival. He left Innsbruck—amazing! Nelda told me how fine Will was, how sensitive, how he'd introduced her to Proust. Utter honesty was part of her; I guess my needs to be loved and admired made me incapable of honesty in the degree to which she achieved it. How stupid it was, in retrospect! I never thought of it then, but she would have let me kiss her. But for me a kiss with Nelda was sacred. It was the door to full sex. And sex was the door to ultimate emotional involvement, which meant the lifelong commitment of marriage "till death do us part." I was slow not for lack of feeling, but because I was *too* passionate, too involved. I could not take sex lightly as Charles could. And if Will were taking Nelda lightly, even no further than a kiss, I could kill him. In my ardent, inhibited way I loved Nelda. We had embraced, but I never kissed her. If I had, we would have had sex. Had we had sex, we would have married. I was not ready for marriage, as I see it now, but did not know it then; and I was not sure Nelda was for me, and my parents were sure she was not, because she was not fully extrovertedly wholesome. They feared that intriguing quality of withdrawal and slight mystery, and they were right, as I guessed, even then. And it seemed wrong of me to think of sex in relation to her. It was years before I began to understand these things; and I have never gotten much beyond a beginning. I think hers was the withdrawness that signals a lonely soul, craving understanding, love and support; and to have sex with her would have been to exploit these needs of hers for my own desires. I guess we all make many and serious mistakes in life, but I still (in the relative calm of my mid-seventies) think this was no mistake. I could not have lived with myself if I had hurt her.

One cannot blame college too much for teaching nothing that is of any use in life. In fact, not much was known then of the emotional life—at least now a little bit is. But even with nothing known, seminars that discussed these feelings would benefit some, would indeed profit many—yet colleges leave these things to student bull sessions. I can only conclude that colleges are not much interested in benefiting students, in educating them to reality, in helping prepare them for life. Nor do they even do a good job of transmitting our cultural heritage. But in one field college is of great value—the field of science.

In Vienna I thought of trying to meet Freud. He was away in the mountains on vacation. I wonder if he would have seen me? Why should he have seen me—a callow, immature, overprotected boy, who could not find himself? But I meant to see Sir Ernest Rutherford, the great experimental physicist, before returning home.

Innsbruck changed nothing between Nelda and me. We were deep friends forever if nothing more developed. I returned to Paris with her and her aunt. There I met Jim, my closest friend. He and I took a little trip to the Midi to see the primitive paintings in the caves near Périgueux. One day, returning from the caves, we saw leaning against an ancient cabin door the all-American girl, fresh and pretty in pastel sweater and cream skirt, right off a magazine cover. Jim fell in love with her instantly, although I did not realize it then. Later on, this girl would have problems, but how can one tell such things? Sex may be simply a physical act, but it involves another human being; and feelings between persons are incalculably intense and complicated. People make each other so happy—but rarely indeed compared to the torment, destruction and death they cause each other. But the sun shone in the Midi, and Pam was there with an American college group, and Jim fell in love with her.

Jim had been studying physics at the University of London, and I asked him about it all. He told me it was a great center for research using the applications of modern physics to problems of physiology, especially the electrical phenomena of the central nervous system, the little electric currents that accompany every impulse in nerve and brain. This fitted in with my interests, insofar as my immaturity permitted. It was exactly my academic interest of the time. I had considered spending more time in Paris to learn the language and get to know this great city, but I had nothing to do there. I was facing an empty existence, being all alone in a city with a foreign language and nothing to advance my studies or to earn money—no progress, no advancement. What Jim had told me of London University decided me at once, without the usual indecisions. The application of physics to electrical problems of that most marvelous of all organs, the human brain, excited me. It used the knowledge I had acquired; it appealed to my egotism; it provided me with a goal. And then, I would not be all alone—I would have Jim for companionship to satisfy my still entirely unconscious dependence and submissiveness.

Jim returned to London. Nelda and her aunt sailed for home and I saw them off at the boat-train; then I looked up Ernest and Sharon and had a goodbye dinner—London was my objective. I took a train to the nearest port and rummaged around the small cargo ships for a cheap ride across the channel, and I found one. There was a crew of three with the look of desperadoes; I wondered if they would risk dumping me overboard in mid-channel for a few nonnegotiable American Express checks and my meager possessions! But my sleep was disturbed only by itching. We docked at London, me covered with bedbug bites. The crossing had cost half a pound or something over two dollars in those days, half the regular fare. I got to a bus and found that I could understand French and German almost better than cockney. I found my way to Jim's tiny flat; he was staying the year and I was to share it with him, lightening his expenses as well as my own during my time in England. We had dinner together at the Isola Bella in Soho.

Next day, after the breakfast of oatmeal, fried fish, toast with marmalade and cocoa (it all came with the price of our room), I went with Jim to the University and obtained an appointment at noon with the new young professor of physiology, a former physicist and mathematician from Cambridge. We chatted and hit it off; I told him I would like to spend a few months, as long as my money lasted, in his department learning what I could. Being a loved child, as I see now, I was not surprised that he seemed to like me and agreed to my entering his department on this basis. He suggested that as I was new to the area of applied physics, I should start in a small way with frogs, under the direction of two young physiologists who were Russian refugees. They turned out to be charming, and one of them became a good friend. I will never forget the terror I saw in the face of the older of the two when Ramsay MacDonald, leader of Britain's Labor Party, became prime minister. He thought this meant a revolution. I saw both the Russian physiologists in later years, when as eminent scientists they came to the United States for meetings. The older one was slowed down then by a heart attack.

My work at University College went along happily. The daily teas were a great and fruitful treat, for I was invited to attend and thus listened informally not only to the brilliant, vivacious professor but also to other world-famous physiologists, anthropologists and biochemists. These contacts were most enjoyable and illuminating, but as the weeks and months passed I got no feeling of being squarely in a career—there was a certain dissatisfaction. I did not know enough physics or enough physiology. Perhaps I should be in one field or another . . . the esthetic appeal of physics and the excitement of its investigations of the atom in those days attracted me. I was spending some time in the library on what is known today as thermoelectricity, the flow of an electric current across the junctions of two particular dissimilar metals when these junctions were at different temperatures. The effect could be used as an instantly readable clinical thermometer, but my interest was not in that effect; rather, it was in the opposite, the possibility of using these temperature differences as a source of electric power. But the current produced was too small. The problem was in determining how to make it workable, and it increased my interest in physics as a practical career. Today, with the energy crisis, I again think of this method of generating electricity from the inexhaustible sources of differences in temperature. I have just read that the Russians have developed a method for making this practicable.

In a discussion with Jim, I realized that I would be financially dependent on a job if I chose physiology, probably in a medical school. But a physician can support himself somehow, anywhere in the world. This random comment from Jim was the first time the idea of medicine as a career had entered my thinking. I paid no attention to it at the time, and we went on with our discussion of physics. Those were the days of Einstein, Bohr, Ehrenfest, Born, Planck, Andrade and other great investigators and thinkers; it was just before Heisenberg and quantum mechanics took center stage, and the excitement of "particle physics" continues to this day.

Jim was my closest friend; he always seemed to know people worth knowing, and had opened much of the world to me. I never expressed to him how much he meant to me in introducing me to the wider world. Of course I only dimly realized my debt to him then. But I have often wondered at characters in books and plays who seem to have no dependent needs. They move about entirely self-sufficient. Are there really such people? Other than hermits and schizophrenics? Or is it that I am abnormally dependent underneath? Here was Jim, for example, settling down all alone for a year in London. Today I would not be alone for long. I would soon find friends. But then I was a student, in other words, a "nothing." I guess I wanted a lot and had nothing to give. I did meet a few people, like Peg. There was not much closeness or rapport. I took her out; with her I hoped to have that first sexual experience, but all I did was show off and of course this had the opposite effect. I meant to impress her, and I did—with being interested solely in myself and not in her. Was it part protective? How would I have felt if she had given me a sign and it had led to bed, and then I had left her to return to America? For there was no question about marriage here, though she seemed nice enough—refined, sensitive, good-looking; or was I again taking it all too seriously?

Then there were Beverly and her brother, David. There was a pleasant friendly cordiality with no thoughts of the relationship with Beverly leading anywhere; therefore it could be easy. They invited me to go to Cambridge with them and stay at the home of one of their relatives. They convinced me it would inconvenience no one. So we set out by a minor chance on a turning point in my life; for Sir Ernest Rutherford, the world-renowned experimental physicist was there, and surprisingly he agreed to see me. I was heading for science as a career, and the romance was with the atomic physicists—also the glamour. How many in youth have a genuine interest, and how many are motivated mostly by prestige? I for one wanted to *be* something great. I didn't know that greatness was a by-product. As I said before, I learned nothing worth anything in college—that is, nothing about living. But I did learn a little about science. And that seemed the finest of human endeavors. It still does, but now not the physical sciences alone: now, rather, the sciences which seek to understand the life of the mind and to reduce man's terrible hostility to man. And I think the cause of their hostility lies in how children are mistreated, especially from conception to age about six. For the child raised with love, security and respect for his personality becomes an adult with love and respect for others. He does not become a murderer. I think all murderers were badly mistreated in some crucial ways in early childhood.

But that day in Cambridge I knew nothing of life and was struggling with choice of career, what to *be;* the choice tormented me constantly, yet so far I could resolve nothing and stewed in indecision. I idealized the atomic physicists; I projected my pride and vanity onto them— to me they were heroes. To my astonishment the great Rutherford with his huge frame and piercing eyes not only saw me, but spent the afternoon with me, from lunch until tea. I had kept up with the advances in the field, studying the writings of its great pioneers, but it was a superficial smattering. It was like knowing only a scale and then hearing Beethoven himself discuss the composition and orchestration of a symphony. I could understand Rutherford just enough to follow and appreciate and be awed. My IQ was high, but not high enough for this. He offered me a place with him if I decided to spend the year in England, and I was overwhelmed that he thought enough of me to invite me, and overwhelmed too at the depth and power of his intellect, which was beyond anything in my previous experience; I was awed at the force of his personality. I went to sleep that night sensing that I should not attempt atomic physics as a career. And a little thought kept entering that I did not want anything so remote from life anyway, even if (with time and long application) I could master it and contribute to it.

When I awoke life looked a little different. My career I now sensed could not be in the abstract; it must have people, must be applied science. Science applied to things, like engineering, was good, sort of masculine—but engineers told me that when they were successful they became business administrators, and I knew that I was no Steinmetz or Pupin. Science applied to living things, to biology, to physiology, was fascinating—but there was no future there, just low-paid jobs in medical schools; those professors married rich wives or else had narrow lives. But in science applied to medicine—*there* were security, a need for doctors all over the world, independence, no lack of jobs, human beings to deal with, public health—suddenly my thoughts of medicine took the shape of the Tyrolean mountains, of vistas and valleys, of charm, challenge, variety. A few weeks later I was stepping down off the sidewalk to cross a street, over which shone sunlight that was exceptionally bright for London in early spring. As I stepped down, in that split second, like a religious experience, suddenly but surely it came to me that medicine was my true career. In that single instant four years of tormenting doubt and struggle were resolved. The pieces fell into place. There were many reasons of course but certainly two of the strongest were the relative security and independence financially and the chance to learn about people. (These reasons have not disappointed me, but have given me the deepest satisfactions of my professional career.)

Looking back after decades of absorption in analytic practice, I can see what went on in at least three layers of my consciousness. In full awareness, I thought: "Rutherford—what a mind, what a personality, what knowledge, what insight, what imagination! This is tremendous. But it is like expecting me, a mere dilettante, to write a Brahms' symphony."

In my pre-conscious, just below the surface and sort of slowly oozing into awareness, was the thought: "But with years—how many years of study—might I learn to do it? And what a privilege to spend this time, if I can find funds to live on, with such a powerful mind and personality—what an opportunity!" And here, then, I think I had a flash of what being grown-up meant: the solitary enormous sustained concentration of energy upon accomplishment.

In my unconscious, strong feelings rather than words, were those forces that might be put into thoughts like this: "You are being tempted to spend your life in a physics laboratory studying atoms. But beware. That is just the opposite of what you really want. It is glamorous, and prestigeful, to be one of these top physicists, but what you want is the opposite. You want life, people, to understand life and people, and to find your way around in the big world. Beware; flee. You have thought of a career which teaches life and provides more financial security than any other, and which will teach you all there is to know about sex in which you are still frustrated, and a lot more about people. Do not hesitate. Take the step . . . go!"

To clarify the dynamics further, one might say that complex decisions, like almost all motivation, usually have many emotional causes (I usually look for at least eight). I did not feel that being a physicist was impossible for my own ability, but felt that to achieve anything would require so many years of such intense learning and concentration that everything else in my life would be sacrificed to it; it would drain all my energies off into a laboratory and I would be moving away from life and living. This much I sensed vaguely even then. What I did not see until much later was that the whole current of my emotional makeup toward life and living and understanding life was threatened by what I saw as a monastic dedication to the atom. In a way I felt atomic physics might be beyond me, but at the same time I was even more threatened by feeling that it was *not* beyond me, that I really could do it, but that the requirements for success ran head-on against what I was unconsciously struggling *toward*. And it was even later before I saw that this threat probably caused a rebound which made me decide so suddenly and definitely to go into what was an opposite direction—medical school.

Out of some such emotional caldron, unconscious and inarticulate, at the same time came the sudden but certain decision as I stepped off that sunlit London curb to flee from the abstract remote laboratory into life and the world. Out of this reaction, of which I was unconscious at the time, came decision. Thus my unconscious decided definitely what my conscious reasoning had struggled with in vain for years.

And it has not taken all these decades of devotion to analytic practice to see that the great scientific problem of that day, exciting as it still is—the constitution and nature of the atom—is not the real problem at all. Mankind has one great problem that overrides all others, and that is the hostility in people's minds and its extreme readiness to break out in cruelty and violence to other humans. The problem is not in the atom but in man's readiness to use the atom for violence against man himself. In a way, this is a far more difficult problem than the atom. I have written and spoken about it for years, but it seems that people do not want to face it; they do not really want to do anything to prevent it, but would rather indulge their hostilities, whether in reality or in the fantasies of paperbacks or TV. But I, as one frail human being, have come from the challenge of the atom to the greater challenge of man's hostility and violence to man.

Having made my decision, I thought of my old chemistry professor, "Pop" Nielsen. I loved him as a father and had helped him with such odd jobs in his laboratory at the college as I could. He had listened to my intellectual gropings, more interested in me than in credits or in recruiting me for his own department.

I cabled Pop Nielsen: "Definitely decided medicine. Please advise."

Fortunately he was in town and replied immediately: "Informed top schools this last chance to get you. Return."

It was done. Jim bid me Godspeed and I left my share of the rent in an envelope for him. Being so occupied with my own problems it never occurred to me at the time that I was deserting him. I saw him as the strong, independent one, who would not miss me; yet now in later life I feel some guilt for deserting him so precipitously. There was no time now to wait on the docks for a chance to work my way back. I booked the first available inexpensive passage. Leaving the house at six that last morning, I saw two cats nestled in a corner of the steps, one on top of the other, silently enjoying sexual relations. Is it so easy for them, and so hard for humans, I wondered with envy, and set off for the boat-train. The path to prostitutes was permanently blocked. The road to a career was finally opened. Thank you, England!

At present I can only regret that I did not write to Rutherford explaining this and expressing my gratitude for the hours he gave me that had such fateful effects on my choice of career—effects that he must have been even less aware of than I as we sat talking about his work and my possibilities in atomic research. Looking back, it is a neat example of the operation of the unconscious—at least, of mine. Years later I realized that medicine is midway between science and the humanities, and therefore appealed to both of these trends in my personality, as it has to so many other young people.

2
SEPARATION

If ever the silver cord be loosed . . .

Ecclesiastes 12:6

The third day out we met a gale. The winds were steady at nearly sixty knots. Although often easily seasick, I now had my sea legs and exulted in the storm and the great seas. No third class was available; my previous skimping enabled me to travel second, which meant a forward upper deck was on limits. It may have been closed during the height of the storm, but as soon as possible I perched there, braced against the rail, watching the bow rise higher and higher against the rushing, dark shapeless clouds of the gray sky, and then slowly plunge into the huge waves. Today I can understand that one way we feel toward people and animals and all of nature is through identification. We respond to what is most like ourselves. The great ship, breasting the immense power of the waves, driving forward against slate-gray skies, represented as in a dream what was in my soul. Here was the inner force and strength of youth, which I felt within me—and here was the force and strength which, never asserted, I yearned for. Here were the power, the drive and the determination that I wished to have and express. Today I see this as the material and method of art. The artist not only responds as I did, to what he experiences, but then he projects his own feelings into his creations. And we resonate to his art if it stirs similar feelings in us. Thank God I had a strong enough ego to ride the inner gale!

One day out of New York I was relaxing in a deck chair, chatting with a Dutch couple I'd become friendly with. A man nearby hawked and expectorated onto the deck. I was revolted. The Dutch gentleman, very poised, very calm, went over and said a few quiet words. The man soon left. This was a knowledge of the world and a way of handling people of which I felt incapable. What was this thing I lacked?

New York shone in full sunlight. It was clear and brilliant after London; it was boisterous and rude and crude after Europe. It was plain, unimaginative, crassly commercial, clean, vital, frank, obvious, part of me, my country, my reality, my home.

Of course my family gave me a royal welcome. Preoccupied as I was with my own problems and leaving London so suddenly, I hope I picked up some gifts for them, but cannot remember. For to them I was the adventurer, returning to the admiring center of the family. They went along unquestioningly with my decision to go into medicine—and I was too self-centered and unaware to notice whether they approved or not. I know Dad had hoped that I would join him in his business. But he was the best of fathers, as I learned over the years; his own disappointment was eclipsed by his satisfaction in seeing me find my direction. His response was: "Every man must carve out his own future. I will go to every length to give you what education you need, but when you marry the support of a wife is your responsibility as a man." I still admire and approve his old-fashioned virtues. But at that time I did not feel at all like a man. Mother directly expressed her hope that I would not marry Nelda, fearing that Nelda was somehow, some way, not entirely wholesome. None of this had much effect on me, for I was still a chick in the nest and encased in my own feelings. Anything I had wanted I had got—from my loving, giving parents. I had only wanted reasonable, healthy things and had done what I could to save money and even earn a little. I loved them, and I loved my "little sister." Self-centered as I was, I had love to give for I had received so much. I never would have hurt any of them, or deliberately hurt any human being or, for that matter, any animal. I just childishly thought of marriage as another thing I would of course get when I wanted it. If it seemed right to me to marry Nelda—or Liz, or someone else—I would have gone ahead and done it, just as freely as I had decided to enter medicine, blindly certain of my parents' love and blessing.

Somehow things had worked out, and, viewing the future through my experience with the past, I never questioned that they would also work out both for medical school and for marriage. I had been too protected to know much about reality. And this was one of the lacks in me which I sensed but could not then define. Slowly and at some cost, I learned a little about reality and that, as Freud put it, necessity is a hard master but makes us potent. But then I was still a child, protected by loving parents, secure in a welcoming home with bills I could not pay met by a conscientious father. I did not know that this very dependence upon them was one great source of my feelings of inferiority, of lack of that which others seemed to have, and of efforts to show my superiority in order to deny the opposite. I did not realize that I tried to charm people as a child, and then felt that I was acting like a child, and hated myself for it. What surprised me was that others saw something mature in me—like Pop Nielsen, my chemistry professor. I phoned him and went over to thank him. But first I called Nelda. My family wanted me for dinner but I would come over to see Nelda after dinner, about 8:30. As usual she said she would be there.

We greeted with a chaste hug. We talked of Europe, and of course of my decision for medicine. She was genuinely pleased, but of course I had not decided to *be* a doctor—that was too limiting for my egotism. I would *be* something much broader, with the knowledge and skills of a doctor added. Babes in the woods as we were, there was something in the ideal, and it worked out that way. But I was so totally unaware of my own strivings for love and admiration, my own needs for dependence, in the family and out of it, that I was oblivious of hers. It never came anywhere near to my consciousness that *she* was dependent on *me*, that *she* might need *my* love. Perhaps I was so used to being on the receiving end toward my mother that nothing else ever entered my mind. I took Jim for granted, and Charles, my two closest friends—and I guess I took Nelda for granted too. In complete innocence I dealt the blow: I was leaving to spend four years at medical school in another city. And she wished me well, was happy for me, as though she had no needs of her own, no needs for anything of me—of my interest, presence, company, support, friendship, love.

There had been a critical instant when our lives might have been different. We had been caught at night once in a downpour. Drenched, we shed our soaked clothes. We were alone. I covered her with a blanket. I could have snuggled in with her. She would have allowed it. In a flash I felt that if I did we would go all the way and have sex together, and if we did that I would marry her; I could not have sex with Nelda unless all barriers were down and I did marry her. But that I could not decide to do—something was not entirely right. I still do not know if that something was in her as I then thought and as my mother judged, or in me, or in both. But my inner makeup decided it. It was unreasoned; the barriers were not breached. And now I was leaving for a new life, and she still was the beautiful child when it is quite serious and concentrated on some little thing, such as drawing a picture or tying its shoe. Possibly I was too attached to my five-year-younger sister and felt the incest taboo, although Nelda seemed totally unlike my sister. At any rate, Nelda was dark, warm, gentle and remote; after Nelda the girls who attracted me strongly were all blue-eyed, extroverted blonds. But I always loved bright gray eyes like those of my girlish, gray-eyed mother.

For some reason, as I left I thought of Nelda's father—a gentle giant of a man with a huge shock of hair so dense that he would hide candies in it for Nelda and her sister to search out with squeals of delight, when they were small children and he came in for dinner.

Before leaving town, I paid another goodbye call; would my life have been different if I had not? Jim had introduced me to Dr. Ralph Ackley, a general practitioner who had become a close and helpful friend. He was a sort of highly sophisticated horse-and-buggy doctor in the great metropolis. He was a kind of "Man Flammond" in the mold of Robinson's poem: "With firm address—with news of nations in his talk—who held his head as one by kings accredited." He was in his mid-thirties. Jim was a year older than I, who was then nearly twenty-one; we were among the many of all ages who were fascinated by him.

I must say a few words about Ralph so you can understand how a passing remark of his could have affected me so deeply. As Jim once said, people either hated him and fought him, or were devoted to him. Ralph was a simple, natural person, good-looking but not strikingly so; he had starred in swimming at college, an activity he still enjoyed and continued regularly. He seemed to know everyone of consequence out in that big world which I longed in vain to enter. He was a man of the big world; he had easy talents. He was an accomplished pianist and could play all the classics. He could also improvise at the piano; you could hum a tune, and he would play it in the style of Bach or Chopin or as jazz. He got around to the art shows and knew many of the artists themselves. He did not have much money, but he helped them by introducing their work where it might be appreciated and purchased. He knew the theater as well as music and art, and he knew people at all levels in life. Some of his friends were poverty-stricken slum dwellers. He really knew his way around, and, additionally, he had a way with people; he seemed always to understand the person and the situation, no matter where or what, and to be at ease and in command—but always in a quiet, unassuming way. He had the true art of living. He taught me how to choose gifts—not by going to the store at the last minute for something, but having a closet in which to drop all sorts of items that attracted one and were good buys. It might only be a nice bit of pottery—but for the right person at a suitable time Ralph's friend the florist would put a well-chosen plant in it, and it would delight the recipient.

Once he asked if I'd like to see a man who wore a size 19½ collar and was starting out on the stage as a strong man. The theater was small and shabby. We saw the act, then went backstage where Ralph introduced himself and me and chatted easily with the man for a few minutes. We left and Ralph said, "He does have phenomenal strength—really extraordinary. But he will not succeed. He is a vain peacock; he has no imagination and won't study, think or work. He is no Houdini! He will never get anywhere. There is no use trying to help him." I marveled at how Ralph could size up a person and situation almost at a glance. "In contrast to this peacock," Ralph said, "just last week I met a young man with an amazing musical gift—I think he is something of a genius. You will enjoy meeting him."

"What is his name?" I asked.

Ralph replied, "George Gershwin. We will be hearing of George without doubt."

I was delighted by this promised contact with the great of that big world out there.

Ralph Ackley has just everything I lacked; he represented so much of how I wanted to be that I almost hero-worshipped him. When I phoned him, he said in his easy way, "Can you come to the hospital about a quarter of five? We can walk to the house together, and still have nearly an hour to talk before I have to dress and go out for dinner." Could I! We spoke of many things. We talked of Paris, of Ernest and Sharon, whom Ralph knew well. I described the painting of what life had done to the waiter, and Ralph told me that the painting showed what Ernest possessed—power, insight and willingness to work. But according to Ralph, Ernest would never make more than a moderate success, for as the waiter in the picture showed, Ernest was cynical and bitter, and Sharon was good fortune beyond his deserts; she was natural, wholesome, healthy, sensible, realistic, and irresistible, and would eventually domesticate him and almost certainly marry him and even have children with him, although at present Ernest was dead-set against this prospect—"unless they could be born at seventeen years of age!"

Then I told Ralph of my sudden decision to go into medicine. He was pleased. Then, stumblingly, with great difficulty, I told him I still masturbated and still had not had sexual relations, that somehow I never could find the right girl. He said, "That's funny, I've never had trouble getting women." He said this almost under his breath, more to himself than to me. The effects were not immediate, but his remark sank in like a slow poison. He went on about having been in a strange city with the college swimming team years ago and how he, together with a friend, had found two attractive girls after the match, and they went to bed that evening; and how once here in his house he had swept his arm around a girl who had just hung up the phone, slipped off her underpants, and just like that, bang-bang-bang, had vigorous sex. He meant to encourage me. We were close friends and he was only exchanging confidences. He was a positive force in my life and never wanted anything but my welfare—as I wanted his. The effects of his remarks would have surprised and distressed him.

Only in retrospect did I connect all this with his being still a bachelor. Only years later did I see that he did not explore my problem with me, but instead showed how easy it was for him, and made me wonder even more what was wrong with me. Of course I took it as my own failure of masculinity—the masculinity I so wanted, was so sure that somehow I had, and yet could not satisfy. What he said meant to me that a *real* man can get women without difficulty. To prove myself then, to prove I was a man, I would have to get women. This determined me. I did not think of it then as purely egotistical, as getting without giving, as a "free lunch." But some mechanism in my feelings had always prevented me from mentioning Nelda to Ralph, much as I admired and idealized him. He did not tell me (could it be that even he did not know?) that masculinity is not merely sexual potency but psychological maturity, independence, responsibility, giving.

That year, medical schools were not flooded with applicants. With my good record, especially in science, and Pop Nielsen's resourceful intervention, I was accepted by the institution of my first choice, reputedly "the best." And now I was on the train and on the way. Not a trip this time, but a permanent step into life, which I had always felt so unreachable because I was so set in the patterns of overprotection and winning approval which I did not then recognize or understand. I looked through the dirty train window at the passing changing scenes. The rhythmic clatter of the wheels had never stirred any thoughts or music in me; the nagging sharp clicks had been a bore to be blotted out. But now, in time to their beat, I heard Nelda's gentle voice: "Corey, Corey, must you leave me—don't you see that we are one?" This kept repeating until suddenly it was replaced by a harsh, staccato, "That's funny, I've never had trouble getting women." I thought of the city I was leaving, the friends, my home, and sensed a certain relief, as if I were fleeing from something—and a presentiment that I would never return again, except as a visitor. A cycle seemed to be completed; was another beginning? The wheels beat on, and, just as in novels, a light rain pattered against the dirty window. As the train plunged on through the mist, my mind turned from the past I was leaving to the unknown future. The man next to me sneezed. I took out a handkerchief and made a show of blowing my nose to hide my tears.

3
BABYHOOD

The hand that rocks the cradle rules the world.

Folk wisdom

You must have a picture of the home I was leaving, explained Corey Jones, in order to understand me. It will not be easy to relate, because no one finds the inner life of a small child very absorbing; yet it is vital for that child's whole future life until the day of his death. As Freud so truly wrote (in *A General Introduction to Psychoanalysis*): "The child we once were lives on in all of us."

What I am going to tell you I did not learn myself until years later, beginning with my training analysis. And for undertaking this I am indebted to Ralph Ackley. He had taken nine months out of his general practice to go to Vienna and be psychoanalyzed by Freud himself. Leave it to Ralph to do something like that!—to explore something new, especially something having to do with understanding people; to spend time in a foreign land and in a great cultural capital. Apparently he was an instant hit in Vienna and had a marvelous time. What he told me about his analysis was not very intriguing. For one thing, he said that "You just talk freely, and then when Freud summarizes what you have said, you see that you've lashed yourself to the mast." Then he added, *sotto voce*, in barely audible tones, "Freud was the father." But I did feel Ralph's sincerity when he said, "Don't let anything interfere with your getting some analysis— with the right man, though—and the earlier in life the better, because it illumines everything that comes after." He did not talk of it as medical treatment for neurotic problems, but as a profound human and cultural experience, as a way of learning about yourself and people and life; learning what I yearned to know and what college does not teach. Finding the right analyst was not easy. During medical school (which I thought was an ideal time to be analyzed) I had interviews with six analysts and felt that I could not trust my mind to any of them. One of them I rejected because he had three telephones on his desk and was too transparently trying to show me what a big shot he was—or at least, so I thought. I will return to that later. Here let me review some of the forces that molded me in my most malleable years. Like our animal pets, we all "reflect" our homes as they were during earliest days, weeks, months and years. Even the prenatal period is important; my mother had an illness and an operation and was down to ninety pounds while carrying me, which probably had something to do with my prenatal development and light weight, never over 138. Seeing the world through the pattern of one's family is natural and inevitable, because as small children we know of the world only through the family in which we grow up.

In my mother I had the best of love and devotion. I knew she would have died for me. But I never thought that way. Her gray eyes were always happy. She enjoyed her responsibilities and the everyday jobs and events of living; the simplest recreations delighted her. She had all the warmth with no need to control our thinking. We were a matriarchy (which I have learned most happy marriages are), and her life was her home. Dad built his own business, an association of manufacturers' representatives. He traveled himself, a long week-end about every two or three weeks. We were always sorry to see him go and delighted when he returned. "We" came to include my sister Judy, five years younger. Dad was strong and courageous, and a leader out in the big world; but the instant he stepped over the threshold of home he fully accepted Mother as the boss. Perhaps it took strength and security to do that—and it is true that only the strong can be gentle—a saying which impressed Nelda, who was not given to clichés. Much about his personality is revealed by a brief remark: a friend of his once said to him in my presence, "You must be proud of your son." I had heard another father, who did not want to "spoil" his son, answer such a remark with the reply, "Yes I am *but* . . . ," and then list some of his son's faults. My father's immediate response to the remark was, "I do not think I am *proud*, but certainly I am very *gratified*."

Although it is not a feature of the conventional psychoanalytic history,* it is a tacit assumption that "antecedents" have something to do with one's personality. Hence a few more words about Mother

*Saul, Leon (1972): *Psychodynamically Based Psychotherapy*. New York: Science House.

and Dad: My mother was, I think, in all ways average—of medium height, not conspicuously thin and never overweight; her brown hair was slightly wavy. Her face was oval, and her eyes were gray— not cold or steely gray, but warm, bright, merry, laughing. In her seventies she wore rimless eyeglasses only occasionally for reading. Even when her heart was giving out and she was near death at seventy-nine, her eyes were still bright and dancing, and lit up when she saw me. She also had a streak of the poker-back Prussian in her makeup, but it was not so much domination as determination. She had no distinguished talents or abilities; she did play a few "pieces" on the piano when I was young (such as Sinding's "Rustles of Spring"), but I have never been able to trace my own enjoyment of and deep love for music, especially the piano, to this small talent of my mother. Perhaps it affected me while I was still an infant. She was American for a few generations back; her early forebears had come from Germany in the neighborhood of Frankfurt and from France near St. Pol de Leon.

I saw Mother as quite ordinary in all ways, which was of no consequence, for she had the one great quality of being able to love; and she loved my father, sister and me unqualifiedly. Because of this my father adored her. For my sister and me it was usually "Mom" and "Dad." What so touched my father was that Mother would choose to love and marry him, "a poor immigrant boy." This was part of his gentlemanly humility, which grew out of strength, not weakness. He came to the United States in the early 1880s at the age of seventeen from his parents' farm in Gloucestershire, not far from Bath. Like me, he was the first-born; but he was followed by five or six brothers and sisters, while I had a brother two years younger who died shortly after birth and then my sturdy sister, Judy, five years younger. I saw pictures of Dad's parents taken when they were both ninety-three years old but still strong. His father had piercing eyes and a black beard cut square across the bottom. Dad's mother had a strong weather-beaten face, but one of obvious refinement. I never learned the details of why Dad left home, beyond the fact that his father used to beat him and made Dad so wretched that he decided to emigrate. When miserable, he told me, he would go to the barn and feel consoled by the horses. This is no doubt where his love for them developed. Riding was his great recreation, and he continued it until his death, despite Mother's teasing about how he smelled of horses when he came in for Sunday dinner after his ride—a complaint he dispelled by shifting the horse routine to *after* dinner.

Dad's 0 to 6 must have been good, loving and secure, for him to have the self-confidence, independence and maturity at age seventeen to come to the United States alone and penniless, to seek his fortune. Perhaps his mother gave her first-born son a good 0 to 6; perhaps his father was not mean to him until he was old enough to work on the farm. At any rate, my mother had the confidence in him to marry him and be his helpmate. From the beginning of their marriage my mother acted as his general secretary and handled all accounts both at home and in the business. When I asked her about this once her eyes danced—"It was one of the happiest times of our life," she said, "those early years with no money, starting out together."

In appearance Dad was no beauty but was something of a paradox: his figure, which never changed, was trim and muscular at a steady 148 pounds, with especially strong hands, wrists and forearms, giving him the look of an athlete. He never seemed to age. At ninety-one his kidneys gave out and in three months he was dead, but he was never really "old." To the very end he moved like an athlete, working, riding, swimming and enjoying his food, his occasional glass of wine and his after-dinner cigar or cigarette. His nose was broken by a horse and therefore broad and flattened, like a boxer's or a football player's. A neat moustache helped his looks. His lips gave an impression of both gentleness and strength, which, with forth-rightness, were in fact Dad's chief qualities. 2002532

I grew up loving him too much even to notice his appearance until I was a young adult. He was never self-conscious about himself in any way that I ever noticed. On one of the very rare occasions when I ever teased him, I asked if he had any Jewish blood that showed in his flattened boxer's nose. There was not the slightest trace of this in the pictures of his parents; but—to my surprise—he replied, "It could be; my parents mentioned that this was possible a few generations back. If so, you may find it an advantage if the accepted traits of that race are in fact as they are reputed to be, sensitive, perceptive, warm and imaginative. America is a melting pot which is an essential of its greatness; England also became a melting pot although far earlier, through being conquered by so many other races, and that is an essential of its greatness too."

I pressed him with further questions but it was always painful for him to speak of his life before age seventeen. I did learn that his mother's maiden name was Wilson; the family had been on that farm for generations, and almost all of them were farmers. Nevertheless, somehow or other, there seemed to be a coat-of-arms in the family, although Dad had never cared enough to inquire into it. "That," he said, "is of no consequence. All that matters is what kind of man you are. I hope you will always be upright, honest and direct. Look everyone square in the eye and say clearly what you have to say. I will support you for all the education you require, but you will have to carve out your own future."

I still kick myself for being in London that year and not looking up any remaining members of the family in Gloucestershire. I was too completely absorbed in my own problems of sex and choice of career, and possibly Dad's attitude of letting the past be forgotten influenced my lack of interest. I do know that I came from undistinguished but long-lived, hard-working yeomen and that is exactly what I am fortunate enough to be myself, I hope, even though I am slight of build and in an intellectual professional field.

I have no memory of my two and a half years younger brother who died shortly after his birth, only of hearing him mentioned later; I have no memory of Judy's arrival.

My first definite memory is of being a small baby, snug in Mother's arms, and then being handed by her to Father. In this memory I liked Father, but his texture was quite rough compared to Mother's— his cheeks were rough, even though shaven, and so was his tweedy suit. I turned back to soft, smooth, warm, cozy Mother.

One picture tells more than ten thousand words. We all have these scraps of memory from very early ages. They always are eloquent if one can decipher them. What this flash from not later than age two portrays is self-evident: the liking for both parents, but the clearly preferred attraction to smooth, warm Mother. Father is no intruder or danger; he is very much part of the scene. Only Mother is sensuously preferred. And the baby, myself, feels loved by both. Obviously here is love, with the sensuousness attached to Mother. These fragmentary memories always reveal a main theme for a person's whole emotional pattern, which repeats in different forms for life. Perhaps we remember—or think we remember—just because the scene is like the statement of a leitmotif at the opening of a symphony which is our whole life. This fragment of memory foretells my close friendships with men and my irresistible attraction to women.

A second fleeting scene is of the baby (myself) lying face down, nude on a bed—apparently after a bath. Mother and my beloved Aunt Edie hover delightedly over me. Aunt Edie bends over and kisses me on the bottom, at which moment I make a loud poop of air and the two women go into gales of laughter. This scene may not be a true memory but an anecdote they told me years later. But it *feels* like a memory. It doesn't greatly matter because it lives in my mind among those earliest fragments, and it portrays the wonderful, sensuous, unconditional love. It reveals in a single stroke the basis of my confidence in women loving me. Accustomed only to such treatment, naturally I grew up with deep warmth and sensuous (later on, sensual) feelings for women. Knowing nothing but such love from women as an only child might enjoy for the first five years of life, how could I initiate sex with a prostitute or any girl to whom I was but one of many, and whom I did not to some extent love? And if I once married, how could I ever be anything but closely intimate and single-mindedly devoted, just as my parents were to each other and to me—and as devoted to my parents as Aunt Edie was, as she was also to her own husband, who in turn loved me and whom I loved. I have always gotten on well with men, but have felt closer to women and more at ease with them.

There has always been some readiness in me to be dependent, and this doubtless was also derived from being the object of so much love. This is depicted in a third scene, definitely a memory: Now I was nearly four, but certainly not any older, because my sister was not yet born. I was flying a kite. It got away from me. Father ran with me to retrieve it; that is, I had a pattern of a man as companion, protector and helper to provide a model for later friendships and for getting on well with father-figures.

Probably nobody's childhood is a garden of Eden without a snake— at least a little one. My next memory is of sitting on the floor with my sister, Judy. She was then about one or two, which made me nearly six. She had thrown a little toy at me, an iron engine, and it had hit my forehead, drawing nearly a whole drop of blood. But I was gratified. Apparently I was the only one who was always blamed for some mistreatment of Judy, but here at last she was the one who had injured me! I had my triumph, and we went on playing.

Judy was a character! I loved her dearly. I would also get exasperated with her on several counts. The first was that she complicated my peaceful, hitherto only-child existence. Second, she got into my room, my toys, my privacy. It is back to this that I trace my fierce jealousy of my privacy and my personal possessions—and later of my friends and the restaurants I'd discovered and tried to keep secret. One thing was not her fault: I was supposed to accompany whoever took her for walks in her baby carriage. This insulted my boy's pride, of course, as well as being a restriction and a thorough nuisance. I hated trailing along after her and did not relish her trailing along after me, especially when I got friends of my own.

In a memory from age six or seven, I was in a high old hassle with Mother, over what I felt were unjust controls and restrictions. At this point Judy pulled on me from behind, demanding some attention or service or just trying to join in. Suddenly I was fighting on two fronts instead of one, and got pretty angry at her as well as at Mother. In retrospect, Mother may have been a little too overprotective, controlling and restricting. I do not know for sure. But she never interfered with our freedom of thought. Most decisions she just made, and we all, Father included, went along and didn't even question them. Only years later did I learn that they had lost a child, a son, after I was born, and this loss no doubt increased Mother's anxiety and solicitude and protectiveness of me, to a point where I rebelled. It made me a thorough-going Jeffersonian democrat, with hostility to all forms of tyranny over the minds of men and resentment of dogma and unreasonable authority, although Mother imposed mighty little of it. It was mostly my own extreme needs for love and dependence upon her that required my submissiveness.

To this day if a woman suggests I do or don't do something, my tendency is to comply at once without thinking and then, shortly after, to rebel. But with insight into this I have learned to recognize the tendency and beware of it. Since Mother wanted obedience only for my own safety and not brainwashing to exercise her power, my rebellion has led to good results—questioning of authority and a certain freedom for original thinking within my modest capacity. I can see in myself how my feelings in response to Mother have shaped my political and social outlook—the sympathy with all, as individuals; the rebellion against tyranny; the love of democracy, of reasonableness and agreement; the hatred of hate and violence.

There is one more vivid childhood memory which I almost forgot to tell, but I know it is true because it happened well before any continuous memory, and is a discreet, isolated, fleeting scene, unrelated to anything I can recall at that time. I must have been about four, and remember doing something of which Mother disapproved. It is my only memory of her being thoroughly angry at me. She had often spoken of using the hairbrush to spank me, but she never did so; I could not comprehend it as reality until this scene occurred. I was in the front room and she was determined to act. She went into a back room to get the hairbrush and a towel (which also always figured in her threat; the brush for the spanking, the towel to dry the tears). Mother was only of average size, but when she returned to me she seemed a huge, towering figure, all-powerful, with me totally helpless. As she bore down on me, what I experienced was less physical fear than a feeling that my whole world was collapsing, a sense of complete devastation. Beyond that, I can recall nothing. I have a faint lingering idea that she went ahead with the spanking, but I cannot be sure; she may have perceived my panic and let me off. From this memory I deduce a trend toward submissiveness in myself— to do anything rather than become the object of rejection and attack from the very person upon whom my whole life and security were so largely built and founded.

What has not been a beneficial residue, though, has been guilt. Mother loved me so and I loved her so that I could not help but be guilty for the rebellion and resentment against her. The same for Judy—I loved her deeply, and as I got older I felt just awful about the ways I rejected her and flared up at the little thing. I'd like to think it toughened her, but it left me with guilt—and perhaps with a pattern of rejecting girls and guilt for that. Many years later I wrote Judy about my guilt, and she diminished it by telling me all the good, loving, helpful influences I had had on her. She diminished the guilt but did not fully allay it, because I knew that she was trying to relieve it out of love for me. But I do think we both felt better after bringing the guilt into the open.

When I was about eight, I'd just gotten my first two-wheeler bike. I'd learned to ride it on our deadend sidestreet, at the shore where we used to spend a month or more during the summer. We were having an early dinner, and I was excited over riding it a distance as soon as we finished. But Mother thought the main road too unsafe and forbade it. In a "pet" I shoved a dish of prunes, spattering the brown juice all over the white tablecloth, which we still used in those days.

It was a childish, silly thing to do, but Mother was magnificent; she simply ignored it. And the rest took this cue from her. I was spared not only punishment but embarrassment. For this I was so grateful that it was a step toward more mature relationships, and I do not remember venting such petulance again.

All the devotion from Mother and Judy, however, would not tie me to their apron strings. I was already in rebellion. Already strivings for independence, to leave home, to be out in the world were stirring within me. And I had a model in Father. At home he was strong but a willing part of the matriarchy; out in the world, however, he was independent, a leader, the gaffer, the boss. He never worked for anyone else; he was always his own man. His was a simple, puritan outlook. Father loved his work; it was also his recreation. He was good at it; he controlled it—it never controlled him. He loved his home and whatever it involved for him, but he left its management to Mother. He was superb as a husband and father. Mother said he was unsentimental, and smilingly called him "dead slow." In my later years I once wrote Father a letter on his birthday, stating with complete honesty and sincerity that he was the best father any boy could have. I meant it from my heart. Years later I found that he carried that letter with him always.

When I was ten or eleven he took me with him on one of his trips. It was after dinner and we were on a bus going across broad empty spaces to the center of some small city. The bus was quite empty. We sat on the left. Two seats in front of us were the only other passengers, two young men in their late teens or early twenties. The one on the left at the window was heavy and husky with tousled black hair. In a loud voice that carried clearly he was telling his companion and the world: "I'm going to town tonight for some good humpin' . . . ." He kept repeating the idea. "I'm going to find a woman and get some good humpin' . . . ." Father was embarrassed. He shook his head in a characteristically deploring manner and said to me, "An animal, just an animal."

Fortunately, the young buck did not hear him or chose to ignore us. Father was deceptively light. He knew how to stay out of trouble, but he had done hard physical work on the family farm and had always taken excellent care of his body; he was a light middleweight who could take care of himself. Once on the beach a big man boasted that he would toss Dad over his shoulder, and reached for him. Father quietly grasped the man's hand and executed a move in Indian wrestling, throwing the boaster over his shoulder and landing him supine, but unhurt, on the sand. But Father usually handled situations with his personality alone. About a year before this scene on the bus I was attacked on the street by three much older and bigger boys who held rocks in their fists. I was fast on my feet and ran. Mother was glad I got away safely. But Father's smiling response when he heard my description was, "Did you hold your ground and fight? My legs were too short to run so I always had to stay and fight."

After I'd had sexual experience I told Mother about it, although without any details. She took it with a smile, as something naughty but cute and to be expected. I thought of it as proof of manhood (remembering Ralph's statement, "I never had trouble getting women"). But I never could tell Father. I could not bring myself to refer to it in spite of our free exchanges on every other topic. There must have been some feeling in me, from his silence about sex, that it was not proper, not to be mentioned, and this may have led to some inhibition of it in me. After learning a little about the world outside of my family, I wondered how Father, growing up on a farm, became so refined and how, beaten by his father, he became so gentle. I suppose it was some sort of reaction against his father and a loving relationship with his mother.

We all take into ourselves so much of the feelings of those who rear us. We *identify* with them; we do this even though sometimes we fight against it. But Father never imposed anything whatever on me. He never pushed, cajoled or pressured me on anything, nor denied me. He loved walking, and we had rambles many miles long together. He taught me to swim and to ice-skate, and I was an eager pupil, who grew up loving sports. Sometimes he took me on his trips, and I was an enthusiastic traveler. Occasionally he told me stories from Greek and Norse mythology, and I have enjoyed those stories all my life. He conveyed his puritanism in his opinions, but never tried to impose any of this on me. Therefore, no doubt, I accepted all that I wanted to without rebellion or conflict, for I completely accepted *him*.

With all his travel, Father could have found or made or been exposed to many opportunities with women. I think he felt that he was blessed in his wife and children and in his work and associates, and would not tamper with these foundations of his life. So his rule was simple: sex only in marriage. My wife was brought up with the same rule, and maybe it played a part in our love at first sight. We have lived by this rule, never broken it. We have always had a cocktail hour together before dinner. The "hour" might be only twenty minutes if I were busy, and was usually fruit juice rather than alcohol, to keep my mind clear for the evening's work. But this daily time together with or without the children was sweet to both of us. We discussed any and every thing, but never pried into each other's deeper feelings without invitation. One such time, when we were in our sixties, we decided that henceforth our lives would be measured in years rather than decades and there was no need for the jealousies of our mutually passionate, insatiable youth; we could each accept the other's doing whatever desire prompted if tempting circumstances should arise. But they have still not arisen. Any temptation would have been something purely physical, though; but neither of us could ever be anything but loyal to the other—loyatly is the base of any true marriage.

Judy was one of my great educators. She was born when I was five. From that age, therefore, I was well acquainted with the female body, including the genitals. This worked out as a fine and natural thing. We were bathed together in the same tub, and on trips we slept together in the same bed until I was seven. Any sensual feelings I may have had for Mother were turned to Judy. Compared to Judy, Mother although actually still young was relatively big, old, controlling— Judy was all fresh, pink and appetizing. Often in afterlife there would be two women in my life—one patterned on my loving, giving Mother and not primarily sexual—and another, young and sexually compelling. This split probably contributed to my indecision and failure to marry as early as I so ardently desired. I could not fuse the two images—neither alone was entirely satisfying. There was always an unattainable ideal, somehow just out of reach. Another possible reason for my failure to marry early was my mixture of feeling toward Judy. My resentment of her presence, of her demands on me, of her disrupting my privacy, of her getting into and borrowing my things, was far overbalanced by affection and acceptance of her as a beloved and integral part of the family. But this continuation of feelings toward Judy, the love and resentment, has I'm sure shaped my pattern of loving individual girls but of being on guard in some way against them.

Another powerful force in my feelings toward women and my difficulty in finding a wife was the undying pattern toward Aunt Edie.

I did not think she was with me enough to have so strong an influence. She and her husband, my mother's brother, lived about one half mile away, and soon they moved to another city where one of my great joys was an all-too-rare visit with them. Aunt Edie was of a more delicate beauty than Mother—a gentle blue-eyed blond, childless, who doted on me and whom I adored. At their house a half grapefruit never appeared plain, but always with a maraschino cherry. The top crust of an apple pie was always latticed, and when there was no ice cream to put on it, there was whipped cream or a pitcher of light cream. Their bathroom always smelled so good. It was not until long after I started dating that it began to dawn on me that finding delicate gentle, blue-eyed blonds so irresistible was a revitalizing of my love for Aunt Edie. After I was married, she once came to visit us, and my wife, although a great sceptic and critic and slow to intimacy, loved her at first sight.

All these feelings bound sex with love so that I could not have sex freely with prostitutes or without love, or shared with another man. And these feelings also left me with an identification with young children and an abiding delight in watching them grow, which almost led me into becoming a pediatrician. In medical school on the pediatric wards I thought I was treating angels. These patterns also gave me a great reservoir of understanding and appreciation and love for my own children. Judy, my innocent instructor, I did not treat as well as I might have, or half as well as she deserved! Toward Father I felt no resentment and no guilt, at least consciously—he was my best friend. And love easily won out with Mother, over the resentments of her authority. Whoever is so fortunate as to have lived as a child with acceptance and unquestioned love is destined by this for a good married life, and for friendship and goodwill to men. Wars do indeed start in the minds of men—they start in the hate that begins in early childhood as an automatic response to what is done to the child.

I have tried to review only a little bit of those attitudes which had been grooved in me and would therefore provide the channels for the great drives when they came, the drives toward making an independent life and career; for sex, for girls and feminine companionship; for mating, for marriage, for reproduction, for a home of my own—drives that impel so many animals besides man. From Mother came unconditional love and warmth, even if not always with entirely wisely administered control. From this love poured in I got much love to give out, as well as much need for it; I got a deep need for women and appreciation of them, and, as with Judy, the fusion of sex with love; and some rebellious tendency to be independent, and a residue of guilt for it. Judy attracted to herself much of my feelings toward Mother, thereby fixing the sex appeal for me onto younger women; with some residual elements of my rejection of her and of guilt for it, which also came out toward young women in my youth. From Father (and of course, Mother) came simple basic monogamous mating with unswerving devotion as husband, father and breadwinner. Even this little that I have so briefly described I learned only later in my analysis, and that was just a small beginning in seeing the patterns that had shaped me and how those patterns lived themselves out in all I did and felt, and in how I behaved toward men, women, children and animals.

4
CHILDHOOD

Deep in the man sits fast his fate
To mould his fortunes mean or great . . .

Ralph Waldo Emerson, "Fate"

Men are but children of a larger growth,
Our appetites are apt to change as theirs,
And full as craving too, and full as vain;
And yet the soul, shut up in her dark room,
Viewing so clear abroad, at home sees nothing . . .

John Dryden, "Mankind"

That I was aware of a difference in my feelings between women and
men before the age of two at the latest, said Corey Jones, is suggested in my first memory of Mother and Father. This is quite
different from concern with the anatomy of the genitals. This anatomy was no problem for me after the arrival of my sister, when I
was just five. But the intriguing thing is not merely the anatomy.
It is the overall fascination that the female holds for the male and
vice versa. This I noticed when first I was able to toddle along the
street past the corner house. For in that nice house lived a brother
and sister about two years older than I, named John and Mary
Brooke. Curiously, we always waved to each other but never played
together. I always saw them together and heard them referred to as
a unit: John-and-Mary. But even at age three I felt a difference—
like that in the first memory between Mother and Father. John was
nice; but Mary, whose quiet dark eyes and wavy dark hair I can still
see, had that softness and indescribable something that was dissimilar and alluring. Not that I thought any more about it than in
the feelings of the moment; for, as I grew up, my life was centered
on the boys of the neighborhood. This was a great blessing which

no child should be denied. There were about ten of us boys on "the block"—enough for all kinds of games, which over the years developed from tag and hide-and-seek to the many street games and sports of adolescents.

There were two of the boys on the block where I lived who very often were late in coming to play with us after school. That was because they had to go somewhere with (as I recall it) a rather rhythmic, poetic-sounding, two-syllable name. It turned out to be some sort of instruction in Hebrew, whether in the language or something else I never learned. (I have asked about the name since, but none I've heard sounds quite right.) I was sorry for them because they were regular fellows, but while the rest of us played they had to spend time on something which sounded strange and useless. I never did find out the point of it, or see that it made any difference. A little later there were boys who had to go to church very early in the morning while the rest of us took our ease. Some of them seemed to feel superior because of this, but we did not see why. Then we met boys who looked different because they were black-skinned, but who were either good guys or bad guys, like all the other boys. And that was the upshot of knowing all these different boys—we got used to their peculiarities, and these were unimportant. What was important was whether we liked them and whether they liked us and fitted in with us, whether they were friendly and fun or hostile and dangerous. Today I would say personality is everything.

Absorbed with the boys, three of whom were close friends, I had no sustained interest whatever in girls. In fact, at about age seven, apropos of some discussion at dinner, I announced in all seriousness that when I grew up I would marry no one except my sister Judy.

One summer about two years later, when I was nine or ten, we were at the shore as usual for a month or two and my closest friend, Andy, was there with his family—his younger brother and his parents. They rented a house directly across from ours. His cousin Della, who was about our age, came to visit them for a weekend. It was afternoon; the weather was warm, the sun shining. Five of us were out playing one-o'cat with a soft ball. Della joined in. And she was good. My male superiority, formed possibly in part from Judy's being so much younger and more helpless, was shaken. Della could throw and bat with the average, but what speed!—she ran faster than any of us. When she came near me in all the activity and fun of the game I felt something different. Her eyes sparkled as she concentrated on the ball, she was sweaty as we all were, and I was aware of the difference. She exuded something. It felt pleasant, disturbing, fascinating. She was the first girl, exogamic, outside of the family, that I was fully conscious of physically and as a person, with all the magnetism of healthy animal femininity. After the weekend she left. What if she had stayed? She might have become the girl next door whom the boy finally marries. And meanwhile, had our immature needs been channeled to each other, what companionship might we have found, and what frustrations might we have encountered or been spared? But she left and I forgot her, or almost forgot her.

Life in our bunch of boys on the block in the city was pretty idyllic, always having friendly kids to play with and later to wander about with. I wonder if it exists at all in the cities today, swollen as they are by the great immigrations from rural areas. But we soon learned that the world is not always idyllic. I have referred to being attacked without provocation by the three big strange boys. This might happen if one strayed into other areas, where "gang" meant more than "bunch." Here we sensed fear by instinct, and learned it from reality. Election nights we would search for wood to build a fire and would roast potatoes in it. Two of us were out of our neighborhood looking for wood when we saw two big boys stop an old man with an empty pushcart. We recognized one of the boys, named Landers. The big boys said the cart would make fine firewood, and they grabbed it. The old man of course hung on, whereupon Landers, who wore an ironnail ring, swung at him, and the head of the nail ripped open the old man's cheek. He screamed, people gathered, and the boys fled with the cart. We had learned to stay out of such things, and we quietly vanished. Why should our group of boys be so friendly and a group nearby be so heartlessly violent? At the time I was learning self-preservation and did not think about that at all. But in adult life I have studied the question, and feel sure that there is one main answer: our bunch came generally from loving homes. But those other boys were taking out on each other or on a stranger or an "enemy" the burning anger they felt against their own parents for the way they had been, and perhaps still were, treated. That is the basic reason behind seriously dangerous teen-age gangs and adult gangs, and the main cause of crime and even, under certain conditions, war—the main reason, in fact, for human violence. Few problems are solved by violence, and few would not be solved peacefully if all concerned were of goodwill.

The violence of these boys, as we learned from experience, came out against anyone, even against animals. They beat up smaller boys and boys their own age if they outnumbered them. They shockingly showed no respect or consideration for age, nor even for women.

Women and sex interested us hardly at all then. But we were not ignorant of these things. Ideas, information, experience, flowed pretty freely among us. We had a pretty good idea of intercourse. Somehow I had the idea that the male organ rubbed on the outside and left its juices there, rather than entering. Some of us could still not believe that our parents had sex relations, although we all knew where babies, ourselves included, came from, so that it must be true. Probably this attitude was due to no more than the home atmosphere against sexual interest in mother and sister. At any rate, we heard of hostility to girls, even to gang-shags. Those teen-agers who would kidnap a girl and all of them rape her. I don't think this sounded like much excitement or fun to most of us. Our love for our mothers and sisters had formed too much good feeling to be intrigued by sex when it was so flagrantly a vehicle for the brutality we knew and had always to be alert against for our own protection. Of course we knew about masturbation and tried it. But that was long before puberty. Nothing happened. There were no juices. It was no fun—we dropped it.

Not too much later on, an older boy and a big one, named Danny, asked me into his room. Thinking nothing of it I went. He lowered his pants and wanted me to stroke his genital, which was partially erect. I did not. He reached for mine. Automatically I pulled back forcefully. He dropped the matter, and I went out into the sunlight. This was something I had never heard about, but I felt that somehow it was all wrong. I didn't think in terms of morals, of course, but just felt it was unhealthy, disgusting. It did not touch anything in my makeup, which was all shaped to friendship and helpfulness and companionship with men, via Father—with all sensuousness firmly bound to women, via Mother, Aunt and Sister. I remember clearly, though, that although I was only a little kid, I lost all respect for

Danny. I never said a word about this to anyone, but I had no use for him anymore. Ideally, a child should be able to discuss anything and everything with his parents, but the parents ideally would have to remain calm. This was a transient incident; forgetting it was best. Sex and women remained something we were aware of but as yet had no real interest in, beyond occasional stories and jokes. Our preoccupations were with athletics—walks, bicycles, baseball, hockey, street games, explorations—a beginning discovery of books, and, of course, autos, which were only just appearing on the streets. Puberty gathered slowly, like a storm, and like a storm it burst suddenly, in a flash.

But first I should tell an incident of earlier childhood. Four or five of us were lounging for a few moments. I was then seven. Sam was also seven; he was not a close friend but was nice. He leaned over good-humoredly and grabbed the ball I was holding. Also in fun, I shoved him down on his back in retaliation. In so doing I felt an erection. It was pleasant, but nothing I was impelled to continue. Having no idea about it as good or bad, if the impulse had been there I would have continued the friendly scuffle. But we sat up and went on chatting. And that was that. I mention it because like so many of these passing trivia, it seemed to hold a clue to a problem of potency I had later—or what I thought was such a problem. Fourteen years later this incident occurred to me and suggested that male sexual potency certainly in me and perhaps generally is connected with mastery, control and power over another. This is why a girl can usually seduce a man sexually if she can provoke his aggressiveness, even his anger, and probably why weak, childish girls often have strong sex appeal.

From age about eleven, Andy was my best friend. In the summer especially we were inseparable. His family and mine both came to the shore—if his family did not go, then he came alone for long visits with me, and vice versa. So we both had long, beautiful free summers together. Our fathers took only short vacations. The rest of the time they commuted, usually coming down only for weekends. If our parents thought they were doing something good for the children, they were deeply right. Father worked; Mother ran the house; Andy and I were big enough by now to do just about everything—and we did so with zest and relish. Few chores were required of us. The smaller children were by then amusing and no longer interfered in any way. We swam, fished, crabbed, hiked, bicycled, played sandlot baseball, flew big "wing and angle" kites on the beautiful, clean, little-frequented, out-of-the-way beach—an outdoor life, free and clean as the wind. Those were the halcyon days!

Whoever suggested that the Garden of Eden is analogous to childhood was very perceptive. The idea is that all was provided then, and life was innocent. But Eve tempted Adam with the apple of sexual knowledge. With it came the snake, symbolic of the phallus and sexual desire. Thus came maturation and the need and command to leave the home of childhood, to go forth into the world and earn one's way by the sweat of one's brow. Responsibilities for survival and then for a wife, children—the end of the carefree years is heralded by the stirrings of sex, which, for all its pleasures, messes up so many lives. Only today the years are no longer so carefree; for it seems that the schools, with short supplies for the demands of the increasing populations, unconsciously and rapidly impose such pressures as to defeat the true purposes of education.

But in a carefree summer at the shore when we were eleven or twelve we had some new interests. We would collect our urine in bottles and hide it. I think this was doing one forbidden mysterious thing instead of another, which we could not yet do. In a primitive way, it may have formed a basis for my later interests in the mysteries of chemistry. At night, before going to sleep, we had fantasies of control of others and even of cruelty to them. They were sadistic, but I think they also expressed unconscious germinating sexual impulses. Finally, and I don't know when or how it started, we began clear strong curiosity about young women. I think we were as clean-cut as boys come. But we evolved a code of secret signals: for example, "select" signaled a chance to look up a girl's leg; "seaboard" referred to breasts; the ultimate was "cedar" for genital. If one of us noticed something, he would work the appropriate word into a sentence.

One day two girls were at a neighbor's to help out with preparations for weekend house guests. They rested sitting on the porch. Andy and I were below on the ground, looking up. The view was unobstructed all the way. No signals needed. We kept the girls talking as long as we could. The one—Rena—about twenty-two, was sort of hard. Toward her our response was crude physical sex, as to a female body. But Alice, about eighteen, was a gentle, pretty, lovely friendly girl, with golden hair and a sweet dimpled smile.

We had no scruples about the sexual curiosity for Rena's anatomy. We did not like her; we even disliked her a little. But Alice was different. She was so pretty, so nice, so friendly and clean and innocent. We were a little in love with her. Even such an opportunity to see everything could not push aside regard for her as a lovely girl and the feeling that we must not do anything at her expense. Sex then must be part of the totality, the unity, of love and mating, home, children. Does it ever break loose as a force in itself without making problems, because of being directed against a body, without consideration of the personality that body is part of, that personality which, like all others, wants love and respect as its deepest needs? If a man has been loved and respected in his home, then he has love and respect to give. But if he has been provoked into anger and hate as a child then heaven help the girl he thinks he is "in love" with! For no word is so misused as "love." True love is a generous, altruistic interest in another. It is a capability of maturity. But often the word is used to mean sex attraction, even if there is no love, even if there is underlying hate. Sex and hostility are not love. And not all that is attraction is love. It may be dependence, or status, or other things also.

The glands were beginning to pump. The bedtime fantasies of controlling others were becoming outright sexual fantasies of girls, now accompanied by erections. Urges to hold, disrobe, see, clasp, kiss a girl were becoming almost unsupportable. Erections might occur at any time and be embarrassing. Mac, a little cruder but a little more direct than some of us, chuckled in the corridor at school, "Gosh, I have a hard on and can't keep it down." The urges grew stronger. I decided that since I could not take off a girl's clothes in reality, if I dreamed of a girl I would do so in the dream. I tried but of course it never worked. I did not know that what we permit ourselves in dreams we permit ourselves in life. If I were a delinquent who could attack a girl in life, then I would be able to dream it, but I couldn't. I could only have done it with the girl's permission and I did not know any girls of that kind, or so I thought. The mounting instinct with all its intense curiosity was entirely exogamic, directed only to girls outside of the home, not at all to Mother and Judy, with whom my relationships continued unruffled. The storm was boiling up from within, but showing on the surface to others not at all, so far as I knew then or know now.

The tension was becoming almost intolerable. One night when I got into bed with fantasies of a girl and disrobing her I rolled over on my abdomen for a comfortable sleeping position; suddenly there came my first orgasm. It took me by surprise and in almost complete ignorance. I had heard of the seminal fluid, but had no concept whatever of the *feelings* associated with it. So this was it. And how would it be with a real girl instead of a fantasy?

Nobody had told me, as I've said, that I'd have several of these a week, no matter what, even if I tried to control them. Nor did anyone say that since this was so, I should go ahead and enjoy them. Of course, I did pick up some of the opposite ideas, that masturbation rots your brain and makes you crazy. But my family was too realistic, too down-to-earth, for me to take any stock in that kind of talk. I was supported, as so often and in so many things, by the wisdom of the streets, where the word was this: ask a man if he has masturbated; if he says "no" then he is a liar, or else sick. So I lived with it and enjoyed it, except for the shame; but kept it secret or thought I did, or did as best I could. It probably would have been a relief if Mother and I could have talked about it. She must have seen the spots on the sheets. It would have cleared the air. But I never mentioned it, and neither did she. And neither did Father. And the shame about it built up; when I was older, I felt that other men got women but I only masturbated.

I don't know if the boys who were more open about it were better off or not. There was a circle of older boys who made no bones about it at all. About a half dozen of them took it lightly and would strip and all masturbate together in a contest to see who could ejaculate farthest. I don't know if this is healthy frankness. I do know that some of those boys had serious emotional problems later in life; maybe there was no connection though, and the more repressed boys have problems too.

For me, sex has always been—if only because of its very intensity— an ultraprivate thing. It is something from the inner depths and fastnesses of my mind, my personality, my body. Therefore, in unrestrained abandon with a woman it is a wild animalistic thing, but also it is something so personal, private, special, the ultimate culmination in feeling. Because it means so much to me and always has, I can never share it with a woman who does not feel the same about it. If she does not, then it is a tawdry thing and a secret depth of the soul has been profaned and cheapened, its mystery and treasure made dirt and dust.

Perhaps the fathers are right who take their sons at this age to a prostitute to learn about sex. I wanted to know badly enough, but with my feelings about it I doubt if it would have worked. Something I've treasured all my life might have been smirched, even destroyed, at age thirteen or fourteen.

What of these very nice girls, of refinement and feeling, warm and loving, who start off at fourteen or so to have love affairs, lasting about six months, in which they have sex with the boys? They seem to enjoy it and appear to show no ill effects at the time. Are there any ill effects later? My sister Judy and her friends were not that way. She dated the field, married at twenty-two and waited for intercourse until she was married. She and her friends did not think much of the girls who were free sexually. They thought they all came from upset homes; they even predicted which girls were destined for trouble. I never met, consciously and effectively, one of these willing ones; perhaps I did not recognize them because I was too naive. Whether that has been my loss or gain I do not know. But it was a long wait from thirteen to twenty-one to begin a sex life with women. Now I have lived through the early decades of the pill and of permissiveness and of the "drug culture." Do these developments make for increased happiness and maturity—or the opposite? I do not know. But I suspect that they do not decrease emotional problems. Rather, this freedom usually increases them by exerting a corrupting influence and impairing development to maturity through weakening the character and providing too immediate a satisfaction of the pleasure principle at the expense of the reality principle. Freud wrote of the restraints of civilization, and thought they required too great a sacrifice—but the pill and drugs may well have lifted the restraints too much and too rapidly for the long-term good of the individual, our nation and humanity. For "he who conquers himself is greater than he who taketh a city."

I still wonder if there is any solution except early marriage— but that involves meeting the right mate! And just that I tried to do, beginning at age thirteen—but not entirely consciously and determinedly; rather, at first, with the vague searching of childhood. But it was the biological instinct to mate and form a home which we know as marriage and family. How this was operating in me, without my knowledge, was soon evident.

I had no idea how long the road would be to marriage and children. But I can describe this long arduous, strenuous path and some of what befell me during the search because it is a part of biography that has been neglected, and cries for understanding. It seems rather silly to devote endless research two centuries later to disclosing the sex and love lives of Jefferson and Franklin. The sex and love life is of vital importance for one's understanding, especially by the adolescent who is struggling with his own sexual growth and might be helped by reading how it worked out in other, more contemporary individuals, people who are relatively healthy and have succeeded in solving the problems of the sex drive and have mated happily at long last.

5
ADOLESCENCE

At first, it appeared that I might be the type of personality for whom mating would be the first of life's three great problems to be solved, for I fell in love early at about thirteen as nearly as I can recall. Some friends of my mother had a big party or were all attending some sort of function. Their children were included. My mother was pretty good about letting me off from such social gatherings to play with the boys; but this time, for some reason, she insisted that I go with her. I kicked like a broncho, but she won and I went. The whole gathering was even then only a mist in my memory, out of which stands as a sharp, clear image a girl my own age whom I saw and did not even meet. I found out her name: Minerva. My father had told me a little about Greek and Roman gods and goddesses. I connected Minerva with Pallas Athena, and for my whole life I have had a special fondness for these goddesses. Minerva was to me a beautiful name that just suited this girl's perfect little figure, her serious but bright gray eyes, her freckles, the frame of light-brown hair, all blending with the tannish color of her cloth skirt and jacket. New feelings swept over me, such as I had never experienced before. I think I did not show them, but inside I was transfixed. She moved with such vitality and grace! And then the party was over; we left; and I had never met her. How true can be that sweet, simple song: "There is a lady, sweet and kind, was never face so pleased my mind. I did but see her passing by, but still I love her till I die."

Suppose I had been told from an early age that I would sometimes see a little girl for whom I would have special feelings. And that when I did, I would be shy, for that was natural. And that she would be shy too. But that if I were friendly and gentle and considerate, it was all right to talk to her. Suppose my communication with Mother had been such that I could have told her. Suppose, suppose—"the saddest words of tongue or pen. . . ." But I was overwhelmed by my own feelings and hid them from the world, kept them in that deep vault of unassailable privacy reserved for my feelings toward girls I especially care about.

What is there that makes one girl so different from others? The female moth, or bird, waits, and the males come. She selects and accepts only a certain one. In other species, males do the selecting, or, as in humans, both do. Part of it relates to feelings to family. Was Minerva enough like Mother, beloved Aunt Edie, and sister Judy to fit into my deepest feelings for them—and at the same time, enough strange and different and exogamic to be outside family sexual restraints so that these deep feelings were attracted outward and over to her? Had she similarities to myself, kindredness of spirit and perhaps qualities I sensed which she had more abundantly and freely than I? Was there a similarity in our feelings toward our families so that we would have understood one another? Of course, I did not ask such questions until years afterward. At the time there were no questions. I did not know what was happening. I was swept into loving and being in love. We call it "puppy love." Perhaps it is always so sharp and clear and intense; perhaps it is always doomed. "But our love it was stronger by far than the love of those older than we. Of many far wiser than we. . . ."*

I thought I would see Minerva again, and meet her. But I took no steps. I was too shy to tell Mother, which would have been the only way. Was this a defect in my character, or an inhibition of some sort? I think that it was more a lack of knowledge, that if Mother or Father had told me of these feelings that I would simply have said I wanted to meet Minerva. I think I would have said it without confessing the depth of my feelings for her. But maybe not; perhaps I would have been too bashful to reveal my feelings, to ask to meet a goddess, even one who was my age.

And what if I had met her? Was I in love with a vision? What would have happened in reality? Being so loved at home, probably I assumed every girl would love me. But maybe she was already in love. Maybe I was too overprotected, had too little independence, too little knowledge of the world, was still too much of a child to interest her. If so, was there a deficiency in me or in my education, and that provided by my parents, that I had not learned what was mature and what was childish? Is there anything more important to

*From "Annabelle Lee" by Edgar Allen Poe.

know? Had Minerva and I met, I might have lost a beautiful illusion. We men all have fantasied ideals which embody the anticipated satisfaction of our childhood desires and of the frustrations of our lives, and they are apt to be very different from how real women actually are, namely, suffering children like ourselves. At thirteen I had never heard about illusion and reality. More and more I now value reality. But with man's hostility to man, sometimes reality is intolerable, and even the strongest must look away at times and find solace in illusion.

So I was left without the real Minerva and with only my dreams of her and a special feeling for Minerva and Pallas Athena, the loving, understanding goddesses of wisdom.

One evening soon after this I had just gone to bed. I was alone on the third floor. The sadistic kind of fantasies had vanished, and I was falling to sleep thinking of Minerva. We were married, and in some lovely pastoral country, walking hand-in-hand, communing with each other and together communing with nature. It was very pure. But we were married and it was going to end with sex and sleeping together. At that point I heard a sound. My door was open. There was a hall, and on the left a bath and then another bedroom, which Rena was using while she was staying with us temporarily as household help. It was a favor to her, but she was helping us. Her face was not pleasant but the solution of the street was "put a towel over it." At the sound I looked. She came out of her room; the light in her room shone through the sheer nightgown she was wearing, and I saw everything as she snapped the light on in the bathroom and moved slowly in. I could hardly control the impulse to leap up and grab her and try to have sex. From what I later learned she might have yielded. But what complications might have ensued I cannot guess. It might also have been that kissing that face might have cooled my urges. She disappeared into the bathroom. Nothing came of it. But next day at dinner Rena was gone. Mother was indignant. We would never see her again. Somehow, Mother had discovered that Rena had gonorrhea—and dared live with us and expose us all to it, especially us children. Of course I'd heard of the "clap" and of syphilis. But that was only in people remote from us, the kind of girls I heard about but never saw. This was close to home, even *in* the home. I'd learned something.

That winter I went to a party at the home of a pretty girl named

Winnie. She was small, dainty and perfect. I was attracted to her, but only as a pretty girl, with no sudden deep feelings such as I had had for Minerva, no dreams of roaming over beautiful hills with her, hand-in-hand, on into marriage. Winnie was a little stand-offish and very much in command of all situations. We played "spin the bottle." Since the awakening of my feelings for girls I had felt so ardent and passionate that I had to act the opposite—very controlled about them. Maybe I thought that if a girl knew I had any sexual feeling toward her, she would be offended, insulted, and would reject me—and love, acceptance and admiration were what I wanted above everything else. I never saw touching a girl taken so lightly as this—spin the bottle, and kiss whatever girl it pointed to when it stopped. So simple, just like that. I spun it and luckily it stopped at Winnie. She got up, led me out into the hall, presented her cheek just for an instant, for a quick peck, and whisked back into the room. It wasn't much, but I was amazed at how good it felt!

It is striking to recognize today that I still have a vivid memory of Winnie. I think I could pick her out of a picture or out of a crowd. But I have no memory whatsoever of any other girl at that party. I see the room, the circle of us sitting on the floor, spinning the bottle, the hallway and the split-second kiss—but only dim figures except for Winnie. It is the same for the party at which I saw Minerva. I remember her vividly in every detail, including the colors and textures of her hair, her eyes, her skin, her little suit—but the others were only a confused crowd, through which I saw Minerva. And so it is with this selectivity. Of the many, many girls I met as a youth, only these certain ones are alive in memory, as alive as they were then. The others meant nothing to me and passed out of my life and mind.

The summer when I was fourteen, I went one evening with another boy and his date to the home of a girl who was about thirteen, named Lorie. The night was hot. We sat in the living room chatting. A balmy breeze coming through the wide-open windows furled the curtains; I wondered why we were not outdoors. The boy sat on the couch with the other girl. Lorie was in a big overstuffed leather chair; I was on a pull-up chair near it. She said it would be cooler with the lights out and turned them off, leaving the room dimly lit by a lamp in the hall. I had a vague feeling I could not understand; the evening ended tamely. While saying goodnight to

Lorie and thanking her for the evening, she got me aside and said, "Why didn't you come sit in the big chair with me?" I said, "May I come by and see you tomorrow?" She said, "Yes." So I had missed a wonderful opportunity, but I thought, "Next time I'll know what to do."

Next day I rode over on my bike. Her much older sister said, "No, Lorie isn't in." I asked when I might catch her in and left. Well, I returned about five days running, but Lorie was never there. Then one day in a pickup baseball game I saw her on the bench. She was quite obviously friends with a boy named George. He was a nice fellow, quiet, a little older than I, a little more assured. I guessed that he had known enough to join her in the big chair. But then why had she made the little play for me? At the time I did not even guess. She seemed so refined, but could she possibly have been one of the friendly, free, easy girls? Suppose I had known enough to take the cue and sit beside her? Would it have led to necking, petting, and, before the summer ended, even intercourse? And if so, what would the effects have been on her? Presumably none, if she did that sort of thing anyway. On me, then? I think perhaps excellent. But we never know where sex will lead, what dark forces it will awaken, or what silent guilt it will generate. Willy-nilly, I remained chaste and freehearted.

Lorie was only a missed opportunity, but with Lucy I was briefly just a little in love. She was in my class in the country school I attended and enjoyed in the fall, before returning to the city. I had never formally met her or spoken with her. I came through the big city school system, which in those days kept the sexes strictly separated; high school was an all-boy school. And mostly male teachers were hired, tough men to handle those tough, violence-prone boys. Lucy was my age, a trifle heavy, but so clear-eyed, so serene, so demure, and the little gold crucifix emphasized the purity of her breast. We were classmates; each grade had only one class and one teacher. One day on the street I saw her at a distance. We were walking toward each other. We would certainly pass. I must say hello to her. Then she was there and I managed to smile and stammer some greeting. She smiled so demurely and said hello in such a friendly way. Then we had passed each other. I felt warm and good; I realized that I should have turned and asked if I might walk a little way with her. Was it too late? I looked back—she had turned the corner. I froze. It did not seem right to run back after her. I walked on, blushing, reproaching myself. An older boy, also a classmate, came along and asked if I'd seen Lucy go by. I said, "Yes." He was gentle and friendly. He said, "You're in love with her, aren't you?" And what came out of me, without thinking, was, "No, of course not!"

"Yes you are, admit it," he said.

"No I'm not," I lied.

He smiled softly and went on. I was in a turmoil. I still remember it. I felt dishonest denying what was most certainly true. I felt like a fool, for he was sympathetic and would have helped me meet her. But at the same time my treasured privacy resented the invasion. How could he, almost a stranger, dare ask me something so personal, so deeply felt? And then the thought—how did he know? Is it so obvious? Or can he read people in a way that I cannot and never will be able to? So the summer passed, and Lucy went out of my life— no goddess like Minerva, yet she was so relaxed, so sweet, so beautiful. If we had met, might we have given each other what we needed and saved the turbulence of many later involvements? Was she already committed? Did her heaviness melt away, leaving her lissome and svelte? Or by the time she was twenty was she seriously overweight, a condition which has always repelled me? Would I always see and love and nothing more? What the after effects are, I do not know, but I still carry demure, clear-eyed, beautiful Lucy vividly in my memory.

At sixteen I was part of a little group of fellows and girls. A few went steady; others dated as they wished, i.e., "played the field." That summer, some of them went for a while to a spot where there were a lake and a river, with swimming and baseball, and canoes that could be rented. I joined them for a few days. One of the boys was named Randy. He struck me as weak. Probably I especially disliked this weakness because of hating my own weakness—especially disliked that sense of not being as assured, not knowing my way around or how to handle people and situations as well as others seemed to. Randy smoked cigarettes. Most of us didn't; we thought it an affectation, a show of sophistication. But it was all right; no one then thought it harmful. One day in casual chatting Randy said he was unable to stop smoking. That was the limit—how could anyone have so weak a will? But a few minutes later in the conversation, Randy was instructing me on what to do on my canoeing date with Rita that evening. He told me where and how to rent the canoe. "Then," he advised, "you go from the rear seat where you've been paddling down next to Rita. Take the cushion along. Make her backrest low, or get rid of it entirely. Then put your arms around her."

I was pretty surprised. How did Randy know this? He must have been out with her. Or was this a regular procedure they all used? But Rita, I thought, was sweet on Rob and only gave me a date as an old, platonic friend. Well, Rita was pretty and I certainly had urges to touch her. I called for her, and when it was dusk we set out for the river. It was a pleasant sight, with a few colored lanterns here and there. I followed Randy's instructions to the letter, and to my amazement, Rita complied. If Randy had instructed me further, to kiss and to neck, pet and go on ahead to intercourse, I'm not sure I would not have done it, and I'm not sure to this day that Rita would not have gone on complying. She was pretty and I liked her and had wanted to touch her, but she meant no more to me than that. The feeling was purely physical. There was no such feeling as for Minerva.

I didn't think our group went on to all-out intercourse. That was long before the pill, of course, and before antibiotics. It was a time of fear of pregnancy, and fear of venereal disease. But it was not only those externals that restrained me, I think. It was also my internal fear of rejection, of not being loved, accepted and admired because of moral superiority, not only by the girl but by my inner image of my father and the atmosphere of my home—from which I also got a love for women that could not stand the possibility of hurting them or of being rejected by them. This was perhaps not all love, but part of the pattern toward Judy, of loving her but also defending psychologically against my early hostility to her.

Next day, Rita was the same as always, and quite obviously sweet on Rob, despite lying in my arms, though nothing more, the previous evening. I still don't know whether this kind of enjoyment, even all the way to full intercourse, is a great thing or not. Maybe I missed an opportunity. Maybe I missed years of all-out sexual enjoyment by not knowing what was going on. It didn't work out too well for Rita, however, though maybe it does for others. She married at eighteen, and at twenty-five I met her by chance. She was not with her husband, but with one of the boys of that old group. She had a child, five years old. Two years later our paths again crossed; she was with a still different man and was in the process of divorce. I told my sister Judy about this. At the time of the canoe incident Judy was only twelve, but Judy remembered: "Why are you surprised?" she said. "Wasn't she destined for it? Wasn't she the one whose father was never home? Didn't she have something all wrong in her family?"

The anatomy and physiology of sex is nothing at all to know and teach. Any elementary biology course does it fine, with the birds and the bees and the flowers ("Yes, they do it too.") I still remember "the pollen that the bee carries from the anther of the stamen to the stigma of the pistil." We all understood that in terms of humans, sex and babies. But the *psychology* of sex, why all the individual differences, how it works in different people, the deep *feelings*—we don't know much about this, and that is why there is all this controversy over "sex education." Who knows that much about the part of it that is the real problem? Is that not the connection of sex with love—and with hate? For example, why did Rita—a sincere, generous person, and a good friend—mess up her whole life and that of her child with marital infidelities and divorces, which brought so little happiness and so much suffering? Does the difficulty all lie in the personal emotional relations with oneself and with another person?

Like so many others, I grew up through puberty in ignorance and confusion about the tremendous phenomena of attraction to girls and different reactions to different girls. Thus we grow up struggling with our instincts. I used to think only that I was a fool to have missed those opportunities, but now I do not know whether in man's battle with his instincts the ones who are stronger than their instincts do not have the better lives. Certainly I was fortunate in having only the great attraction to girls to struggle with, and not (like some of the boys and girls) also hatred and guilt to parents and (in some tragic cases) attraction to the same sex—which some persons give in to, while others suffer horribly with it. It is fortunate to have such good mental health, stemming from good relationships with parents and siblings, that one has only to struggle with a normal instinct: the physical and psychological attraction to the opposite sex; for that is tremendous, powerful, complex and confusing enough. As the longings and sexual urges became almost intolerable in me, I emerged from adolescence with no single-minded devotion to a "girl next door," with whom I would join hands and walk into the sunrise. The solution of the problem of mating remained as remote for me as ever.

6
LOVE

Pity me that the heart is slow to learn
What the swift mind beholds at every turn.

Edna St. Vincent Millay,
"Pity Me Not"

Then came college, said Corey Jones, and the war and the SATC, although I was underage. My experience seems to show that every decision and sustained activity is the result of eight or ten motivations and reactions, some mature, others derived from the emotional patterns of childhood. My temperament fitted the peace testimony, yet I volunteered for officer training. The cause was partly sincere patriotism, which I have always felt deeply while also recognizing that its abuses lead to jingoism and even wars. Then a powerful motivation was the pattern of feeling inferior to the "big boys," and the drive to sign up with them to show that I was equal to whatever they could do. And part of my decision resulted from the exhibitionism of the uniform, of being recognized as one of the earliest in the service. Of course I believed much of the propaganda about stopping the Hun and what "he" had done to Belgium. The rest of my decision really lay just in being caught up in the emotions of the time—not to be an evader or shirker, but to join the others in doing what needed to be done, in spite of the difficulties and dangers. An essential element was what later received the correct label, "masculine protest." All these dynamics, then, impelled me into the Student Army Training Corps (SATC) almost without thinking, and freed me from my usual struggles with doubt. It was also characteristic of me that once my decision had been reached, I acted on it without delay; such action was often to put me in a position of leadership, contrary to my opinion of myself as just a childish follower.

But none of this solved anything in my problems about women. How could it? (In fact, had the war lasted another year, I would have gone overseas and might not have returned in one piece, if at all.) My juices gathered and burst forth three or four times a week in complete privacy, but never in intercourse. I met new attitudes in the men I encountered. Mort was frank: "Why should I spend time or money on a woman if I don't get anything out of her? Why, that girl wouldn't even kiss me goodnight!" I thought a little about this philosophy of going out for what one could get. I remembered Rita in the canoe and how easy it was as far as I went. But I didn't think highly of it. For I was the son of my mother and the brother of Judy Jones; and if any fellow of any age were to take that attitude toward either of them, I could only think that, peace-loving as I was, I would want to strike him one deadly blow. I thought Mort was an animal as Father had once used the term, and I was sure the girl couldn't stand Mort. (My father, as I have said, came from a farm and should have not maligned animals that way.) I hoped the next girl would not only refuse to kiss Mort goodnight but would push his face in. Perhaps I was only an inhibited idealist, but certainly I did not like Mort.

The rest of life, though, apart from women, expanded gloriously. I seemed to be well coordinated and got to be reasonably good at sports and enjoyed them enormously, although I was too light for the college teams. Also, the sense of well-being sports gave and the good fellowship were satisfying. Always a participant rather than a spectator, I lost interest in following major league baseball as the worlds of art, music and drama opened up. I no longer saw much of Andy. Our paths diverged. But I met Charles and we explored together. And then I met Jim, a classmate. Jim was outstanding. I wondered that he bothered with me. He was only one year older, but knew so much more of the world. We hit it off marvelously, and thought it great to phone each other any hour of the day or night if something was afoot. He introduced me to politics, economics, social thinking all over the world and the key books in each field. He questioned and studied what I'd blindly grown up in and taken for granted. This was way beyond the ignorant guesswork of freshman bull sessions; he introduced me to Ralph Ackley, and the circle widened to acquaintance with artists, musicians, actors and, above all, science and scientists. We moved through college. With science, athletics, Charles, Jim and Ralph and the great urban cultural worlds of artistic and scientific creativity, my life was full and rich in spite of the sexual frustration.

Summer vacations I found jobs of one kind or another that took me to far parts of the country. These vacations yielded so much experience, enjoyment and refreshment that I have continued two-month vacations all my life, regardless of financial sacrifice. After the age of about fifty I would take along my notes of the previous winter season and begin to shape them into books. The writing has been pleasurable and never interfered with the activities of the vacations. But I was still protected. The realities of poverty, of the struggle for existence, of the "toiling masses," did not penetrate the fog of enthusiasm for all the marvelous things of life I was exploring. Jim and I scrimped and saved and got to the best of everything—theater, concerts, ballet, opera (where we stood)—even an occasional expensive restaurant where we ordered the least expensive meals we could devise. Our families were lower middle class; Jim's father was a biological scientist on an academic salary; my father was still starting up the ladder in business. Our families had enough for the necessities and could spare a little more, which we were loathe to take but learned to put to the best possible use. This was just before and then after 1920—the post-World-War-I period, when the behavior of youth generally was very different from the excessively self-indulgent egocentricity of our later so-called Age of Affluence. Adolescents of the post-World-War-II period seemed to feel that wanting something was reason enough to receive it, without consideration for others, especially one's parents; in this later age the pill released sexual activity as well as self-centeredness, as seen partly in drug abuse, hostility and violence and the suddenly mounting crime rates of the sixties and seventies.

In my adolescence, as the wider world opened up to my view, most of the people I knew seemed banal. The fellows and girls I'd gone with and most of those at college seemed unimaginative; they were good people in ways I could not then define, but somehow they were limited, also in ways I could not define. Most were headed for this or that business. Dad was a businessman. I admired and respected businessmen, for I knew that success required effort, a lot of sense of reality, understanding of people and maturity; but they seemed interested in nothing but business. We began to awake to the dire poverty of most of the world, to the hate in people, to the worldwide ferment that could make revolutions and wars that might destroy all culture and leisure and the people whom we loved. We questioned.

We explored. We thought. I was confused, but I enjoyed. And with Jim or alone, if I had no summer job, I hitchhiked everywhere, to Montreal, to California, exploring and meeting people, seeing things. Our population was then only about 110 million, and one met only hospitality in the vast spaces of the Southwest and the West Coast.

I still felt inferior, not really a leader, not really in control of situations. Unconsciously I still put myself in the position of the child wanting love and guidance, although I didn't realize it then. But with this inferiority I felt a certain superiority to the unimaginative ones of my generation. And all the girls of those years were in that category. They are a gray blur to my memory. I can recall individual ones, but only with deliberate concentration. They were all so ordinary— differing in size and shape, all young and most of them attractive, but with no mystery, no excitement. Even I, unobserving as I was because so wrapped up in my own thoughts, feelings and problems, noticed that some girls made plays for me. "Why aren't you interested in so-and-so?" asked one of the more mature boys. "She is a good, motherly kind of girl." She was, too, and sexy in a buxom way, but I felt no spark. Maybe she was a simple person who did not satisfy my vanity, now so engaged by the great cultural areas. To me, she was just another girl.

The summer after my sophomore year at college I used not for travel but to attend summer session, taking a course in biology. I hoped it might help me in choosing a career and still allow for lounging and sports. It was delightful—a slow, easy pace—school the way it should be, except for one thing, delightful in itself: it was coeducational. In one of my classes were a half dozen girls, young teachers mostly, each more beautiful than the others. Now, a lifetime later, I still remember them vividly—even the names of those I felt most strongly about. They were a little older and more mature, and I was inhibited in approaching them; they were not the kind I could approach for sex, nor was I thinking of marriage with any of them, although I always thought of getting married. I just didn't know how to get into a relationship with any of them. So I did nothing—except stare, and see the pink cheeks and spun gold hair, and nearly burst out of my skin. In class I could hardly stand it, sitting so close to them day after day, longing almost beyond control and not knowing what to do about it. I never could have stood a co-educational college. I was glad to go back to life as it was in the fall.

In the middle of that year, my junior year when I was nineteen, Charles and I were visiting a somewhat older girl he knew, who had just become engaged—Nellie. She was a superior person although not my type, good-looking enough, with remarkably high intelligence and a lot of judgment, insight and wisdom about people. It was always a privilege to visit with her. We respected and liked Nellie. I think she in turn liked us for our spirits and humor. That evening she turned to me and said, as though thinking it over, "I know a girl who's only seventeen, but whom you might possibly like to meet." Only half interested, I wrote down the name and address. Time has taught me that one of the greatest gifts any person can give to another is a carefully thought-out introduction to someone he might like. I took the name, but for some reason, perhaps because I thought I was superior to seventeen-year-old girls, I was in no haste to use it. Perhaps seventeen sounded uninteresting, being too young for sex and not old enough for sophistication. Now I can see that her age probably put her in a class with Judy in my mind, and therefore made her a "little sister," inferior to me. Association with her might make me feel inferior myself. Anyway, I'd sort of given up on women and my abilities to deal with them; I'd met so many, and nothing ever came of it.

Then something happened. Brent was a classmate and a very good guy. I liked him more and more; so did Jim. A real friendship was developing among the three of us. It was his birthday, and Jim and I and a few others had planned to take him to dinner in celebration. I had just learned about batiks, and found a pale blue-green batik tie for Brent as a present. In midafternoon, there was a phone call for me in the chemistry office, which was most unusual. It was Jim. He said, "Brent was operating an autoclave. It just exploded and killed him instantly."

With the loyalty of students all over, we did what little could be done; his home was far distant, making it impossible to visit his parents. We were shocked and sick at heart. We went our separate ways; Jim left town that evening for something or other. At five o'clock, for some reason, I thought of Nellie and of the young girl she had mentioned. Although usually cautious and given to much inner debate before reaching a decision, this time I acted and phoned the girl. She herself answered the phone; I heard a voice like a clear gentle bell, poised and at ease. After introducing myself I asked, "Is it too last-minute or would you come out for a bite of supper with me?"

She hesitated briefly and then said, "The family won't mind. I can be ready at 6:30." Then came the doubts. Wasn't this a stupid thing to do while still shaken by Brent's sudden death? But I showered, dressed and went out to meet the little seventeen-year-old.

She opened the door herself, and the impact startled me. This was not just another of those run-of-the-mill people. Neither was she a crazy, artificial bohemian, nor a self-assured career girl, nor . . . she could not be typed. She was slender, willowy, perfectly proportioned, brunette, with soft dark eyes. She was natural, gentle, quiet, perceptive, sympathetic. She was beautiful. Perhaps her most striking feature was a calm serenity. She was the "child of the pure unclouded brow." We ate somewhere—we talked and talked and still talked; it got late; we went somewhere else—and talked some more. Then we went home. And I, the sophisticate, so superior to a seventeen-year-old, was unaware of time, and to this day cannot remember where we went or anything at all that we talked about so long and so earnestly, except that it seemed very profound. I was only conscious of this lovely, unassuming girl. What affected me most were her naturalness and her utter honesty, and perhaps, without my realizing it, her high intelligence—probably far higher than my own. I told her about Brent. With a look alone she made me feel that I was somehow sentimentalizing the tragedy, somehow using it to pity myself, to gain her sympathy. I guess it was true: my old childhood need was asserting itself, to get love and attention and admiration as I once had it in babyhood from my adoring family, especially the women. This was Nelda—fearless in facing reality. She never attacked anyone for being hypocritical or artificial; she sensed that if they were, it was because they had to save themselves some kind of pain. ("The lie is the shield behind which the coward hides.") She was kind; she always allowed a person a way out, myself included. Nelda was special not as the word is twisted, bandied and misused for flattery, but in the most honest, sincere sense. As our friendship deepened and I got to know her better, I found that she was more than special, she was *extra*-special, distinctive, singular, unique and extraordinary, at least for me. She was unlike any other girl I had ever met. We made a date for some days thence.

The next afternoon about five I finished some studying and stood at the window for a moment, planning a swim in the college pool before dinner. I suppose every man has stood at a window and felt lonely in spite of all his friends and interests, and thought of a young and lovely woman appearing and slipping her hand into his and smiling up at him. Just then the phone rang. It was Nelda. Would I like to stop by for a few minutes that evening? I forget what the reason was, but it did not matter at all. She was perfectly natural on the phone, there was no element of invasion of privacy, nor of demand on me or my time, which I was always sensitive about. What mattered was her taking the initiative, her presence. It had happened. The lovely girl had appeared and, as it were, slipped her hand into mine. With her, dating was no formal thing; we just called each other freely and freely met, with no wondering, no hesitations or doubts, no struggles, just honesty and freedom.

The rest of my life continued expanding just as it had been—the life of the college, sports, being on the college newspaper, the loose friendships and interesting contacts. The latter included the son of an opera singer, also a tall strong athlete, who rowed on the crew and later became a sports writer, then a writer of some very fine short stories; and there were two very pleasant intelligent fellows, one of whom became a very successful publisher and the other a successful author, and a short stocky fellow, not an athlete but strong, with whom I once made a bet that he could not carry a trunk, and he tossed it onto his shoulder and carried it with ease. He went into the banking business and became outstanding. And there was a tall Swedish boy with quiet blue eyes who improvised delightful melodies on his violin. Sometimes we would sit in a booth in an inexpensive bohemian restaurant, and he would play softly—to the delight of everyone, especially if it were late in the evening. Summers he would take a trunk full of books and work as radio operator on a freighter. Thus I first got the idea of working my way to Europe. It has been my loss to have allowed that loose friendship to slip away.

In high school I was drawn to prestige organizations, and was a member of an elite one, but in college I was not attracted to such groups and never joined a fraternity. My primary interest was in science and the labs. I reveled in the rich close friendships with Jim, Charles and Ralph, devouring all the cultural activities the great city had to offer. And through it grew an awareness of nature and the problems of the world. But something wonderful had been added, the most wonderful for any man: the companionship of a sincere, honest, truly superior girl, Nelda. I feel sure now that it was the love of a noble woman, but I did not fully realize that then. As I have seen men with marital problems in my practice, I have realized the tragedy not only for the wife and children but for the man who is unable to achieve closeness of spirit with a fine woman. It is one of the greatest experiences in life, but for most it is fraught with frustration and struggle and pain.

We were happy. I think I provided the extroversion, the outward thrust into life that Nelda wanted. I was older, but oblivious of that now; I had more facts, had been more places, knew more people, but she was far ahead of me in her perception of people and situations. For my mind was not yet free to observe. It was too engaged in daily living, with studies and all the interests and activities of school and town, and in searching for a career to provide enjoyable work as a means to relative financial security; and when I was with people I strove unconsciously to win love, attention and admiration for myself, the pattern of early childhood which caused me increasingly unendurable feelings of inferiority and kept me in an impotent rage.

Ralph could look at a painting and tell us about its composition, its draftsmanship, its use of color, its technique, its effects; but Nelda could catch instantaneously the feel and conception in the mind of the artist who created it. She was quite an artist herself. It was amazing to me how she could catch the essence of a scene or face with a few strokes; and she could roll a bit of clay between her fingers and in a moment make a perfectly shaped head or perfectly formed hands, gesticulating, idling or praying. Her creations were projections of her superb perceptiveness and sense of reality; of her honesty, her ability to see through sham, while remaining sympathetic to it as a human need. If a face, figure or scene impressed Nelda, hours later she could sketch what she had seen with just a few lines of her pencil, pen or brush. She could represent solid things, "realism," but also managed to convey human feelings, like fear or affection, doing this sometimes by abstractions, sometimes with face or form or group or scene.

I skimped and saved and took odd jobs, mostly in the science departments, so there would be enough money for us to do things together. That included nearly everything. We had no car but that did not seem to impair our getting around. City streets were safe then. Public transportation was adequate and cheap; we were young and indefatigable. We had long talks; we explored introspective things, like Buddhism; we read about psychic research. We experimented with extrasensory perception long before it was widely known, and read each other's thoughts far beyond chance. And in the spring we went out into the country. We hiked; we rolled down hillsides. Nelda sketched ideas for paintings, but we always traveled unencumbered.

One mild Saturday in early April we were out in beautiful country; spring was ready to burst. We walked hand-in-hand. My going-to-sleep fantasy of Minerva had come true with Nelda. A lovely superior girl was walking with me over spring hillsides, hand-in-hand, just as I had fantasied with Minerva when I was only thirteen years old. A few years later, when I had sex relations with various girls, I found sex even more enjoyable than I had expected; but the deeper more lasting, soul-satisfying gratification in life comes, for me, from this closeness and companionship of a true and pure woman. It is this which satisfies the soul. Had Nelda and I gone on to sex together, we would truly have been one and, as I have said, we would have married. And for that I was not ready—nor did I know what "ready" meant. But that fine day we did not think, we only enjoyed, and we enjoyed together. Hands clasped we walked and chatted. Suddenly a cloud appeared, the wind shifted to the northeast, and a blinding snow squall caught us. We were lightly clad, and I had to think quickly. It seemed to me that we were not over two miles or so from the cabin, if we could only find it, of a young Dutch chemistry instructor and his artist wife. We fought the wind, the icy cold, the snow; and somehow there was the cabin. Ed and Elly took us in—we were frozen to the bone. We all had hot soup together, and visited. They would not hear of our going on, but bedded us down for the night, in separate rooms.

That summer, through Ralph's genius for creative ideas and personal relations, I got a job tutoring in the West—helping a boy prepare for some exams. I earned a little money, and we both traveled and had a great time. Nelda was away with her family. Her mother was a strong personality. At first she seemed antagonistic to me; I felt it but could not understand it. Now I see that she didn't know me and only saw that her daughter was sort of swept out of the home. Later, she saw that I had a serious interest in Nelda's welfare, that I wanted Nelda's happiness, and then we became friends. Nelda's sister was nice but prosaic; for me, she was just another girl without the spark and the mystery. The mother once told me when referring to Nelda that she felt like a hen who had hatched a swan.

That fall Nelda and I exchanged notes on our summer. Nelda caught me up on her observations on people, life and art; I filled her in on science. Jim informed me of the affairs of the world with all their many disturbing undercurrents, which I did not yet recognize as manifestations of man's shortsightedness and unquenchable hostility to his own kind. For we were all loved children and loved our parents, and were free of the hatred most people were full of because they had been badly treated as children and grew up hating their parents; this hatred they turned against others. I got a regular job helping in the labs and so could save a pittance; I did not know how the idea developed, but I felt that Nelda must have a studio. I came up with a third floor back room in an ancient private home in a rundown neighborhood—but in those days the city was safe to walk around in at night. The whole place wasn't much; it was old and rather dilapidated. But the room was large, with a tiny kitchenette and a bath, and had north light. I showed Nelda, and she approved. Where the sparse furniture came from I can't even remember. There were a few chairs, a table, a lamp or two and a huge, broad couch. We each had a key. It was super-secret; no one ever knew we had it. It was marvelous to have this retreat, this place to be alone or alone together—especially with my insistence on privacy, which I had had to fight Mother and Judy for in my home. But deeper than that was something Nelda probably observed but I never knew, and that is the mating instinct. It was this and not sex alone that drove Nelda and me to this nest.

It was a marvelous year, but toward the end it was painfully frustrating. For we were so close to consummation, so close to sex, and to having a home and children together. I was now nearing twenty-one. Nelda was nearing eighteen. We still adventured together. In the studio she painted or sculpted, and I studied. We traveled about, going to parties, and coming back to lie in each other's arms for a little before going home. What was the inhibition in me? Late that fall we'd played tennis one afternoon. Maybe she was not wearing a bra. Anyway I was very conscious of her breasts, but this did not seem right to me, not right to think of Nelda lustfully, and I pushed the sexual element out of my mind. Once we were caught in the rain that spring and drenched, and repaired to the studio to dry out; we lay on the couch together, nearly naked—and yet I did not take her sexually. My parents thought something was not quite healthy about

Nelda and begged me not to marry her. Her mother thought Nelda had a problem. I had sort of felt so too, before any of them said anything to me. I had no career, no established course, no path to regular earning. I didn't know how I would establish myself in the world, or even if I could. But although torn by conflicts and doubts I knew for certain that I would never use Nelda sexually unless I married her. And I still believe that if sex had been added to our closeness, we would have been sealed together forever. And then would my father have held to his principles of a man supporting his wife? Was I too far from being a man? Would I have found my career? Was Nelda indeed too introverted? At the time it was no intellectual problem at all; it was all instinct. I was so unconscious, I didn't even realize that we were deeply in love. Instinct alone said definitely, "Nelda is not for sex." And so the closer we became, the more frustrated we were. Also I was driven unconsciously to escape my dependence upon my family and my dependent attitudes toward others—like a child trying to be admired and taken care of, not quite knowing how to do it himself and not knowing that this is what conflicts so sharply and painfully with the adult independence and masculinity that he strives for so desperately.

I felt I was bursting and had to break away from it all. After graduation I packed a bag, said goodbyes, and went down to the docks at five-thirty one morning to wait for a job on some ship to Europe, because I had heard that foreign sailors so often jumped ship here in the United States in the postwar days of the early 1920s. Dad, busy man that he was, had come to the docks with me. He looked wistful when he gave me his sturdy embrace, which conveyed so clearly, "I love you, good luck, take care of yourself, till we meet again." Later he told me that he felt "bad" leaving me all alone that morning. No doubt I looked forlorn, sitting on the cold stone of the curb, my feet in the gutter, waiting and hoping.

At three that afternoon I was called and signed on to a ship ready to sail for Antwerp. It was a passenger vessel of 30,000 tons, built in Belfast and on its maiden voyage. What great good luck!

So I was off—for what and for how long I did not know. Nelda, Nelda, I know you have forgiven me, but I have never forgiven myself. Yet I was so unconscious of what I was doing. I only saw it much later. You enriched my life, gave me the greatest thing there is in life for a man—you made no demands whatever; from you I got much and learned much. You would have given me sex too, and it would have been perfect, I know for sure. We slipped into a relation that was like a limited marriage, except that it was all romance and no element of "accustomed" or taking for granted—but always new and exciting. And then in the end I went off. I involved you and then deserted you, without knowing that I was doing so. I wish I could be sure that I did not damage your life; you were only eighteen, and that sounds dramatic, but I fear that to some extent I *did* injure your life. Can you imagine not realizing until many years later how much I loved you, and how you must have loved me? And I threw away this undemanding, freely generous gift because I was still too much of a child to know what was happening, too immature as yet to have found my own way, let alone to take the responsibility for it? Sex education! Forget the anatomy and physiology—it's nothing at all. A child can get the idea in no time. But the psychology of it, the psychology of living, what is in the mind and in the instincts, what is childishness and what is maturity, what is their cause in living, and how sex fits in, and work, and loneliness, the need for a woman and for mating—for all these questions we have many answers to find before we will know what to teach. I have spent a lifetime getting a few of these answers, but I did not have them then as the ship headed into the open ocean against a stiff wind, and I looked to the bosun's mate for clues as to what I should do.

7

SEA DUST

I did not look long for the bosun, said Corey Jones. He immediately ordered me aloft. I had no idea what I was to do on the top of that soaring foremast, but there was nothing for it except to start up. By now the wind had so stiffened that it was all I could do to clasp the iron rungs with grim determination and keep climbing without blowing off. When I was about halfway up, the bosun called to me to come down. Apparently the captain on the bridge had ordered it, seeing that I was not an able-bodied seaman, a rank obtained by three years of experience, or even an O.S.—ordinary seaman. Tragedy may have been averted, for I knew absolutely nothing of what was wanted or how to do it. I did not even know that one arm and both feet must be firmly secure, while the other arm is needed for the job.

The bunks below deck were in pairs one above the other, in the fo'c'sle head, the very prow of the ship, against the massive bulkheads, which were all that separated us from the cleaving waters of the ocean. As the waves grew larger, they pounded against the prow with tremendous force. But the pounding seemed to disturb no one's sleep. The seamen were long accustomed to it, and I had been up since 4:30 in the morning, so that by the time eight bells sounded and the watch ended, I dropped into a sound sleep as I hit the bunk. I was oblivious of all but a dreamless darkness until suddenly, two minutes later, I was abruptly awakened by a clanging bell and a shrill whistle. I jumped up, startled, but it was only the signal for us to come on the 10:00 P.M. to 2:00 A.M. watch. Our job was to hose down the decks and "holystone" them by pulling a heavy square stone on a rough mat back and forth over the wood. The water poured from the hoses like a magnificent spray of cold fire—for the water was filled with phosphorescent organisms. The others were amused at my delight in this sudden unexpected beauty. But the water was cold—icy cold on my bare legs and rolled-up old trousers. After four hours of this I was frozen. We ate something, I forget what if anything besides the white bread and jam in big tin jars. Again I was asleep almost before hitting the bunk. When the bells clanged and the bosun's whistle blew to get us up at 6:00 A.M. for the next watch, it seemed to me that I had been at sea a full three days instead of only overnight. The next night, though, we drew the six hours off, and enjoyed the luxury of sleeping uninterrupted from 12:00 midnight to 6:00 A.M. I began to get into the swing of the four-on, four-off, four-on, six-off shifts.

I was settling in. A big Portuguese seaman offered to rent me his extra pair of rubber boots for our nightly swabbing of the decks to save me from freezing. He asked five dollars for the trip. The first night it was a great relief from the icy water to have dry warm feet. But the very next time the boots leaked so they were useless.

After what seemed to me to be a full week, but which was in reality barely three days, my thoroughly upset circadian rhythms must have begun to reorganize themselves. For I found myself with a few minutes to myself, salvaged from the icy deck-swabbing on the night watches which froze my feet and legs and the cleaning of all the white paint by day. I had not known what I was getting into, had no idea how tough a bunch of sailors would be, did not know whether or not they hazed a landlubber, especially a lightweight and an intellectual. They were indeed muscular physical types, but each seemed to mind his own business. In these first few free moments I came on deck and had the good fortune to see a whale surface and blow his great spout of water. At my elbow was the Portuguese who had rented me the leaking boots. He was trying to straighten out a fouled line. It had surprised me to see how much heavy hawser and regular lines were used on such a modern ship. Another man tried to help the Portu- guese, who gave him a murderous look which said, "This is my own problem and I can do it myself; don't insult me by implying that I need help, yours or anyone else's!" That reaction impressed me, struggling as I was, although unconsciously, for independence; I often recalled it when I had a responsibility and found myself tending to ask for help.

It had been immediately evident that the seamen, ordinary and able-bodied, considered themselves an elite, much superior to the "sissy" stewards and to the "black gang" who shoveled coal into the furnaces below decks. While waiting at the dock, I had met a callow young fellow who seemed somehow weaker in makeup than I, although I could not have defined what that "weaker" meant. He had been signed on as a steward, and it pleased my egotism to be identified with the more masculine seamen.

After deeply enjoying my break on deck I went below. McDowell, a hard-bitten young sailor about my age and size, sat on his bunk, feet dangling, playing very badly a few simple airs on a concertina. "Well," he asked, "are you going to become a sailor?"

"No," I replied, "I think not."

"Why not?" he asked me. "The food is not like home, but it's good, and the men are good companions."

"True," said I.

"Then why not; is it that you don't like the sea and the ship?"

"No," I said, "I like the sea and ships very much."

He looked at me as though I were crazy and picked out another tune as he pumped the concertina.

Before the day ended they thought me even more peculiar. Working at our job on the foredeck, I heard a passenger call to me from the first-class ladder. It was a beautiful, perfectly groomed young woman. Doing what I thought was only courteous, I went up to talk with her. It was the sister of a friend in the chemistry department, who was crossing the ocean with her mother. Her brother was not a close friend, just a good acquaintance, a little older than I and very handsome, with a good build; he was physically strong as well as poised, and a fine chemist, married, apparently happily—a sort of ideal for me, for he had solved problems with which I, in my immaturity, had hardly come to grips. His sister asked me how I liked working as a seaman, and I questioned her as to how she and her mother were enjoying the crossing on this maiden voyage, hoping that she liked the ship. I almost said "our ship." Whereupon a youngster in officer's uniform ordered me to report to the captain immediately. I did. I give the captain credit for picking up that I was an American.

"Don't you know enough not to talk to a passenger?" he challenged harshly, as though my simple courtesy would be punished by walking the plank or swinging from the yardarm, or merely twenty lashes, or maybe only being put in irons in the brig. I found myself keeping my poise and explaining that I did not know the rule of not talking to passengers and was sorry. He did not move a muscle but glared at me with, "Well, now you know! I don't care what you do on your damn

Yankee ships, you will not do it here!" It was a shock, this first encounter with hostility for being an American. This was no situation
for an argument. I did not know whether to salute, so did not, and
quietly left. At the end of the watch, going below, I found a gorgeous
basket of fruit on my bunk—oranges, grapefruit, apples, figs, dates
and other delicious delicacies. Of course I passed it out to all the men
of the watch, getting kindly but strange looks in return.

Then at the opposite socio-economic pole a tall powerful mulatto
with whom I'd exchanged a few words asked, "What are your plans
when we dock?"

"I'm not sure," I replied. "Why, what are yours?"

"I plan to go to France as a 'stick-up' man," he replied, "and I'd
like you to join me. We would do well together."

"Thanks," I said, "but I can't do that because I have to get to
England. But just how do you operate, what do you do?"

He said, "Mostly on the roads . . . hold-ups . . . ," but then we were
interrupted.

I had struggled for years over choosing a career, and here in half
a week I had been offered two that I had never considered: seaman
and robber. It took no great mental stewing to turn these down and
forget about them.

Early one morning a few days later we came on deck and saw green
fields, cows and windmills all around us. It was like a picture postcard, but for me terribly thrilling—this first sight of a foreign land.
We were in north Belgium, gliding up the Scheldt to dock in Antwerp;
only in Belgium it was spelled Anvers and pronounced in French. I
said goodbye to the bosun, the Portuguese, McDowell and the
mulatto, expressing regrets at parting (partly sincere because it would
have been an adventure to join them). We were paid off. I checked
my duffel bag somewhere and roamed about Antwerp, got to a channel
port and found an inexpensive crossing to England.

In England, with the guidance of the marvelous "bobbies," despite
my difficulty fathoming the cockney tongue, I made my way by
bus to Jim's. We took up as close friends where we had left off. Jim
asked me to share his rooms in that house which served breakfast,
and we ate together; we had dinner out, inexpensively, usually in one
of the foreign restaurants of Soho. Jim was temporarily a vegetarian
"on principle" he said, which saved a lot of money.

One evening about a fortnight later we dined out late, and Jim went on to a meeting at the University of London, where he was studying. I walked home alone, and that is how I came to be alone in London that evening when I encountered the well-spoken, brave little, sad little girl, in tasteful brown, peering in the shop window.

CYCLE II

Tell me, what is the name of the highest mountain?
Name me a crater of fire! a peak of snow!
Name me the mountains on the moon!
But the name of the mountain that you climb all day,
Ask not your teacher that.

Edna St. Vincent Millay
"The Cairn"

8
SCHOOL

It felt, said Corey Jones, as though a cycle had been completed. As I saw it then, the progress was only intellectual. Not that this was unimportant—my liberal education in school was complete and I had some slight grounding in chemistry and physics. I had had my *wanderjahr* abroad. I had some background in music and art, drama and literature from the great metropolises. My career was taking direction. But emotionally there seemed to be little or no progress in my life. I had not found a mate and I had not found myself; I still felt inferior and full of impotent anger from being unable to understand this, or to do anything about it. Now I was traveling in the gathering gloom toward four more years of school, medical school, and the hard row to hoe which I had been warned to expect.

I neither struggled nor drifted through my schooling, said Corey Jones, but just progressed methodically, mostly unaware. No doubt I was too occupied with the conflicts in my own mind, as I have stressed before, to have much attention for the outside world. However, the efforts to solve these conflicts in my dynamics caused a great deal of thinking about them. Possibly all this thinking was not a total waste but developed my intellect. It made me feel a certain identification with thinkers, a liking for thinkers and a feeling of fellowship with them—with those great names in all areas of the sciences and also with other intellectuals whom I met and with whom I had this interest in common. Paradoxically, it seems to me the struggles with my inner problems made me walk so unaware through the schools, doing what the schools were supposed to be encouraging their students to do: developing my intellect. More paradoxically, by this introspection I found school work relatively easy. As it now seems to me, I was thinking then only about my own emotional problems (my inferiority and what to do about it, my relations with girls and my choice of career), and all I had to do was turn this thinking toward my homework—it became easy compared with the problems with which I constantly wrestled! For problems of one's emotional life are so much more abstract, elusive and confusing than an external problem in any field.

I think that is why physics so attracted me but also did not satisfy me. Physics, compared with the emotional life, was as clear-cut, clean, orderly and aesthetic as a near-perfect piece of architecture or some other infinitely complex but perfectly composed and executed art form. That is why I still enjoy physics as bedtime reading occasionally, if the mathematics does not require too much effort.

At any rate, it may be that the struggles to solve my inner emotional problems increased my intellectual abilities and gave me a taste for them. This taste was reinforced by the schooling and by the intellectuals to whom I was attracted, either because of their accomplishments or just as friends. These people placed a high value upon thinking. Therefore I got the idea that thinking was desirable just for its own sake, an idea which was pleasant balm for my sorely wounded egotism, buffeted by feelings of inferiority.

I even had an occasional transient fantasy that although slight physically, I could be strong mentally in thinking and self-control. But I never accepted this as reality nor made it a conscious goal. I never believed that one could strengthen his mind by exercises—no doubt if I had, I would have tried it. In reality, I have been extremely skeptical of all such exercises, in fact, of any tampering with the mind, without the most expert knowledge and the greatest care to do no harm. Such things as Dale Carnegie courses or speed reading seem to me to be artificial, to say nothing of the hundreds of drug, group or religious "therapies" which claim or unconsciously imply a quick and easy cure for the ubiquitous emotional sufferings of desperate humanity (while taking in annually many tens of millions of dollars). So I moved mostly unconsciously and blindly through my schooling, doing whatever was expected or required, but never knowing what it was all about—how some students became class officers, for example. I eliminated myself from athletic teams because of the feeling that I was too slight physically to compete in sports on that level with "big boys." I always enjoyed sports for myself (swimming, tennis and running) but felt I could never be good enough for a team, and felt that intense competition spoiled the enjoyment of the sport for its own sake.

This slight physique of mine may have been more traumatic than I ever realized. We all have known or read about persons who became heroes or daredevils, whether successful or self-destructive, as an overcompensatory denial of feelings of fear and weakness. I had a flicker of this in an early memory: I might have been about four. A great mound of snow had piled up along the edge of the street from being shoveled off both street and sidewalk. I stood on top of this mound, when along came a boy about my age. Some sort of difference developed and I challenged him with "Will you come up here or shall I come down there?" He went on and there was no fight. I have had a trace of this challenge in my makeup but only a trace. Basically it is out of character, for I could not fight or hurt anyone weaker than myself, possibly following inhibitions of hostility to my five-years-younger sister. And I was too sensible to fight someone bigger and stronger.

As I remember it, it was with much patience and love that my mother taught me to read. I can see the book as clearly as if it were this evening:

IT IS AN APPLE

and then on the next page

APPLE AN IS IT

Perhaps this pleasant introduction to reading was of some consequence in my life-long enjoyment of reading, which has never been really excessive, for I am fundamentally active. But to my astonishment, writing has become a great outlet late in life. The immediate upshot of Mother's teaching was that I entered into Grade 3A of the neighborhood public school at age seven. Of course this also meant that I was in the home and protected for that much longer and lacked the preceding two years of experience out in school with the other boys. Also, I was younger than they were, and as I did well scholastically, I graduated in a half year's less time, thereby being that much younger, smaller and less experienced than the other boys in the class. And then I went through high school in three and one-half years instead of the customary four, winning a scholarship to a great metropolitan university, which solved the problem of choice of college.

The only significant event of those early grade-school years occurred within days of my starting school. I was at the stalls in the lavatory urinating when a big, older boy rushed in, unintentionally (I assume) lunging into me and throwing my head against the rigid stone partition on my left. Dazed, I rushed to the very maternal-seeming teacher, threw my arms around her skirt and buried my head in it—just as I would have done with my mother. She was mildly sympathetic, but nothing more and quickly detached herself; and it struck me even then that this was not going to be like home, that I could not run to her but was pretty much on my own.

From the time of entering Class 5A, I went to a different school about three-fourths of a mile away. My mother wanted me to have a "hot lunch." So I walked back home at lunchtime and back to school again, walking morning and afternoon as well; fortunately, I have always enjoyed walking. There were only two incidents worth mentioning from then until I graduated from 8B, as the system was then. For the first and only time I felt a quiver of love for a teacher. I thought of her as not quite middle-aged. Probably she was about 35, slightly plump, with a round pretty kindly face, golden hair and pink cheeks. For a while she was my teacher; then, very soon, she was not.

Of more consequence was the dignified teacher of physics whom I have already mentioned. He looked rather like the usual present-day pictures of Lenin—well-shaped bald head, Vandyke beard and intelligent eyes. His name was Mr. Beech. He could not keep order, nor did he seem to try very hard; probably he had given up long ago. He assigned very little homework, but he taught in what was for me a new way: he did actual experiments before our eyes. This way was much better than my having to study and just memorize a lot of books in order to pass exams. My seat was toward the rear. Through a pandemonium of big boys yelling and throwing things, I witnessed in simple form the basic experiments in mechanics—the inclined plane, the lever, the wheel, pulleys, gears, etc. And I discovered basics of sound as Mr. Beech (called "Nut" by the boys) exhausted air from a bell jar containing a buzzer, making a vacuum and the vanishing of sound. I found the experiments themselves and the principles they demonstrated fascinating, even seen through the vulgar roughhousing of the pupils. Possibly physics was the only subject I got anything out of during grammar school. Before this, at home, I had experimented by mixing everything I could find in the medicine closet; I think "Nut" Beech was also one reason why I observed how the striking mechanism worked in one of our large mantlepiece clocks, which I went so far as to disassemble, adjust and reassemble in good working order.

How important that my parents let me do this, for it signified a potential interest in things mechanical, which is the basis of science and engineering.

The incident with Mr. Beech is remarkable. Here I was, a relatively unconscious, dependent, submissive child of about thirteen, not knowing what life was all about, just doing what I was told, suddenly showing a flash of entirely independent interest and thinking. I cannot remember ever not just flowing with the stream. But in this rowdy uncontrollable class I alone of the thirty or forty boys sat silent in rapt enjoyment of the demonstrations of elementary physics and paid strict fascinated attention. All the rest of the yelling mob threw things, from spitballs and paper airplanes to books; and they yelled. I can distinguish two possible reasons for my attention: the first was a genuine interest, coming from where I don't know, in these simple demonstrations of how things work; and the second was a lack of identification with the toughs of the class. I loved and respected my parents, and because of this I believe I respected all authority figures who in the least invited my respect or even permitted it. I held this elementary physics teacher in high esteem, respected him, learned from him and to this day vividly remember his simple, clear demonstrations.

There must have been other incidents of independence, but I cannot remember many, except possibly taking long walks alone into neighborhoods I thought to be relatively safe, trusting to my skinny legs and light weight for the speed to flee if need be from the omnipresent toughs and gangs. I remembered the fable of the deer who admired his beautiful antlers but despised his thin legs. Yet in danger his legs carried him to safety—until his antlers, of which he was so vain, became entangled in tree branches and vines and caused his end.

There was the time, though, when my first bicycle had just arrived. Good friends and I lent things quite freely; but there was a neighbor boy, somewhat older than I, whom I did not like, who was what I learned later to call a "chiseler." He insisted on trying out the bike on its arrival, before I could ride it myself. He begged and wheedled and I gave in, saying "O.K., twice the full length of the block."

After riding these two lengths he did not stop but sailed by me asking for another. I said, "O.K., but that's *all*." He repeated this ride and I assented to a fourth lap, but added, "Then I will *take* it." The fourth time he also tried to pass me, but bigger though he was I grabbed the handlebars and turned the bike around. He did not fall, but what an air of injured innocence—how could I do that to him?! As for myself, I was dimly aware of asserting myself in an unusual way and with a bigger boy. But the determination that was in that act seemed familiar to me as a recognized part of my makeup. I think an element of that showed decades later when a clique tried to oust me from a professional society and I decided I would "bull" it through and never be one of those who by resigning yielded to those for whom I had no respect. But whence that determination derived I am not sure. Such assertion with a baby sister, five years younger, could not have been required or occasioned; nor could it have been occasioned toward Mother or Father. It seems most likely that it came from an *identification* with Mother or Father or both, because they both, with all their love, tolerance and understanding, also had a no-nonsense, "so far and no further," firmness of fiber. They could be definite and firm with people although gentle. I may have absorbed that element of their attitudes, and this was but the first occasion to bring it out.

In high school my sense of not quite knowing what it was all about did not diminish, but increased. There was a very bright, attractive-looking gentlemanly boy in my class. One day he was at the blackboard and took a piece of chalk and made a few lines and, behold! there was a sailboat on the water. I did all my homework without trouble and got good grades, but I could not do that kind of drawing. One day the teacher asked a question that I could not understand at all. The boy I've mentioned, named Stowell, answered the question with, "the power of the press." The teacher said, "Yes, of course." I had only the vaguest idea what they were talking about; here was a whole world of which I was unaware. I felt that it had something to do with that big world into which my father, incomprehensively, ventured and earned our livelihood, but of which I knew nothing whatever and perhaps never would, and perhaps never could. I felt very inferior. I could pass exams and get grades, but could not comprehend the realities of life.

I could and did do well those things I was expected to do. I did my studying with ease and passed the exams as a matter of course. Only much later did I learn that many students of all ages "clutch" and "freeze" at examinations, their minds going blank. Only then did I realize how fortunate I was. I felt anxiety before the exams, but it was like the anxiety of an athlete before a competitive event. It seemed only to spur me to greater effort. Although I took the special exams routinely like any other, it was a surprise to be informed that I had won a university scholarship which paid tuition at a top college. Happily, this settled early and without struggles, doubt or indecision the choice of college.

O. Henry's famous story "Roads of Destiny" starts with words to the effect that "I seek on many roads that which will be." In the stage play of this tale, Florence Reed said, "No matter where you go, no matter what road you take, I will be there." Perhaps . . . perhaps if I had not won the scholarship and had gone away from home to a distant college, my life would have taken a different course and its story would be different. But perhaps not, for to a considerable extent our lives are lived for us by our own basic personalities, by our major childhood emotional patterns of motivation and reaction, that is, by our central psychodynamics.

There were a few sharp, outstanding highlights of my years at college. The first of these was my continuing to live at home, which was nearly on the campus. It certainly slowed up my achievement of the independence I so strongly but unconsciously desired. Or did it? Perhaps the tension from failure to achieve independence made it burst out all the more vigorously when the time came and drove me to Europe, so that in the long run this road *did* lead to the same place and just as quickly.

The next big fact of college was the setting: a great metropolis with the best of everything, the most variety and most intensity in all areas of human life—industry, finance, art, music, theater, opera, ballet, as well as business; a city with the greatest wealth and direst poverty, a melting pot of all nationalities. I have only touched on its influence, but even that was more of an education than I received or was able to accept from the college.

The college was also benefited by being part of a great university, enabling it to have contact with graduate schools in science, engineering, the arts and the professions. This arrangement was of educational and also practical value to the callow student like myself who had not found himself and had no set goals.

I did not figure out for myself all of this but recognized it when it was pointed out to me. It was Jim who brought me to this recognition. And this brings me to the four persons already mentioned who were the personal highlights of my life at the time, enriching it so that the effects have remained throughout the more than fifty years since. I have never felt that I benefited much from going through the schools that were supposed to provide a "liberal education," college included.

I feel now, in my mid-seventies, that the purpose of a liberal education is threefold: (1) to acquaint the new generation of youth with the main features of its cultural heritage; (2) to educate it to the salient realities of life (what I so much wanted and seemed unable to grasp); (3) to prepare the student for life. None of these benefits did I get from the schools; but out of (or maybe in spite of) the emotional struggles generated in me by my childhood emotional patterns I think I've acquainted myself with each of the above-named purposes.

Today there is still confusion: should there be "law and order" or permissiveness in schools? There are all sorts of experiments in education. It seems to me that it is the job of the faculty to know more about our cultural heritage than the entering freshmen. In that case, the faculty should organize the essentials, which should form a *required* course; for no one who is unacquainted with the essentials of our cultural heritage deserves a B.A. degree. However, for learning his own tastes and interests, and choosing a career, the student should be free to explore the whole range of subjects. Education to reality and preparation for life require a mixture of the required and the elective. The greatest thing I got out of school was, apart from science, the leisure to explore knowledge and life.

Jim was only one year older than I. His father was a biology professor at a different university. Jim was an only child, as I had been for the first five years of my life, which may have been one element in our hitting it off. He seemed to have everything I lacked and wanted so badly: the acquaintance with life and knowing his way around in it. He opened up so much of reality to me. Through Jim I learned what was going on in the campus, the city and the world. He became one of the vivid highlights of my life. As he was another student, I have college to thank for my luck in meeting him.

The next great highlight was Nelda (also the oldest child in her family, as my own father and mother were also oldest children); the third highlight was Dr. Ralph Ackley, the young worldly physician, the friend of Jim's who became a friend of mine also; and there was Charles, the hedonistic sophisticate. Jim, Nelda, Ralph and Charles—how could one want more, how could one expect so much?

Like almost every confused student since courses in psychology were introduced, I signed up for the introductory psych course in the hope, however inarticulate, of learning something that would help me understand myself and life. I did so before Freud's discoveries were known in the United States. The professor turned out to be a delicate, prissy and slightly doddering, feeble little old man, devoid of any force of personality or intellect, who gave the immediate impression that he knew even less about life and people than did I, whom I considered almost the ultimate in naiveté and ignorance. I stuck it out and passed the exam, but felt that all I had gotten from the course was the certainty that whatever field I ended up in would have nothing to do with this "stupid" psychology stuff. So little do we know about our own destinies!

The other subject to which the confused turn for help, for something that might be called "wisdom" but is also an avenue for help with their own emotional patterns, has traditionally been philosophy. So I tried that. The professor was an unsophisticated youth, remarkably less sure and less forceful than myself. Amazingly, in spite of everything, I have always been aware of a certain force in myself, a certain drive and determination. What he taught and assigned for us to read seemed to be futile intellectual exercises, which bore no relation to real life and living. I lost interest after the second lecture and got nothing whatever out of that course. It made me think of philosophy as an intellectual exercise, useful only as an escape from life and as a rationalization for the particular philosopher's own makeup: pessimist (Schopenhauer), hedonist (Epicurus), power-seeker (Nietzsche), and so on.

Next I turned to world literature. It was most pleasant, but I found that it did more harm than good, because it spoiled the books for me; instead of reading them for my own pleasure and enlightenment I found myself reading them with ulterior motives, to be prepared to pass examinations. This idea of reading to pass an exam utterly ruined the pleasure of reading, and the possibility of learning naturally through that pleasure. The only way I can enjoy a book and learn from it is to do so at my own pace. I know almost nothing about speed reading, but the idea of tampering with a person's natural rate of reading horrifies me. Maybe that is only because I read fairly rapidly compared with most people, but not nearly so fast as my wife, unless it is to skim a professional article for its basic technical data and ideas. We seem to read different material at appropriately different rates of speed.

While in college I read for my own pleasure Romain Rolland's *Jean Christophe* and thought it the most beautiful book I had ever read, especially the first volume—"Dawn, Morning, Youth and Revolt." I was so happy that this experience had not been ruined for me by my having to read it as part of a course. It was a personal experience, esthetic in feeling for self and others, yielding insight, understanding and knowledge. It would have been sacrilege to make it a subject for intellectual dissection and tests, and examinations. It would be like never enjoying music or the stars through one's feelings in response, but only observing and thinking with the ulterior motive of passing an exam. But one student told me that Shakespeare's plays meant much more to him since taking a course in them. *Chacun á son goût.*

The only really solid, valuable result of my courses was my education in science. I soon learned to prefer selecting and reading my own books, going to my own concerts and art exhibits and meeting the people I gravitated toward naturally; but what I did not have was a laboratory, and what I could not or did not know was how to set up by myself the scientific experiments. The experiments done with "Nut" Beech in high school were repeated with far more complexity and depth in college, and quantitatively using mathematics. I had feared calculus as exceedingly difficult, but found the first class no less than thrilling. How could anyone invent such a concept? I still remember the first problem: a man six feet tall walks at three miles an hour past a lamppost fourteen feet tall. At what rate does his shadow lengthen? and how exciting it was to find how simply and easily differential calculus could give the answer.

One morning in chemistry class I was sitting in the front row, just in front of the professor's desk. It was a routine lecture. He brought together glass containers, holding, in his left hand, some ammonia vapor and, in his right hand, some hydrochloric acid gas. Both of these gases were invisible. As they met invisibly, a white powder (ammonium chloride) precipitated out. I had often blown on a cold window and seen visible fog from invisible breath. And of course I had seen water change to ice and ice to water. But all this I had taken for granted. This demonstration in class was different. It had great impact. I was fascinated. For one thing, it was quantitative. You could take exact quantities of the ammonia and hydrochloric acid gases and predict exactly how much ammonium chloride would appear as a solid. For another thing, through Jim I had gotten a new sense for the sciences and probably already had the mental set to be impressed by such a bit of drama. The effect was to consolidate my interest in chemistry and in science in general, to make me feel that whatever I did as a career would somehow involve science.

With all my immature patterns and inferiority, I can say one thing favorable in retrospect: there was never any doubt about my deeply wanting a career. The struggle was over what to choose. From the time of that chemistry demonstration, I felt that my interest in chemistry would be connected in some way with living things, and possibly sensed that this reflected in part my curiosity about people. Hence, I moved from this course in inorganic chemistry (in which the professor tried his best to get me to take a Ph.D.) to organic chemistry, which is so much more directly related to the chemistry of living things. Organic chemistry was taught by "Pop" Nielsen; we quickly hit it off and became friends in spite of the age difference. At the same time, influenced by discussions with Jim, I began taking courses in biology and in physics.

That's how I came to attend the summer session and sit with all those attractive young women. It was a course in biology. What I remember most vividly is the reek of formaldehyde, the dissections of the pickled small fish and my struggles with my reactions to all the young women—reactions that continue pleasantly, in memory, fifty years later.

We all have our individual dynamics, our emotional patterns shaped in us by our inherited potentials interacting with the emotional influences upon us from birth, in fact, from conception through earliest childhood (through approximately age six). Of course these influences include the physical ones of health, shape, looks, size. Certainly I was not handsome; yet I gathered from people's reactions to me that I was reasonably attractive, and certainly my life would have been very different if I had not been, or had I not been blessed with health and abundant energy. It would have been different if I had weighed 200 pounds instead of 135. We have our dynamic patterns formed in us during early childhood, and they unfold especially visibly from adolescence on, sometimes slowly, sometimes rapidly. Just how this process of unfolding works is not clear. I have told something of my own dynamics: the sense of inadequacy in grasping the realities of the big world; the needs for dependence, protection and direction and the difficulty in making decisions (which my mother had always made for me); the sense of inferiority caused by these needs and attitudes and the reaction to this of efforts to overcompensate. The striving to grasp reality and for independence sent me out to get a job on a ship to Europe, but I ended in London dependent on Jim. But now at least I had made a decision, chosen a career and entered medical school. How did the pattern unfold further?

The previous indecision was in some part because of a feeling common to youth. As I felt it, I feared losing my identity. It was largely egotistic. I did not want to be limited to *being* "a lawyer," "a doctor," "a chemist," or the like, submerging myself into a circumscribed profession. I wanted to be a complete person—maybe Corey Jones who knew and practiced medicine, but *not* Corey Jones narrowed down to *being* a doctor and nothing more. I do not know whether there is any reality to this fear—I doubt it, but I do know that I have often seen it used by youth to avoid the responsibilities of learning a profession and earning a living to support themselves and their families. Many misguidedly want to take a year or more doing nothing, to think out what they want to do. I think most of these youth really want to do nothing, for they are passive-dependent personalities, who want to continue in the childhood position of being supported. Usually work is just the opposite of limiting: it becomes essential to development. In fact, responsibility and work provide the path to the development of an identity and of the entire personality. And they do this in part by providing a comprehension of and experience in reality, and responsibilities for it. The kind of reality that must be faced and learned and for which one must take responsibility changes constantly. Each generation must find its own way in a somewhat different setting.

Maturity, I have learned, can almost be spelled "responsibility." Alan Gregg wrote a book about doctors with a chapter titled "Responsibility Matures." When I saw that, it struck me as the essence expressed in two words. Could I have been helped in college by that information—I and the millions like me? Yes, I think so. There was something else I read that expressed it, but that was decades later, after I had learned it slowly and often painfully for myself, so that I already knew it and it was no longer a help. That was a line in a short story ("Flight") by John Steinbeck. As I recall it, the wise mother told her adolescent son, "A boy becomes a man when it is required of him. I have seen boys forty years old because there was not need for a man."

This knowledge began to dawn on me after medical school and became a little clearer when a man told me with some pride of his son in the Navy, saying that the son handled the full payroll for a crew of three thousand men. His pride, I began to see, was that his son could handle the responsibility. I do think that school should teach the essentials of at least this element of maturity, for it sometimes seems that emotional maturity is what everyone is striving for.

9

MEDICAL SCHOOL

The Art is long, Life is short, the Occasion instant,
Decision difficult.

From the Latin

In youth, said Corey Jones, I did not realize how long and hard is the way to grasping reality. I thought others just had that grasp and I did not. Possibly this feeling was due to my growing up with adults who had a sense of reality, while I was a young child, over-protected and too small to rely on my physical prowess for self-protection on the streets. Nor did I realize that one only learns over the years to grasp certain limited aspects of reality. Medical school started me on the road to at least some of its aspects. It seemed to me that the first year alone provided me with more of a "liberal education" than all my previous schooling, even college. But it is conceivable that I somehow absorbed more from the previous schools than I realized.

As a cultural experience, as part of a liberal education, on the very first day we began by learning gross anatomy through the dissection of a cadaver, in well-lighted rooms, on convenient tables, with proper instruments. Just think of what Michelangelo and Leonardo da Vinci went through and risked for this then-forbidden privilege! Michelangelo dissected in the dark of night with only a candle in a paper cone perched on his head for light. It appears he wanted this knowledge only for his art, and his thoroughness is reflected in his painting and sculpture. Leonardo, it seems, was interested in anatomy as a science also—one of these fascinating borderlines between science and art. For the first four months in medical school half of our time was spent on this gross anatomy and the other half on the equally fascinating microscopic anatomy, on the structure of the tissues we handled as seen through the microscope. How intricate and beautiful they are; what an esthetic experience it is to see them! And what a lesson from the microscope itself. For at first one sees nothing but confusion. And one learns only slowly and by assiduous practice how to use the microscope to discern the great realities of nature and of the human body in particular that lie invisible except beneath its lenses.

So, too, one can go through life, blind to the greatest realities of existence because one has not learned to see them. This is true in every area. Not everyone can really hear the music or appreciate the art or, what is really important, recognize the human feelings and motivations.

Later, when I studied psychoanalysis, I realized that I was again learning to use a microscope—a psychological microscope to perceive what went on in the human mind and spirit, heart and soul; I realized that I was blessed with the capacity to learn to see through this psychological microscope while many are not. Like any science or art, some have a gift for it, some can learn it through arduous study, and others never get it. I was of the second category. Ten years of intensive studying and of agonizing to understand and help my patients, and then four years in the Navy, which provided the base of broad practical experience in life for developing an ability in this field—this plus the prior years of introspection brought to fruition what talents I had.

During that first step in medicine, in the study of gross anatomy and microscopic anatomy (or histology as it is called—the study of cells), we would often murmur in awe, "We are wonderfully and fearfully made." Not from the first day on did the slightest doubt enter my mind about having opted for medicine. This was an amazing change after being torn with doubt for so many years as to what field to enter and the fears of what I would become. Nor did I even realize the change at the time. Suddenly I was totally absorbed in the school work. My conscious efforts were all directed to trying to build a single, unified, integrated, comprehensive and complete image of the human body, with all its bones and muscles and internal organs; I tried to fit every bit that I learned into this image of physical man.

The second half year was devoted to physiology, the behavior of the organs, and to biochemistry, the chemical changes the organs produced to make the more detailed processes of life.

Demonstrations like those "Nut" Beech gave in elementary physics and the dramatic introduction to inorganic chemistry in college—the synthesis of ammonium chloride—were suddenly and unexpectedly to thrill me again. Such an event occurred in physiology, where we were studying the kidney. We could not use a human kidney but viewed that of a frog through our microscopes: there it was, in actual operation, the cells of the blood moving and stopping as this amazing machine which filters harmful chemicals out of the blood operated by its own laws and principles. There was an essential chemical process of life before my very eyes. "We are wonderfully and fearfully made."

As I learned more pieces of the puzzle and how to fit them into the coordinated comprehensive picture of man, different wonders appeared. The marvel that is the human hand we saw in the anatomical dissection. What an intricate piece of machinery, how beautiful, both scientifically and esthetically! How can anyone kill, I thought; how can anyone destroy such a wonder? Also awe-inspiring were the ear and the eye and the lungs. In fact, no part was uninspiring if one could see it and contemplate it. Then there was the whole area of pathology, of what goes wrong with the body in sickness and death, learning what we must know to help our patients get well and stay well. And, another thrill, acquaintance with the vast unseen world of bacteria, in which we unknowingly live and much of which lives inside us, some helpful and some potentially harmful, able to lay low and kill even the most vital and strong—and not just humans but, as in the case of the tubercle bacillus, for example, all species, even innocent birds and fish. What a beautiful, mysterious and terrifying world is bacteriology! And today this microscopic world of bacteria is expanded by the addition of the whole new world of submicroscopic viruses. Recently even these have become visible, at least indirectly, through the electron microscope.

Thus the first year and a half of medical studies expanded and deepened my view of physical man and his environment infinitely more than all the schooling of all the previous years.

But perhaps I would have been too immature to appreciate what I was being offered if it had been set before me earlier. I did not think of it at the time, for I still felt so callow and immature, but medical school was after Jim and Nelda and Ralph and Charles and

Europe. The other side of the coin was my disappointment with my classmates; they did not seem to be of the caliber of Jim or Nelda or Charles or Ralph. ("Caliber" is a word that has a clear meaning to me when used in comparing personalities, but which I have never been able to define closely. In part, I mean sensitivity, sympathy, understanding, breadth, depth, freedom from narrowness and rigidity, open-mindedness, love, constructiveness.) But from the moment I crossed the medical school threshold, I admired and felt at one with almost all members of the faculty. They were the "caliber" I could identify with and strive to be like. They seemed to do everything so well.

During the first one and one half years of medical school the central cultural aspect was the thrilling study of the forms of life, not only human life but also that of viruses, bacteria, molds and parasites.

Another great cultural educator was the gradual acquaintance with death. No doubt there were practical reasons why the "stiffs" on the tables in the great lighted anatomy laboratory were all face down and the dissections by the teams of four students at each table began with the muscles of the upper back. Psychologically it softened the shock of entering this room and having to stare about thirty dead men in the face. They had been preserved, I believe, in formaldehyde, the same as the little fish, amphioxus, we had dissected in the biology lab in college. Yet all humanity was not missing—we might joke, give the cadavers names, but I think this was a psychological defense against realizing that these men had been like ourselves and that someday we must be like them. Thus some of us also felt a little queasy, a trifle faint. It would not be the last time we would feel that way, but such a weakness passed of itself or was dissipated by professional interest as soon as we began to concentrate on studying their anatomy, and later, in surgery, on the operation at hand.

Fortunately, we had already become a little used to death by witnessing, close up, the autopsies. These were worse than dissecting the cadavers because they were performed on people who had died only a few hours or days before and had but recently been passionately alive. Now each was just a body, a specimen, whose organs we must study the better to understand and combat whatever condition had brought that body to this table and this grim room.

Freud said the dead looked to him like those who had completed a heavy task. Maugham wrote that they seemed to him like puppets tossed aside. To me, they were something totally different, completely remote, unknown, "something else again," "a whole different ball game in an entirely different kind of ball park." The dead can be made by the undertaker to look as though they are peacefully asleep. But plain death without the mortician's skills awed me; after I left the first postmortem with vast relief and as my feelings subsided, I thought with Omar Khayyam:

> Oh threats of Hell and Hopes of Paradise!
> One thing at least is certain—this Life flies;
> One thing is certain and the rest is Lies;
> The Flower that once has blown for ever dies.

One of our professors, Dr. Francis, was known to have an advanced, then inoperable, incurable cancer of the lung. Yet he came before the class and lectured in his quiet, brilliant way. He was an inspiration. In a few weeks or months he would be cold and stiff and lying on that autopsy table, and we would see his lungs and try to learn from them something to help another man or woman to live out his or her life without dying prematurely like this youthful, wonderful man. All families were asked to give permission for postmortem examinations because that was how medicine learned—and therefore it was taken for granted that every physician and medical student would offer his own body after death. I have never liked the idea, but of course could never betray this obligation. I would prefer immediate cremation, probably out of irrational fear. But I was already part of medicine, body and soul, and would do whatever was expected of me alive or dead, as I would today. What really struck me was what I have said, that death was something totally *different*. However angry I might feel toward someone, however much I might wish him out of the way, it was always "out of the way" in life. Being dead was an entirely different area, a totally different realm and concept, and I knew that whatever fantasies might come, I would never want to kill anyone in reality or even wish anyone dead.

Suddenly, unconsciously, I was a physician in spirit. And I had not lost my identity as a person. Because medicine is not simply a body of knowledge but a way of seeing and living, I was beginning to find my identity, my true self. But it would be a long road yet, as the road toward mating continued to be.

I enjoyed every subject we studied in medical school. All were highly educational, and most opened new worlds. But I never felt comfortable at the autopsy table, nor could I quite understand how some of the students were attracted to pathology, although it was fortunate that they were—the field is fundamental for understanding disease and for preventing it, so that when a postmortem examination was scheduled, we all dropped everything so as not to miss it.

On one occasion I rushed a little late into the autopsy room where the body of an ancient, emaciated old woman lay sprawled on the table. My guess was that she had wasted away with cancer or tuberculosis. The pathologist approached the other side of the table, scalpel in hand. He noticed that she was entirely unclad and automatically and with delicacy draped a large white towel over her middle, covering her genital area as though she were a blushing young girl. In a few moments it would not matter—she would be at the mortician's. I could not imagine that anyone would have the faintest shadow of sexual response. If her internist had thus protected her modesty even though she was now far beyond it, the gesture would have been intelligible; for he would have known her as a person and probably have seen her through long, painful, wasting illness to a death that was probably merciful. But to see the pathologist, scalpel in hand and mind focused on learning from mere dead remains, show this unconscious automatic respect for a woman in death was poignant.

Among the marvels medical school presented, one stood out among all others, possibly because of my own pre-formed interests. This was the CNS—the central nervous system, including that wonder of wonders, evolved over so many millions of years, the master tissue of the universe, which can put men on the moon, relieve suffering and pain and prevent disease, and also produce murder and crime and war—the human brain. Somehow, locked in this lump of milky jelly that I could hold in one hand, were the secrets of that great, complex, real world which I felt unable to grasp and also the secrets of my own problems and struggles, and the key to their solution. My scientific interests and my neurotic problems (if the mature and the childish could be separated at this time) combined to form a deep interest in this wonder beyond all others. Unless the student wanted to become a general practitioner (a noble choice, but not for me), he had to specialize. For me, this specializing in the brain was a quiet choice, made without my previously characteristic doubts, indecisions and conflicts. In fact, it was no choice at all, for it felt like a strong interest that had always existed. The CNS was a clean, esthetically pleasing organ, complicated but clear-cut, like electricity and electrical engineering. Indeed, it seemed an intricate yet orderly, highly organized, eventually comprehensible tangle of electrical circuits. And so the choice of the nervous system, chiefly the brain, continued my two already familiar interests: science and people, life. My approach to its problems would be along the lines of these interests, namely, via electro-neurophysiology. The teacher of the CNS was a relatively young man, Clark, hardly more than ten years older than myself. He quickly became my friend and was soon my mentor. Thus my move into this specialty fortuitously brought the good fortune of a life-long friend.

Trying to analyze the motives for my interest in the nervous system shows the difficulty of distinguishing the infantile and irrational from the mature and realistic and also the accidental (the meeting of a new friend).

And so during my first years of medical school I had an entirely new state of mind about a career, as though the slate had been washed clean of all the tumult of indecisions. I no longer gave it any thought at all—it was as though a complex arrangement of well-greased gears had slid into place, meshed and was turning silently. There was nothing to do but follow each step as it came. I had found a pleasant room in a substantial house on a good street, and now there was never a thought as to how I would like medical school—it was great from the first moment.

I wish they had explained to us the new philosophy of the medical school. I had met the dean, who impressed me mightily—a tall somber man, slow in his speech and movements but a powerful personality and mentality. He had initiated a schedule of classes extending from nine to five, Monday, Wednesday and Friday and only 8:30 to one o'clock on Tuesday, Thursday and Saturday. He believed that the students would use the free time in the library and laboratories. Later on that is precisely what I did, for my interest

and drive were strong and I tended to overwork then, as now—
but it was *after* graduating that I started research in Everett
Dalton's neurophysiology lab. He is now eighty, and we are still
close friends.

At this point, as a first year medical student, I was forced out
into life by the irresistible sex drive. It probably worked out better
in the long run, for life is what I needed to know about and experience.
Libraries and labs could not give me that knowledge of life; for immature me, it was much more important than books. It happened
this way.

Jay was a boy who roomed near me, and we frequently walked
to the school and back together. He was bursting sexually as I was.
Being alone in a strange city was one stimulation; knowing no girls
as yet was another. And then the whole medical atmosphere of dealing
with the body physically, even though starting with the dissection of a
dead one. And the nurses . . . we were in hospitals very little as yet,
but from our few experiences the nurses were young, and (as I see now)
also kept aroused by constantly dealing with bodies, men and women
and children of all ages. And there were patients, too, some beautiful
young girls. We did very well, I think, in sublimating our sexual
interest in a woman patient into sympathetic medical interest. However beautiful a woman's figure, her breasts, her round arms, she was
sick, and our concentration went into medical knowledge and
reasoning.

There were certainly wonderful girls among the nurses, but I never
set out to find them. I wanted to find a wife. It seems to me now that
some snobbery entered here. I had turned twenty-one, I was a
lordly medical student; the nurses were only little high school girls
from the sticks, not too knowledgeable and intelligent. I passed them
by. Stupid, ignorant egotist that I was (I guess I reacted to them with
my dynamics toward Judy—only a little sister, the old egoistic sibling
rivalry with me being five years older). "Too soon olt, too late
schmart," as the saying goes. Much later I found how many superior
girls go into nursing.

At any rate, the whole situation made Jay and me, and I'm sure
many others, into sex-mad medics. One day he told me he'd met a girl,
made a pass, was in bed with her, had no rubber, withdrew and shot
halfway across the room, and held her as she looked at him with big
grateful eyes. Well, now! Was it that easy, really? And the "grateful

eyes." I'd always thought women had something that men were dying to have, and yet here *she* was grateful to *him!* I had never realized that in general women want men as much as men want women. The mythical Tiresias said that women enjoy sex ten times as much as men do (and having been both, he was in a position to know).

A month or two later I saw Jay with a girl. Quite a girl—full-blown, full-bodied, full-blooded, exuding sex. A classmate confided to me, "I understand Jay is sleeping with that girl regularly. He's been over every inch of her body." Later Jay told me all about it. In three months they were married. They had a hard time of it after that; it looked as though the sex drive had ensnared Jay into a marriage that was not working out. He dropped out of school after the first year.

I felt isolated in my room, a mile-and-a-half-walk from the school, and I lost a lot of time trying to locate a place near to it. I found a one-room apartment, an outside one facing the street a few floors up in a slightly shabby building. But it was a room of good size, with a tiny kitchenette and a bath. With secondhand furniture and the few Indian blankets and pottery accumulated from the summer I tutored in New Mexico, the apartment took on a certain character. A poor thing, but my own—and my need for privacy would be satisfied. It would be available in two weeks.

I wrote home briefly about once a week, if only on a plain postal card, to please my mother; but among my most intimate friends there was never correspondence except for a reason, and then it was brief and to whatever was the point. So a letter from Ralph was a surprise. It was typically laconic:

Dear Corey,

Myrna R., career girl, will arrive Thursday. Staying at Hotel ———.

   R.

Decoded this meant: "There is a person I don't know too well, who will be alone in a strange city, and she and I would appreciate any gesture of courtesy you might extend her." I wrote her in advance at the hotel, marking the note to be held until her arrival.

Myrna phoned me Thursday evening. She had a meeting Friday until five and another at 7:30, but was free in between. I took her to dinner. She was beautifully built, but a little overweight and somewhat older than I, a strong personality who knew her way around much better than I did. She had a presence; she was in command with the waiter in a way I wished I could be. She was good-looking: "pretty" would not be the word and "handsome" would be too strong—just very good-looking. We were not really on the same wavelength, but she had a lot of feel for life and art and a good sense of humor. The conversation flowed. I went with her to her hotel room, where she wanted to stop before the 7:30 meeting. No decision, no thought—I found myself slipping my arms around her, bending over her and then kissing her. She did not resist. I don't know if her eyes were grateful, but they were certainly full of surprise. So was her voice: "Why, I didn't know you had that kind of interest in me!" she said. She did not discourage it, and I urged it. The result was that she promised that she would come back in a month and stay with me in my new apartment. When I put my arm around her and kissed her, it never entered my awareness that it was no great thrill. It was not even like that brushing kiss on little Winnie's cheek. I was too intent on getting her to agree to sex to notice that embracing her was not exciting, good-looking though she was.

The day arrived at last . . . I met her at the train. She was all smiles. It was a Saturday afternoon. A family I'd met were having some young people in and asked me to bring Myrna. I thought she might enjoy it, and it was a chance for her to meet people in the area. And, as I did not recognize until months or years later, I would show her off, or really show off myself via her. As I expected, she was a great hit; the couple insisted that she and I stay for a bite of supper. We did, and then on to the apartment and then to bed. This was the moment I'd waited years for, but I was not fully potent. I functioned, but that was about it. It was a disappointment to me and to her, and trying to excuse myself I said, "This is my first affair." She sniffed depreciatingly and said sarcastically, "Hah, your first affair!" She put the accent on "affair," and I knew she misunderstood. It never occurred to her that it was my first sex. But I said nothing. A little later she said, "It's good for you I didn't come. If I had, you would have been scared out of your wits." That hurt. She thought me such a child that I'd be scared by her orgasm. Probably she was also boasting how good she was at sex and what I'd missed, and that it was not her fault but mine. Maybe she was a little frigid and had to emphasize how responsive she was. But I didn't think of all that until a long time afterward. She was a good sport, and kept good spirits throughout the rest of the visit. We slept well, and the morning together was happy. I was happy in spite of everything, for I'd had the experience and could face the world with that knowledge. And I must have been happy too because such a beautiful, knowledgeable, worldly girl had freely given me her company and herself. I kissed her goodbye at the station and even as the train was pulling out, it began to dawn on me that I'd given her nothing, not even sent her the railroad ticket. I had never stopped to question what I, as a poor medical student, had to offer to her, yet she freely had taken this whole weekend to spend with me. Thank you, Myrna, for so much.

As a loved, respected child I knew I was basically sound, but my sexual performance worried me. It was not like the irresistible force of the sex drive I had been accustomed to feeling. I was depressed and frightened. I feared I might be impotent to some extent. I wish I had gone to see a good doctor then, for one visit could have saved me weeks of doubt and fear and shaken self-confidence, if it had been the right doctor. A few simple facts would have helped, such as that forty percent of men and women have *some* degree of disturbance in their sexual functioning at some time. But especially this: that a man is not always fully potent with every woman. But I did not know where to turn; no one told me; nowhere did I read that second simple sentence. So I suffered. It was months before I learned from experience what I could have read in a few seconds. It never occurred to me that I went to bed with Myrna only because I wanted to try sex, rather than because I was attracted to her sexually. I never thought that the lack of full potency might be connected with the fact that there was so little thrill in first kissing her in her hotel room and then her surprise that I had taken "that kind of interest in her." She was right; I did not.

But when you are young you want sex so strongly that you feel sure you can have it with anyone at any time in any circumstance, and this is almost but not entirely correct. According to a vulgar expression of the day, still good as far as I know, "even a knothole will do." But why was my potency laggard when at long last I had what I sought so urgently? I think because the sex drive was only for a female. It did not take into account that "a girl" is not simply a female body but another person with all the complexities of a personality. My egotism wanted a superior girl for the first sex experience. In that it was satisfied. But Myrna was so superior to me in knowledge of the world, in presence, in strength of personality, that she did not stir up my impulses to domination and to mastery, which in me were part of the sex drive. Instead, having had a strong dominating mother, I probably quite unconsciously took a slightly submissive attitude toward her. Thus to some degree, but enough to blunt the zip and zing of potency, she was like a mother-figure to part of my unconscious, awakening that much of the old childhood submissiveness and the old incest taboo. This is now known to be a biological reaction. Fully potent young male monkeys show no sexual response to females that are older and dominating, like their mothers, i.e. "mother-figures."

When I went home from medical school for the Christmas holidays it was pure enjoyment to see my close friends. Charles was his usual delightful pleasure-loving self. Jim was full of news and insights into people and world events. Ralph was vital as always. "Did you get to see Myrna?" he asked, and added, "Did she go to bed with you that weekend?"

"No," I started, meaning to tell him that she did go to bed with me a month later, but he interrupted me, which was very unlike him. He said, "That's funny, why not? Did she have the clap?" Ralph was an extremely sensitive refined man. I was surprised, shocked and offended. Could Myrna be that promiscuous? My only-child psychology was easily revolted, but I remained silent. I felt loyal to Myrna. I still do. She had done her part in giving me a wonderful weekend and the experience of all a mature young woman can offer. That it was no soaring success was because of my own immaturity, self-centeredness and inhibition. Ralph knew nothing of all this, surprisingly, since he was such a "menschenkenner," such a keen observer and accurate reader of people.

When I next saw Jim, he cast some light on this. Jim remarked that he thought something was bothering Ralph; Ralph didn't seem to be his usual self. This was rather upsetting; Ralph had such security and strength that I could hardly imagine him not being on top of any situation or problem that might come his way.

Then the visit with Nelda—child of the soft eyes and the pure unclouded brow! She was like a cold, clear spring of pure water. It's a hackneyed simile, but that is how I felt. Yet somehow, our feelings for each other remained latent. We were only deep, good friends. That much was sealed forever. I babbled about medical school and my classmates; she said she's been seeing something of a young man named Tad. I felt a touch of ice, of fear, but brushed it aside. Fear for myself, losing her? Fear for her? Yes, the latter. We were so finely tuned to each other—strike one tuning fork and another vibrates. I sensed something; was it in her tone, her manner or her expression, or something in her soul which even she did not sense?

"Nelda, we are one. Now I have a career; I love it and know I will be good in it. I have a little apartment. I don't want to be searching for women, searching for a wife. Let us get married now, and come back with me. We'll manage financially. As you know, my parents have reservations about you as a wife, but this is easily solved. You have only to come and spend some days living in their home. And then they will love you as I do." Why did I not say just that? Why? Was my head guiding me correctly, although contrary to my heart? The decision to marry requires certainty of both head and heart.

Again I sat alone on the train back to medical school. Again the sky was slate. The passing landscape was wintry, bleak; it reflected my inner feelings. I thought of returning from Europe through the gale on the Atlantic, the great dark waves and the plunging ship. But now I felt no exhilaration; as in the landscape, gray and dark moods drifted by within me as I went through this second parting. I now see that it was not only the parting from Nelda; it was also the breaking of the dependence upon home, parents, and close friends, to move out on my own, to be alone and to be truly independent. To break the dependence can be a painful process, although it is a necessary one for maturing. For dependence is one of the strongest of human needs, although at that time I knew nothing whatever about it, nor did I realize that to be adult is largely to be alone. It was never mentioned in my schooling—I was a graduate of one of our great universities, a college which required, for a degree, swimming a certain number of lengths and diving from a ten-foot board, but did not require an understanding of one's self and of man's deepest needs. The fear for Nelda continued to nag me. My mood blended with the bleak scene. It must have been somewhat depressing, since I was losing the dependence on my home, but I was too much the optimist, too much loved, to know that. Always having so much to do and having been trained by my mother to finish a task before relaxing, I invariably carried a book to read or study so as to avoid wasting time. I was going back to medical school to finish a task, an absorbing and satisfying task. I took out my bacteriology text and read.

10

GIRLS

*"Oh,—Mary, thy laugh was sweet
In the days long remember'd
When a fire burns safe, complete,
There's warmth in its embers."*

Irish Folk Ballad

In her kind, selfless way Nelda had given me the name of a girl whom she knew only slightly, but Nelda guessed I was still a little lonely at medical school and thought I might like to meet her friend. Bette was my age and a beginning sculptress. I phoned her and went to see her in her studio—strong face, beautiful complexion, nothing lacking in looks, energetic, outgoing, dynamic. Her right eyelid drooped ever so slightly and gave her a slightly knowing sort of look. We hit it off at once, but there was an element of wariness in it. I didn't quite know where I stood and felt that she was stalking me. We made another date. I took her to dinner and we talked. I didn't know then how enormously I needed admiration and acceptance (does everyone?). The conversation led into her asking me, "What do you think of sex?" This caught me off guard; I was trying to make an impression and thought of something I'd heard recently that sounded clever: "Sex is a reflex from the waist down." I guess my unconscious was saying, "I am very superior to all that, and therefore, admire me."

I went on trying to make an impression, not noticing what was going on. The third date I asked her to come to see my apartment, but she refused. I was never the arguing type, but I argued this time, and then it came out. Bette had decided that it was time for her to try sex, and during that first meeting she had chosen me to initiate her. But then I'd said that sex was a reflex from the waist down, and she had no intention of being interested in anyone who thought that little of it. I felt like an idiot. But I was speechless. I couldn't tell her the depth and breadth and burning that sex meant to me really. I couldn't tell her I was trying to say something smart and that she had taken it literally. I could not discern whether she had picked someone else in the meantime. I was very upset. We did have rapport, and I did get her to come to the apartment, but nothing developed. She was adamant.

But she came again, and this time she made herself at home—she took off her shoes. She was wearing a loose blouse with a big tight belt. She loosened the belt; I made advances. She was not coy. She was strong and definite and said, "No." I don't know what got into me or whether she aroused it, but I was indignant. I felt she had led me on, gone to the brink and then tried to say no; it was just not fair, and couldn't be. This time I was determined—in part because I was angry at her. Suddenly her defenses collapsed like the wonderful one-horse shay, all in one piece. She stripped and I stripped and we were in bed together. Full potency this time. I was so excited I don't know to this day whether she was still a virgin or not; I think so. I was pretty fast the first time. But about a half hour later, the second time, it was perfect. I had no idea it could feel so good. She was a keen mind, a promising sculptress, a dynamic masterful personality, a beautiful girl with peerless, smooth skin with the tints of Raphael. Now the dikes were down! We were twenty-one; our energies and enthusiasms were inexhaustible. So was our desire. We drank our fill of passion and sex.

No impairment of potency now. But there was one curious exception. I would sometimes put my arms around her when she was standing, and in full desire bear her down flat on the floor—and then, strangely, before entering there would be some loss of desire and some detumescence, which lasted until entering, when all was lusty and full-blown again. But there was no reason to prefer the hard floor, and in bed there was no problem.

After a month or two, it was evident that Bette was always insatiable, and she was becoming dissatisfied. She had her home with her parents and had her studio too, but she practically lived with me. She became critical for no reason that I could fathom or that she could or would explain. Sex two or three times at night and again in the morning, almost every day, yet somehow she wasn't satisfied. She began talking about Barnes, one of the justly famous sculptors of the day—how virile he seemed, how she was thinking of studying with him and sleeping with him. I wondered if all this was to tease me; it wasn't too pleasant. Barnes was in his mid-forties, a married man with several half-grown children. I saw a picture of him; he had a big, powerful build and must have had a strong personality as well as outstanding talent to be dominant in his field. I decided that I didn't care if she talked about him or dreamed about him just so she continued to sleep with me. I didn't care who had her soul so long as she gave me her body.

In the spring she became even more insatiable. June was approaching and exams. She was adding an unwelcome element to our sex relations, being so insatiable and so vaguely critical as to make it sometimes for me a chore. She flaunted before my eyes some dates with another fellow and made up to him very openly in public at parties; I've rarely been jealous in my life, but Bette gave me the experience. I was really mad with jealousy; it was made no better by fearing, with my awareness of my immaturities, that maybe he was a better man than I—I even had fantasies of killing him. Yes, with all my love and goodwill and reason I had such thoughts, but of course they were only fantasies, bearing no relation to reality. I would never *do* anything.

But Bette never did develop anything with him. It passed, but I overdid sex trying to satisfy her. One day, urinating, I passed a clot of blood and nearly fainted. It was a warning. I told Bette, and we both went for examinations, but of course we both were healthy. I decided that if nature overflows about three or four times a week, it is unwise to push too many times beyond that for any long period of time. Twice in an evening is natural—if the first should be too fast, the second was always perfect. And usually again in the morning. But then rest a day or two or three; Bette agreed. But she still had Barnes on her mind: I heard all about his art, his concepts, his techniques, and how he turned these into financial success.

Then Jim came to town and the three of us spent an evening together. Next day he told me flatly: "I do not like your girlfriend." Jim was my closest, most devoted, most respected friend. He would not say that unless out of loyalty to me. I appreciated it, for by then I had come to the same opinion and only needed Jim to articulate it; but I did not know what I would do without Bette—I didn't see how I could again live without a woman and feared that I might not find another. In spite of her willfulness, her lack of consideration, her self-absorption, she slept with me, and that was still great. Then she went away for a long weekend visit. She was vague about where she was going; but that following Monday during lunch I went into a local store, and there she was. Her back was to me, but I was so keyed up in relation to her that, incredible as it seems, I knew for certain that she had gone away to sleep with Barnes. She turned and saw me and blushed crimson. I said, "You slept with him."

Before she could think she said, "Yes," and I turned and walked out. I was in a rage. It soon subsided—unfortunately, for I think I would have gotten it out of my system faster if it had worked itself out slowly. I thought it over. What had I to complain of? We offered each other sex; I was satisfied, she wasn't. She was free to leave. But I was vaguely aware of something I learned later in life, that women go for men who have status, not always so much for what the men can *give* them as from their own need to gain power and position by association and identification with successful men for egotistical reasons, for identifying with their fame. However good Barnes was in bed, I'm sure that at forty-five he could not compete with me, a twenty-one-year-old, although I did not think of that then.

I returned home for a visit before the summer recess. I was now aware of feeling somewhat depressed. I talked with Ralph and tried not to tell him about Bette, but of course with his worldly knowledge he guessed it in a moment. "You are having some trouble with a woman," he stated flatly. "Tell me about it." Once it was in the open I saw the controlled, even repressed rage I felt at the rejection, at the hurt self-esteem, and out of jealousy, I saw my fear that I would not find another woman as a sexual partner and my fear that I could not live without one. I saw a more profound thing too: how emotionally dependent I had become on Bette. This was my first inkling of any reference to me in Freud's discoveries which I had just read about in his *Introduction to Psychoanalysis*. Bette's behavior, unconsciously, said, "Corey, you are only a little boy. You cannot satisfy me. It takes a big, strong, successful man to do that, a man like Barnes." What I did not see was that there was something childish in a beautiful twenty-one-year-old girl going after a married man in his forties. Nor did I see that she might be plotting to marry him—a prominent, financially successful artist. Amazingly, my pride and independence and thrust for life all came back to the fore in one sudden rush. Never again would I be so dependent on any woman that I would let her upset me like this—gone was the depression, gone the fear of not getting another girl. On with life! Ralph had given me a "blitz analysis" in one chat. Small wonder that he had suggested that I be psychoanalyzed as soon as I could, with the *right man.*

A few years later I was tested in the same way. I had a first date with Audrey, a nurse. We had worked together in the Children's Hospital, of which more later. Audrey was a stunningly beautiful girl. She attracted me sexually almost more than any girl I had met. I borrowed a car from a classmate for this date. I stopped the car to kiss, and a policeman appeared and gruffly told me to move on. I guess he was the forbidding, punishing father-figure. I overreacted. I let it ruin the atmosphere, the mood between us. When I saw Audrey to her door, she was totally cold and rejecting. I thought possibly I had acted the coward with the policeman, but when I saw her, accidentally, the next morning, she was not just angry at me for being a coward, she was in a barely controlled rage. I had never been so directly rejected by a girl or anyone, except for physical attacks in childhood on the streets by much bigger boys. I could not understand it whatsoever. I was demolished and depressed. But even then I found it hard to believe her rage could be directed to me, the naïve, the immature. After two days I said to myself, "It is ridiculous to let this get you down. Don't let it; forget it. You're not interested in marrying any girl with such a vile temper and so inconsiderate, so what does it all amount to? Don't let yourself be so dependent on anyone. Forget it." And from that very moment I did forget it, this time without the need for a Ralph Ackley to tell me my feelings. The depression vanished in that instant. Only the problem remained, and I never learned the answer. What *had* I done that was so bad? Had I rejected her that much through overreacting to the policeman? That is my guess. Is it possible that *she* desired *me* so passionately that she counted on going to bed with me that first date, and was in a fury because of sexual frustration? That never occurred to me as in the realm of the possible. It was years before I learned how desirous a woman could be. Happily for me, I had quickly reduced it all to a puzzling incident. In a few months Audrey was married, and I thought when I heard the news, "Lord help her husband!" In fact he died in his forties, and I can't help wondering if she had something to do with it.

She and Bette are the only two girls I do not remember with much warm tenderness and affection. I was an only child for five years and was so wanted and loved by my mother and beautiful, childless Aunt Edie that I responded with much love for women as part of my dynamic pattern. Also loved by my father, I have always had good relationships with men, some close friends, and many who were less close. The intimate ones like Jim and Charles and Ralph were, I think, persons I could identify with in extensive areas of personality, although they were very different from each other: Jim the scientist, with the deep broad human insights; Charles the businessman, with his love of pleasure; Ralph the physician, with his vast interest in people. I felt close to them because I was so much like them; we were so companionable because we were alike in many ways, especially in our interests and what we enjoyed.

Jim was special, though, and I have never had another friend like him; for he was not only like me so that we identified with each other, but he was superior to me in his knowledge of the world, and was a leader and a guide for me in introducing me to the world. He was invaluable for me in doing this. He taught me to find my way around, introduced me to people, opened my eyes. I sometimes wonder if they would have been opened at all had it not been for Jim—certainly they would not have been until many valuable years later. Because of him I emerged from a narrow, constricted life into the worlds of art, science and personal, social and political understanding. I used to wonder what he saw in me that kept us such close friends. I guess he enjoyed things better having companionship, and he must have liked feeling appreciated and admired. Damon and Pythias, David and Jonathan. When the time came, some years later, that I felt able to handle my own life alone and was married and Jim was also married, we drifted apart. If I had been stronger, more mature, truly more independent, I never would have let lapse this closest friendship of my life, to which I owed so much. It seems now, in my mid-seventies, the memories of those I have loved and by whom I have been loved provide a constant background glow, as though I am living in a beautiful sunset.

Each of these friends I would like to see again, and all the girls toward whom even now I feel the sex urge and a love which has never died. I yearn to see each of them and apologize for any hurt I may have done them because of my sex drive, and express my gratitude and tenderness and affection. The sex drive remains in full force, and the machinery still functions although the performance wanes.

But Bette I have no great wish to see, except out of interest in what her life has been like. Why not? She must have gone too much against my dynamics. Perhaps she committed *lesé majesté* against my royal egotism. I was my mother's darling, not displaced in her eyes by my father or, after five years as the only child, by my baby sister. Now Bette did not fit into that but took the opposite attitude: I was nothing much compared with the powerful, successful, prestigious, wealthy father-figure—Barnes. And this played into my own feelings of inadequacy as a mere student in a world of knowledgeable, powerful father-figures, a dependent child in a world of independent men. I went into a rage, which, pent up, made me depressed; but after the chat with Ralph I think my dynamics extruded the whole thing and said, "To hell with it!" and I forgot it, even in the face of losing my sex outlet and fearing that I would never find another!

This shows, I believe, how much more fundamental love is than sex. I do not remember Bette with the love and affection which is my memory of the others, not only because she did not touch a chord in my dynamics but because there just was not that much love in our relationship to remember.

I think love is the more fundamental because it is experienced much earlier in life. Normally it starts at conception and certainly enters the child's life at birth. In general, the earlier the influences upon the child, the greater their effects. Even if sex enters at about three to five years of age, as Freud maintained, that is much later than the experience of love. And for most people, physiologically functioning sex does not start until puberty, so that it is mainly a matter of how the previously formed childhood emotional pattern leads a person to channel and deal with his or her own physical sex drives.

I guess my desires to get away from it all, to get back to nature, prompted me to get a job for the summer, not in a hospital but on a farm near the sea. The farm was owned by the Holdens, Steve and Estelle, an extremely nice family I had come to know. They were in their forties and had two charming half-grown children. I looked to the land and the sea and the sky, which I loved, to refresh me and give me strength, and they did.

11
SEARCHING

The summer served its purpose well. I returned to face the year re-freshed and tan, bursting with vitality and sex; but for some reason, powerful as was the drive, I no longer feared being without a girl. Back in town, the Holdens had open house every Sunday evening. Only one or two might drift in—or a dozen or more people might show up, of all ages. The Holdens were so easy, down-to-earth, open. They could do almost anything without ever giving offense. They could shoo you off early, or ask some and not others to come early the next time for a bite of supper before the evening really began. If you wanted to bring a friend, they were delighted. It was there that I had taken Myrna. And it was there that I had met Everett, the neuro-physiologist who became a lifelong friend. I wonder if they knew how much it meant to some of us, young and without roots in the city as yet, to have a home to go to where we felt wanted and welcome— not a duty invitation, but a home in which their warmth made us feel at home, made us feel as though we unsophisticated students gave them something, as though they got something from us.

Of course I went to visit them to check in shortly after returning to medical school that fall. Among the six or eight present was a very nice-looking girl, Penny. She was a little younger than I and "all girl." She had the noticeable accent of the society people of the area, but was friendly and natural, not exciting as a personality, but attractive sexually to me, sex-starved all summer on the farm. We made a date. It went fine so far as congeniality, but was not very intriguing personally. I didn't know why. It never occurred to me until many years later that sheer intelligence has so much to do with rapport. I did not know then that when we took IQ tests to learn about them in medical school that I would score over 155, or that this was pretty high. I don't remember the test used, and this may have been ten or more points above a reading on today's standard tests. I didn't think of Penny's going only to junior college in terms of intellectual ability. I just never thought of people in that way. She seemed to have the average intelligence of youth who went to college, and quite enough for most practical purposes. All I knew was that we enjoyed each other in a casually friendly way, that I had no interest in marrying her (searching though I was) and that Penny was a tempting morsel sexually.

I invited her to the apartment, and although upper crust socially she came. I was about to learn that just about every girl I invited did come. She was very simple, not noticeably seductive, but pretty irresistible. We chatted. I eased my arm around her, and she did not object; I eased her to the bed and we sat upon it. She had some remaining traces of adolescent acne, but her lips were perfect. In order to completely avoid any scars from the acne, I kissed her full on the lips. It was luscious. I lit up like a flame, and with two or three more such kisses I began to take off her dress, unbuttoning the buttons. This was the most perfect sexual situation I had been in—if I could only keep control and go slowly enough, it would be utterly gratifying. No impairment of potency this time, just pure desire. I came to a little pin and started to unfasten it. She looked at me full in the face and said, "I have never had relations. Do you think it is all right? I trust you, Corey; I'll do whatever you say if you think it's all right."

I went into the bathroom, turned the cold water tap, filled the washbowl and stuck my head in and out several times. I dried with a big towel, then opened the window, put my head out and looked out at the lights of the city and the passing traffic. I took a few deep breaths. They say an erection has no conscience, but this was not true for me. I did not dare button her dress, though. I said, "Penny, you button it and let's take a walk."

She said, "Thank you, that's a good idea." My decision was too fast for thought. Afterward I knew part of it was the vain show of being noble. That was the *ignoble* part of it, but also I did think that I could not in the heat of my sexual arousal let her, a virgin, go ahead with sex with a young man who knew he would not marry her. I could not take advantage of her trust and her desire to let her plunge into a dead-end relationship. I sensed that she needed a good husband, that she could not take care of herself in the world too well. Later I learned to inquire into a person's home life, especially in childhood, but at that time I didn't know that people tend to repeat in their marriages with frightening exactness the emotional patterns of their childhood.

We walked. She was warm and friendly. I was let down and in quite a state. I took her home and kissed her lightly goodnight. Her kisses were delicious. She said, "Let's do outdoor things together." This made me feel awful. I enjoyed sports hugely, but with the boys. With sex out, I did not have enough interest in Penny. A week later she called and invited me to a place where we could get freshly steamed clams. She was nice as could be, but without sex the spark was gone. Thank you, Penny, for your trust. I hope you soon got a husband worthy of your trust. Thank you for sweeping away the last vestiges of doubts I had about my potency. Even today I cannot think of that moment of desire with you, so luscious, in my very hands, the thrill of undressing you and your yielding, without becoming all aroused again and impelled to plunge my head into a washbowl of cold water. And so it was a girl I never slept with who finally gave me full confidence in my potency, just as Nelda—with whom I never slept—gave me the experience of early love. Resisting that whole desirable temptation is a great loss—I wish I had the memory of possessing you, of our intermingling that night. But I think my unconscious reflexes made what was the right decision for you, Penny. I hope so. For we denied ourselves at the last minute the ultimate in pleasure that sex can offer. But perhaps you might have been afraid and guilty, and then too involved with me for it to end without your being badly hurt.

Why did my unconscious make the decision of denial? I think it was partly that the atmosphere of my home was that sex outside of marriage was not right. And this was reinforced by my having a younger sister. I certainly felt that if any fellow took advantage of her only for his own sexual satisfaction I could kill him. Of course I knew that this was a mere fantasy, but my feelings must have been that sex without marriage was somehow taking advantage of a girl, somehow hurting her; it was something the girl would regret and feel demeaned by, because I was somehow *using* her. My dynamics included so much of loving and being loved by Mother and Aunt Edie and later by Sister Judy that I really have always loved women. This love for the girl conflicted with any feelings of mine for seducing her into sex because of my own desires alone, seducing her into something in which she would surely be hurt. Even that early I think I had some recognition of how readily girls confuse sex with love, thinking that a man's sexual interest in them is love and then expanding this erroneous interpretation of love into a likelihood of marriage. Because of my childhood emotional pattern I could never tolerate the idea of a man's hurting a woman. That has always seemed to me the depth of the despicable. In that moment I did not know what I was getting her into and therefore reacted against the responsibility of letting her do it. And then too the inevitable egotism entered and wanted me to show Penny how noble I was, and thereby win her admiration and love, which were residues of childhood and probably still my strongest motivations toward everyone. Where I learned that there were rules for seducing women I don't know. But I knew such rules existed. For example, I knew men tried to get girls drunk to get them to give in to sex. But the rule I knew was that a real man does not take advantage of a girl sexually when her defenses are weakened by alcohol or unhappiness of some kind.

There was something else I learned in retrospect but did not see then, namely, why I felt so completely free and potent sexually with Penny. I think the reason was revealed in her saying that she had complete confidence in me and would do whatever I said. By this Penny showed that she was emotionally in the weaker submissive attitude toward me. In other words, she put me in the position of control and power that was an important part of my (and every man's) sexual potency. Her personality, her feelings toward me, took me out of the position of being overly submissive to a too-controlling mother and helped put me in the controlling, dominating position over Penny, just as at age seven I had an erection when pushing Sam to the ground to get my ball. This is why Penny unconsciously attracted me so strongly when I was introduced to her at the Holdens'. That is how I learned, although not at the time, why a man is not necessarily potent with every woman. It depends not only on his own freedom from inhibitions but upon how her dynamics fit into his own. Penny had put herself in my hands to do as I wanted with sexually, but with the promise that I take responsibility for her welfare; this I could not do on split-second notice in the heat of passionate arousal.

At a large party I met Molly, an unusually attractive girl, vivacious and with bubbling good spirits and an ever-ready sense of humor. We chatted and hit it off instantly. She invited me for an early supper the next Saturday. It turned out that Molly was divorced and had two small children. She was certainly fun to be with, and almost irresistible sexually. But she was not for me. She just had to be seeking another husband, and I did not want to be ensnared. The fact that she was divorced probably meant that, happy and wholesome though she seemed, something was not quite right somewhere. For why should a girl with every desirable quality make so bad a mistake in choosing a husband and then not find it out until after having two children? Any girl can goof on her first choice, but having two children before discovering it is something else. Maybe I was learning something—or maybe it was only my instinct, ever alert when it came to self-preservation, and maybe I did not consciously think that until much later. At any rate, as I was leaving, the door from her living room to the hall was about halfway closed. I opened it wide with my left hand and extended my right arm in what was meant as a gallant social gesture, as though sweeping her through. But she took it as an invitation to my arms. She threw her arms around me, pressed her body against me and kissed my lips ardently. I reacted reflexly by pressing her even tighter to me, bending her over backward, returning her kiss. It was ultrapassionate, and I could not control having an instant orgasm.

This of course enormously increased the temptation to see her and have her with me in the apartment. I tried to keep a distance but she sometimes got through my defenses. Unquestionably, she was trying to seduce me sexually in the hope of marrying me; she was so attractive that I could not help but give it some consideration. But I tried my best not to let her think that there was the least hope, even though she had to know that I liked and respected her and could barely control myself sexually when with her.

One warm Saturday afternoon in the springtime I was in the apartment studying and happened to look out the window. A police car was pulling up. I watched it. It stopped at the entrance. An officer got out and then Molly! He escorted her into my building! In a few minutes she was at my door, alone. "I've been in an accident," she said; "I was thrown out of my car . . . look." And she showed me her legs, the stockings torn and her legs slightly bruised. As a medical student I was all solicitude, starting to examine her bruised legs more closely while asking her if she hurt anywhere else, and asking whether I should not take her to the out-patient clinic just to be sure, and in case any legal questions should arise. I tried to think of everything medically and legally. But she had no interest whatsoever. No sooner was she seated on the bed than she pulled me down on top of her, wanting sex. I yielded immediately without even disrobing. It was wonderful. But why, just out of an auto accident serious enough to be thrown out of the car, did she disregard the medical and legal problems, and why, when the officer offered to escort her home, did she direct him to my apartment? And then why come to me not for my care or sympathy, but, directly undistracted by anything else, for sex? Did she think I would become more likely to marry her? I got no feeling of anything calculating, but only of spontaneity. I still wonder if it were not that she was trying to relieve her anxieties and tensions, and *escape* her problems of a damaged car and everything else in that great diversion and reassurance, sex. For sex can be like alcohol and drugs as an escape from troubles and sorrows. Can it be that sexual acceptance by the partner has a meaning in the deep unconscious, of a return to and acceptance by the original source of love, help and reassurance—one's mother? And certainly sex drains tensions of all kinds. Did Molly come because she was so stimulated sexually, by the accident, so impatient for intercourse?

Molly could be characterized by two words: delightful and irresistible. But she should not be tied up with me, for all her needs should be in the service of finding a good husband who would also be a good father for her young children. "I don't do well without a husband" she once blurted out. Yet I could not reject her. I was learning to let time take care of some things, especially decisions that could be postponed. Meanwhile, selfishly, for me it was great. Was she so irresistible, so full of sex appeal, because her needs for intercourse were so importunately strong?

About two weeks later it was almost dinnertime, and I was waiting in the apartment for Gil to stop by for a book he wanted to borrow. There was a knock; it was not Gil but Molly! She gave me a kiss, not only friendly but intensely passionate. She wanted sex and immediately. I told her Gil was coming any minute, and said, "Let's wait until he has come and gone, it can't be over ten minutes, he's phoned and is on his way," but she was too aroused. "No," she said, "now, please, *now!* If he comes tell him to wait a minute."

"I can't do that," I replied. "And why should we be interrupted?" I did not want Gil, whom I did not know very well, to see Molly there, for both our sakes. She pressed against me. She succeeded in arousing me thoroughly, but I said, "Let's just wait two minutes." Thereupon Gil arrived. I asked Molly to stay in the bathroom. I gave Gil the book and in less than two minutes he was gone, and I went for Molly. The place was now our own, free and clear; we could take our time. Molly came out—in a barely suppressed fury at me—all sex drive gone. She was on her way somewhere, so there was nothing to do but drive her to her destination. She remained in her rage at me, speaking in subdued but intense tones, almost whispering although we were alone together in the car. That was the last time I saw her. She could not tolerate frustration for even five minutes. She had to have sex exactly when she wanted it: otherwise she seemed frigid.

Apparently Molly was sometimes under extremely intense pressure of desire and had to act to quench it without delay. I remembered her telling me that the great sex she had had with her husband for the year before their marriage vanished instantly the moment the ceremony was over. At that moment, she lost all desire for him. Later I recalled her telling me that her father had a mistress and her mother was so submissive to this, almost groveling to hold her father, that Molly lost all respect for her mother and came to despise her. Maybe she was only free sexually when she was in control of the situation and remote from any possibility of being like her submissive, groveling mother. Was this the key—that she used sex to be in control, and the need to control intensified her sex? By contrast, she spoke of her father's mistress admiringly, as though being a mistress were something glamorous, far better than being a wife; and she seemed to identify with her father, the one in control. I could get only these glimpses of her dynamics, and of course knew nothing about her childhood pattern.

My own dynamics in relation to her seem clear. Molly was a happy person at least on the surface, and I think we all feel happier with happy people. She was vivacious, with a good sense of humor and quick wit, so there was no mystery about being attracted to her as a person. Sexually I was so strongly attracted because I was, in large part, reacting to her own intense and free sex needs and her happiness with sex, and probably also to her needs for love and attention, reassurance and security, which were behind them. I felt that she got even more satisfaction from arousing me to orgasm than having one herself. This fitted her need to control. And it was diametrically counter to my rebellion against being controlled as I was by my mother. Therefore, these childhood patterns of ours conflicted and did not mesh. It is no reflection on Molly, wonderful girl that she was, that she was not for me as a wife. She was too mercurial; she felt that she had the fit to me, but I did not feel that way toward her.

While my education in sex and life thus rocked along haphazardly, my medical education proceeded systematically as laid out by the school, with every minute of it thrilling. We marveled at the beauty and wonder of the body and of the forces working for and against it. Cells and bacteria and submicroscopic viruses; the strange life cycles of parasites; the master tissue, the brain—we had all this to learn, and had to learn to use it to "relieve suffering and prolong life." I do not know how many of our class felt the excitement of discovery as profoundly and enjoyed it as deeply as I did, but at least two shared my feelings—Gregg and Chet. We three had become close friends; I used to tell Gregg he reminded me of Dorian Gray, for he was very handsome in an aristocratic way, being in fact an aristocrat of the Old South, and nothing animalistic showed on his calm, poised, proper surface. Chet was equally sensitive, but more earthy and less assured. Chet didn't date very much. Gregg liked only the best; society girls— ultrabeautiful, perfectly groomed, with collars of the finest natural pearls around their necks—were his type. He liked simple people too, but society people were the kind he gravitated toward, and that seemed to drift into his field. There were other classmates too with whom I played tennis and swam. And then there were people I met here and there. The school had great wisdom, providing a relatively light schedule, with ample leisure, to keep us fresh and enthusiastic. And in the national board examinations more of us would place in the top ten than would students from other schools with much heavier schedules. I think all schools should pressure students less and trust them more.

Among the outside people I'd met was Maude. We became quite friendly, in a platonic, asexual way. She was old in my eyes, about thirty. She was good-looking enough, but for some reason the sexual element was absent. I found out that the inhibition was in her, not me. I was never quite clear as to whether she had been married very briefly years back or not. She had an apartment and would invite me there for dinner or just for the evening. I took her out to occasional things she was interested in, like art and music, and sometimes a hockey game. It was very comfortable; if I felt lonely I would go and study in her apartment, and she seemed to like that. One day in early winter she asked if she could stay overnight in my apartment. I think she said hers was being redecorated. I never liked to sleep with anybody in the same bed, except a beautiful girl whom I desired. So I kept a single folding cot in case a friend wanted to stay the night, and I set it up for myself, leaving the bed for Maude.

It was all very easy, comfortable and platonic. She did not leave the next day or the next. The fifth evening of this, we both retired at the same time but suddenly, alone in my cot, something shifted in me. I became aroused sexually. I rolled on a rubber and slipped into bed with her. The same Maude who had never interested me sexually now aroused me to the greatest intensity. But there was one flaw; I'd heard of vaginism, common enough in virgin brides and soon relieved—a spasm of the vaginal wall which clamps the opening closed and prevents full penetration. I found out later that it was not the absence of proper wooing, the suddenness of my unexpected approach that caused this, but that she suffered with it on other occasions. It did not dull my desire however, which was overwhelming. The resistance even heightened it. In spite of the intense pleasure of that night, Maude still did not arouse me much sexually in the daytime when we were up and about. I had no intention of having a girl or woman move in with me. That was for marriage when the right girl came along. Meanwhile, although I might not have known it clearly then, I wanted my freedom and independence.

Maude moved back to her apartment and we saw less of each other, but continued our comfortable, platonic friendship. I do not mean it unkindly, but I can't help looking back on this incident with some amusement. Also surprise, for with no other girl were the barriers to sex ever down once, that I did not ever after desire her. That spring Maude was married. I was so ignorant, naïve and dumb about people and their feelings that I still don't feel sure I can guess what she was up to, if anything. I'm suspicious that she was trying to marry me, despite the discrepancy in our ages. I was then twenty-two. But maybe it was only that she was lonely and found it pleasanter to be in my apartment than alone in hers. Or possibly some undesirable man was pestering her in her apartment. I was too self-centered to think of this last possibility then, and she never hinted at anything like that. So I try to excuse my lack of sympathetic understanding for a friend; Maude was a fine person, generous and always welcoming when I was lonely. I should have understood her better, but I was still struggling with my own needs and problems, and they so filled my mind that there was not enough mature, surplus interest to give out to her. It was gradually turning out that I could have fresh eager young girls, and I was not that attracted to an older, sexually inhibited one, however charming and lovely she might be. The vaginism might not have been a serious inhibition, as it often occurs in girls who for any reason are anxious about sex relations at the moment. Perhaps Maude just had temporary doubt and hesitations. I remember her fondly and wish we could meet and have some chuckles over those days. I certainly hope her marriage was a happy one—I was so egotistical as to think that she might have been dissatisfied with the man who wanted to marry her and thought him a little below herself in culture, refinement and sensitivity; and thought she would have a try for me before committing herself to him irrevocably.

It is hard to be objective about one's self—everything one sees that is favorable is not necessarily egotistical. All that glitters is not brass; one can only try to be as objective about one's self as about anyone else.

12

BEST FRIENDS

The friends thou hast and their adoption tried,
Grapple them to thy soul with hoops of steel.

William Shakespeare,
"Hamlet"

Make friends by being honest. Keep them by being steadfast.

Elizabeth Jackson's advice to her son, Andrew Jackson

The ash-grove, how graceful, how plainly 'tis speaking,
The harp thro' it playing has language for me;
Whenever the light thro' its branches is breaking,
A host of kind faces is gazing on me.
The friends of my childhood again are before me,
Each step makes a mem'ry, as freely I roam.

"The Ash-grove," a Welsh folksong

Home for Christmas vacation again, and Jim had introduced me to a simple but beautifully decorated small, quiet restaurant in a large apartment building. It had booths and was the sort of place where one could be as leisurely as one wished. Most dishes were extremely expensive, but some few were not (if worse came to worst, I had shirred eggs), and I'd saved my pennies for an evening there with Nelda. Our marvelous, absorbing talks continued, and I only wish I had the kind of mind that could remember some of them in detail. A little of that evening's talk comes back to me. Of course, egotistically, I was soon telling her about my adventures. I remember saying, "You know, or perhaps you don't realize how much I admire and love your unflinching honesty. But why is that? I don't think I am *dis*honest, but yet you seem to have something that I don't."

She said, "You are honest, but maybe a little prejudiced."

A trifle shocked, I said, "You know I grew up with every kind of boy and that I like anyone I can respect who likes me, and that's most people, and I do not even notice their backgrounds."

"Oh," said Nelda, "I didn't mean that kind of prejudice, but I think every kind of prejudice interferes with thinking realistically and honestly."

"Then what kind of prejudice do you mean?" I asked. "What other kind *is* there?"

"Why," she said gently, "sometimes I think you are somewhat prejudiced in favor of yourself."

Her words hit a nerve; I knew it was true. Nor have I completely overcome it, although I have learned more and more to leave myself out of things in devotion to the task at hand.

I recalled Matthew 10:39, "He that loseth his life for my sake shall find it," which had always seemed to mean losing one's egotism. I have lived with and by these wise words, and they have benefited me immeasurably. In analytic terminology, Nelda had interpreted my narcissism, my egotism, bringing them into sharper awareness, and this has helped me in working them through ever since. She added, "There is a possibility that your interest in science is part of your striving for honesty and certainty, for you see it as learning with the greatest certainty anything that man tries to know and is capable of knowing— and perhaps that is why, after reading that novel, you quoted to me, 'Oh what a dusty answer gets the soul when hot for certainty in this our life.' "

I told her about Gregg and Chet, what good friends we had become, but that somehow they were not like Jim and Charles. As usual, she could go directly to the reality I groped for and missed: "They are not like Charles and Jim at all," she said. "Charles is ahead of you in some ways, but behind you in most. He is much more worldly than you, but you have some inner strengths and higher aims that he lacks— you're more interested in understanding the world and contributing to it, although you are still struggling to find your way. Jim and you are so close because you have something that supplements him, but you respect him so much and he is a leader—independent—while you are partly still a follower toward him. But Gregg and Chet are satellites of yours."

Suddenly this seemed clear. "I think you are right," I said; "you've put your finger right on it. I need them and we enjoy doing things together, but with them I'm more in the position of leader. I'm surprised; I've always felt that I was a follower, so dependent on someone else for companionship and insights and finding my way and it infuriates me to be so dependent and submissive, so much the follower. But with Gregg and Chet I feel I am the stronger, more free personality."

Nelda smiled. "You are independent and leader enough," she said. "Only it will take time to come out." I was pleased but puzzled.

"I hope you're right," I said. "But meanwhile, I have found my field yet have not found *myself*. And this keeps me from being as happy as I could be. But I'm thankful for the good luck in having found true friends."

"Richness in friends," said Nelda, "isn't luck. It is a quality of the person. It is one of your characteristics, like your hair, your eyes, the way you carry yourself. You will always be rich in friends, Corey!"

Suddenly I felt very sad. I felt that what she had said was, as always, simple and true. I *was* blessed with the quality of having close friends, but I felt sad for Nelda. For suddenly it struck me that one of the barriers between us was a loneliness in her and that it was a quality of hers just as definite as having close friends was a quality of mine. I remembered my fear when she first had mentioned Tad, and that I had said a little secret silent prayer that she would not be lonely. To shake off this mood I said, "Do you remember my telling you of my first night as a seaman, hosing down the decks, and the sea water bursting out of the big nozzle like a huge sparkler on the Fourth of July? And I saw this phosphorescence as it spurted from the nozzle, phosphorescent plankton—little microscopic plants and animals, billions of them glowing like tiny fireflies. That's how medicine is to me. A thing of beauty and wonder."

"It's esthetic to you, and emotional, like art," she said. "Just as scientists like Planck and Einstein are so impressed by the beauty of the universe they explore. But you will use all this, Corey, not for art or science, which are really not so different perhaps, but you will use it to heal."

"Yes," I agreed, "but although I've never thought it through, they all fit together somehow . . . art, science, healing."

"I'm sure they do," said Nelda, "but the healing means your life will be made difficult as well as gratifying. You are a healer already in outlook and feelings, as you are an artist in your appreciation of nature. I can express myself in art, in the beauty that is in the realities I select. But you will devote your life to relieving suffering, and it will be painful for you to live in a world in which there is so much ugliness and in which so many people are so callous and cruel to others. You want to heal, but you must live through evil, and every day you will see what is on the first page of the newspaper—mostly the opposite of what you will be working for."

And so we talked. Nelda still saw Tad, but was not inclined to speak about him. But it was not jealousy that concerned me; rather, it was Nelda's happiness. (This must have been mostly from identification with my parents' wishes for my own happiness.) I thought she did not love Tad and that he would not make her happy. How could I feel that, based on nothing? I guess I could because Nelda and I were so sensitive to each other. But I did feel some reassurance. Our mood turned light. We went out to walk down the dinner. We talked for an hour or two and then stopped in a little shop for hot chocolate, parting at her door with a sense of happiness. Yet underneath there was something new, a faint distance. It was because of me; I was moving no closer to marriage wth Nelda. She could have moved me, but she gave no sign. Possibly she did not want it, but it was not in her nature to be subtle or devious. And so again we parted.

A few months before this visit, Jim had married Pam, the all-American girl we had met while in France. On my way to visit them I learned what a bachelor feels when his best friend marries. We now lived in different cities and would not be seeing much of each other, but Jim could no longer be his free-ranging self. "He travels the fastest who travels alone." Now Jim was two, not one. He had primary obligations. It was a loss to me, but I was glad for him. He had found his mate, while I seemed as far from this as ever. Pam greeted me warmly with a friendly kiss. Now I am old enough to enjoy affection and eroticism in the kiss of a charming woman. I enjoyed it then, also, but too intensely to be relaxed. I was shy. I blushed. I think it was because for me, at twenty-two, constantly suppressing a volcano of sex, such a kiss was enough to stir some tumescence, and I feared that my sexual feeling would show through the affection, that it would be resented, that I would be rejected because of it, not loved and accepted, as I needed so inordinately to be. Sex was too powerful a force then for me to guide it with a light rein. But if I blushed, Pam only showed pleasure. We had always liked each other immensely since that first meeting in the Midi, and she would have accepted me anyway as Jim's best friend. Also, she must have responded to my admiration for her. She was still the all-American girl, with the invisible tennis racquet, so straight, so easy, friendly, good-humored and outgoing. I envied Jim—for achieving marriage with such a girl. But the envy was slight compared with the friendship. Jim was sort of my alter ego, how I would have been had I been more free, more grown-up, whatever that meant. He had opened the wide world for me, more than any other person. In my mind, nothing was too good for Jim. He deserved a wonderful girl like Pam. I think she sensed a little hero worship in my attitude to Jim and liked it. She must have taken it as solid approval and confirmation of her choice.

Jim had become a nuclear physicist. He foresaw it as a great coming field. Even I knew that atomic energy was only a short time off. All physicists hoped it would be used for peace, but were powerless to prevent its use as a bomb, which depends not on power over nature, but on power over other men. I don't know if power corrupts, but I do know that the world is full of people who are corrupt anyway, people with hate and violence in their hearts—and that they often get power over nations, in spite of the people of good will; and I believe powerlessness also corrupts.

I have learned that the differences between those who hate and those who love can be traced to how each one was treated during early childhood, especially from conception to age six or seven. Love and respect breed respect and love. Abuse generates in the child lifelong hostility in his adulthood. Whatever else, that is basic, and it is that simple.

I thought of the afternoon in Cambridge with Rutherford. If my IQ was 155 on that particular test, Jim's must have been at least 165. But what I admired in him and tried to emulate was not intellect alone; it was the way he *used* it, the emotional base on which it rested, his capacity to be interested in people, things, events, rather than always striving for his own acceptance and status and being absorbed with his own problems. He knew what to read. He read a lot of newspapers and decided for himself which were "good" and reliable. He knew where to go and whom to talk with, and he followed through. What I admired far more than his intelligence was the kind of person he was. I knew we would be close friends forever; but I was aware that his marriage and his career would take him in new directions, as mine would me, and perhaps to distant locales, and the future would not be as the past had been.

Before leaving we chatted about Ralph. Jim said, "I may have a clue as to why we thought Ralph was not quite himself. He is seeing a lot of a very young widow with a small child. It sounds improbable, but don't be too surprised if he marries her." I was incredulous and said so. "I just can't imagine 'The Man Flammond' married. I just can't visualize it!" To this Jim replied, "Every personality is full of surprises. But I agree with you, Corey. It's hard to imagine."

My sister Judy was now in college. We'd grown close; the unconscious rivalry of early childhood had waned. I invited her to come see me whenever she could, and meet Gregg and Chet. Occasionally classmates and other friends stopped by to visit while I was home for vacations, but I knew she would enjoy coming on such a visit and meeting some of my medical school classmates. I had never been very thoughtful or active in introducing her to my friends, because I guess I still saw her as little Judy, the slightly-tomboyish, athletic kid sister, rather than as a young lady; I still had some of the old pattern of protecting my toys, my room, my secrets, my friends, where I went and what I did—in a word, my privacy, from Judy's curiosity and her "tagging along," which she had done in all innocence as a small child. I am always surprised and distressed at how these old childish ways of feeling fail to be totally outgrown, but go on and on in adult life forever. But I have learned that once we see them clearly, we can consciously control and change them to a considerable extent. I hope that over the years Judy has come to recognize how much her older brother truly loves her, in spite of his showing it so little until so late.

13
ALINE

Christmas and vacation were soon over, said Corey Jones, and I returned again to my apartment. I enjoyed its privacy but it lacked a fine and congenial woman. And I still was looking for a wife. Soon after returning, at one of the Holdens' Sunday evenings, I met a girl who was not at all attractive sexually to me, but was very interesting intellectually. She had held many jobs, had traveled widely and knew people all over the world. Her name was Amalie, and she was pushing thirty. She spoke of a man in the South whom she was in love with, but it was not clear whether or not she was engaged to him. Amalie smiled a lot, and the smile had an artificial quality. Now I know a name for it—euphoria—a happiness which is somehow exaggerated, usually in order to hide the opposite, some painful unhappiness, even some depression ("We laugh lest we weep."). I could see that when her face was in repose, care and sadness showed through all around her mouth and eyes; they disappeared when she lit up with a smile. She was courageous, facing life despite her inner unhappiness. Amalie had an administrative position in a school of art, a good position in an excellent school. She responded to my interest in art and artists, and at the end of the evening she said that she had to manage a tea for the school, and would I come, because they needed extra men. This was in mid-January, close to examination time; I did not want to encourage anything with Amalie, but she so much wanted me to come that I accepted. Afterward I kicked myself for being so weak and phoned her to beg off. But she was out, so I dropped the matter and went. How often do whole segments of our lives hinge on such trivial inconsequential decisions.

The tea was as I expected: very polite, a little artificial, everyone trying to be nice. I consoled myself with the thought that the weather was foul, with intermittent freezing rain, streets slippery and slushy, so that I wasn't missing anything much outside, and in here it was warm and cozy. I was sitting rather stiffly in a wing chair, rising periodically to be introduced to a student or faculty member. Then a girl came over who was different from the rest. Amalie saw her and introduced us, and she seemed pleased. "This is Miss Aline Clayton," she said, "a good friend of mine." The sparks were already flying. Aline sat on a big leather ottoman, at my feet . . . soft hair of finely spun gold, beautifully tinted natural complexion, no makeup, perfect figure of the rather broad-hipped type, all girl, simple, direct, looking me full in the face, eager, accepting. It takes too long to write all I noticed and reacted to in that split second. It added up to utter femininity in a high-caliber, proper girl, and it was all I could do to control my impulses to touch her arm, her hand. Now I see that I was reacting to something in her also that she directed to me, or which was aroused by me. It was pure masculinity and femininity interacting with each other. When she spoke, she gesticulated very little, but enough to brush my knee with her finger. I saw Aline several times in the next few weeks; and when exams were all over I took her and Amalie to dinner.

We paid a lot of attention to Amalie during dinner. She lapped it up, but I think partly we did it to control the sparks between us, the attraction was so strong. Aline reminded me of someone, someone pleasant, and in the back of my mind I was searching for whom it might be. But then I heard Amalie say something that startled me back to full attention. "I'll be away next weekend," she said to Aline, "and if you'd like to sign out and use my apartment for a change from the school I'd be glad to have you there."

Aline thanked her and accepted tentatively. When I got home I wondered a bit; did Amalie engineer this? She would have made a play for me herself if there had been a chance of its working. She was lonely and had her own needs. She probably sensed that I was not attracted to her. Did she get vicarious pleasure from bringing Aline and me together? Did it make her feel part of it, important? Was that as close to people as Amalie could get—participating vicariously in their mutual attraction, making them grateful to her? She seemed pretty straight-laced and that heightened my surprise. I couldn't figure it out, but if it was gratitude and vicarious participation that she wanted, she had it already—she had made us grateful and made us her friends. We were all pleased.

I phoned Aline every day, and just talking by phone aroused me sexually. Saturday finally arrived. With razor and toothbrush hidden in the pocket of my overcoat, I called for Aline and we started off for dinner, I hugging her arm close to me. I'd given a lot of thought to the selection of a restaurant, and decided on a rather simple one, not expensive—by necessity—but with character and good food and pleasant waiters. We were early enough for a choice and were easily seated at a table for two at the wall. Our waiter felt the situation and smiled benignly. He gave us plenty of time to get settled and to seriously debate what to order. We gave him our selections (lamb chops with all the trimmings and a glass of rosé wine), and he departed with a flourish. In due course, as the lawyers say, he returned beaming and set the piping platters before us. There were little lamps on the table, the room was pleasantly filled, everything was perfect, and then we found that we could not eat. We just could not get it down. We did our best, if only because of the waiter. He was very upset. Was something wrong with the food? Was the lady indisposed? Life's embarrassing moments! There was nothing to do but leave. Once out in the cold air, with me hugging Aline's arm close, we both burst out laughing. And laughing we turned our steps cautiously over the icy streets to Amalie's apartment. Aline had left her weekend things there earlier in the day. We closed and bolted the door. Alone at last.

Aline was utter femininity and utter naturalness, with none of Myrna's surprise that I was interested in her in *that* way, none of Bette's decision to see what it was like, none of Penny's uncertainty—not that any trace of a thought of them was in my mind. I was completely absorbed in Aline. No sooner was the door bolted than we were in each other's arms, overcoats still on. It was as natural as breathing or heartbeat. It was as though it had been fated from the beginning of time. No question, no doubt, no hesitation. Nothing to decide. Something urged, and we followed blindly, unquestioning, unthinking. There was no element of seduction; this was a mutual coming together. We stood there in each other's arms and kissed. What a delicious kiss! She said, "You are inflammable." I said nothing but she was exactly right. If I did not control myself firmly I would explode in the next minute, in all those clothes. So I controlled the kiss, just savored it slowly, and drew apart to help her off with her coat, then switched on the lamp in the hall and the light in the bedroom. I took off my coat. In the bedroom I did not trust myself to undress her, and before I knew it, with speed and grace, she had shed her clothes and was in bed, pillow raised, blanket under her chin, watching my every movement, smiling faintly. I snapped off the bedroom light, leaving only the lamp in the hall to diffuse its soft, warm glow. I slipped off my clothes. Aline said, "Oh, you are just like a butterfly coming out of a chrysalis!" Total naturalness, free of any embarrassment.

I slid into bed, hoping she did not notice as I quickly rolled on a rubber. I was gentle and as slow as I could be; I wanted this to be just right, but the sexual pressure required a lot of control. Slowly, gently, firmly I put my arms around her. To prolong this pleasure was difficult, but how intensely, sensually satisfying it was. The restraints held, and we climaxed together. We lay in each other's arms breathing, relaxing, until the next surge. And after that we slept. I awoke first in the morning. Awoke to a dream come true—and to a daydream come true. How rarely are our sleeping or waking dreams so gratified in reality. To awaken with a gorgeous girl right there in your arms—beautiful, young, in every way desirable and desiring you, and wanting to be desired by you. I relished to the full what I now knew reality offered or permitted only rarely, so full a gratification of our wishes. Gradually the urge welled, too strong to be denied. But the sun was well up outside the drawn blinds, and I thought I knew how this lovely creature would like to be awakened. My guess was right. We lay entwined awhile longer, loath to relinquish our long embrace. But once we stirred we were exhilarated and ravenous; we showered, and I found that she was more free and natural than I, who probably imbibed over-modesty from the attitudes of my father. We decided to prolong our enjoyment as long as possible and not venture out into the dismal world to eat. We would raid Amalie's stores and replace them before leaving.

I escorted Aline back to the school before Amalie returned. We were walking on air, as the cliché goes. We did not want to come down to everyday chores and problems and people. We each wanted to be together or else alone with our feelings. She sped to her room, I to my apartment. Even then I felt that we were one in body. And a faint thought of Nelda flashed across my awareness—that feeling of being one in spirit with her. I really just surrendered to *feelings* for Aline; but some weeks later I had further thoughts: someday I would meet such a girl as could be one in body *and* spirit. That girl would be my mate for life. And then suddenly I knew whom Aline reminded me of—my Aunt Edie! She, too, was this sort of good-humored, natural, all-feminine, blonde, blue-eyed, loving person. Scientists who study animals tell us that sexual desire follows the paths of the first attachments of the young. A sparrow raised by a robin will not mate with sparrows, but will try to mate with a robin. If Aline reminded me of Aunt Edie, who had loved me so when I was a baby, and whom I still loved dearly, that must have added intensity to my attraction to Aline. To how many gatherings had I gone and searched in vain? And from this party that I so nearly did not attend came Aline, came the change she brought into my life, and came aftereffects which never entirely wore away. Like other great determining occurrences of my life, this one resulted from a minor incidental decision of no importance whatever—the decision not to refuse to attend a tea.

An idyllic period opened. For Aline, sex was something so natural and simple, so clean, so virginal. It snowed, and it was clear; in the spring rain fell, and then the warm sun shone; and just as simply and naturally and unthinkingly Aline and I came together. We tried everything, not out of curiosity or experimentation, but just by following impulse. We lived for the moment. Ah, that those days "so soon glided by e'en like the passage of an angel's tear, falling through the clear ether silently."

The week before Easter Judy came to visit. Gregg and Chet liked her, but nothing more than that. Another classmate, Roger, was a powerfully built extrovert; we all liked him enormously and agreed that he would be a "horse and buggy" doctor, and live to be a hundred. I was pleased and surprised at his giving Judy a rush. He seemed seriously interested and followed up with visits to her at school and at home. Absorbed as I was in my own problems, it seemed almost out of character for me to be so responsible toward Judy as to introduce her to my friends and eligible young men. There was another classmate whom I did not know very well named Gerald. He was rather distant and sometimes seemed a little sad. He met Judy also, but showed no interest. Jim was right: every personality is full of surprises. Roger, the extrovert, the strong, the country doctor, the centenarian, never married or practiced, but went into research, for which he won national honors; he died of a rare disease before our fifteenth reunion. And Gerald, the distant, married Judy and became a national leader in his specialty. But the paths to these plateaus were long and tortuous. How long would be the climb before I found a mate and found myself?

Aline and I worked out plans for the summer. I located a job in a small private sanitorium for subacute and chronic diseases, in rolling countryside near a semiprivate lake, where I would have privileges, and not too far from the sea. Since I had finished only two years of medical school, my responsibilities were limited, being mostly for laboratory work. But it was also an opportunity to see patients and learn how such a hospital was run. The pay was not high, but the job was only about three-quarter time. It was ideal for a vacation, in that setting, with Aline nearby. For she had succeeded in finding a position in a shop in the medium-sized town on whose outskirts the sanitorium lay. Considering Aline's beauty and gentleness, she was an obvious asset to any business dealing with the public. Still we thought we were most fortunate in making these arrangements. We both allowed time to visit our homes before starting the summer jobs. Aline lived in a southern state and had a long trip home. I saw her off the day before I left to see my parents.

On the train going home I thought of Ralph. The simple announcement of his wedding had come a week before. The incredible had come to pass! They were not leaving for a honeymoon for two weeks yet, and I went to visit them. I thought Ralph was so special that probably even a demigoddess would not have seemed worthy. Eunice was good-looking, straightforward, a young widow, only a few years older than Jim and me, with one child. A year after their marriage she presented Ralph with twins. I thought of Minerva . . . and Nelda . . . and Aline. Eunice was just a fine woman, and I guess there is nothing better. I regretted not getting to know her well. I still could not visualize the free-ranging Ralph coming home to dinner each evening and being a patient father to three children, no matter how wonderful a wife he had. It was like a stallion broken to be a carriage horse! It just didn't fit.

When I saw Jim and Pam, I asked them about it. Jim had somewhat the same feeling as I, but he said: "Don't forget that you are not too different—and neither am I." This was one of his sudden thrusts, and as usual there was some truth in it, and as usual we argued the point.

"The reason we like Ralph so much," said Jim, "is that he has the freedom and capacities to live as you and I would like to, at least parts of us would. But I admit that he is more than ten years older than we are, and he has had that many more years of experience and practice in living. Maybe it will be harder for him to change his spots at forty than for us at twenty-five."

"That's my worry," I said. "Can a leopard really ever change its spots?"

I had called Nelda, and we made an appointment for two o'clock the next afternoon. After breakfast I phoned "Pop" Nielsen and he said, "Let's have lunch together in the cafeteria at 12:30," which fitted in nicely. The day was cloudy with intermittent rain. I was thinking about Nelda. True, we were one in spirit only and had been for three years. But we could also have been—perhaps still could be—one in flesh also. With her honesty, insight and feelings she would be as free and passionate and clean and beautiful in sex as any girl could be, as I knew Aline to be. Why, then, had I always hesitated? Aline and I could join and enjoy the masculinity and the femininity. But for some reason, as I've said, I felt so profoundly that I could not be united sexually with Nelda without marrying her. Sex with her would be wonderful, I had not the slightest doubt, but once we were joined physically we would marry no matter what, and without delay. And why not? Because she was not as outgoing as I? She had other qualities; we could complement each other. Was she in some way weak, neurotic—why did my mother have reservations about Nelda? Who can judge these things? Could anyone so perceptive and sincere, so free of illusion about others and herself, have anything much wrong? If we were one in spirit but not one in flesh, as man and wife, perhaps the fault lay in some inhibition in *me*.

Well, it was time to meet "Pop" Nielsen. He had been a good friend, helping me locate the jobs in the laboratories, and, once the decision was made, not trying to persuade me to come into his department but writing the key letter that helped get me accepted by the medical school of my choice. I did not formulate it then, but he was possibly the most selfless and least egotistical man I had ever met, as Nelda was the least egotistical girl. It was always good to see him. He continued an interest in my unfolding career, and from him I got a firsthand look, from one at the top, of developments in the physical sciences. Lunch was over all too quickly. Raincoat over my arm, I set out for Nelda's.

She opened the door and I entered, dropping coat and hat. We greeted with our usual little affectionate hug and light kiss. Then she did something quite out of character, for she had never made any physical move toward me—she took my right hand in her left and my left in her right, and stood back with them away from our bodies. She held my hands lightly but firmly, looking me full in the face with that gentle, demure, serious expression, and said, "Corey, a week ago I married Tad. I thought it was better all around if you were not there. I wanted to tell you that myself rather than write or send an announcement. It was rather sudden because Tad found that he would be taking a trip this summer, leaving next week, and if we married we could go together. Corey . . ." She may have said more, I don't know. I felt myself bring our hands together over our breasts. I squeezed hers with deep affection. I felt myself circle my arms around her, and this time I kissed her full on her beautiful warm lips, slowly, gently, a full ardent kiss. Then I stood back a little. I took her hands again, left in right, right in left. I heard myself say, "Nelda, you know better than I myself that I love you and have always loved you since that first evening we met after Brent's death. You know that I have never succeeded in loving you properly. You know I could not love you sexually without marrying you, and something in me has blocked me. But you know how much you have given me and meant to me and always will."

And I heard myself going on, "You know how much I want your happiness although I have not been man enough to try to give it to you myself. But with all the feelings I have for you, I want you to have a good and happy and satisfying life." And then, coming a little out of my daze, I felt something wet on my face. And then I came to myself and realized that tears were running down my cheeks. I stood there a little sheepish, but strong enough not to try to control them. Nelda lightly kissed the wet, first on one cheek and then on the other.

"We will meet again," she said, "with no disloyalty to Tad or to whomever you marry." We could not stay and chat about trivia. We embraced and kissed again, affectionately, lightly, and I walked out into the gray afternoon. Rain was now falling steadily.

Fool, fool, fool, I thought silently to myself. What have you denied her and yourself? Do you expect life to give you this a second time? I raised my face so that the cool rain would wash away the hot tears. I walked and walked. Again melodramatically the gray sky and falling rain reflected what was in my heart. Then came a distant rumbling of thunder, and I thought, is this foreboding about Tad? Why should I not trust him, whom I had never seen, if Nelda chose him? Is it my own jealousy? I looked around to see where I was and turned to walk home. As I trudged along, indefatigably in those days of youth, reassurance expressed itself. If my instincts were against sex and marriage with Nelda, how could I force myself against them? Could I force the issue if it were something in Nelda—or if it were in me? Perhaps I could not have done differently—but what a loss. If only she would be happy!

I reached home in time for dinner as I had said I would. Always so wrapped up in myself, my own feelings and problems, I was a poor observer of others, although not lacking in empathy, warmth and sympathy once I understood them. But Judy, though much younger, missed little. A look from her showed that; but she said nothing. My controls came to the fore and we had a jolly family dinner; I told the news of Ralph's wife and Nelda's marriage, and my tone seemed bright, matter-of-fact, and came out with humor at times. Judy chimed in with her own news and interests, and Mother and Father commented and contributed to the conversation, watching the food vanish from our plates and enjoying our company.

Blessed small talk and chitchat, and blessed family stability! This is the great haven for youth—a harmonious and stable home. It is what every child needs, and for a long time. I was twenty-three, and it was still a needed harbor from the ocean of a life that had thus far been calm; but I had not yet put out far from shore. Those who cannot provide children with a happy, stable home should not have children, for children are foredoomed who lack such a home, foredoomed to neurosis and craziness and crime; and thus they doom the world to crime and hate and wars. I had a happy stable home, and I was grateful even then. I become more so as my life lengthens and I look back over its source and course. I went to bed not alone in an apartment but in a home with loving parents and a loving sister. That is a kind of emotional security. Whatever happened in life, my family truly loved me and I loved them. I am grateful for so much in life, and one thing is that my parents lived so long—until I was grown and settled and at least a little mature. Since they have died, I think of them looking down on me from heaven with all their love as strong as ever, satisfied with how I turned out. Because of this fantasy I have little fear of death.

At home I relaxed, felt safe, knew I would sink into a deep and satisfying sleep; but then just on the verge of sleep I began to think of Nelda—demurely, simply, sincerely looking me full in the face; quietly, gently, steadily holding each of my hands in hers; telling me she was married. And my eyes, though closed, overflowed again. No crying, no sobs. Nothing but a silent, steady flow of tears. Hot tears, the poets call them, and they are right. Were the tears flowing for my own selfish loss? I did not feel that—I felt them as an out-pouring of love for Nelda, as a prayer from my soul that she have a happy life, as gratitude for all she had given me; for teaching me what emotional honesty was, and sensitivity of perception, esthetic feeling, and artistic talent, and generosity—demanding nothing, not even requesting anything; for her ease of seeing life, and freedom from egotism, and more and even more . . . her wholehearted ac-ceptance of me, and the sex she would also have given me if I had taken the step. Now what? Yes, I wept for my own irreparable loss, and I wept for the good life I wanted for her and did nothing to give her, and for my fears of how Tad, the unknown, would treat her. Then it was morning, and, being young and healthy, I had slept and was refreshed and ready to learn to face a life without Nelda—Nelda, always there, and happy when I called, now to be in the arms of another. And the tears came again. And I knew it would take time, and that now I could not indulge them but would have to watch for them and control them.

Judy and I took a walk after breakfast. The weather had cleared; the sun shone. "To the hills whence cometh my strength . . . to the solid ground of nature, trusts the mind that builds for aye." Somehow sorrow is a little easier to bear when one contemplates the great impersonal forms and forces of nature that have been there for so many millions of years, since before human life, or any life, even existed. Always in life, when possible, I have been one of those who end the day by walking in the darkness and contemplating the stars in their beauty and infinite distance and duration. It restores perspective. Walking with Judy under blue sky and warm sun, against a cool breeze, even in the city, I was in full control and told her a little of my feelings. She told me some of hers. Some of the pressures of the boys on her at college for sex. And not only the boys, but the girls who slept with boys and told Judy she was "chicken" not to. She had known these problems came down to mating, to love, to feelings for another, eventually to reproduction, to babies. Many animals and birds mate faithfully for life, so marriage must be at least in part an instinct and not just a social convention; and if sex is part of permanent mating in many higher animals, then it must be to some extent in humans too, unless something is wrong with them. Judy thought there might be a double standard. Judy said that if she had sex with a boy she didn't love she would hate herself, would be disgusted. But if she loved him and wanted sex with him, then she would want to be married to him first. I told her of not having sex with Nelda, desirable as she was, because I could not think of her that way unless I married her, but that I had slept with other girls, and my conclusion was that she, Judy, was absolutely right. Try to concentrate it all on one person—love, sex, parenthood, marriage; that is a tall order, but it is the only happiness. She said she had taken courses in psychology but had found they had nothing to offer toward understanding these problems of real life. I told her that was my experience too, and we agreed that some of the instructors in psychology were afraid of life and afraid of seeing what people are really like emotionally down underneath. Judy and I were babes in the wood. We soon went our ways for the summer, Judy to a girl's camp as counselor and I to the laboratory job in the sanitorium and to Aline.

14
SUMMER IDYLL

For yesterday is but a dream and tomorrow is only a vision. But today well lived makes every yesterday a dream of happiness and every tomorrow a vision of hope.

From the Sanskrit

This time it was a fine spring day, said Corey Jones, as I once again rode the train to the medical school. I had to stop there on the way to my summer job in the small hospital to make the final arrangements for subletting the apartment and also to pick up the model-T that Gerald and I had pooled our resources to purchase. It was second-hand and old, but the mechanic, whom I admired for his independence, was satisfied that it was sound. Gerald had a job in a big hospital in his hometown and could use the family car for the summer while I used the Model-T.

Again I watched the passing landscape as the train sped on, and once again Nelda came into my thoughts. I felt as though I had lost part of my soul; I had lost someone I had never fully availed myself of, but I could not in fairness hold onto a rare person with needs of her own as strong as mine. I did not quite see then that I had held her or that I had rejected her. But I felt a twinge of uncomprehended guilt, perhaps because I had gotten so much more than I had given, or even had it in me to give. Yet Nelda must have received something from me. And then my mind turned away, and I pulled out of my bag a manual of laboratory procedures and studied it assiduously for the remainder of the trip; but the vague mood of depression tinged with anxiety would not entirely evaporate. I had not learned that each of us has only certain things to give and can only accept part of what another has to offer.

Having the car was a lift, for now I felt mobile. Gerald and I had heard that a classmate, Don, was turning it in for a new one, and we offered him whatever the dealer's allowance would be. At the time I asked Don why he was turning it in while it was in perfect condition, tight all around, the body still shiny, and he lived so near the medical school that he usually walked and used the car but little. He said, "For the girls, that's why. In fact, that's why I have a car at all, and why I'm getting a new one. That vicuna coat I got—why did I buy something that expensive and unusual? Why do we do any of these things? For the girls!" I could see his point, but something indefinable struck me as not exactly right about it. It was certainly true and proper to a point, but beyond that point his statement seemed not entirely honest; in fact, it sounded a trifle meretricious—not entirely masculine. Nelda would have been able to see clearly, where I groped. I had noticed Don's dapper dress without thinking about it. Now I thought, "Dapper Don." I didn't mean it unkindly; I liked him, although we never became close friends. Perhaps it was that Don was playing a feminine part—dressing up to attract girls— instead of assuming a masculine attitude of giving something. And perhaps I was critical because, although it was foreign to my makeup to criticize others, I was critical of myself; for I, too, was only a student with much less money than he had, and what did I have to give a girl?

I picked up the car and drove to the bookstore. There I got the textbook of medicine that we would use the next year and also a few books in the specialties we would be studying. I thought these would help me understand the patients this summer and that seeing the patients would immediately relate the reading to the reality. Then I phoned the couple who were subletting the apartment, Richmond and Gail Gates. He was a fourth-year student from out of state, with a summer job in a hospital near the medical school. He seemed like a substantial if pedestrian citizen, very nice and friendly. But Gail impressed me. She was entirely feminine, warm, friendly, with a sparkle in her eyes; but she also gave an impression of strength of body and of personality, as though with charm and grace she could run a home with six children or two or three hospital wards, a fine combination of the eternal feminine and the maternal . . . quite a girl. I envied Rich for being married and for having such a wife. Chet was still around and I stayed over where he roomed. We had a pleasant dinner together. But afterward I thought about Gail; not really about *her* but about what meeting her had sharpened up in my mind about Aline.

I never thought seriously of marrying Aline precisely because she lacked these qualities of Gail's, the strength of body and personality, the ability. Had I been strong enough myself or of different temperament, this might have meant little. But I was egocentric; I was devoted to my own goals, or rather, I hope, to the goals of science; I was grounded in research and dedicated as if to a religion to the faith that truth will make us free if anything will. I vaguely sensed that the wife for me was one who had the independence and strength that I struggled to achieve for myself, one who could take responsibility, run a home on her own. All this we would share, of course, but I could not do her job and mine too. The home, the children, the accounts, the good judgment—these would be shared, but it would be a joint responsibility. In a small way I had a sense of medicine as a mission, a call, although I did not yet know that consciously. I knew I had to have a go at research for the purpose of trying to contribute my bit toward alleviating the ugliness and hate and violence that were all around us. For this I needed a wife who was a true partner, an equal, and not only a lovely child to devote myself to. It is an old problem—how to divide one's energies. This was the feminine, maternal, sturdy kind of girl I was searching for as a wife; but it was not clear to me then. What *was* clear was Aline's lack of these strengths and that marriage with her would not work. Meanwhile, *carpe diem:* we made the most of our wonderful relationship, although it was based mainly on sex; nor did we heed the rumble of the distant drum. Perhaps I should have taken more responsibility for the future, but fortunately—yes, fortunately—we lived entirely in the present, and so experienced for a summer an idyll such as life rarely affords.

I reached the hospital in Hillfield a week before Aline, and got settled in the job. The young man in immediate charge of the clinical laboratory, Dale, was great, always helpful, never pushing. We became lasting friends. He went into the Public Health Service. Decker was the resident in charge of the patients. He was too good-looking, in what used to be called the "arrow collar" fashion. We never hit it off. He was always critical and suggesting things for me to do. If Dale had suggested them, they were good ideas, and I executed them willingly; but there was something in Decker's manner that antagonized me. I don't know if he had the same effect on others. He seemed to think he was perfect, was superior and could boss me; but I had had a loving but slightly dominating mother and had developed the dynamics to handle this. When he ordered me to do something, I rebelled automatically and angrily; I hated giving orders or receiving them. One thing I admired and envied Decker for: every day he would phone his wife, and he spoke to her with such ease and pleasantness. He must have had a fine wife and a good marriage. He had the home I had not yet achieved; I guess I was not ready for it, but I didn't know that. I still didn't know what "ready" meant. I think though, that if I had met a Gail, I would have been ready and would have concentrated on her and home and children all the enormous energies that I expended on women without marriage, with still plenty of energy left over for my calling. That summer was just suspended in space and time, like the stars.

I met Aline at the train and drove her and her baggage to the small apartment in a renovated private home that she had located through the store where she was to work. It was reasonably private, but we would have to be careful of her reputation. We were bursting for each other. My job was only three-quarter time, as I said, with few emergencies because most of the patients suffered from subacute or chronic disorders. A young woman named Sally had applied for and obtained a job as lab technician in the hospital; she was willing to take the position at a low salary to get experience for a bigger job she wanted in a large medical center beginning in September. Sally and I got on fine; there was no sexual element. One soon tired of blood counts, examining smears, running urines, even growing cultures. The blood chemistries and spinal fluids were more involved, but the procedures we used were pretty well standardized. I far preferred everything that had to do with seeing the patients. Toward the end of the summer I left most of the lab work to Sally, which suited her, and spent all possible time with the patients, helping in any way I could. During those nights I was on call I learned to spend the early evening just visiting with patients. This I enjoyed greatly; and I learned a lot about each one of them so that they no longer were incidental personalities attached to diseased organs, but real people. And they in turn, isolated from normal living, greatly appreciated my visits. Some years later I would concentrate on and even help in pioneering a new field called "psychosomatic medicine."

Life outside the hospital with Aline was as perfect as life allows. We had the car now, and we were not far from the ocean. We were near the semiprivate lake where, through the hospital, I had privileges. I rented a canoe for the summer. We were careful; no word of gossip ever got back to us. Dale would have told me as a friend if he had heard anything, and Decker would have warned me sternly. At the ocean we located a cottage that took guests, and Aline turned her ring so that it looked like a wedding band. We came often. We were distant but friendly with the owners, and when we left, we gave them a small present. Grown-ups, if a serious quiet young couple comes and stays the night with you, don't examine them too closely; you do not know how much such nights together may mean to them, both then and in their memories for the rest of their lives. Take them in . . . do not make it too hard for them. It would never have occurred to me to ask this of the medical school, yet today, college students ask it of the college. Would I say the same thing to a college administration as to the grown-ups who have a cottage such as we stayed in? I don't know. But having the room in that seaside cottage gave Aline and me the sea and shore and each other, each day more beautiful than the one before. "Today well lived makes every yesterday a dream of happiness. . . ." I have thought many times in later years about that poem's meaning, and tried to achieve its essence. To live each day well is not easy, perhaps even impossible.

The lake and the canoe . . . there was no weak-willed Randy now, telling me the mechanics of procedure! We enjoyed the setting, and we always carried two blankets and ponchos. A zephyr off the lake sufficed to free the lakeshore of mosquitoes. When the air was balmy we made love on the fragrant pine needles under the stars, all clean and cool, and we would dip in the lake before returning. That summer, work was play and the time off was rich and full and carefree. I cannot think of it with any regrets. I hope, I pray, that Aline thinks of it as I do. She must, for it meant as much to her as it did to me—or more.

Lovemaking under the stars . . . once, apropros of something, I had made the remark, "Sex with clothes on is indecent." That touched something in Aline, and she picked it up; afterward we always were guided by that principle. Sex only full and free and naked, clean and unashamed. No insinuations among clothes.

Ted was an intern. He joined the dozen or so of my lifelong friends, never so close as Jim and Charles, but the kind of friend one might not see for five years at a stretch, who might be off in other places and yet would write to ask if he could stay over for a few days; it was the kind of friendship that resumed unchanging, except for deepening, whenever and wherever we met. Ted was surprised when he found out about Aline. He thought I was too innocent for that. He had a girl, a nurse named Fern, straight, strong, beautiful. It may sound as though all the girls I tell about are beauties, and that is true—for those I tell about. But for each of them I would meet perhaps one or even two hundred who were ordinary and whom I never mention. I'd seen Fern only a few times, and wondered if Ted would marry her. Then he told me that she was sleeping with another fellow besides himself, and I was shocked. He said that this was ideal, that he much preferred it this way. My vanity and only-child psychology made me puzzled at this. "No responsibility," Ted explained. "Or anyway, a whole lot less." I didn't know if he was referring to pregnancy or obligation to marriage, or what; but I could see he had a point. But how could a girl like Fern be so promiscuous, or was it only a sort of bigamy? And how could such a good person as Ted accept it? I had not yet learned the many different ways people handle their sexuality. For some it is love, for some it is prostitution. Some make themselves happy with it; others ruin their lives with it. I had seen it, but didn't clearly understand it then. I didn't even know if there were reasons for it. Judy had told me long ago about a girl we both knew who was illegitimately pregnant: "Of course that girl is in trouble. Just look at how her father treats her." But I had not made the connection of that insight with what I was seeing and experiencing now. Later I understood something of the effects of the home life on the child's behavior in the world forever after.

September came. The golden summer had glided by. The last ten days before leaving were busy ones; Sally had left the lab, and Dale was away most of the time. I was on duty without relief and didn't really mind it, except that I could not see Aline. We could not meet until the last Saturday, and the next day we would both leave. I reserved the room in the cottage at the ocean. Nine days . . . how could I last? I was determined to have no sexual overflow, to save it for the last night with Aline. I have always had a strong will, at least in some areas. Once I told Nelda how as a child I looked at a box of candy, smelling the chocolates and not taking one, just to prove that I had the strength to resist. Nelda was revolted by this. I saw it as strength; she didn't agree. During that week before seeing Aline I took cold showers because I did not dare risk hot ones in my libidinal state. By sheer determination I even prevented wet dreams. At last, Saturday came, and we drove to the sea. The sexual pressure was almost unbearable, but the release was worth it, and that experience was of such intensity that I have never forgotten it. And I doubt if Aline has.

The next morning, Sunday, I said goodbyes at the hospital, packed my things in the car and went to pick up Aline. We put her things in the car and went back for a last kiss and look around. She paused at the window, looking out. There was no hurry. I sat on the bed to wait quietly. But there was no wait, for she suddenly said, almost to herself, "Will you love me like this when we are old?" I was stunned. Then she picked up her pocketbook, and we went downstairs and out into the brilliant sunlight. There, looking at our car, was a girl of about twelve in charge of an especially cute little boy of about two who was probably her brother. Aline saw the child toddling about and lit up with warmth and enthusiasm. "Look," she exclaimed, "a tyke!"

So we set off happily in the old car, rolling over the open roads in the sunshine. But in my heart I thought, "What have you done? What have you done?" I did not dwell on it. We reached the city in good time, and I saw Aline off on the train to her home in the south, then left the car for Gerald and checked in with Rich and Gail Gates, finally catching a train for home.

On the way I tried to figure it out. Did I think too much—or not enough? The world celebrated great thinkers and I would have wished to be in their company. Did I not observe? Did I not know? I never seduced Aline. I did nothing to make her have sex with me. No word was said. We both just felt it and merged together. I never said I loved her; I would never use that word to any girl except the one who was my wife. With Aline, marriage had never been mentioned, nor had the future. Yet, from that one remark Aline seemed to take sex as love and love as marriage. Did she want marriage to me from the day we met, or did that wish only develop out of this blissful summer? Did all girls take sex to mean love and marriage? Did Fern? Was Fern loose, promiscuous? Or did she too anticipate love and marriage? Fern seemed of high type—how could she not be? I felt pain in my mind and pain for Aline; I could not marry her. Was that the only alternative to hurting her? She was too lovely a person to hurt, even for such a summer. The sun shone, but I was sad and confused and felt a little lost.

Again the blessing of having a good, solid family! Whatever happened in life, whatever threatened, there the family was, strong and constant and loving, overjoyed to see me, giving anything, asking nothing, only that I have a good life. Because they gave so much to me I had something to give to others. Because they loved me, I could love. And because they gave me only selfless love, it caused me pain, hot and guilty pain, to hurt another person, especially one that I loved in the way I loved Aline. For of course my heart loved her although not with that utter abandon and that unremitting day-in, day-out consistency which marriage requires.

The visit with Jim and Pam was wonderful as always. Jim was still my most intimate friend. Pam was busy with a lot of details of her own, so Jim and I had one of our old-style talks. We spoke of instincts. There was no doubt at all about the need for food and shelter; that was simple self-preservation. But was it a source of conflict? It seemed to become so in people who were driven to more wealth than they could use. No doubt about sex either; but did it make conflicts as Freud said? To some extent, yes; look what it had given Aline and me. The idyll but now the problem, maybe the pain. Was there something still more basic? Something that made a higher-caliber girl like Fern sleep with more than one man? Something that made sex part of happiness in some and of misery in others? Beyond food and shelter, beyond bare survival and reasonable comfort, was not the more basic force of love and its opposite, hate and maybe fear? Freud said it was sex, sensuality, the attraction between cells and between individuals; but was it not love and hate and fear that made friends or enemies, marriage or divorce, war or peace?

War and peace, wealth and poverty. We got into a discussion of how our economic system worked. What other systems were there? What of Communism? And how did the economic system of free enterprise and the political system of democracy affect the structure of power in the country? Jim was a nuclear physicist but had always been deeply interested and remarkably well grounded in these things. I admired him more and more, and after I left I knew that this is what was lacking at medical school. I had not found one person or made one friend who was sincerely interested in these problems that affected every human being in our country—in fact, in the world. I had met not one person with whom I could have such a conversation.

The family was great. After his first visit with us Gregg told me, "Judy is so attractive and perceptive, your mother is so maternal, and your father is so masculine and fatherly." Gregg was gallant and always said the right things, but usually they were correct. Even then I appreciated my family, but that appreciation of naïve, self-centered youth has deepened with knowledge of people and what makes their infinite variety. I have said it before and repeat it now: No child should be born except to good, healthy, loving, respecting parents—or else that child is doomed, the nation is doomed, and the world is doomed. "How long, oh Lord, before those in power or most of humanity will act on this insight?" I write, and an occasional response from somewhere in the world shows that there are a few people who understand.

Often Mother and Dad may not have understood me—or did they understand me better than I knew myself? But certainly they did trust and love me utterly, and that is how they loved Judy and each other. Yet, at nearly twenty-three, after some days at home I would sometimes snap at Mom, Dad or Judy and then hate myself for it. I had no idea why this happened against my will, and against my true feelings, which were full of love; but now I think it was because home aroused my old dependent feelings. It tempted me to renounce all the struggles, the problems of career, of finding friends, of finding a wife, of dealing with girls, with Aline. It tempted me to come back home and be a child again, to accept the love and care of my devoted parents, to take their decisions instead of making my own. Of course, my thrust to life, to independence, to freedom from control was much too powerful to be impaired. Mother and Dad had respected me as well as loved me, and had let this thrust develop in full force; but I had not grown far enough out of childhood but that some of these old feelings and needs to return to being a child in the family lingered on, and I rebelled at my temptations to regress and fought my parents because home tempted me. That is why my snappishness only showed after my being home a few days. I was adult enough to know that never again could I return to live in the home I loved; whatever came, short of my being incapacitated, and maybe even then, the force that drove me to the docks and the ship would see to it that I stayed on my own.

My father had told me that he would provide me with the means for an education but that I would have to carve out my own future. I was fighting against my own old dependence upon Mother and Dad.

They ignored my occasional irritability, just as Mother had ignored my shoving the prunes onto the tablecloth the day she forbade me to ride my new bike on the thoroughfare. And I left them with gratitude and love in my heart, fortified for whatever was to come, with Aline or without her.

15
THREE SECONDS PASS

It was good to be independent and back in the school again, back to my small apartment. We were all enthusiastic about beginning the clinical years after the laboratories for the basic sciences, great as those were. The summer had indicated that although my interest in the physical sciences continued in full force, the appeal of patients and their problems would exceed it.

Aline returned from her visit home. Nothing seemed changed between us, but I knew we would have to talk. We checked in with the Holdens on one of their open-house Sunday evenings. Toward the end of the visit, Estelle and I were talking *tête-à-tête*. She said, "I can't help remarking on how beautiful Aline is. She is just made for love." Estelle seemed to hesitate.

"Go ahead," I pleaded, "tell me your thought."

"I was going to say she's just made for love . . . (again Estelle hesitated) but for nothing else."

I said, "Thank you."

Steve would never have given an opinion even if asked. But he and Estelle were close, discussed everything and everybody with each other. This was a joint conclusion, I felt sure. I was in many ways overly susceptible to the opinions of those I respected, especially on matters which puzzled me; but this was not the point. Estelle had put in a sentence what I had thought but had been unable to express so succinctly. Estelle had voiced my own thought. That was why it was all so wonderful, but also why I felt so definitely that Aline was not entirely right for me as a wife. And if that is true one way, it is true the other way also. If I were dissatisfied, I would not be right for Aline either. I saw Aline's limitations of strength in body and mind and personality. But not until years later, as I've said, did I think of the importance of intelligence in people's feelings for each other. If I had been of a different makeup, I would have gotten all the intellectual interchange I wanted from professional associates.

But even then I felt I needed a wife with better and more realistic judgment than mine, an equal, one with whom, I would say today, I could identify.

Memory is a strange and wondrous thing. Some scenes of the past are more vivid than ones of last week. But other memories seem to leave no trace. Perhaps these are not important enough to us, do not strike some strong feeling deep within, are not sufficiently charged with strong emotion to continue in our minds, do not touch our childhood dynamics enough. Perhaps some are too painful, and without our intention they are pushed out of mind. This must be what happened with my memories of Aline. I could not bear the prospect of hurting her. As I recall it, without any pain, I made remarks to Aline that hinted vaguely of my feelings about the future: two more years of medical school, two years of interning, probably three years as a resident. She made clear that she would wait; we could go on apart until we could go on together. But I made clear that it was all too uncertain, not fair to her or to me; how could either of us bind ourselves today for what might be seven years from now? She saw how I felt and handled it marvelously. Or maybe she did not quite let herself realize what I was trying to say. Perhaps she thought I would change with time. She kept her dignity and self-esteem and seemed to continue as we were; it threw me into terrible conflict. Body said, "Yes"; heart said, "Half-yes"; head said, "No, no, no." Thanks be that I had that strength of will to keep this turmoil of indecision pretty well walled off from my studies, athletics and other friends. "For man it is a thing apart, 'tis woman's whole existence."

One day in early December, after weeks of foul weather only rarely relieved, I was late in leaving the school and rapidly strode the mile to the apartment over ice, through slush, around dirty snow. A freezing fog hung in the air. When one is young and vigorous, bad weather is only a challenge; it stimulates impulses to meet it, to drive through it. A boy has become a man, it is said, when he walks around a puddle instead of through it. But this late afternoon the dismal streets touched something similar in my heart. Thinking of Aline, I was glad to reach the apartment. To my joyous surprise, Aline was there and had dinner all ready to put in the oven and on the stove; she had taken a chance on my coming and had it ready but not yet cooked.

"I like food cooked slowly," I said facetiously, "so adjust it for an hour." It took her five minutes to get things adjusted while I washed, and then it took us two minutes to be stripped and in bed. And then in three seconds something fateful happened. I don't know what play of forces suddenly made me abandoned. In one second I exclaimed, "The heck with it, I won't use the contraceptive; we'll let go, have a baby and get married." For better or for worse . . . the pain and strain of indecision was ended. In one reckless second it was done, for better or for worse. I rarely let my feelings bypass my head, but the next second, instead of pressing me closer, Aline said, "Are you sure? Are you certain that this is what you want?"

The balance arm was on a knife edge. A breath had tilted it one way; now a breath tilted it the other. One does not take enormous fateful irreversible steps when there is doubt and hesitation. Not if it can be helped. The third second my resolve was abandoned; the rubber was on in an instant. The lovemaking was gratifying as always. The dinner together was warm and intimate; the moment had passed. And strangely it was she who had tipped the balance. It was definite now—some way, somehow, it must end. My search for a mate must continue, with no end in sight.

Christmastime was upon us. Aline was going home for the holidays, as were most of us. I drove her to the train and kissed her and saw her off. I returned to the apartment. Sometimes it was a refuge, my castle of privacy. When Aline was there it was something of a home; tonight it was lonely. There were no good, inexpensive places to eat in that run-down area, almost all were unbelievably drab; it was too late to call Gregg or Chet, everyone was getting ready to leave for the vacation period. I went through the refrigerator to see if there were the makings of a meal before it was cleaned out for my departure. I ate alone, in silence, turned in early and awoke in the same lonely mood, which was unusual. "Sufficient unto the day. . . ." Each day was a fresh start, but this morning the mood lingered. I went down for the mail, and a small package containing a beautiful billfold was there from Aline. It blurred as I looked at it, for tears had filled my eyes and I was deeply touched. I have often thought of that moment and wondered why I felt such a pang. It is only a guess, but perhaps the reason was because I was rejecting Aline, whom in so many ways I loved; I was hurting her, God help me, and here she was showing her love for me with this affectionate thoughtfulness. Aline, Aline, can you forgive me? Did you get something from me as

I did from you? Often I have felt that you gave me more than affection, sex, love—that you were there in my time of need; and in some way I cannot discern you gave me life and stability. For while strong in some ways, I felt within me crosscurrents and undertows that I could not understand. Without you, the tensions would have been almost unbearable.

After that vacation we grew apart. We saw each other less frequently, sometimes not for two or three weeks; it had come to marriage or nothing for me. In my own mind the scale was tilted. Indecision was over, it would not work, it could not be forced, and now I see why, or think I do. It is because in the end everything rests on personality and the fit of personalities; sex alone cannot do it. Affection alone cannot do it. Love alone cannot do it, nor can all three of these together. The personalities, the childhood emotional patterns, must be right in themselves and right for each other; right in the fit, in the mesh, like gears, of strengths and weaknesses, intelligence and sense of reality and judgment and abilities, maturities and immaturities. Only then can permanent closeness endure in humans as it does in other, psychologically more simple, animal forms. Although I did not see it clearly then, this is why I felt we would not be a fit. I hated to hurt her, but a wrong marriage would hurt her more and for longer, and would doom the children. For a male not to hurt a female has seemed to me to be a biological, instinctual thing. That a man could hurt a woman, could strike her or rape her, could in any way injure her mentally or physically, always seemed to me, with my childhood emotional pattern, to be against nature, against instinct, against biological law. It was evil. That men could do such things was a measure of their depravity, or as I later learned to see it, in nonmoralistic terms, a measure of their neurosis and their criminality and their emotional distortions. And these, I learned, came from how the men were treated, mistreated and abused in early childhood. Freud selected the tragedy of Oedipus, but the greatest crime in Greek mythology was that of Orestes. His killing his mother, even for cause, was the crime that gave birth, through Athena, to the jury system. I loved my mother; I loved my sister; I still suffer pain to think of hurting Aline who gave me so much that was invaluable. But in my own mind the die was cast, *ilea jacta est*. But now Aline would not accept it.

It was April. The weather had settled a little. The sun shone warmer again. Aline came to the apartment, and I could not reject her; I could never do anything but welcome her. Now she pleaded. She said, "You will never get anyone as beautiful as I unless you have a million dollars." I began to feel what it is to go cold in one's feelings; for then for the first time, although I still desired her, it was without intensity. As she pleaded, I even felt a shadow of distaste. Unbelievable that I could have even the shadow of such a feeling for Aline, but she must have felt it. Even sex could not hold us now, and that is how it ended, coolly, calmly, disappointingly, with us as friends. "Not with a bang, but a whimper."

But that was not the last time we met. It was a month later, in the last weeks before the school term ended and the summer recess began. It was early evening; I was alone in the apartment. A knock, and Aline appeared. She was not angry; she was not sad; she was smiling in her touching, irresistible, girlish way. She was her old self. She said, "I'm so glad you are in!" I felt the overpowering surge of the old magnetism. I took her light coat. I tried not to take her in my arms but was losing the struggle. She smiled and said, "You are still inflammable." Then she disengaged herself, and it took all the will power I had to release her. And then she gracefully shed her clothes, slipped into the bed and pulled the covers up to her chin, raising the pillows so she could comfortably look at me. And she smiled. I shed my clothes. She happily said, "Just like a butterfly coming out of a chrysalis."

I slid into bed, rolled on a rubber rapidly, hoping she did not notice, and slowly put my arms around her. And slowly kissed her. Gently, strongly, slowly for it was more important that this be perfect even than that first time; it *was* perfect. Only we wept. Our flesh mingled and our tears mingled. And we were strong enough not to control them. We did not sob at all; only the tears flowed, and then we fell asleep locked close in each other's arms. In the morning when I awoke, she awoke. We smiled. We had breakfast together there. I offered to see her home, help her pack, drive her anywhere, do anything for her, anything. But she said, "No, please don't, it has been too perfect. Let us part here. I wish you the best of everything in life."

We kissed slowly, lightly, affectionately, and she was gone.

Aline was wonderful. She had regained herself. Although I could not marry her, I now loved her with all my heart. I forgot school, I forgot my appointments, I forgot everything but Aline. Again a part of me was gone. I was not wept out. Nature's safety valve . . . I threw myself on the bed where she had lain in my arms and wept freely. Yet youth is resilient. About noon I made the bed, did the dishes, straightened out the apartment and, enveloped with the feel and scent of Aline, went out into the sunlight and walked briskly to the school to finish what needed doing before I left for a visit home.

But I was troubled. Again I was so close to a girl but knew (for by now I was entirely certain) that marriage would not work with her. So I was close to her, but then rejected and hurt her. I was concerned about her and guilty. She needed a strong husband who would take very good care of her and treat her gently. Would she find him? But what about myself? Was something wrong with me? Did I have some neurosis or block that kept me from marrying, urgently as I wished to? I thought the reasons for wanting marriage were obvious and realistic: to satisfy the normal sexual and mating instincts—to have wife and children. It was also to escape this waste and turmoil of finding girl after girl. It was to settle down and be able to devote myself to wife and children and to my profession, which was becoming ever more absorbing. Why then had I not found a wife, a true companion? I had met hundreds of girls, one out of each two hundred being outstandingly beautiful and attractive. Was I asking the impossible, because of some conflict in me? Could it be that Aline was so perfect for me sexually and egotistically because of her weaknesses arousing my masculine dominance, but that if she were stronger than I, then I would be less responsive sexually, as with Myrna? Was my egotism searching for a perfection that did not exist? I had read Freud's *Introduction to Psychoanalysis.* He said that there is much in our minds that we are not conscious of. I now knew this was true for me. Something in my mind was interfering with my achievement of what I so much wanted and needed, but I did not know what that block was. I recalled Ralph Ackley telling me not long after his own analysis with Freud: "Don't let anything interfere with your being analyzed, and the sooner the better, because it illumines everything that comes after." My interest in the brain was now expanded by a supplementary interest in the mind. Could Freud be right, and was it really possible to study directly the in-lying spirit and soul of men? I wanted to get analyzed sometime; my medical education and interest, my gravitating toward the patients at Hillfield, the limitation of a knowledge of the brain in providing an understanding of people, reading Freud and now my personal problems were all moving me away from the laboratory in the direction of the clinic. But it was some years before I went the whole way and went through the arduous training and study and began to devote my career to understanding patients in terms of psychodynamics. Thus, I came to study professionally for both therapy and research the basic realities of human nature that I had always felt inadequate to understand.

One day, as I reflected with a bittersweet sadness on the relationship with Aline, now gone forever, I remembered a remark that Amalie had made to me: "From that first time Aline met you, she has always been aflutter when in your company." Unaware as I was, nonetheless I saw the dim outlines of a truth. I could recognize that Amalie's words had hit the mark. With that as a starting point, I could see that I had an effect on most women. This was a tremendous discovery for one who had felt immature, physically and emotionally; had thought girls would not look at him twice; had felt rejected in adolescence by Lorie, who wanted me to sit in the big armchair with her on a hot summer night; had been rejected by Bette for the middle-aged successful sculptor, Barnes.

Now all that seemed to have changed. Mother had centered more love and attention and physical care on me than on Father. Although I still saw many men, especially those who were more mature, as big, strong father-figures, I now felt that I could compete with them for the love of women. In fact, it was dawning on me slowly and vaguely that just about any girl I felt strongly about and wanted would soon yield and go to bed with me.

I still do not know whether they responded because they wanted to marry a healthy, energetic, promising future physician, or whether I was taking advantage of this unconsciously; or whether they were merely yielding to a strong attraction. It was probably both. Even now that I have passed seventy, young women from seventeen to thirty are not completely indifferent to me sexually if I show any interest in them. Once, while I was in the hospital as a patient and dressed in what I considered an ill-fitting, unattractive dressing gown with my right arm injured, I was chatting with a woman patient across the hall. She introduced me to a beautiful girl of about twenty-one, a friend who was visiting her. What luck for me to have two charming women to chat with! But the young visitor proceeded to pull the curtain between the beds in the room and tried to get me into the far bed with her. I refused out of loyalty to my wife and fear of compromising my reputation as a physician. Later my wife repeated what she had told me when I passed sixty: that she would not have minded. Of course I told her the same thing, but neither of us has taken advantage of this. This experience, which ended with only a good French kiss, gave me an enormous lift—to feel I still had appeal for a young woman, neurotic as she must have been. I have always been extremely discriminating in my appreciation of women. Mostly I am either attracted intensely or completely uninterested, or even repelled. It is still only one in two hundred.

I have often wondered why some men affect women so strongly while others do not. It seems to me that, in general, the observations on "imprinting" in animals are supported by clinical observations of humans; for the sexual feelings follow the earliest and strongest emotional attachments. A man like myself, whose first and strongest attachments were to mother and aunt, tends to have his sexual urges follow these channels. If it is overdone, then disorders and psychopathology can result, for example, through excessive identification with women, which impairs the masculine identification. A girl's earliest emotional involvement, whether love or hate, if too strongly tied to her mother may develop into homosexual tendencies later in life and difficulties in relating to men and responding sexually to them.

What specifically heightened the attraction in me for certain women was quite a complex of strong feelings. First, there was all the childhood affection I had been given by females and my response to it, leading later to unconscious seductiveness toward women (always very discriminating) to win affection, combined with a strong urge to express affection. Sexual feelings followed both of these channels, creating a stronge urge to get and give the affection in sexual form. The somewhat overly strong needs for love and dependence caused some inferiority feelings and a reaction against it of "masculine protest," drives to be masculine and independent like my father, whom I loved and admired and sought to model myself upon, consciously as well as unconsciously. These drives to independence and masculine activity absorbed a certain amount of hostility because of the feelings of inferiority, but the hostility which entered the sex drive and reinforced it was overcompensated by love, sympathy and identification. The girls felt the assertiveness, mastery and hostility, but also felt safe because of the love, sympathy and identification: they sensed that I would be protective and never knowingly hurt them. I never realized at the time that I was hurting any girl, and in retrospect, when I see that I might have inflicted hurt, I am filled with remorse and guilt and a strong desire to make amends. Incidentally, just such complexes of emotional forces can make a marriage work if they "mesh" or destroy it if they clash. The first few years of life, by forming the childhood pattern, can make or break a life as well as a marriage.

16

ANOTHER SUMMER—THE PATHS CONVERGE

It was summer again, said Corey, after I had worked hard at the clinical studies which occupied the third year of medical school, getting a feel for the fundamentals and a smattering of the specialties: eye, ear, nose and throat, skin, bones, joints and muscles, nervous system and so on. I was constantly trying to fuse all this knowledge into a single comprehensive picture of the human body in health and then to understand all these disorders as I came to see them. The more one knew, the more fascinating were the body and its problems— and also the great unknown area of the personality in that body and how it worked in illness and in health. My job that summer was in a big hospital right there in the city. Here were patients of every kind, from accident victims brought in by ambulance to those with puzzling subtle diagnostic problems. I could now be useful with patients as well as in the laboratory, even covering for brief periods for interns who were out or away, or assisting on wards that had a rush of admissions.

And then I saw Elaine. It was early July. She was an occupational therapist playing ball with some children in the little courtyard of the hospital, outside the rehabilitation center. These children had been injured by accidents or diseases like polio, and were on a supervised plan of increasing activity. Some wore braces but were well enough to be outdoors and forget themselves playing ball. Elaine was twenty years old, I learned later. She had a trim figure with the consummate grace of the born athlete. Her face was the prettiest I had ever seen in life or art—all beauty, health, vitality, goodness and sweetness. She was wonderful with the children. I glimpsed her for only a few seconds because I had to take blood for testing from an acutely ill man just admitted, and fortunately my mind could turn and concentrate completely on him; but the scene is as vivid as if I had just turned away from that window. Were I a painter, I could portray it today—the children, excited with the game and a little in love with this beautiful, vital young goddess; and Elaine, the fresh young beauty with sun glinting yellow gold from her thick hair, her arm raised to throw the ball girl-fashion, with that slightly awkward but still graceful motion, her face glowing with love for the children, her supple vigor, all so girlish, so tender, so vibrant, so alive.

My absorption in my patients was never disturbed, and rarely has anything interfered with my sleep. But that night in my little room in the hospital I tossed about; the image of Elaine in my mind was as vivid as when I glimpsed her through that grimy windowpane. I had never known before that to be "crazy" about someone, "mad" about a girl, is a very correct use of the terms. I dozed off a little toward morning, and there in my dreams was Elaine! one arm poised in that girlishly graceful awkward fashion, so appealing and full of youthful health. The iron was pulled to the magnet. It was irresistible. I *had* to meet her; did I dare think I had to have her? Yes, I was thinking of her sexually—this was one girl that I must have, this vital young goddess. It was out of my hands; Corey of the irresistibly strong willpower was swept along unthinkingly, desiring more intensely than ever before. I went to the center while she was on duty. I saw her, tried to control my feelings, tried to chat casually. "I saw you playing ball with the children in the yard yesterday."

"Yes, that's a pleasant part of my job."

"I thought you were enjoying it, that it's more than just a job for you."

"I love children, and I like the work here in the center. I hope I will be kept here a long time and not transferred somewhere else in the hospital."

"Can the chief here at rehab help keep you?"

"I don't know, but he seems friendly."

"Are you involved with anyone, or would you consider going to dinner with me, this evening?"

"I'd like to, but I can't this evening."

"Tomorrow, then?"

"Yes!"

"Where and when shall I pick you up?"

"At my apartment any time after five."

It was not the distance from window to court or distortion by the grimy glass that had lent the enchantment. She was even more beautiful and appealing face-to-face: simple, naïve, with the enhancement of utterly charming dimples. I did manage to do my work that day, but I slept only a little this second night also, for the vision of my sun-drenched dimpled goddess in the courtyard with the children, throwing the ball, never left my mind's eye.

At last the hour came. She lived alone in a poor little back apartment, which made mine, by comparison, seem light and large and almost elegant. She wore a white summer dress, no makeup or so little I could not see it. She needed none, with her freshness; she was so lovely I felt every cliché there is about love—swept toward her by the tide, forced toward her by inner compulsion. I did not know anything so intense existed. I drove out to a simple inn in the country. The evening was balmy, not hot; the clouds were pink in the sunset and afterglow. We ate and chatted of small things. We drove back and I asked if I could come up to her apartment for a little while; she assented. She sat on the couch and I came over to sit next to her, hesitatingly but driven by irresistible forces I put my arms around her, around a perfect girl, a goddess, and amazingly she put her arms around me and we kissed. I said, "Can you . . . will you . . . is it all right?"

She said, "Yes," and then said something that in my ecstasy at the thought of possessing her I did not hear or understand. She turned out the lights and went into the bathroom. I undressed. She emerged nude. There was faint illumination from the window. She was utterly perfect, and I was unable to be slow this time. For two days I had been so obsessed with her that I could not sleep. She was bitterly disappointed, but the second time a half hour later was perfect. Her hair there was short. Then it began to come to me that she had said something, ending with, "Does it matter to you?" And I, caring only to possess her, had said, "Of course not," not knowing what I was replying to. Now I knew it was a recent abortion. But my answer was still true—it made no difference whatever in my feelings for her—then or ever.

The blue-white flame had ignited between us. Sex was not lovemaking. The affection, the lovemaking, came afterwards. Sex was a huge tidal surge that became nearly overwhelming when we only spoke on the phone or when I stopped at the center to confirm our date. And once we were together it overpowered all controls; the first time I always had difficulty waiting for her climax and sometimes could not do so. The sexual attraction between us was so violent—I did not know that such intensity could be. And then finally we could be together. And each time was as intense as the last. We could barely endure separation. We always used her apartment because mine was again temporarily sublet; she referred to our sexual union as "going to the South Seas." She would awake in the morning and say, "Last night I went to the South Seas," and the words seemed to come happily from the depths of her feelings.

About two months after our first dinner together and our first night the weather was warm enough for us to go to the shore. It was Sunday. Sky and water were blue, sun and beach golden—and Elaine was golden, with that beauty of face and figure, that vitality, a child of nature, a goddess of the sea. As I thought of this, walking with her, with Elaine occasionally bounding about with sheer high-spirited animal energy, she said, "I love the ocean! I love all water. I have no fear of it at all. I will never die in water. But if I should, it would be all right; I would not mind dying because I love it so."

We ran in and dived side-by-side under a breaker, swam out to the rolling swells beyond the breakers, dived to the bottom and joined hands on the sandy bottom, rising together. We caught waves coming in and rode their crests. Then we found a secluded hollow in the sand among the small dunes and dried with towels and lay in the sun. "Tonight," she said, "We will have dinner somewhere and go to the South Seas." Just the thought of it was too much for me. Swimming in cold water seems to stimulate sexual desire strongly anyway, certainly in me. And I always assume that I am just like everyone else. Sex seems like an excess of energy. Cold water stirs up the whole body, making it tingle, and much of that energy over-flows as sex. However that may be, the cold water and the dip together, the warm sun and the seclusion in the dunes and her beauty were too much for me. I took her in my arms and kissed her. I should have torn away at once and raced into the waves again, but it was too late, and I exploded then and there, myself relieved with her only the more keyed up. She was disappointed, but I said that by the time we reached her apartment it would be the same again. It would have been, for it was a forty-five-minute drive back. But Elaine was inconsolable. We swam again, had dinner; but now she did not want me to come to the apartment. This was the first disharmony between us. We drove back in the traffic. In her apartment I was sure she would feel differently. I slid my arm around her and was aroused. The irresistible power of her magnetism on me . . . and then we heard a step on the stairs. She went to the door. It was a man in his late thirties, who seemed rather a nice gentle, considerate person. I had noticed him before, an attendant at the hospital. Elaine said she was just saying goodnight to me and was sorry but she was busy. So he and I left the apartment and went our separate ways.

Back at the hospital I phoned Elaine. For me, I could not stand anything wrong between us, and for her I could not stand the thought of a goddess of the sea all alone in that poor little back apartment in a dingy building; we made a date for Tuesday for dinner.

The next day, Monday, one of the woman doctors told me directly that "Miss Hinchly, the head nurse at the rehab center, is worried about your seeing Elaine. She doesn't want that lovely girl hurt. And I agree with her." I admire people who are direct, but these were fighting words to my ears, because they were so contrary to my image of myself. I took them in silence. I forget if I said nothing or just, "Thank you for telling me." I was jolted because I had to admit there was something in Miss Hinchly's fear. I saw myself as a kind and sincere person, not a seducer of women, and I certainly didn't mean to hurt anyone, above all Elaine; yet here I was in a violent sexual relationship with her and no thought of marriage. Would she be hurt in the end—as Aline was and as Nelda must have been? Was I all wrong about myself—was I not the hero but really the villain? It was a disturbing thought, and I feared there was some truth in it. Yes, I must study it, for it was fundamental to my makeup and image of myself. If I were not virtuous, I would not be admirable or lovable and therefore not emotionally secure. But in the press of work I forgot about it. Tuesday at dinner Elaine said, "Why don't you show me your apartment? I hear you have marvelous works of art in it. And why don't you take me to town to things and to meet some of your friends?"

Dear Elaine, a goddess, but so human, such natural questions! But I, deaf and blind and egotistical, was threatened; threatened in my egotism, in my prestige. To her my second-rate apartment was luxury. I did not see it clearly; I only felt that she was on a lower "level" than I and would not enhance my esteem in the eyes of the world or in my own. She was somehow less than I, a little below me—but how? in what ways? Oh my goddess, how could I think that way? How could I feel that way? May God forgive me. I felt threatened and reflexly I pulled back emotionally, thinking of myself and not of her. I never could believe Oscar Wilde's line that "each man kills the thing he loves," but what *had* I done?

There was a rush of patients, with many acutely ill. Caught up in the work we did not see each other for four days. At last a free evening, a drive into the country and a leisurely dinner—leisurely for us for whom this volcano had so suddenly erupted. We knew our bodies and some of our feelings but not much of our personalities. For example, I hardly knew her well enough to ask if the abortion had been caused by the hospital attendant. I barely hinted at it, but when I did she answered openly and without embarrassment: "No, by a friend of mine, whom I expected to marry, a fireman."

I did not mind this, but again was slightly aware of a difference in levels. She, a goddess, a storybook princess, refined and poised, who would grace any social circle, who could walk with the elect of the earth—why was she moving on that level? The attendant seemed like a nice person but was already in his thirties, nearly fifteen years older than Elaine; what more would he ever be, how could he offer her more than the poor apartment she had? I see so many of my faults, and looking back they pain me sharply, but one I never had was snobbishness or financial or social climbing. Penny's family was social register. I'd met girls of all levels. One, very healthy and attractive, a debutante, was coming into three million dollars in her own right. Incredibly, she made a play for me. She even told a mutual friend she wanted to marry me—knowing he would relay this to me. But I passed her by; if the spark was not there, I was not interested. A great flame was there with Elaine; had she been right for me to marry, I would have given not the slightest thought to her poverty or her friends or her past. ("Love is love in ermine or tatters, dear; Love is love and nothing else matters, dear.") But there was some kind of difference, which I felt as a threat. Perhaps it was only her lack of formal education, her youth, her disadvantaged background. I was too blind to inquire. Perhaps it was her IQ, less than my own—a characteristic that for years I kept ignoring in evaluating people. Was Miss Hinchly right, then, in fearing that I would hurt Elaine? And what should I do? These were fleeting thoughts, gone in a moment as we ate and glowed in each other's presence. And then the apartment. It was a hot night. I would try hard to hold back the first time. As usual, she disrobed in the bathroom and emerged nude, a nymph, a naiad, strong, firm, soft, perfectly proportioned. She came into my arms and said, "No rubber tonight, please. I want a baby, your baby, our baby."

In my turmoil I sensed even then that this was her instinctive response to my emotional withdrawal, to the sudden distance that was coming between us. This was not a scheme to hold me; it was instinct— if she were losing me she would have a child. I said, "No, I can't take the responsibility." But it was too late. I let myself go completely and did what she wished. It was tremendous and beautiful. But afterward, after the explosion and the relief, came fear. What had I done? What trouble had I made for her, for me, for a child if she had one? Then I would have to marry her, and this was no way to marry, or was it a deep instinct leading me truly? I cried out, but in a whisper, "Elaine, Elaine, what have we done?"

And she murmured, in pain, "You can go now, you can go, I have the child." I rose. She sat up on the bed, her knees together, totally flexed, her feet together on a line to her left, so that she just missed sitting on them, like the statue of the sea nymph sitting on a rock in the harbor of Copenhagen, only far more beautiful. Her gorgeous hair poured down over her shoulders and breasts like distilled June sunshine. Could such beauty actually exist in the workaday world of reality? I had seen nothing that even approached it in all the museums of Europe and the United States. The most perfect girl one can imagine. She sat there, so sad, a few tears dropping; I could barely see them in the half-light. I felt for her, I was never more "in love" with her, and never loved her more, but was impelled by fear to save myself. Automatically but more truly than I realized I murmured again, "I cannot take the responsibility." And I left—left her so perfect, so lonely, so forlorn. Fortunately she did not become pregnant. My search for a mate was still not over.

Today I wonder at my blindness. Could I not see her loneliness the first time I saw the dingy apartment? Could I not see that beneath the passion her accepting me on our very first meeting was a plea for help? Could I not hear the piercing cry to save her when she asked if it mattered? And again, when she asked me so simply to take her to town to do things, and to meet my friends? I don't know how many men she slept with, or for how many years. She was young, just twenty, pure and virginal in her heart, and I loved her so far as I was able. But I was too intoxicated by her to see her dire need. I too was lonely and a little lost and hungry for the love I had had as a small child. Down underneath, each of us is the child he or she once was. Were we, then, two children underneath, each crying out for the help and love that a small child cries for, and must have or die? Perhaps we both had a hunger so strong that we blinded each other even as this hunger pulled us together, erupting between us through the overwhelming current of sex. Could I not see that this rare girl, the likes of whom I have never met again, was alone and lost, earning a pittance by her nursing, living so frugally, but yet so full of life and love and so indomitable? Could I have saved her by doing what she asked, helping her in every way to escape into the light from that drab back apartment? Could I not do it short of marriage? Or even then? I did not know enough then to ask her for her story. How could a goddess have come to this situation in life? Is it possible that beneath all that health and freshness were serious problems with her family, problems that left scars, problems that made her injure herself? Problems like weights on the feet of a fleet, strong swimmer? Problems that I could not have helped? Even if I knew enough and were mature enough and loved her enough, could I have helped? Perhaps not—but I should not have been swept along by my own desires for her so that I did not at least ask and try to understand. It was a long time before I learned that my own violent reactions are not only out of me—that they might then have erupted volcanically toward Elaine because she herself was a volcano, because she so passionately desired something and turned to me for it, because of something she saw or imagined in me, because of the intensity of her own frustrated needs; but perhaps something that did not exist, like perhaps the love she did not get enough of as a small child. Maybe I was only answering unconsciously her desperate call, which I could not hear, overwhelmed as I was myself. And perhaps the violence of my sex urge for her was in part a reaction to her own free, irresistible sexual desire through which she was trying heroically to palliate all of her own desperate needs.

And as I tell this, it suddenly strikes me that Elaine reminded me just a little of Alice, the pretty, sweet girl who came in to help our neighbors years ago when Andy and I had our code word for seeing parts of girls' bodies. We looked and enjoyed, but could not be crassly, aggressively sexual as we were with Rena; for we loved Alice in our puppy way and did not want to take furtive advantage of her. She was open and sweet with us. There was already a channel in my mind to this fresh, sweet, vital kind of girl. Perhaps this funneled the over-powering flood of feeling into such concentration on Elaine, and possibly behind Alice was my lovely, blonde, blue-eyed Aunt Edie.

If I were a chemist I would try to understand that intense beautiful absorption in Elaine in chemical terms. But my field is psychody-namics, and I must try to explain it in psychological terms. At the time, it swept me along with the inexorable power of a huge ocean wave. I was too young, too untrained psychologically to be equipped to understand anything about it at the time; but of course the idea of analyzing then would have been almost sacrilegious. This was an elemental passion that carried me on its crest. It was to be lived blindly; it lived me. My life would have been poorer spiritually with-out it. I do not try to understand it by coldly dissecting it too much even now, these decades later, and only analyze it for what help it might possibly be to other young people, so that the boy will not hurt the girl and the girl will not let herself be hurt, but both will gain from it one of the richest experiences of a lifetime.

Sexual attraction is still a great mystery: certainly it can be in-hibited by emotional forces, but also it can be enormously intensified by them. I cannot guess what forces could have intensified it so, except along the lines I have mentioned. I had loving parents and friends, but nevertheless I had lived a relatively lonely life, very lonely compared to all the preceding years in home and college; also I'd led a tense life, and sex is the great outlet for tensions. I had worked very hard day and night for three years. Probably there was more competi-tion in me than I realized. It was a good life, then, but lonely and tense. As Aline had said, I was "inflammable." And I think this played into something in Elaine—perhaps my need awakened something similar in her. Only twenty, she should have had the security of a parental family. If I were so tense and needy with my background of loving parents, how must she have felt without them—if she had not had such parents, had been deprived of that love and security in childhood, and now was not, like me, heading for an established career as a physician, but only barely keeping her head above water as an occu-pational therapist? It breaks my heart to think of it now, more than fifty years later—she, a child so far as I could see, all alone, without family, without emotional support, an ineffably beautiful child. Cherish such a child; understand her; help her; do not exploit her sexually; do not awaken her hopes, whether they are realistic or unrealistic. For what she wanted of me might not have existed in me or in anyone for that matter—maybe, as I have suggested, it was only the love she craved which her parents had not given her adequately as a child. But I doubt whether, should I have tried to give her what she wanted by marrying her, it would have worked out. Maybe this thought is only to excuse and console myself. I am also influenced in my thinking by other men who had strong rescue impulses. One married twice because of these impulses, and neither marriage was good. The first ended in divorce, and the second was very difficult because these girls were frustrated by deprivation in early childhood, and therefore they continued feeling frustrated internally and were insatiable in their adult lives.

However that may be, for two whole months I possessed a goddess. How I pray that this daughter of the sun and waves went on to a good marriage and a good life, up in a light and airy home and with many trips to the sea and the sun, which she loved as her own true parents.

Work is the great stabilizer, especially work that is demanding of intense concentration on patients. I was soon absorbed in life without Elaine. If I'd thought about it, I would have surmised that I was pretty well burned out for a while by the conflagration of the two months with her. But the dynamic unconscious, as Freud called it, is unquenchable. Gradually, with absorption in work, a degree of calm returned. I welcomed it and wondered whether ever again a girl could inflame me to such blue-white heat.

There was a secretary in the administrative side of the hospital. She was tall and straight. She had beauty and character and was surely "true blue." It was easy to make her acquaintance through a proper introduction, by simply being near at the right time. Her name was Joan.

It was instantly evident that we had a lot in common. She was of highest caliber in every way; this was the kind of girl I might marry. But some spark of excitement, some element of the irresistible did not compel me. No iron snapped to a magnet; rather, it was like two boats drifting down the same stream coming together. Again I was under the old sexual pressure. But this girl was a "straight arrow"; I might marry her, but I would never try to seduce her. That is, I would never bypass *her*, her personality, just to enjoy her body, perfect as it was. We became good friends (one of the best bases for a marriage, although I was too immature to know that then). She was nearly my age and had substance and strength.

There was some hospital business with a family in a tough slum area. Although beyond the call of duty, Joan characteristically said she was going to see this family herself, and I said that I'd drive her. She agreed. I was scared but she insisted on going in alone, and disappeared into the dark doorway of a tenement, while I waited at the curb, doors locked, motor running. Maybe it was an unrealistic fear of mine, born of defenseless early childhood, when the nail on Landers' fist ripped through the cheek of the old man on election night. She came out of the building and we drove off.

Joan and I did the healthy outdoor things that Penny wanted to do with me. Joan, completely feminine, was in fact an athlete, with the speed and coordination to be good at every sport. We played tennis; we swam; we jogged; we hiked. Her job was nine to five with weekends free, and I managed to make my time off fit hers so far as possible. I began to wonder where it would lead and why it was not developing further, and I wondered if I were still too full of Elaine. Joan was more on the same "level" I was on: we were alike in outlook and background, in the amount of our exposure to formal education, to music and art and books, to people with more income, who did not have to support themselves as Elaine did; and probably Joan and I were more alike in intellect.

My path and Joan's crossed frequently in the hospital. One day as I put my tray on a table in the cafeteria and sat down to lunch, thinking how cool and easy and comfortable it would be to see Joan again, a fellow intern named Grant sat down with me. His opening remark was, "I feel like a king." I was quite willing to "bite" and asked, "How so?"

"Because," he said, "I was out to the theater last night with such a queenly girl."

"Who?" I said, "Do I know her?"

"Yes, Joan Bradley."

I wondered why this confidentiality. Had something serious started between Joan and Grant? Would I be infringing if I saw her? I decided to see her anyway, for Joan was a straight shooter and would tell me frankly if I should stay away. She didn't. She was glad to see me, and we resumed our platonic, athletic, outdoor, companionable relationship; but we were becoming closer. One day about two weeks later, I finished a little before five o'clock and stopped by her desk. We walked together to her apartment. She asked me if I'd like to come in. I said, "Very much so, but I can't guarantee what might happen if I do."

She smiled faintly. She shared an apartment with another girl, who would not be in until late in the evening. I put my arms around her. Everything platonic vanished. I said, "I will make night," and pulled down the shades. Her marvelous lithe, strong body! There was a slight hesitation in my potency. But only for a split second. Then all barriers were down, and I was amazed and delighted. Sexually we were exactly compatible. It was perfect. Now we were each other's, and I thought seriously of marriage. Only one little reservation held me back— the spark was not there. Perhaps it was absent because it was too soon after the flaming volcanic month with Elaine; it might have grown with time and developed. I believe it would have. Perhaps the best love in marriage is this cool, comfortable kind, the passion of sex combined with day-in, day-out friendliness and good humor in the face of all we endure in life. But I hesitated in my ignorance. There was a head nurse in the hospital, a little older than I—Celia. We had become very friendly, on a platonic basis, and chatted freely on occasion. She was extraordinarily perceptive. One day she rocked me by asking, "You're not going to marry Joan, are you?"

I said, "Why? Yes, I am thinking of it. Why? Tell me!"

She said, "Don't, because she is so wan."

This was a little like what I thought of as absence of spark. I wondered, though, if this were Celia's opinion, told me in friendship for my own good, or whether she might be expressing some jealousy because of interest in me herself. Joan and I continued and were happy. One day I said, "Let's go on a schedule as nearly as my job will allow. Let's make two evenings a week and weekends for us for lovemaking." Joan was delighted. There was a party and we went; a girl was there who exuded sex. All the men flocked around her; I was fool enough to do so too. The girl meant nothing to me, it was pure sex, it would have been good to go to bed with her, but I would never reject a princess like Joan for a girl like that. Today I know such girls are usually very neurotic—something is oversexing them. Sometimes they were terribly deprived and unloved as children and still feel that way inside. And their cry for love comes out as sex. For others, sex is a way to rebel against their parents. For some it is even repressed hostility to men. But then I knew nothing of this and reacted automatically. I was so stupid, so inconsiderate of Joan, who couldn't have been a better sexual partner; this girl might have been more intense, yes, but could not have been more satisfying than Joan, with her perfect lithe body and loving, eager compliance, and strong orgastic satisfaction.

After the party I felt miserable for what I had done, but Joan ignored it. Was that because of lack of spirit in her, or because she saw how childishly I had behaved and thought it best to ignore it? More and more I thought of marrying her. I took her to the Holdens', sort of the way a son introduces to his parents the girl he is beginning to be serious about. I think Joan sensed this; it was a fine evening. She was radiant. As we left, Steve looked at me as though he was impressed and approving; to my amazement, however, Estelle murmured, "Go slow!" Can people really tell anything from an evening's visit of what will work or not in a marriage, for a lifetime? This struck me because it echoed my own faint reservations. But also did Estelle's opinion carry weight because she was a mother-figure to me?

Then external chance swept decision from my wavering control.

The first minor event was again the result of one of these totally inconsequential incidents: Pete, a talented pianist turned law student, whom I saw only two or three times a year, phoned. He said there was a mixer dance at the university and would I like to come with him on Saturday evening. I knew he was shy about attending these usually futile functions alone; and as it was a mixer, he did not want to ask a girl for a date. I was off duty that evening, while Joan was occupied. The idea did not particularly appeal to me, but out of friendship for Pete I accepted. But at the dance, you guessed it, I found myself dancing with quite a girl—"Dawn." We chatted, and she revealed a brilliant mind, a deep interest in music and the arts, a fine singing voice and the fact that she was an heiress. As I have said, that never influenced me; but for some reason this time it represented a great temptation. I invited her to the symphony, for which I always had two season tickets. I told Joan about this girl, as a man might confide in his wife. But Joan did not take it that way: we were riding in the roadster; Joan burst into tears and told me to stop and let her out. I said, "Wait . . . wait , , , wait!" She quieted down and said, "Just when we were going on a schedule!" There were fresh tears which, however, gradually subsided.

After my second date with the heiress it was obvious that we had nothing but superficialities in common. When I phoned for a third date, she asked if it might not be better to discontinue seeing each other, and I agreed. Three months later she sent me a wedding announcement. Ours was a transient, inconsequential meeting, like that with the sexy girl at the party. But why did Dawn accept the first two dates at all?

There was a deep and momentous event that *did* influence me profoundly: after interviews with six psychoanalysts, to none of whom I would trust my mind, I finally found the right man, or so I thought, and started my own psychoanalysis. I told Joan about this, and also that I was anxious. She smiled and said she would stand by me. Of course I told my analyst, Dr. R., about Joan. He was totally unresponsive. He said experience showed that it was best not to make irreversible decisions during an analysis; but he never commented on the question of whether breaking off with Joan might not be just as irreversible as marrying her. What happened dynamically I had no idea initially. I dreamed of Dr. R.'s face, and it merged with that of my mother, and then blended with the face of my father. The dream showed that I was seeing Dr. R. as my mother and father. In those days I completely denied that dreams had any meaning; I thought the idea was patently absurd. Dr. R., in retrospect, was more concerned with my "resistance" than with what my dreams meant. It was not until long afterward, after I had acted my dreams out, that I could see what had happened: starting the analysis with Dr. R. stimulated regression, away from responsibility back to the wish to be a child cared for by his mother and father, as the dream showed. It stimulated the old fear of father because of my sexual activity. It was both the regression and the "castration fear" that blocked my drive toward Joan and marriage to that healthy, wholesome, straight arrow of a girl. To reemphasize, at the time I was utterly unconscious of these feelings, motivations and reactions. It was especially my tendency to relinquish the effort and yield to the temptation to regress to a less effortful, less independent life that caused my reaction in meeting the heiress at this time, although it had not done so previously.

If Joan did not see these dynamics, so unconscious to me, she did probably sense them. A few weeks later I came to Joan's desk at the hospital and apologized for my behavior and for hurting her and said I had learned my lesson. But I had no awareness whatever then of my neurotic reaction to starting my analysis and said nothing about it. She smiled and was sweet and warm. She said, "I've found the man who is right for me, Corey, without any doubt or questions. Although I've just met him, we know we are right and are going to get married." I thought to myself, "So much for you and your indecision, Jones, you fool."

I heard myself say, "Joan, I am so very happy for you." And I smiled and could say nothing more. But I still thought that if I really tried strongly enough to marry her, she would have me. Maybe this was unrealistic and was the old pattern of being so sure of Mother's love and preference that I thought I could marry any girl I wanted to. In actuality, I never tried further with Joan, which is in itself significant. We talked a few times briefly after that, and remained friends. She told me she wanted no secrets from her future husband and had told him all about me, and wanted him to meet me. She was wonderful, strong, open, honest. She brought him to the hospital to meet me; his name was Frank and I liked him. I was a little embarrassed, though, and every time I saw Joan after that or thought of her I reflected: "Corey, you fool, you fool, you have thrown away your happiness." At night I wept a little. Not for her, because she was radiant and I knew she would be happy, although she would have a quieter, less exciting life with Frank than with me. I wept for myself and for my lost happiness. Through Grant and other mutual hospital friends I got word of her now and then. She was having a good life, thank heaven; only the gorgeous athletic figure had become (in Grant's words) "a little maternal."

Looking back, I see that Joan and I may have missed not only because of confusion in me, but because of crosscurrents in Joan too. In fact, who doesn't have such conflicting drives and needs? But I am thinking of the courageous girl whom I drove to the dangerous slum on an errand, beyond the call of her duty, the girl who introduced me to her intended so that there would be no secrets when they married (the wisdom of which I still question); and then I contrast this with her complete willingness to follow my every lead as though she had little personality or judgment or willpower of her own. She had graduated from a top college; she was from a stable, loving home (and how I have learned to value that!). Did I ask too much, want too much strength in a wife, so that I would be more free? Did I want that strength because I grew up with it in my mother and father? Once Joan said a peculiar thing: "I feel that if anything ever went wrong with me, with my health, it would be my mind, a mental disorder." This from straight, courageous, open Joan! I remember it, but happily she was mistaken. Like me, she is past seventy now and nothing has ever gone wrong in mind or body. Her marriage remained excellent, as have the lives of her children and grandchildren.

The void Joan left in my life was filled only with chaos, and in the months ahead I began to wonder about my own stability. I still had no idea of how much of the turmoil was in reaction to the beginning of my psychoanalysis.

Then in late autumn came a great stabilizing experience, and as usual it came from work. Whatever happens in life, if a person can continue working, he stays on the track and is never completely thrown.

It seems curious that I cannot remember today just how I heard about it—there may have been a notice on the bulletin board at school, but more likely some student told me. An intern in Children's Hospital had to be away for one month and needed a replacement, someone to "strike" for him. With a snap decision, free of any doubt, I sped over there and was accepted, and *then* got permission from the dean's office to serve a month as substitute intern in Children's Hospital. Another week and I was outfitted in white and on the job. Of course I knew the basic principles of medicine: the anatomy and physiology and some pathology, a little about the infections and less about immunology. But along with my strong drive to mate went a strong drive to have children, although both drives up to now had been frustrated. This inner emotional state was complemented by an increase in polio, which at that time was reaching epidemic proportions. Internal needs meshed with external circumstances to give me intense motivation, and I was happy to plunge in, doing all I was able to while learning all I could. I read and reread furiously from cover to cover Holt's *Diseases of Childhood* and used it as a reference for what I did not know. But the contact with the professor and his next-in-command was a remarkable experience. A child would be lying, seriously ill, on a litter-type table. The pediatrics professor was a silent, taciturn man. I do not recall ever seeing him smile, but he was kind, gentle and generous. He would stand about ten feet away from the litter and describe what he observed and his thought processes. Sherlock Holmes could not have done better. He would make a diagnosis at ten feet by merely looking at the sick child, and he was always right. His second-in-command was less spectacular but also top-notch, and eventually succeeded to the top post.

The little patients themselves seemed like angels to me. Children are really people like anyone else: some are well-behaved and attractive; others are brats. But almost all of these children seemed to me to be stunningly beautiful. Working to help them was a great pleasure. I thought I could easily spend a lifetime in practice with children, and seriously contemplated staying on in pediatrics. But in the end my childhood emotional pattern, generating my interest in psychology and dynamics, determined my professional life. Helping these children included helping their distraught parents. Often the parents were unprepossessing even though their children were angelic. Handling the adults was in itself a fascinating and important initiation into this essential area of medical practice, one close to my growing interest in people and in the big world out there, from which I still felt overprotected. But the death or crippling of a child by disease was almost too harrowing to bear. Often we kidded and joked lest we break down so far in tears that we would lose our efficiency.

Clinically, every child that came in sick had to be examined, most especially for symptoms of polio. I soon was able to recognize the signs almost at a glance; rolling a child's head to find if his neck were stiff was often enough to signify some meningitis. Seeing so many children with polio provided a sort of baseline, and I soon learned to differentiate those who had it from those with other conditions. If there were any sign of polio, I had to do a lumbar puncture to extract spinal fluid for lab tests and to decide whether to give anti-polio serum, which was just then being developed and tested. At first I was afraid of these procedures, but I quickly learned how to do the puncture so gently that the sick child, lying on its side, did not even feel that anything was being done. Once, before entering medical school, I nearly fainted when I saw an intern in a hospital stick a big needle into a patient, but now I was becoming expert in using needles, a skill I developed further during my internship year.

My experiences with these children and my love for them strengthened an impression I had even then that the drive to parenthood is often as strong in the male as in the female, and sometimes stronger. But this might be only a reflection of my own dynamics.

The head nurse at Children's Hospital, that is, on the ward when I was on duty, was much older than I—tall, thin, gaunt, unfeminine, almost masculine and all business—and I loved her. The nurse who was second-in-command was the opposite—young, luscious, gorgeous. I identified with them both, kidding them, working with them together as a team. It was hard for me to give orders, and I found myself making "requests": "Will you do something for the Fatherland?" I once asked the head nurse, and she replied in a like vein, "The Motherland will always do something for the Fatherland!" She was Irish, a wonderful nurse and person. I made one big mistake: I defied the old dictum, vulgar but so true, "Do not excrete where you eat." The gorgeous young nurse was too irresistible—her name was Audrey. I had a date with her, as I have already described in detail. But something went wrong—whether it was my intimidation by the policeman while kissing Audrey in the parked car or whether I was not seductive enough, I never knew. Anyway she was furious with me, and her rage continued for days. I had inadvertantly broken up our excellent, effective, jolly team and failed to get it repaired before my marvelous month was over and I had to leave the wonderful world of the Children's Hospital for the everyday but still fascinating life of a medical student.

17
CONTRE COEUR

Sometimes . . . to get a stream back into its proper course you have to explode it out of the wrong one.

Linda Triegel,
"I Can Show You Morning"

If I asked you to imagine a young woman in physiological research, I doubt that you would visualize Clara. She was twenty-eight, with no great figure, but such a calm, intelligent, kindly, understanding, lovely face. She had a fine mind, and discussion of any topic with her was a pleasure. We were friendly in an entirely nonsexual way. She was married to a brilliant young chemist, Ronald, and they had two small children. I was chatting with her as she prepared to leave late one afternoon. She knew I shared a car with Gerald, who was using it that day, and she offered me a ride in hers; I accepted with pleasure because I was going to see someone who lived near her. It was early October. Clara took a detour, leaving the direct route, and I wondered why. Then she turned up an old dirt road through some woods, pulled off to the side and parked, while I looked on amazed. She moved that calm, intelligent face toward mine and kissed me warmly on the lips. I had been without a woman's love and tenderness since Joan left, and I had been lonely for it, even somewhat desolate. This was like manna. It was pure affection with sexual overtones— or undercurrents. I thought, "What about Ronald?" She was five years older than I, and seemed to know the world much better. I said nothing; she must know what she was doing. We necked lusciously for half an hour and then she said, "I'd better be getting home." We disengaged, and she added, "Two years ago Ron began his old pattern of philandering. He seduces what women he can, and I see no solution to this except to feel released myself. I would divorce him if it were not for the children; I may someday anyway, but for now what he can do, I can do. What's sauce for that gander is sauce for this goose!"

(What she said seemed reasonable to me then, but from all I've seen since, I've come to a different conclusion. A lovely girl in a similar position, who tried this solution while a patient of mine, hit the mark more closely when she said, sotto voce, "It looks good but it's a shitty life.") Clara and I smoothed our hair and clothes, she started the motor, and we were off.

This was like a gift, such a superior woman, but what was I getting into now? I was alone, she had taken the lead, I trusted her judgment. I thought she was much more mature than I, so despite considerable doubt, I went along with it. A few weeks later she wanted to come to my apartment. It was an inevitable development and was arranged. Clara was older and her figure was slightly dumpy. I was not strongly aroused physically, but I embraced her a little aggressively. Joan would have thought that was great. Sometimes there were toothmarks on Joan's shoulders afterward, which made her happy and proud; but Clara got aggressive back. "If you pinch me, I'll pinch you," she said, so sex was not much; I functioned but not very potently, and Clara was a little dejected. "Cheer up," I said, and she replied, "I expected champagne and got dago red!" By now I should have seen clearly that I was not potent with every woman, especially not with controlling mother-figures who did not attract me sexually, and that Clara's attitude was not basically sexual. Rather, it discouraged my own sexuality. Maybe she gave her husband cause to philander, if there ever *is* an excuse for doing that to one's wife and children. But all I sensed until later was that my masculine pride demanded I be potent with her, with any woman, else something was wrong with me. Maybe something *was* wrong. I think she was indeed a mother-figure for me in my mind, with all the resulting inhibitions. How could I have failed to see this in the perspective of the perfect sex of the past years with those wonderful girls and the sobering first experience with Myrna? And for this failure, why did I feel inadequate? The answer was because I *was* inadequate toward women who were mother-figures to me, and I wanted to be potent to satisfy her, not only for the sex but also for the ulterior motive of holding or winning her admiration.

Now instead of pure sex with minimal personality, I had an outstanding personality with very mediocre sex. We saw a lot of each other for three months, but the sex got no better and at last it began to dawn on me that there might be nothing wrong with me but that she just might not be sexual for me, that I really did not think of Clara in terms of sex, really had no desire for her "in that way," as Myrna had once said; and I was fully potent only with someone who was femininely seductive to my masculinity like ultrafeminine Aline, goddess Elaine or athletic, courageous, straight-arrow Joan. But until that dawned I was again, as with Myrna, in agonies of self-doubt and struggled to break down an inhibition that did not exist except toward mother-figures. One incident helped:

I went to the Holdens' on a Sunday evening and met a father, mother and daughter. They were a socially prominent, wealthy family. The daughter, Grace, was an extremely pretty, starry-eyed girl of about twenty, who attended a top women's college and must have been intelligent. She was nice but without much strength of personality, and her intelligence did not show much in her conversation; I liked her well enough and made a date with her because the situation called for it. Girl meets boy who shows enough interest to take her around a little, and who reacts sexually to her fresh beauty—that was the story. I took her out a few times but never touched her or had any intentions of so doing, not because I did not want to, but because by now I was even more sensitive about not hurting a girl in any way. I only watched to see if, after all, she might not be a wife for me. I did not think she would care to come to the apartment, or that she would come if I suggested it; but she asked where I lived and said she wanted to see the place. I felt nothing close or personal in her interest. The apartment was only another sight to see. We never touched except when I took her arm crossing a street or stepping in or out of the car.

Grace did come to the apartment and was interested in my tiny kitchen; she busied herself with something there and was so pretty, so feminine, so desirable that I could hardly keep my arms from going around her, and my instincts felt sure that she would not resist; we would kiss and be fully aroused, and she would trust me, and we would move to the bed—and yes, probably go all the way together, and it would be warm and delicious; and once we started sex together she would be irresistible, and we would continue. She would become deeply involved with me. (A blind alley for her so far as marriage; I would have to make a marriage I was not confident of, or reject her and hurt her.) It was clear to me in a flash. But I was not going to marry her, lovely as she was, and she was too fine and sweet to use sexually without marriage. Having her, the next months, would be wonderful, but after that what would there be in it for her? Not marriage but heartbreak. I felt sure she was a virgin; I might have been wrong. So I used that willpower to the utmost to hold my arms tightly against my sides, to prevent them from going around her, moved about to quiet the erection and said we'd better go out—there was a good movie to catch. After that I saw Grace infrequently and finally not at all; I think it would have been a pleasant, wealthy, social marriage with everything except close rapport. Bodymates, yes; soulmates, no; therefore we both would have become lonely. But perhaps I read it all wrong. About Grace I still have regrets at missing the sex, which I am still certain would have been wonderful for us both. At the same time, I think I did the right thing.

But the relation with Clara was now pretty clear. Unthinkingly, I took for granted the old, barely controllable surge with Grace. Later on I began to realize that it showed nothing was wrong with my desire or potency. If anything, I was oversexed, and girls reacted to that. Clara was a friend, but for me she was more a maternal than a sexual kind of person. I was beginning to see these two sides of women. Sex with Clara would never be anything exciting or deeply gratifying, and it was only agonizing to struggle to understand it, and free it, and change in me what was so free and strong with other women. I thought of Maude, who was older than I but terribly exciting for that one night in my apartment when I crawled from my bed into hers. That must have been the revivification of some incident of childhood in bed with Mother. Clara and I could be friends, but for me sex and marriage lay elsewhere.

Incredible as it may seem, Clara was so wonderful a personality that I had thought about marrying her, and even discussed the pros and cons with her, but we knew it was folly. So we talked, and I said marriage was on my mind although I was not yet sure of the girl. To my amazement, Clara—under her gentleness, sympathy and understanding—was furious. Again it took me a while to guess at the reason, for we could be friends anyway; sex did not amount to anything sufficient to miss, and marriage was out. But then I began to suspect that Clara, the mature and the independent, had her own needs for love and pride, and took what I said as rejection, and that it was a blow to her as it would be to anyone; she also had feminine jealousy, and later still I began to think that Clara might have had a sexual inhibition and my leaving was one more proof of it to her. Clearly, personality alone is not enough for marriage, anymore than sex alone is. It takes both. But it also takes a compatibility, not of surface opinions, but a compatibility of bodies, souls and of minds, and it takes confidence and trust based on stability; it takes qualities complementing each other, for marriage is like the meshing of very complicated gears, the meshing of each partner's psychodynamics, that complicated interplay of feelings,motivations and reactions, formed by our childhood emotional patterns, which make up our highly individual personalities.

We separated then but, unusual as it is, did remain friends, for the mutual respect and admiration had contained elements of love. Again I was free. I seemed unable to marry, although it was what I had wanted more than anything for so long.

Easter was late that spring, and before it came I reached a low in behavior which left regrets not for what I did not do, as with Grace, but for what I did do. There was a medical meeting at one of the hotels. At such meetings, experienced secretaries supervise registration, handing out of badges, delivery of phone messages to doctors in a large audience, and so on. They sometimes have girls to assist them. There was a message for me during the evening meeting, and by the time I took it, the meeting was nearly over. I had no wish to return. A girl named Billie had brought the message; usually I was mixed up with the men at these medical meetings, and several of us would go out for beer together, but this particular evening I was alone. I started chatting with Billie. She was not so young as I'd thought at first, but about my age; and I offered to take her out as soon as she was off duty. She accepted. We left the hotel and found a small cafe. Fool that I was, I found myself making passes at her, and she was not rejecting. I never saw that for her I might be glamorous, nearly a doctor, and she was just a working girl; all I was aware of was my own desires and that she was not rebuffing me. I saw her home. She lived in a small, unprepossessing apartment with another girl, who was gone for the weekend. She was happy—how could I fail to see her loneliness, her weakness? She straightened the bed, turned the lights out, and we slowly undressed. When our clothes were off she said, "Now we will discover each other." I was horrified. Here was I, only waiting for sex, purely carnal, desiring a girl's body, and she said something to me that was full of such enjoyment and such *intimacy*. She thought that I cared for her. No doubt she expected warmth, closeness, tenderness, friendship, possibly even eventually marriage; it was all in her tone and in her touch. She was quite flat-chested. The sex was not much. How could it be, when I despised myself? It was soon over.

I did not even stay the night with her. I could not feign love and affection; I was overwhelmed with remorse. Cowardly or not, I could think of nothing but escape. I made some stupid excuse and dressed, and as kindly as I could I left and went home. I felt like a thief, despicable. Billie, I hope you are a bigger person than I was and have forgiven me. I had learned a lifelong lesson.

I learned to have a new respect and deep sympathy for these lonely girls, struggling along in life, so often confusing their immediate physiological sexual needs with their great fundamental biological need for love, and (like me, one of the fortunate ones) not only a need for love but a need for security in love and finances, plus self-esteem justified by the respect and esteem of others. When I see a young working girl with some frilly ribbons, in terrible taste, I no longer feel revolted—I feel a great tenderness, for I know that she is trying so hard to win admiration and love. And I think it is utterly cruel and despicable to seduce such a young thing sexually, which probably means arousing her hopes for love and then dashing them and her self-esteem. My father was a rock. His strength supported and protected my mother, and my sister and myself. I think that is how it should be and how history shows it to be. But men do not always take care of women. How can I expect it to be so if even I, with all the love that was given me, could hurt a girl by doing the diametric opposite to what I wanted? All girls should be taught these realities of life and learn to protect themselves and take care of themselves. From what I have seen of marriages (which cause the highest happiness or the profoundest misery, and so often end in divorce), every girl should have some skill with which to make a good life for herself, so that she is not completely dependent upon a man for financial support. And I think that even if the marriage is a good one and the woman never uses those skills, it gives her an interest and makes her more of a person, one who gets more satisfaction from this life.

My behavior with Billie, filling me with remorse, brought to mind a verse* of Robert Burns, whose lyrical sense and earthy wisdom have long made him one of my favorite poets:

> The sacred lowe o'weel-plac'd love,
>   Luxuriantly indulge it;
> But never tempt th' illicit rove,

*"Letter to a Young Friend."

Tho' naething should divulge it:
I waive the quantum o' the sin,
    The hazard of concealing;
But, och! it hardens a' within,
    And petrifies the feeling!

18
AFTERTHOUGHTS

It seems, said Corey, that we all try to concentrate all our feelings and needs on one single person. In marriage we expect one single person to satisfy them all. But these feelings of each of us toward others are so compellingly powerful. A woman divorces a husband who is ruthlessly cruel to her and the children, and then finds her loneliness worse than the marriage she left. We each all but die if we do not have love; we need the esteem and respect of others, and affection, and physical sex; perhaps there are other inexorable instincts. We seek one single person to provide the loving and being loved, the companionship, the sex, the sharing of responsibility. No wonder it is hard to find such a person as a mate! No wonder it is almost impossible—yet if one does not find a partner who fits one's needs reasonably well, if there is serious incompatibility, if hostility replaces love, then the marriage is a lifetime of hell, and the children are doomed to emotional disorders. The strife, however, of a bad marriage can for some be worse than the loneliness of no marriage at all. But it is a wretched choice, either way.

Many of my violent urges had found satisfaction in one girl at a time, each girl superior in some way. Not all of these deep needs had been satisfied by any single one of them, and I did not know if this was because of something in them or something in me. Therefore, I had not married. But there had been enough concentration on one girl at a time for profound satisfaction, such that I am still in debt to each of them for life, and some of that love lives on in the embers and makes me what I am today. Now, with the loss of Joan, there was no one point of focus. The result was months of chaos. It is all a blur in my mind; I can untangle the threads only with a deliberate effort.

But first a few retrospective comments about Joan, points never thought of at the time:

In spite of my gallantry toward women, my friendship and identification and championship of them, perhaps I did have some unconscious hostility toward them, for I began to feel that Miss Hinchly might be right and that I started heavy affairs which ended by my rejecting and thereby hurting those girls who became close to me. Of course, at that time the concept of unconscious hostility had no meaning for me at all. But I was beginning to see that I made a play for those girls who attracted me, and then, when they began to make demands upon me, I did not fulfill the demands but rejected the girls.

Was this following a pattern toward my sister, whom I loved but who, when I was struggling with some problem of my own, exasperated me by making some kind of demand so that I felt, "What, now *you* too?" and wanted to be rid of her? I loved her dearly, but I did have some hostility in my emotional pattern to Judy, for her demands and for taking my things, and for bothering me and also no doubt because of sibling rivalry.

And I loved my mother, but there was a pattern of hostility to her for what I felt as her domination and restrictiveness, even though they may not have been excessive but only for my own realistic protection. As George Bernard Shaw remarked, "The Church added new zest to life when it made sex a sin." Sex for me contained this element of rebellion and defiance of overprotection, overcontrol and restrictiveness, and this augmented its intensity.

The only woman of my childhood for whom I felt unadulterated love with no resentment whatever was beautiful Aunt Edie. There is no doubt that many of the girls who especially attracted me did so because they reminded me unconsciously of Aunt Edie as well as of Mother and Judy. Aunt Edie often wore a muff, a winter style during my childhood, and I walked with her with my hand on her arm, at times in the muff. Sometimes Aline put the fur-trimmed sleeves of her winter coat together, like a muff, and when my hand was included, I was swept by a surge of feeling for her, although at the time I did not connect it with this loved aunt of my early life.

But was it only the pattern toward my mother and sister that led my affairs to end in rejection and hurt for the girls whom I basically loved? I know I loved Mother and Judy and I loved the girls. Could it have been a form of "spoiling," of self-indulgence? My mother, despite her restrictiveness, unquestionably said yes to everything she reasonably could. It was not easy for her when I stuffed an old duffle bag and set out alone for the docks to try to get a job on a ship sailing for Europe. But she assented. Now was I naively asking these girls for sex and getting them to indulge me, without my having sufficient grasp of the reality, which lack was the source of so many of my old feelings of inadequacy? I did not adequately see the realities, and therefore was not master of them: "For that which is invisible is that which is invincible."* Did I do something *contre coeur*, against my own heart, and hurt the girls I loved, not so much out of unconscious hostility as out of childish selfishness, thoughtlessness and ignorance?

I must again emphasize the fact that only about one girl in two hundred attracted me sufficiently for me to look at her twice, and it must have been fewer than one in four or five hundred that I found truly beautiful and irresistible. I met so many in the hospitals and at the university—why was I attracted to just these particular ones, and so strongly?

This brings me to the positive side of the relationship with Joan. Should I feel guilty about hurting her when, in the end, it was *she* who rejected *me?* As a friend of mine commented to me later, "You still thought you could marry any girl you wanted." It was true. And Joan wanted me until I delayed too long and she met Frank, who seemed so much less complicated than I, and who had no doubts or hesitations about Joan, or at least none that Joan could not quickly dispel. I was indeed "going slow" on marriage, but marriage for me had been so profoundly meaningful for so many years that I could hardly rush into it. Instead, with all my doubts, crosscurrents and turmoil, I could only hope that I was nevertheless moving toward it. I did not know what I was looking for in a wife—except perfection. If Frank had not appeared, I still believe that Joan and I would have gotten married and that it would have been an excellent marriage in all ways. Why then was I moving toward marriage with Joan? I can only list a few reasons:

Consciously, eugenics had always played a primary role in my vision of a wife, as I should think it does in anyone who wants children. I had deeply enjoyed my good coordination and reflexes. Running down a mountain had been exhilerating, as my feet seemed to pick their own way without conscious will, among the stones and rocks, crevasses and tree trunks and other debris of the wild. But I was unhappy about being so slight that I could not play football or even college baseball, although I had always been good at pickup games

*Robert Hichens, "The Charmer of Snakes."

on the lot and even boxed and wrestled a little. Perhaps my egotism was offended more than I realized by my meager 138 pounds and my height (5'7"); so my first surprise was that girls were attracted to me in spite of the slender physique. I think my feelings of being so light physically became mixed with my feelings of psychological inadequacy for being immature, not sufficiently independent and knowledgeable about the big world, too much occupied with trying to get people to admire me. I was past my mid-twenties before I realized this, and also that physique has little to do with success in life, unless you are a professional athlete or in a job requiring brawn. I had a good instrument—a good mind and a basically healthy and well-proportioned body, light but well-coordinated and full of drive and vitality. *Mens sana in corpore sano:* the Greek ideal. Why should I complain? The instrument was adequate; it was only a matter of how I *used* it. I could be as good a doctor, husband, father, friend, citizen, at 135 pounds or at 125 pounds as at 235 pounds. This realization helped a great deal in counteracting my feelings of inadequacy.

When I was moving toward marriage with Joan I very much wanted the children to be perfect. In a way, it was not entirely rational. My parents were of perfectly normal build; I was so slight because my mother had an illness during the pregnancy, and her weight had gone below one hundred pounds. My sister, Judy, was sturdy, full-muscled and a good athlete. Nevertheless, I saw Joan's straight athletic build as how I wanted my children to be. She was entirely feminine but strong and well coordinated, and when we played tennis together, she could hold her own in singles with me. She attracted me eugenically.

Another reason was that we were friends; we *liked* each other. Liking is different from love or sex. But it is very important. In fact, from all I've seen of marriages, in the long run being good friends in a marriage ranks with love and sex. It is a cooler feeling but deep. We liked each other. Part of this was my admiration for Joan, and I think she had some for me. We would have been close friends and unquestionably loyal.

From my experience, when people actually take the step of marrying, it is almost always because they have a great deal of their dynamics, their childhood emotional patterns, in common. Joan was the first and oldest child, as I was, and had a younger sister just as I did. But that is about all I know of her background. I guess I was so concerned with my own feelings that I never delved into her family, what her father did for a living, her life as a child and her life before we met, except that she was a graduate of a top college. I only knew her in her interrelation with me. I wanted the right wife for me and, egotistically, nothing else seems to have entered my head. I had no ideas in those days of "childhood patterns" and of "dynamics fitting." It may be just as well. If one has to do it by intellectual study, it may be that something is wrong with the relationship.

Today of course I have a pretty good idea of my own dynamics and can say that the identification with each other was very important. We enjoyed doing things together. I was always the leader—in going to the shore, going to dinner, going to a movie, going to bed—and also the leader in ideas, politics, discussions of what was going on in the world, all from the path Jim had helped set me on, which now I could begin following alone. That kind of leadership, as I now realize many years later, was part of my emotional pattern to girls. But Joan did have ample strength, and I felt I could always count on her as she could on me, if the need arose, but it never did. When she once had to have a wisdom tooth extracted, it was natural for me to be with her, standing on the left side of the dental chair, holding her hand through those bad moments when the dentist had to find some bits of tooth or bone that had chipped off and were somewhere in that blood-filled hole. I admired her stoicism and patience and uncomplaining acceptance, and afterward took her to a movie to distract her. We were simply drifting into acting like a married couple.

One of the conflicts over finding a wife seems to have lain in wanting a woman who was stronger and more mature than I, like Mother, but also one who was younger, fresher, looking up to me, like Sister Judy. The weaker sister-figures were the sex objects but did not satisfy my needs for support and mothering. The mother-figures, like Clara, were not sex objects, did not appeal to my physical or psychological masculinity. Obviously no girl could combine both, or so it seemed.

I can understand why I wanted to marry Joan but not why I hesitated, knowing that she wanted to marry me. In part I guess I was too preoccupied with myself. But even though, after Frank appeared, I still felt that I could win her back, I didn't try. I seem to have changed, no longer panicking at the idea of being without a girl and unable to find one immediately. And now the stakes were higher, marriage itself.

What I thought of as a "spark" just wasn't strong enough between Joan and me to make the desire a compulsion. Maybe that was what my platonic friend meant when she described Joan as "wan." Yet the other girls, the ones with the spark and the intense sex appeal who were ready to go to bed with me, began to seem flawed with emotional problems. But I loved Joan then, and still love her. I feel no guilt or disloyalty to my wife of nearly half a century because Joan still lives in my memory. By the greatest good fortune, unlike the situation of those men who cannot stop philandering after they marry, all my experience with girls has only strengthened my deep, unwavering, unquestioned love for my wife.

It seems to be a characteristic of the human mind to dwell on whatever is a problem and ignore what goes well. Perhaps this preoccupation with problems helps develop the intellect. The emphasis in this story of my life has been upon what was my main problem: the sex drive, girls and the search for a wife. Of course there were other whole areas of living that were relatively free of problems. All moved ahead smoothly in career and in friendships with men, both father- and brother-figures. No struggles and indecisions there, but the truly blessed freedom to observe, study and work with full ease and undistracted concentration.

19
CAREER: THE END OF THE BEGINNING

Although I was still struggling to find a mate and to find myself, said Corey Jones, I had found my career, or at least the basis of it.

The enjoyment of the studies and experiences in medical school continued to expand and deepen in the clinical years—learning the rudiments of the medical specialties in third year and of internal medicine and surgery in fourth year. In medicine I recall once going on rounds with a professor who was seeing a puzzling patient, a man recovering from a serious infection that seemcd entirely overcome and was no longer detectible. But the man was incredibly weak because he could not eat. The professor said, "Is there anything at all that appeals to you, that you think you *could* eat?"

The patient replied, "I sometimes get a hankering for some salt pork." The entourage, thinking in terms of anatomy and physiology, an irritated lining of the stomach, and of biochemistry and the need for easy digestibility, were slightly shocked; but the professor said, "*We* have not succeeded. Now let us try *his* own instincts." And he said to the patient, "Fine, you may have the salt pork and whatever you want, but at first only in small amounts. Just start gradually." The patient recovered his appetite quickly. One can never be certain about biology and can be even less so about psychology, except that the childhood emotional pattern will somehow, sometime, surely assert itself for better or for worse. The old aphorism is fatefully true: "As the twig is bent, so is the tree inclined."

This professor was a huge, blond man with a strong impressive personality, not always easy to get along with. One of the other professors, with whom I had a close friendly relationship, was having trouble with him and remarked to me, "I'll just *make* that bastard like me!"

In surgery I was just learning to scrub, get into the gown and mask and stand in at operations. The first was the removal of an ovarian cyst. It was the size of a grapefruit, transparent, filled with a clear fluid and attached to the ovary by a filmy membrane so thin as to be barely perceptible, like a soap bubble. The professor turned to me and asked, "Do you think I can dissect it out without breaking it?"

I thought he would feel bad if I said yes and then he failed, so I said no. He put on a mock scene of weeping because I had no confidence in him. I was shocked that with the patient's abdomen open and this tissue out the doctor could clown like that. But then, with astonishing skill and incredible speed, he dissected out that soap bubble of a cyst. He could afford to clown in order to teach, because of his justified confidence in his undeviating concentration and in his skill.

Gregg and Chet and I were very close friends, but of course we each had friendly relations of various degrees of intimacy with most other members of our class. An occurrence with Gregg and Chet is dynamically interesting and instructive enough to relate here. In our fourth year, dormitory and dining room facilities were expanded to include us. After some discussions it turned out that Gregg and I would share a double apartment in the dorm, and Chet preferred a single to having a double with a roommate. The doubles were two separate rooms with connecting doors, so that it was easy to have privacy, which continued very important to me, probably because, as previously mentioned, in childhood my mother kept such close watch on me, and Judy as a toddler got into my things. Even having my old upright piano at one wall worked out. I never played well enough for anything but my own pleasure in keeping up an intimacy with the great music. Occasionally Gregg would help himself to one of my shirts. One was special for me, an oxford gray, attractive in texture and color, which I used for dressing up informally, when white was not indicated. But I liked Gregg so much and had to admit that this shirt went extremely well with one of his suits and a tie with a bit of red on gray; so I made no issue of it, even though it did strike my emotional vulnerability of Judy's getting into my things as a toddler, and later her interest in my friends and the restaurants I preferred.

After graduation Chet surprisingly decided to take out a year or two and spend it in a famous school of drama. Gregg got an internship in a big private hospital in another city, which treated many wealthy, socially prominent and important people. I thought it just suited

Gregg, and he would soon marry his beautiful socialite with the choker of choice pearls around her neck. I felt Chet, by detouring to a top school of drama, might in time join those eminent writers who had M.D.'s, like Conan Doyle and Somerset Maugham. Then Chet showed me a play he had written. I do not know if it was his first. It was about a young man who was heartbroken because he felt left out of things by his two best friends, who roomed together while he was alone. Part of writing is transforming one's personal frustrations into something artistically creative, but it was a distressing shock to see that Chet had felt rejected by Gregg and me to that degree, that much quantitatively, to write a play about it. How little I observed of what was going on in the feelings of my closest friends, and how powerful and sensitive are the *dependent love needs* and the need to be included! Maybe a specific emotional vulnerability left over from Chet's childhood had been touched. After two years he returned to medicine and became successful and even modestly prominent in a huge metropolis. Two years in drama school and writing was a fine experience for him, probably giving him something very much like that I had always had with the piano.

Poor player that I was, I could nevertheless read music, not fluently but haltingly, and did understand basic chords. I played through almost all the great music, including symphonies, piano concertos and vocal music such as lieder. And I accumulated a library of this music, which I think I understand emotionally and esthetically, and have enjoyed for life; it has often provided me with a needed emotional outlet and support. The end of Bach's passacaglia and fugue never fails to infuse me with determination and perseverance. So does Sibelius' "Finlandia." I seem to get more from stumbling through music myself at the piano than from passively listening to records of fine performances—probably because when I do it myself I select what fits my mood; it is a form of self-expression, a participation in that whole strange other world and a way of speaking its mysterious, beautiful and effective language. We all relieve our tensions in different ways. Athletics—tennis, golf, swimming, ice-skating—have been my chief outdoor ways, and piano has been the main indoor way. The only creative way has been by writing professional articles and books, trying to select, organize and formulate what I have learned from assiduous study of my patients. Years later, when I mentioned to Jim that I never thought I would write, he laughed and said, "Of course not. In those days we did not know enough to have anything to write!"

At that time, the fourth year of most medical schools was filled with anxiety, distractions and wasted time and effort by the merciless and chaotic competition for the best internships. The Great Depression was just beginning, but only a very few, rare people had the slightest idea of the dimensions of what was to come. Even among my classmates, many were telling of how they had bought a certain stock on margin and in two months made enough for the year's tuition and a new car. But my father's business was one of the first affected, and I felt the need to become self-supporting as soon as possible for his sake as well as mine.

My good friend, Lars, a physiologist from Iceland, proposed that he and I spend a summer crossing central Iceland on Icelandic ponies before settling down in our careers. This was a great idea and temptation. But when the "crash" came, I could no longer indulge myself with such a delay. I had no choice but to head directly for the goal of establishing myself in a career that would enable me to be self-supporting and to contribute if necessary to my parents, who had so unstintingly given to me. As I faced a life of independence, and hard work I thought of one of the songs Maude used to sing so beautifully:

O sing me not the old Circassian songs, love haunted;
They only fill my soul with dreams of distant shores and life
  undaunted.

Any letter in my father's strong handwriting was an honor, for my mother gladly handled the correspondence with Judy and me. But when my father's letter arrived telling of the loss of his business, the suit by his creditors who were trying to take every bit of his personal property in addition to the assets of his corporation, it was a shock. For my conscientious, devoted, completely honest father I felt terrible. I got a few days off and returned home to be with him. My esteem for Dad rose even higher. Through it all he was his usual unruffled, stable self. His sleep was disturbed for only one night, the one before the meeting with his creditors; they acted like ravenous beasts while trying to save themselves, but they failed to disturb Dad's quiet composure. Bad as I felt for us all, paradoxically I felt a certain lift in myself, for now I was up against it—now there was no choice—suddenly it was mercilessly necessary for me to make my own way in order to survive. Thank goodness in another month I would have my M.D., but my internship was not yet firmly arranged. Now I *had* to be independent and self-reliant, just what I had been unconsciously striving for. I had not yet read Freud's remark that "Necessity is a hard master, but under him we become potent." But I now learned through experience, the most painful but most effective teacher, the truth of that statement. Until then, in the back of my mind persisted the idea that, if worse came to worse, I could still fall back on my strong father. Now life forced me to mature to the extent of being self-supporting.

My mother was so happily girlish that one forgot her own inner strength. She maintained her quiet cheerfulness throughout the grim proceedings, and was an unfailing source of calm and support. I have always believed that the wife and mother is the spirit of the home. Certainly my mother demonstrated it; doubtless she was the source of my belief. Dad's creditors were soon satisfied, and every cent was gone. Only then did Mother reveal that over the years she had saved money out of the household accounts and kept it in a separate bank account in her name only. "I saw enough of business," she explained, "to want a little something set aside for a rainy day—what a downpour this 'Crash' is becoming!" With that Dad faced the world again at sixty-five as he had faced it penniless nearly fifty years before. But it pained me to see my parents relinquish the apartment they loved and move to a dingy dark one, with the furniture covered over and of course no help at all, scraping to put together tasteful wholesome meals and facing the ever-deepening Depression. No enjoyment of "golden years" for them.

Yet they were happier than many—happier than their friends, the Norrises. Mr. Norris had foreseen the Crash, sold short in the market and cleaned up. With their fortune they moved to an exclusive neighborhood of millionaires. But their marriage began to go bad, and soon they were miserable and divorced. That did not improve matters for either of them or their children. Life is primarily human relations: I did not appreciate that then, but I returned to my career with a new urgency and determination, for now life had put me entirely on my own, and I felt that whatever the disadvantage of that, it would save my soul. This it did by forcing me toward maturity. Psychotherapy only helps us make the best use of life, but is no substitute for it.

Whether I went into psychiatry or a different specialty, I wanted the shortest possible requirement, an internship of only one year in medicine or surgery. I thought I would get a broader view in medicine. But there were no internships for just one year in the teaching hospital connected with the medical school. In that situation I went to Clark, my friend and mentor.

Success in life, as one of the professors had once mentioned, comes from a combination of personality and ability, usually in about equal proportions. Clark had a full share of both. I was not the only one who immediately liked and trusted him. When we met at the end of my first year, he was a young instructor only about ten years older than I. Now he was already one of the outstanding leaders not only in the school but nationally. As usual he had a quick, realistic answer to my problem. He said, "My friend Bill Yardley is professor at the new medical school and hospital at the University of _____, and will be looking for interns. Why don't you go and see him? I will write a good letter for you if you like."

He did, and I went the next weekend, a nine-hour drive. Clark's friend, the professor of medicine, seemed extremely young and boyish. We met in his office and then he asked me to take a walk with him next morning, Sunday. As I think of that walk, it seems to me that I was trying to impress him all the time. I discussed Spengler's monumental *Decline of the West*, just recently published, to show my broad interests, and there were other such exhibitionisms. He debunked everything with a few simple obvious observations. I felt like a fool, but at the end of the walk we sat down and he said, "You have the job. And do you have one or two classmates whom you like and could recommend who would like to come too?"

The surprise was so sudden I was almost speechless; on second thought I was flattered and enormously relieved. Now I would have no struggles and uncertainties for the next months, because this vital problem was solved. As I have said, besides very close friends like Gregg and Chet, there were many whom I liked a great deal but who were not quite so close, two in particular. After Gregg and Chet, who were still seeking longer internships, declined the offer from Yardley, I asked the other two friends. They were happy to accept. One of them, Karl, stayed on with Bill Yardley, married a local girl and became one of the most prominent professors at that new school and hospital; he won national recognition for his investigations of some little-understood diseases. We remained good friends and stayed in touch for life, although we rarely had opportunities to meet.

Graduation came in June and passed, and now I faced the next step, internship in a new world. But I had sudden doubts, the first in my medical career.

"You fool," I said to myself. "Here you are at the school of your choice among the greatest men of medicine, at one of the greatest medical centers in the world, and what are you doing? You are leaving it for a far-away, unknown, untested little place that has not yet even graduated its first class of medical students! Act before it is too late!"

Was this good judgment, or was it hurt egotism at leaving so prestigious a center for a place with no standing? Or was it partly also a protest against breaking the dependent ties to what was so familiar after four years—ties with the Holdens, the friends, the teachers, the accustomed halls and familiar faces of school and hospital, Gregg, Chet and the area where I had so passionately loved and been loved? I was leaving the roots and all I was dependent upon to go out into a void. I told nothing of my doubts to anyone, even to Clark. I quietly investigated other possibilities and found that nothing could be done.

But such separations have never been too painful or difficult for me, nor, except in the Navy, have I ever felt the slightest tinge of homesickness. Those persons and places that I love seem to become an intrinsic part of me—they live in my memory as do my feelings for them; that, I think, is due to my relating so largely by *identifying*. My loving home is an ingrained part of my makeup. I need never think of it consciously, for it is always with me, a living part of me; this lovingness of home is the core around which accreted all the later loves, which have become intrinsic to my makeup and live in full vividness beneath the activities, challenges and tasks of everyday life, coloring the emotional atmosphere of my daily living and all its decisions, all I do and feel. What I feel and think and do is, in part, an expression of profound heartfelt gratitude to all those by whom I have been loved and whom I still love. That is the essential of my childhood emotional pattern. As E. A. Robinson wrote, "We never know how much we owe to those who never will return."

CYCLE III

20
MEDICAL INTERNSHIP

Down, down, down into the darkness of the grave
Gently they go, the beautiful, the tender, the kind;
Quietly they go, the intelligent, the witty, the brave.
I know. But I do not approve. And I am not resigned.

Edna St. Vincent Millay,
"Dirge Without Music"

Together with graduation from medical school, Gerald and I had graduated from our Model-T. Eddy Petty wanted to sell his four-cylinder open Dodge roadster, and I happily purchased it from him for the rather high price in those days of 250 dollars. It appealed to me for many reasons, especially my "masculine protest," for it took a certain ruggedness to drive an open roadster in those winters. Now, however, it was the end of July. I bowled along across three states to whatever the internship held. I still felt that it was a terrible comedown from the great medical school and center I was leaving, and I had mixed feelings about driving alone. Partly it was great: the independence and freedom I had always wanted and always known. But no mate sat beside me, no insightful transcendent Nelda, no quintessentially feminine Aline, no vital golden goddess Elaine beaming with joy at this adventure, no comradely Joan. I was entering the next step of my career, the step into the big world, without having found either myself or a mate.

I often think of Churchill's remark, "How hard it is to know our own self-interest." For what then seemed a terrible comedown turned out to be one of the best years of my life—a place with top men, top medicine, a youthful spirit, and colleagues even more congenial than those I had before. Two of them (Hugh and "Shag") joined my circle of very intimate friends which has persisted to this day. After so many years of the intensive study of books, it was a huge relief to try now to use some of that knowledge practically to help patients.

203

During that year I did not read a single book of any kind and used books only as references.

There occurred a few incidents that were minor in themselves but which affected me deeply and permanently. I was to draw some blood from the arm of a young man. I put on the tourniquet carefully and well, not so tightly as to obstruct the arteries but tightly enough to stop the flow back in the veins, so that the veins would be tightly filled and make the insertion of the needle quicker, easier, less painful. Then something distracted me, I forget what—perhaps the right needle was not out. I turned away to get it and had to search. At that moment Karl came by. He stopped and reprovingly said, "You left the tourniquet on the patient's arm—but don't worry, I took it off." I was merely embarrassed at the moment, but afterward I felt the way you do after escaping a danger. And I have never recalled the incident without anxiety and humiliation. After four years of intense study and concentration on my chosen field, how could I be thoughtless, distracted and childishly irresponsible even for an instant in the care of a patient? I determined that nothing like this would ever happen again; and in my practice every patient I take responsibility for gets my complete, undivided concentration, down to every detail I can recognize and encompass. At that moment I saw that Karl was more mature and responsible than I, and I began to get an inkling of the fact that responsibility was a very large part of the maturity I so yearned to achieve.

The other incident occurred in the dead of winter when the hospital was full to overflowing. In some internships there are a senior, a junior and a "pup." There is division of labor: the "pup" or newcomer does the routine lab work, mostly urinalyses and blood counts, which soon becomes boring. But where I was, the intern had a whole ward, and every patient on the ward was his, as though he were in private practice. Of course, a close watch was kept on him by the resident and everyone else up to the professor of medicine, who had the ultimate responsibility. This was by far the best system, I thought. But in the pneumonia season, in those days before antibiotics, keeping up with all the work was extremely difficult, as there were at least thirty acutely ill patients demanding care. A patient died of pneumonia and came to postmortem examination, which most of the staff attended. The pathologist, in examining one kidney, reported some kind of damage. Bill Yardley, the professor, turned on me with a scathing tone: "Your clinical record says the urine was normal. It could not have been. There must have been red cells in it."

This was a direct attack and exposure to public humiliation before the whole staff. Of course it was unpleasant; but for some reason I took it calmly (as, I learned later in life, I usually took direct attack). He was right. I must have been too hasty in my microscopic examination of the urine. Not that it made any difference in the case; it had nothing to do with the patient's pneumonia and his death. But my negligence may have revealed a carelessness in the medical department that reflected on the professor. What struck me, though, was that the other interns supported me. One whispered to me, "Just tell him that was your finding." I said nothing but I appreciated the support. Also I was pleased that Bill treated me as a man whom he could attack and not as a child with a father attachment to him whom he must baby.

This incident did not humiliate me so much as leaving on the tourniquet, so that I feel shame even now; but it did show me that, even though the patient was dead, under pressure I could be careless and even somewhat dishonest, writing "no abnormal cells" without doing a sufficiently painstaking microscopic study to be absolutely certain that there were none. Carelessness and the least dishonesty are incompatible with my makeup because they were so with my father's personality, with his straightforwardness. Both of these hospital incidents were basically a matter of "responsibility," and I knew I would have to be meticulous if I wanted to be a doctor. I did not know that they would help me so directly to emotional maturity, of which responsibility is such a large part.

Perhaps I was learning a little more rapidly now that I spent less time in books and more time among people. As Goethe put it, "A talent is built in solitude, but a character in the stream of life."

Another problem involved Albert, a surgical resident in the room next to mine in the interns' quarters. He had a radio that he played very loudly. Its blaring prevented me from sleeping soundly, which has always been of great importance to my physical health and mental sharpness, both essential to good productive work. All my life, provided I have gotten nine or ten hours of sleep, I have been indefatigable physically and mentally. I spoke to Albert in a friendly way about it, but he paid no attention. My mentioning it only served to give him something he could torment me with. This was a kind of open hostility I had not known since the streets of my boyhood. One night it was worse than usual; I hated to say anything but was furious, could not sleep and went to his room—it was vacant! He had gone out and left the radio blaring. I switched it off and retired. Some of the boys thought this humorous, and I had no choice but to go along with them and take it in good part. I was much too busy to take time to give it any thought. But if it worsened, it would threaten my efficiency. Meanwhile, I did nothing but let my silent attitude toward Albert show what I felt and what I thought about him. If success is ability plus personality, I wondered how Albert could ever be a good doctor with proper sympathetic feelings for his patients if he could be this inconsiderate of a fellow intern. Even though a few of the resident staff could see humor in this, Albert's general insensitivity was beginning to damage his reputation. For me the whole problem was solved by his leaving prematurely, for reasons I never discovered. I still think of him with resentment, but do not wish him ill.

Another incident occurred during that year which left a permanent effect. It was midwinter. I was the intern in charge of a male ward overflowing its capacity. A nice-looking, gray-haired elderly man with a powerful physique was admitted in a coma; he had pneumonia. Everything that could be done for him had been done, in those days before antibiotics. He had been seen by the entire staff, including Bill Yardley, the professor. In those days life-sustaining machines did not exist—not even oxygen tents, let alone machines to continue breathing, heart beat, kidney function and such, long after natural death would have occurred; nor did we use heroic but usually hopeless measures, such as massaging the heart or injecting adrenalin into it. Certainly not when his coma was caused by a massive lung infection for which nothing could be done. But I gave him all the time I could. I was listening to his chest with my stethescope. It was evident that his heart was failing; his breathing was shallow; he was dying. Nothing could be done. As I listened, his heart gradually stopped; his breathing stopped. There was nothing dramatic, no death rattle. I knew that in a few hours rigor mortis would stiffen his body and limbs, but his death, of which he was unaware, was no more than going to sleep. He silently passed from the sleep of unconsciousness into the sleep of oblivion, from unawareness to nonexistence. The film on which his perceptions were recorded was no longer in the camera. Since that moment that is how I have thought of death, as I saw it then at his side. He merely "slipped away." Of course any incident which has an important, even permanent, effect does so because it falls on fertile ground, because it fits one's dynamics. As interns we had often quoted, "So live that when your time comes to join the innumerable caravan, that moves to that distant bourne from which no traveler returns, you go not like a quarry slave at night, scourged to his dungeon, but as one who wraps the draperies of his couch about him and lies down to pleasant dreams." (This is not quite as Bryant wrote it, but does not suffer from this dash of Shakespeare.)

This is the kind of death, without pain and with dignity, as we say today, that everyone is entitled to. For me, it is inexcusable and cruel that anyone of advanced age, with no hope of recovery, should lie in a hospital bed with all the resources of modern medicine available and be ignored when he or she prays for death. But the doctors cannot "pull the plug" because it is against the law. A woman I had known since her youth and loved as a friend had cancer of the liver. The blood could not get back into the circulation. Many quarts of serum collected in her abdomen, distending it until she suffered terribly. Nothing could be done about the liver, shot through with cancer. But the doctors dared not even drain off the gallons of fluid in her abdomen to ease her pain because it meant removing protein and might hasten her death, for which she prayed.

My father, after a healthy, active life with hardly a sick day (only a hernia in his late eighties, which was easily repaired) had his kidneys suddenly give out at age ninety-one, and in three months he was dead. After a month in the hospital it was obvious that there was no hope, that nothing could be done. Indomitable spirit that he was, now he prayed for death, knowing this was the end. But the doctors dared not spare him the agony by a simple, merciful shot of morphine, for it is against the law.

Of course the deeper reason, my dynamics, formed by my childhood emotional pattern, of why I see death not as threatening but only as a simple going to sleep, is that my parents were so kind and loving from my conception through earliest childhood, and for my whole life. Therefore I see, sense, *feel* death to be in their image—like them, with arms around me in which I can sleep and return to the nothing I was forever before I was born. Life has been good, so I expect the future, even death itself, to be that way. But I cannot stand pain or suffering, in myself or in others. Of the dual part of the Hippocratic Oath, "to relieve suffering and prolong life," the relief of suffering is for me the more important, at least after a certain age and certainly in hopeless conditions. Now in my mid-seventies, I am more concerned with avoiding suffering than prolonging my life, or at least I think I am. It depends upon how bad the suffering is and how much I am needed, and on unconscious reactions which one only knows when the time comes. As always with the feelings, motivation and reactions, it is the quantitative balance of forces. I think of Shubert's great song, "Death and the Maiden": "Be of good mood, I (Death) am not cruel, Softly in my arms sleep, sleep." (That is the nearest I can translate it from the German.)

Back working, golfing and swimming again after my heart attack at seventy, I found a reaction in myself that I abhor. Recently I saw Bromley, an acquaintance but never an intimate friend. Bromley is nearly ten years older than I, and had been distinguished and eminent in his field. He had a stroke a few years ago. It looked as though he would not survive, but he did, just barely, and endured the long road back from the brink. He and his devoted wife tried living in various ways and places but had to settle for a retirement home. He was a terrible burden to himself and to his wife and still is; he can barely move. Although his mind has come back and is usually clear, there is no sparkle any more. A gaunt skeleton, his loose flesh hanging on his huge bony frame like clothes long ready to be discarded, his expression glum and depressed, he yet endures. I was genuinely happy to see him again and greeted him warmly, but he was moribund and soon he repelled me, and my true wish was to avoid him. I do not feel that way toward patients; why should I feel thus revolted by a friend? I think the dynamics are these:

In the first place, Bromley is now in personality and mentality like a dead weight that takes too much out of me. He is still interested in the events of the day and has sound, interesting opinions, but he seems to hang on me, taking more than I can give. Also, his feebleness, his lack of spark, his glum expression and controlled depression prevent my identifying with him. I do not think he will live more than a year at most. He barely drags himself when he walks; he is a burden. He is so sick, so pathological, what is the sense in it? I still love him in a way, but just to be with him is a burden to me. There is no spontaneous interchange any more. Could it also be that there is a biological revulsion to a moribund condition, which a doctor does not feel toward a person who is his patient because he sublimates it into sympathy and professional care? Bromley was an old acquaintance, yet I felt this aversion, not daring to think that in ten years, when I reached his age, I could well be like him. Do he and his wife pray for death and lack the means to achieve it? Realistically, what is the sense of it—whether they go now or after another year of suffering? He has nothing more to contribute to life and nothing more to take from it.*

Decades ago, in youth, while vacationing at the ranch of friends in the Southwest, I was riding a horse alone on the plains. He shied away from something near our path and refused to approach it. It was part of the bleached, dried-out carcass of one of the cattle. Do we humans also have such a biological reflex to shy away from illness and from death and its remains? If so, how awful it must be for the old and ill, because how rejected and how lonely they must feel, ostracized by their own species, able only to associate with others who are old and ill, when what they must still want is acceptance by the healthy, the young and mature. I still react strongly to attractive, healthy women and especially blooming girls, and they still respond to me with some appreciation of my interest; that is part of what makes life worth living, just as it was when I was so loved as a baby and small child by my mother and Aunt Edie. I still have beloved friends and my patients who need me, and people whom I can help. I have my writing, at least parts of which I still think may be of some use to those who read it; I have my children and my grandchildren and my wife. I feel relatively young and vigorous, and amazingly there is still a sexual element in the response to me of some young women. When I offer a cheek to kiss as a social greeting, after they seek my lips and frankly make it a sensual kiss. I enjoy it, for no matter what good care I take, what regular exercise, how clear my skin, how youthful I feel at seventy-six, how much the sexual juices continue to flow, this cannot last a great deal longer. Meanwhile, I only hope that nothing changes, until I follow my blessed parents after many more years of this good life. It is because I am so fortunate that I dislike feeling any aversion for those less so.

*Bromley has since died, four months after the visit just described.

The internship was one of the best years of my life. The entire staff—medical, surgical and all the specialties—were my kind of people and welcomed my joining them. They were in fact more congenial than the students I met in that top medical school, more like Jim, Charles and Ralph. And the staff treated me as an equal. They were all relatively young but outstandingly able, and many were brilliant. They soon developed the new hospital and medical school into one of the most eminent medical centers in the country. And I liked the system: we callow interns were not started out in laboratories on minutiae but, as I've mentioned, were given the responsibility for whole wards. The outpatient ward ran on a schedule, just as a doctor runs his office practice. We each had an appointment book, as we would have later in private practice. The nurses, too, were of top caliber. Most were experienced and knew lots more than we interns did. They protected us and interrupted our sleep only when it was truly necessary. I soon felt that this place was not only no comedown from the center I had left, but was in many ways superior to it. My fellow interns became lifelong friends. Hugh was one of them. We used to go out at night when we could and contemplate the stars and philosophize. Hugh went into Public Health. There was also a Danish boy, nicknamed "Shag." One day, bursting with energy, I suggested to him that we run daily before dinner. He agreed enthusiastically. We soon worked up to encircling the adjacent golf course—a distance we clocked by speedometer as best we could at three and one quarter miles. He set the pace, and I still see his legs working indefatigably like pistons while I struggled to keep just behind. During the internship we had a week's vacation. A friend of Shag's had a cabin in the wilds, which Shag arranged to use for the week, while I supplied the car. From him I learned the basics of roughing it far from civilization. We had a grand time. Our friendship has continued, and despite the present geographical distance, we still see each other occasionally. It has been nearly five years now since arthritis necessitated his retirement.

A month or two after my arrival, in September, before the chilly weather arrived, the staff organized an outdoor picnic. That was easily done in those days because the medical center was on the southern boundary of the city with only farms and open country to the south just beyond. It was easy for Shag and me to tramp the country roads on evenings off. The picnic was jolly from the start;

freed from the confinement and pressures of the hospital, everyone was in high spirits. The professors were young but so secure that they felt no need to stand on their dignity. Everybody mixed with everybody else. (Of course in those days it was stag—there were no women doctors.) There was lots of laughter; lots of toasts were offered with punch made from gin and orange juice. When it was time to return, I offered to drive whomever could fit into my two-seater roadster. But for some reason they proposed driving me. (I knew from that summer in the Southwest that I had a strong ego, judgment and controls; when no one else could drive because of drinking, I was coordinated, so it always fell to me to do the driving. The custom at a fiesta was to pass the bottle for short snorts all day long from just after breakfast, as we drove down there, until everyone was saturated by the time we arrived.) But at the hospital picnic why didn't they trust me? Finally my father transference to young Bill Yardley broke through. I said to him, "I don't understand why I can't drive, but if *you* think I shouldn't, I will let someone else drive me and my car back." He said, smiling, "Yes, please do that . . . that is the thing to do."

By the time we got back to the hospital it hit me! They helped me get to bed, and the room spun. Next morning I was too sick to get up and so hoarse I could barely whisper. Archy came in to see me. (He later became an eminent surgeon, but while entering a hospital elevator he was shot and killed by the paranoid husband of a patient whose life he had saved with a successful operation.) He reported, "You drank up all right! Did you notice that they were ganging up on you with all those toasts and chug-a-lugs?" The light dawned: the immaturity which I felt in myself they had all recognized, and they set out to get me to drink. They thought me a sissy—and, as I later learned, a virgin. They set out to break down my inhibitions and make a man of me by getting me intoxicated. Well, there was nothing to do but take it in good part and laugh at my innocence in being so easily gulled. It all worked out well and was the first time in my life that I felt taken in as a full equal and as a man by those who were a part of the big world.

The chief of radiology, John Staff, was a huge, quiet and gentle giant. We felt immediate rapport that increased when I inquired about his investigations and he found out about my training in chemistry and physics and my research interests. We quickly arranged for me to join him in his research with X-rays and their effects on the metabolism of simple plants. As mentioned before, I can only work rapidly and efficiently and enjoy life if I have nine or ten hours of sleep. Somehow that overloaded life of an intern permitted it, and I was able to run daily with Shag and do the research with John Staff, at least until I went on the Emergency Service. We both hated to see our association stop. That year I did not need a wife and probably could not have fulfilled *her* needs—I was closer to the old Viennese medical idea of being married to my profession.

That great practical, happy year was drawing to a close. I had become a little less provincial; I saw there were many excellencies outside the center in which I had attended medical school. There were as good or even better ways of doing things and lots of other top people. I would miss the cameraderie of the whole staff, and of the skilled nurses, and the new close friendships, especially with Hugh and Shag and John. I could have stayed with great pleasure and benefit there as a resident or even for life, as Karl did. But the Great Depression had deepened. I had to finish my training and get established. The year which had been only a formal requirement had been rich beyond belief. But now it was time to move directly to the goal. After a serious talk with Bill Yardley I decided to take the psychiatric internship in the mental hospital that was near my former medical school and which, although supported by the state, was affiliated with that university. Its chief was professor of psychiatry in the medical school.

Alone in my open roadster I again drove through the lovely hills back to the medical school and center that I had left the year before, and now might be settling into for the rest of my life.

At home for a brief visit I found the same wonderful security and love. Judy was interested in Vernon. He stopped by and I met him— brilliant, interesting, articulate, knowing a lot about everything. I did not particularly like him; I thought him not responsible enough, too dependent on Judy. Gerald was quietly in the background.

Ralph and Eunice were leaving for a short trip. Ralph was available only for a few minutes at the office, so I went there and saw him alone. "Well," I asked, "How do you like being married? Free for nearly forty years, is it, and suddenly a husband and the father of three?"

"It's great," he said, and then continued, "when I am attracted to some other woman I say to myself, 'Why should you want her? You already have everything in your own wife. Eunice has looks and brains and why should you want any other woman?'" I said nothing, but what I got from this remark was that Ralph had not changed and was having a struggle. Although married, he was still just as tempted as ever to have affairs with other women, and was trying to talk himself out of them. His life had been with women, plural, taking all those he desired. Could he ever make it with one woman, singular? I still could not visualize it. An acquaintance, one of those men whose practical understanding of the world I envied, had once said to me, "Sure, I had a lot of girls. But at least I learned what I wanted and all that is out of my system. And now I have it with my wife." Some men, and women probably too, have their affairs while they are single and this takes care of much of their curiosity and of their urges to promiscuity, so that they are glad to settle down when once married. In others, philandering is an established pattern that they cannot change. Ralph, I guessed, despite his great worldly knowledge and wisdom, although he married a wonderful girl, was not so fortunate as to be of the first type, ready to settle for just one woman. Maybe it was in part because he married too late. But I thought it more likely to be something in his dynamics, his childhood emotional pattern. Whatever part this played in his conflicting drives between monogamy and philandering, I believe he had reached an adaptation as a free bachelor—and a highly successful one so far as enjoying his freedom. He had been a "successful bachelor," but now was it too late for him entering his forties to settle down to a wife and three children? I was so identified with Ralph that I gave little thought to Eunice, beyond recognizing her as a superior girl in every way. I thought her privileged to be married to Ralph with his incredible charm and brilliance and his range of contacts with the great, the near-great, the ordinary folk and those of the poverty-stricken whom for some reason he liked and respected, and his helpfulness to everyone, regardless. I did not know Eunice well enough to think about what Ralph's struggle to be faithful, even if successful, might be doing to her.

On this visit home I did not phone Nelda. It did not seem right for me to call. Tad, if not Nelda, might have felt it an intrusion. I could have phoned her mother to ask about her, but after debating this I finally dropped the idea.

Jim and Pam were in fine shape. It was a warm feeling to see two friends whom I loved so much so happy together.

At one point in our talk Jim said, "Jones (he occasionally used my last name in an affectionate way for emphasis), I'm glad you are getting interested in people more than the laboratory. I'm a little disturbed. Physics is beautiful and marvelous in itself, but it has consequences. We have airplanes, and therefore death from the skies; very soon now we will realize the goal of splitting the atom. This means we will have in our hands the power that keeps the sun burning but not consumed—the burning bush. The study of the physical sciences is dangerous for it gives people power—the wrong people. Why are there good people and evil people? Don't tell me everyone is a mixture. Of course, but some are ninety to ten and others are ten to ninety. We have got to learn what makes people as they are, what makes the evil ones."

"You're a step ahead of me," I said. "As I see patients now with physical disorders, I think, if medicine helps and these patients are all healthy again, then what do we have, how do they behave? I had a boy only nineteen years old who already had stomach ulcers, but he said he couldn't stop drinking a quart of strong coffee a day and also a lot of beer, nor could he stop smoking. I'm beginning to think that a lot of people make *themselves* sick. Later I saw a gangster as a patient. I'm sure he was a gangster. Doctors are like physicists, amoral, blind. Is it right to heal a murderer so he can go out and kill innocent people?"

Jim said, "I'm glad to hear you think this way. All we've learned of scientific method from physics should be applied in different ways but with equal care to learning about people. That is not entirely safe either. The evil men might use that knowledge also, but if there is no hope in science showing us how to make better people, then I don't see much hope for survival after we split the atom. You talked with Rutherford and you know how near that is, only a few years off."

We talked on, exploring the sources of power in societies, and Pam was in and out, bringing us beer, cheese and crackers and sitting to chat with us.

21

PSYCHIATRIC INTERNSHIP

In the light of knowledge attained, the happy achievement seems almost a matter of course, and any intelligent student can grasp it without too much trouble. But the years of anxious searching in the dark, with their intense longing, their alternations of confidence and exhaustion, and the final emergence into the light—only those who have experienced it can understand that.

Albert Einstein
Essays in Science

I have always been sensitive to neighborhoods and to buildings. This sensitivity is probably due in part to the childhood years when I first emerged from the shelter of home into streets with the ever-present danger of attack by sadistic bigger boys. I was in my teens when Dad sold the house in which I had been born and had grown to adolescence. I felt no pang at the separation and rarely recollect it, although occasionally it appears in my dreams. In part this reaction probably was caused by my liking so much better the neighborhood and apartment which Mother had found and into which we moved. And our bunch of boys had now grown up and was scattered anyway. Our apartment was on a quiet side street in a good neighborhood, near the corner so that we could see the river from the big bay window of our livingroom. As my mother said before I saw it, "It is small but perfect, like a gem." It was indeed—compact, bright, sunny and cheerful.

The hospital I had left after the year's medical internship was only three years old, spic and span. The medical school I had attended was spacious and light and clean. My apartment some blocks from medical school was on a dreary thoroughfare, but the Indian blankets and vases from New Mexico gave it warmth and color, and the tall windows made it bright and light.

Psychiatry was the stepchild of medicine, but surprisingly this relationship did not wound my egotism, probably because my father just worked at his business with no thought of comparison of its stature relative to any other profession. Neurosurgery, particularly brain surgery, was the newest, most prestigious specialty; but I had scrubbed as an assistant to one of its greatest pioneers and had no taste for it. Gradually human nature was attracting all of my interests, doubtless because of my own problems. Of course I was totally unaware of any connection at the time. The mental hospital expressed the position of psychiatry. It was on the very fringe of the new, clean, spacious buildings of the medical center, lying just beyond their boundary in an old semi-slum, deteriorated neighborhood, with dust and old papers whirling down the drab, dirty, windy street. The darkness made the ungracious interior even more dingy than the outside. It was cut up into dim rooms, everything old and poorly maintained and not too clean. Here I would be sleeping and eating, working and living for at least a year—not an auspicious beginning in my chosen specialty.

The professor, Dr. Camp, was animated and quick-witted, with twinkling blue eyes and a good sense of humor, and not in the least authoritarian. Very soon another intern, named Paul, became a good friend of mine. Living conditions were such that there was a tub but not even a shower in our quarters. Paul had been in residence some weeks before me, and he agreed to be spokesman: we got a few of the other interns to come along to Dr. Camp's office, where Paul, in his mature way, broached the subject of a shower. Dr. Camp at first seemed threatened but quickly smiled and replied that he saw no reason not to have a "spray bath." We never got really close to him but we had a pleasant relationship, and later he recommended me for a fellowship, which, together with Dr. Ford's help, made my early years of psychoanalytic training possible. The food was pretty miserable but a linen tablecloth covered the round table and the dining room had some intimacy. One nice touch was the toaster which stood on the table for every meal, so you could always offer to toast someone's bread.

Before I was even aware of it or could define it, I could begin to feel that my interest had always been in the forces of the mind, in "psychodynamics" (to use Freud's term). And I have always been eager to get on with all the training I could get to understand those forces and to use that knowledge for treatment and for prevention. Little did I think I would write one of the first books on the subject. From experience I learned that problems of sex cannot be solved without solving the problems of hunger and dependence and pride and love and hate, i.e., of society and especially personality. We are not exhorted to breathe for we do so without thinking. But we are commanded to love because resentments from childhood make loving something that most of us strive for but which few achieve. I was blessed in this, for all the love poured into me from birth. It filled my cup and made an overflow to pour out in turn to wife and children, if I ever achieved these, and to friends and patients and, with profound humility, to suffering humanity, by what I could teach or write or organize.

We interns rotated in admitting patients; then normally we were in charge of those patients. I was assigned first to the female ward. After I had been there some weeks, a depressed young woman came in who agreed to appear at our daily staff conference, which was always conducted by the professor and attended by the entire professional staff: doctors, nurses, social workers, psychologists and attendants.

Elsie was about thirty years old, and it was difficult to find anything attractive about her. Her depression was not so severe that she was uncommunicative, nor was she so agitated and psychotic that she was delusional, like one woman who rocked back and forth on her bed in an agony of guilt, blaming herself for every ill of the world. Elsie's was more an extremely gloomy mood and withdrawal of interest without gross distortion of thinking.

Following the routine, I presented the history; then the patient was interviewed by the professor. The general discussion covered what was then known of depressions and what bright ideas any of us had about it. It included the tendency of depressions to recur and to alternate with manic phases, i.e., excessive and often uncontrolled elevations of mood, the possible endocrinological causes, and so on. After the conference Elsie was escorted back to the ward by the buxom middle-aged head nurse, Mrs. Burns, who had a way with patients and whom I already liked enormously. Mrs. Burns put her arm around Elsie maternally as they walked, and talked to her in an easy, sympathetic, friendly way. I followed them to the ward, and when Mrs. Burns was free I chatted with her, as I usually did, about the patients. She was down-to-earth, matter of fact: "If you had been through what she has been through, you would be depressed too." This startled me like a sudden shaft of light; the patient could be understood in terms of simple human feelings! This was undoubtedly true; this was what Freud was fighting for. It made psychiatry the most fascinating profession in the world.

Something else also dawned on me because of Mrs. Burns' remarks: all these women on the ward were there after commitment because they were psychotic; i.e., their sense of reality, judgment, reason and responsibility were so askew that they could not communicate or relate to other people well enough to get along in society, and many might do damage to themselves or others by crazy behavior if not by violence. In some form, mild or severe, they were a menace to themselves or others. But except for those in the extremes of withdrawal into their own fantasies or of being entirely out of control of their feelings (as in depression or manic ravings or unrestrained violence), all the rest could be spoken with if you treated them as though they were ordinary, mentally normal persons. This was tremendous—it meant that one could learn about the emotional life by study, observation and clinical experience with patients, not only by personal experience in living. I had not yet found how much could be learned from the great writers of good literature.

My first reaction to Mrs. Burns' insight was a somewhat egotistical hostility to the conference. Here was the professor and all the more experienced staff fumbling for unknown biochemical factors and for esoteric causes, while Mrs. Burns went naturally and directly to the central issue. And they had discussed what sounded like abstruse psychoanalytic theory about incorporation and attacking introjects while missing Freud's main point, that mental disturbances could be understood in human terms, even though the human emotions producing them might not be conscious to the patient himself.

But as I thought about this further, it looked less simple. It was really too egotistical of me to think that I saw more than the staff. Maybe I did, but they were not dumb; the professor was a kindly, perceptive, generous person. He certainly had a high intelligence, and a sense of humor. He had had many years of experience and reading. He gave us lectures on Freud. Something did not quite fit; I began to think further about this patient, Elsie.

Other individuals had been through a lot also, but had not been committed to a mental hospital. Had Elsie been through much more and worse? Had she reacted more extremely to what she experienced? If so, why? Could this have been partly because of her being so unattractive, which is bad enough for a man but just terrible for a girl? I was only beginning to think in terms of childhood background, and fleetingly wondered if that might have somehow *predisposed* poor

Elsie to such a pathological depression. Thus my interest in understanding people was further awakened, being in part a reaction against my years of feeling inadequate in such understanding. It is not too much to say that my interest in psychodynamics, the interactions of human feelings which underlie our lives, emerged into more clear awareness at this point. But it was decades before I saw how these feelings expressed individual emotional patterns, shaped in early childhood.

As I saw other patients with the extremes of depression and of manic attacks, both so completely uncontrollable and so far from any resemblance to rational behavior, I could easily believe that these were like a delirium or drunken state and might well be caused by some form of internal biochemical intoxication, such as some disorder of the metabolism or endocrine secretions; therefore in my thinking I always specifically excluded these extremes of manic and depressive and schizophrenic reactions from discussions of the specifically emotional causes of disorders, and also perhaps some extremes of paranoia. But this does not mean that there cannot be emotional causes also, and in the milder cases I think there are, regularly. A frind of mine is convinced it is all pharmacological and that he can stabilize such patients if he can only keep adjusting doses of drugs until he gets the right combination.

But in my experience, if the patient is brought sufficiently under control by drugs to work with me on the emotional causes, then eventually as he gains control of these powerful emotional forces and resolves them to an appreciable extent, he gradually stabilizes without the drugs; that is, as he resolves the basic causes in his emotional forces, he no longer needs drugs. This psychological treatment of the disordered psychodynamics is at best a long, slow process and successful only in properly selected patients. But in my particular experience it always comes down to the person's psychodynamics, to correcting a warped childhood emotional pattern. The earlier in life this warping occurred, the more forceful and consistent it is; the greater the absence of counteracting, favorable forces, the more difficult it is to correct and the longer it takes. Needless to say, it need not be one thing *or* the other, not all biochemical or all psychological. Good psychiatry is truly comprehensive and uses all diagnostic and therapeutic approaches simultaneously when indicated. Many patients require drugs to keep functioning while they solve their basic emotional problems. But I do believe strongly that psychodynamic understanding, i.e., understanding in terms of human feelings and motives, can never be justifiably neglected, any more than a complete physical examination can. In other words, in every patient one can no more neglect the personality than one can neglect the body. Such observations and such reasoning marked the beginning of another major professional interest, namely, psychosomatic medicine. Looking back, I realize this development was inevitable, because it was merely the fusion of my two long-standing interests, the physical and the psychological.

After about three months in the psychiatric internship I saw, but did not then realize fully what I was seeing, the major dynamics of a manic attack. The patient was a young woman, Wilma. She was a large, strong girl, handsome rather than pretty; she had been quite calm and rational for the five days since her admission, and I had begun to wonder what I was missing and even whether her discharge to the outpatient clinic might be considered. But then one afternoon when I was on the ward, Wilma's three older brothers came to visit her. They were great, stalwart fellows. The one who was just a year older than Wilma clearly rubbed her the wrong way. She began to get angry with him; he handled it poorly and continued to provoke her. There before my very eyes Wilma rapidly got more and more angry for reasons I could understand and identify with, and suddenly she stamped her feet, shrieked at this brother in an uncontrollable rage and went right into a manic attack. I saw it happen, but did not entirely grasp its significance. I was still thinking too medically and not sufficiently psychodynamically. And there was no one to teach me. No one else seemed to see that one component of the manic phase was rage, that one manifestation of rage or one defense against it was the manic attack; no one saw that when an emotion, in this case rage, became excessive, it could disrupt the orderly operation of the reason and warp the sense of reality, thus deranging the mind.

Soon after this experience one of my patients was an angular, scrawny, unattractive young woman of about thirty. Her name was Mona, and she was almost totally withdrawn. It was impossible to communicate with her or to find out what was going on in her mind. She lived in a fantasy world, to the content of which I could not even get the slightest of clues. But every once in a while she would look me straight in the eye and in her low even tones declare with great earnestness, "You are a lizard and a rat." One morning I saw that she looked physically ill. Immediately after rounds I examined her. I took a throat stick and flashlight and said, "Mona, please open your mouth and say ah-ah-ah." She did. I was startled, for she seemed to understand me perfectly and cooperated fully. "Now I want to feel the glands in your neck," I said and proceeded to do so. "Are they swollen?" she asked.

"Yes," I said, "and you have a severe sore throat and a fever of 102°." It turned out that this severe schizophrenic state had suddenly vanished and that Mona seemed entirely rational. Our regular clinical conference of the entire staff was scheduled two days later. I asked Mona if she would be willing to appear and talk to me there. She assented and did. She remained thus rational for ten whole days. Then she recovered from the sore throat, her temperature returned to normal and she relapsed right back into her withdrawn, bizarre, schizophrenic state; when I tried to talk with her she was again inaccessible. And soon thereafter she would again at times look at me seriously and declare: "You are a lizard and a rat."

Mona also appeared at the next general staff meeting, where I presented her case with the question of how and why she could have become so entirely rational only as long as she had the severe sore throat. Was it the fever? Was it some counteracting poisons from the infection—perhaps the ones that caused the fever? Was it self-preservative instinct aroused by fear of physical illness? Was physical illness the only way she got any attention when she was a baby? But not one person out of the psychiatrists, psychologists, social workers or nurses had the smallest suggestion or idea of how to explore this further. Something could produce a remission of a severe schizophrenic state, but no one had any idea of how to investigate it. As one with a research-oriented mind, I was frustrated; but I was only an intern, and we were forever overloaded trying to keep up with our patients, the new admissions and the conferences on diagnoses and disposition. And I was still too immature to do more with this secret of nature that we had fleetingly glimpsed but could not find a way to understand.

Today, in the light of what I have seen of the childhood emotional pattern, it seems possible that there was a psychological reason for Mona's recovery during the time of her sore throat. Her childhood pattern must have been very disturbed at an early age to make her so inaccessible now in her psychosis. Was it possible that in childhood she was given solicitous attention and good human relations when she was physically sick—and that now her physical illness enabled her to relate to me, although she could not do so otherwise? It is not uncommon to see a mother with poor relations toward her child, irritated and resentful, suddenly become overly loving and affectionate when that child is ill. This is probably the well-recognized dynamic of "over-protection."

There was another patient of mine, Jane, in the women's ward, whom I still puzzle over. She was passed on to me for some reason by Dr. K., one of the senior staff who had been carrying responsibility for her. When he introduced me to Jane, it was apparent at the first glance that her situation had to be one of life's poignant tragedies. She was pretty, almost beautiful, with an oval face, perfect complexion, dark hair neatly arranged and pastel-blue eyes to match the whole picture. Jane was still in her early twenties and moved with suppleness and grace; she was in the process of divorce. By what irony did life produce this charm and beauty and then cause such derangement as to consign and confine it to a mental hospital? She was still on a locked ward but no longer on the most disturbed ward. Jane was dressed attractively in her own trim clothes instead of a shapeless gray hospital gown. Ordinary conversation did not reveal why she was committed, but from the record and from further questioning it was soon clear that she was confined for a suicidal depression that still lingered. I had read that the danger of suicide is greatest just when a patient is emerging from a depression. I saw Jane on daily rounds, but at that time I had no analytic training and no idea of her dynamics or why she would have been suicidally depressed. Even then, I had seen or heard of many women of all ages who got divorces and never became that depressed or suicidal. Jane claimed, and honestly I thought, that the divorce had nothing to do with her depression. She had goofed in marrying her husband, was glad to be rid of him and had no regrets whatever, only a sense of relief. She was pleasant, affable, considerate and cooperative, and she obviously liked me. I liked her in return, and when she asked for various privileges which seemed entirely safe, I saw no reason not to consent and order them. She seemed appreciative and continued to improve noticeably. Then suddenly one night I was called—Jane had attempted suicide. Lacking all knowledge of dynamics, I reacted with rage at her; I felt betrayed. I had trusted her, and this suicide attempt was like a stab in the back. Without hesitation I immediately ordered her back to the most disturbed ward, while I returned to bed and, being young, to sleep. In the morning I saw Jane on rounds: she was back in the most disturbed ward, back in the shapeless gray hospital gown, but she was also in fine shape, calm and rational and acting almost as though she were in love with me. I did have sense enough to be quiet and listen. She said, "You are the only one here who understands me. I could wind Dr. K. around my little finger. But you have just sent me back to this ward, which was the only thing to do."

Again I felt that terrible frustration of knowing there must be some way to understand her, but also knowing that no book and no one on the staff could guide me. Since then, I have spent my professional life studying the emotional forces and writing what I have learned, working toward the development of this new subject called "psychodynamics." Jane continued as my patient and, through no wisdom of mine, recovered her stability sufficiently to return to life. She kept in touch with the social workers at the hospital in the outpatient clinic, and I followed her progress through them. One social worker told me Jane confessed she had fallen in love with me (technically, what I later learned to call "positive transferences") when I got angry at her for the suicide attempt and punitively, unceremoniously and harshly ordered her back to the disturbed ward. Her reactions toward me might have been because Jane wanted some other person to give her the strength to control her feelings and impulses; yet from what part of her childhood pattern this derived I was at that time not knowledgeable enough to find out. In fact, I then knew nothing whatever of psychodynamics and childhood emotional patterns and could not even ask her illuminating questions.

Jane's divorce became final without her having to return to the hospital. I moved to a distant city for my psychoanalytic training and lost track of her for about five years; then I got word of her from one of the social workers who had continued to keep in touch with her that Jane had committed suicide, under what circumstances and by what method the social worker did not know. "One more unfortunate gone to her death. Rashly importunate, weary of breath . . ." But why? Why? Why? My curiosity about her dynamics continues. How can such things be? My years of experience in studying psychodynamics and childhood emotional patterns have by now led me to think that if Jane were alive and I could interview her, I might today elicit some answers.

Not until later did I realize the wisdom of the professor, Phil Camp, in just turning us loose to observe and study for ourselves instead of trying to teach us a lot of half-truths and half-baked theories. He said frankly: "No one knows the causes of these deranged minds, but there they are. Study them for yourselves." At the time it was very frustrating. In medicine, as an intern, I had had to watch helplessly while patients died of pneumonia; but there was promising research on serums for prevention and cure. And many other conditions were understandable and also curable. But here, these disorders of the mind could not be understood either in psychological or in physical terms.

I thought that perhaps in the end the longest way around would be the shortest way to understanding, and got Professor Camp's permission to spend time in Everett's neurophysiology laboratory, studying the electrical operation of the brain. My interest in the interrelations of the physical and the mental and emotional was further enhanced and deepened. I made a small discovery and because of it I became known in the physiological circles of the medical center and received an invitation to present a paper and demonstration at the annual meeting of the national society. Everett and I became close friends. We went to the meeting together, and of course it fell to me to demonstrate the experiment. I was in the pit of a lecture amphitheater. It was packed—and in the audience were many of the most eminent of the nationally and internationally known physiologists. The experiment did not go quite right; the sweat poured off my face onto the brown laboratory gown I wore. Suddenly it struck me that for me and my medical school this just *had* to work. With this thought I concentrated intensely upon the task and became calm. Nothing else existed for me—neither the amphitheater, nor the audience, nor the eminent scientists whom I so admired—nothing mattered but the subject. Suddenly I heard a loud noise, but even that did not cause me to look up. Then it dawned on me that it was the audience applauding; the experiment had worked. I had learned the difference between egotism, wanting admiration, and "task orientation," also called "object interest," which succeeded when I completely forgot myself in my concentration and devotion to the task at hand. This capacity to be interested in persons and subjects outside of oneself can be added to responsibility as an essential of maturity. Again, "Who shall lose himself shall find himself."

One day I heard that an eminent psychoanalyst had come to spend a year at the university on interdisciplinary research, with some time available to see patients. During medical school, as I have said, I had been to six different psychoanalysts because I was interested in the field and thought it might help with some of my own problems, such as immaturity, girls and my failure to get married. But I simply could not trust myself to any of those people. The last one had told me, "You have a resistance; you will *never* be analyzed." He felt rejected, I decided later, and said this out of his own anger. Ralph Ackley had told me sincerely, "Don't let anything interfere with your getting analyzed." But I did not think that Ralph, who had gone to Vienna to Freud himself, would approve of any of these six, who seemed to me to be groping and fumbling themselves. And it turned out that my instincts were correct here.

Now the visiting analyst was here, and I arranged an interview with him—and got a very different impression from what I had from the other six. Here was a man of the caliber of Nelda and Jim and Ralph and Clark. He seemed to have a real head on his shoulders, and had a vast cultural background as well as good scientific training in physiology. I had no money, however, and as usual took my problem to Clark. He said, "I think you are doing the right thing. You should get this training. Go talk to Dr. Ford. I will phone him." I did as he said. I knew Ford slightly. He was a big, impressive, very active man, past middle age, an excellent scientific mind and a leader in neurophysiological research. First I talked with Dr. Camp, always kindly and a man of quick decisions. He offered me a fellowship that would permit me to continue the neurophysiological research in Everett's laboratory, which was still going very well. In this way I could also get the training analysis. The fellowship paid two thousand dollars the first year, twenty-two hundred the second year and twenty-four hundred the third year—barely enough to live on. Dr. Ford, after asking me my plans said, "Can you come back and see me tomorrow afternoon?"

I said, "Certainly." I think he phoned some people about me. When I returned he said, "I will take care of the cost of your analysis. Now do not thank me and make a fuss. You have already done good work in neurophysiology, and I think you are a productive person. But if you are, you will, and if you are not, you can't; so it is a matter of my own judgment, and I want you to simply go along with your training and work."

What a man! I knew that he was a multimillionaire, but how gracious of him and what knowledge of people and the world. Would I ever achieve a fraction of that? Of course I thanked him, but "without fuss," for I knew he was right. The only thanks would be scientific or at least professional productivity. It is one of the deep gratifications of my life that his confidence and expectations seem to have been justified. For I study and have investigated, written and taught, all by nature and by my dynamics, with enjoyment and without conscious effort.

And thus, again without fully realizing it, I took a fateful step in my career, a step which set it upon the course it has steadily held to ever since. For once I began this personal analysis, my interest in this new field of the psychological study of the mind never wavered, any more than did my interest in medicine from the moment I started medical school. Chemistry and physics had given me the outlook of a research scientist, and I had become a clinically minded physician, interested in patients rather than in the laboratory; thus my specialty and subspecialty were set: a psychiatrist with therapeutic and research interest in the psychological understanding of individual patients. My old inferiority about understanding the world led me to an interest in applying hard-won clinical knowledge gained from individuals to world-wide sociological problems. This is the greatest good fortune in my fortunate career. All that I learned when floundering around in the different fields, trying to choose a career, was finally integrated into one central interest that encompassed all of it; and it has given my life a steady direction, and made it so enjoyable professionally that I hope I never have to retire. Practicing analytic psychiatry, reading, thinking, writing, with a sense of well-being from athletics, at that time lacking only mate and children, I echoed Faust, who finally said to the passing moment, but with less reason, "Stay, thou art so fair."

"Blessed is he who has found his work." I had found my work, but not my mate, and not, really, myself.

CYCLE IV

22
HEART'S DESIRE

Darlin' you can't love but one,
You can't love but one and have any fun;
Darlin' you can't love but one . . .

American folksong

I was giving much thought to the reasons why I had not yet married, said Corey Jones, and why I behaved as I did with women. Too strong needs for Mother's exclusive love and admiration, perhaps? Too strong dependence? Too much concern for myself and what I wanted and not enough concern for others? Strong, conscious wishes for marriage but unconscious resistance against its responsibilities? (The intellect, however clear and sharp, is useless if emotions do not let it observe and work.) My feelings of inferiority because of trying to get everyone to love and admire me, instead of "object interest" in them and their feelings . . . anger from this sense of inadequacy and also too much competition to disprove it . . . perhaps some hostility to women from anger at Mother because of her overcontrol and restrictions, and fighting for independence from my needs for her love? Love for Judy but some resentment of her and the need to be superior to a little-sister-figure? Maybe all women were only little sisters for me and not good enough, not strong enough, but like little sisters whom I loved but also wanted to get rid of, when they became dependent on me? Or else women were mothers who were strong but sexually taboo? That I was looking for a girl who was all three figures for me—Mother, Aunt and Sister—never crossed my mind. I had some nightmares. In retrospect, I think they were derived in part from guilt about the girls. I feared to tell my father or even (except in passing) my mother of my experiences. And now I am inclined to think that each experience may have added to the guilt. My vanity alone could have led me to outstanding girls—I loved them—and hurt them. I blamed myself; I felt my parents would blame me. And I envied and was hostile to stronger men for being more manly than I, for being men and not like me, a child trying to win love and impress everyone, always thinking of people watching and praising as Mother used to do. But what I was learning was invaluable: I was getting an inkling of how the emotions work. At least I was learning enough to ask relevant questions. I began to see my underlying dependence for love, help and admiration, and therefore wanted to see what use I could make of these insights. I knew that at heart I was a person of good will who yearned to mature and did not shirk responsibility. I knew that what I had done was not evil in intent, but was a problem to be resolved so that I would not cause hurt but could be free to love and be loved.

I managed to arrange a long weekend off to get home at the time of Judy's graduation from college. We were all happy. Gerald always got in a visit with Judy. After Dad lost his business, I took no money from him; the psychiatric hospital provided board and room and paid me nine hundred dollars a year, which I got by on very well. Soon I would be permanently independent financially.

Judy was beginning to suspect that Vernon, her brilliant, fascinating semi-crush, never would be economically on his own, that he was too dependent underneath and clung to her because she was strong. I was gratified beyond words to hear her say this, for I saw that somehow she already knew better than I what I had struggled all these years just to begin to understand. I wondered if anyone ever did mature if he never made his own way financially. Was good loving and respect by his parents in childhood enough? Or is responsibility what must finally do it? Must one have the actual experience of giving something valuable enough for people to pay for it?

I went to visit Jim. Pam was away, visiting her parents, and Jim was not quite himself; I asked him about Ralph and how his marriage was working out. Jim said, "He has a fatal illness and has only two years to live."

I was a little toughened by all I'd seen through four years of medical school and the year's medical internship, but this was a close friend, this was Ralph, the incarnation of perfectly controlled and directed vigor, still a youth and an athlete, barely in his forties.

"It can't be!" I exclaimed.

"It is, though," Jim said. "There is no doubt and no hope. I've spoken with the doctor who examined the microscopic slides." I was shaken. It was my first close tragedy, and the first since that day six years before when Brent was killed and I went to meet Nelda. I recalled being unable to visualize Ralph married; was it possible that he, who knew better how to live than anyone I had ever met, had gotten himself into an impossible situation? That he could not live in nor adapt to marriage—to a young wife and three children? That he could not exist without his old free life? I mentioned this to Jim, and he was thoughtful. He never threw out any idea without closely examining it. Finally Jim said, "Emotions are to the mind what electrical particles are to matter. I am committed to the atom. Maybe someday you will study the forces in the mind; they are so unknown and so powerful. Freud has shown a way to do it even if what he has found has not always turned out to be correct; at least he has a kind of microscope which lets us look into this cauldron of the mind."

Jim spoke with feeling. He started to say something but stopped, and asked about me. I learned the reason for his abrupt change of subject a year later: Pam had begun to show slight but unmistakable signs of instability.

Jim and I drifted apart. We were finding our careers; he was married; we were living at a distance. I was less dependent on him and finding my way despite many difficulties.

Charles was the same as ever. He stopped by in late afternoon to say hello and propose going out to dinner together. Then again a minor incident occurred, a mere remark that he might have better saved until dinner—a simple remark that affected my whole future life. Once again the most momentous consequences for my entire life eventuated from a totally trivial, inconsequential incident—a remark he might never have made at that moment. Charles said: "I proposed to Josie but she rejected me." I had known Josie for a long time and liked her enormously; she and I had maintained a loose, easy friendship, seeing each other only rarely since I'd been in medical school. I could see why Charles proposed; I wondered if he were really in love with Josie and why she had refused him. I guessed that she was not in love with him. I was sorry that two such good people had not solved the problem which I had not solved either. "Are you still friends?" I asked.

"Sure," he answered. I debated silently for a moment and then made a trifling but fateful suggestion: "Should we take Josie to dinner? I haven't seen her for two years and she won't inhibit our conversation any."

"Good idea!" he said. "I'll phone her."

I was slow in learning what complications develop when one starts including people. Charles was on the phone. "Josie says she would be delighted to see you and would love to come, but she has a guest." Then, in a whisper, "I guess we'll have to take them both."

We pulled out our wallets for a quick check of our finances, laughed and agreed.

"May we come for you both at six?" Charles asked. Five seconds later he hung up and said, "Done!" Already it seemed like old times. "It's so late," I said. "Why don't you stay here until it is time to pick up Josie and her friend?" "Happy to," replied Charles. We chatted and laughed until the time came, then washed up and left.

Josie greeted us at the door and it was just like Charles to be relaxed and comfortable, just as though the two of them were old friends, and as if he had never proposed and she had never rejected him. Josie gave me a light kiss and a warm hug of welcome; and over her shoulder, standing near the window of the living room at the end of the short hall, I saw a girl, what a girl! Instantly I took in the perfect figure, the narrow waist, the clean straight legs and upright posture, the fine shoulders, the curves of bosom, the gorgeous thick golden hair, all the setting for a beautiful face, which radiated character and intelligence. Before the quick hug was over I knew I would try to have this girl, but with a difference from the past—I read in that face what I wanted in my future wife.

We went in, and Josie introduced us to her. "Evelyn Holling," said Josie, "and we call her Holly."

It had been a long time since I had felt so irresistibly the spark, the surge and everything else too. It was sexual seduction, but marriage might be in the background. There was no inhibition because of this. I just had to have her. The idea that she might be otherwise committed never crossed my mind. I was my old self, sure I could be the only one. "How do you do?" I said. She was reserved; whether she saw my excitement I do not know; maybe she was used to such reactions from men.

Of course it was Charles who selected the restaurant, and of course his choice was excellent. It was not expensive; we could let ourselves go. There were booths for privacy, and it was not so quiet that we would have to suppress laughter and ebullience. Charles and I always set each other off anyway; like schoolgirls, we would get into a mood in which everything seemed humorous. Josie we knew was an appreciative listener, and Holly, although reserved, turned out to be a good listener too; but it seemed to me that she observed far more than she revealed. (Years later I realized that she combined the sex appeal of Aline, the vitality of Elaine, the good sense of Joan and the perceptiveness and artistic sensitivity of Nelda.) The exhibitionism of Charles and me was stimulated by the girls. We were silly and witty, showing off to impress them. They responded with humor in the way they listened and occasionally contributed a bit of sly wit right to the point. In the booth I sat on the aisle, Josie was on my right, Charles opposite her and Holly opposite me. It was a great evening. We went back to Josie's for a short while before Charles and I left.

Holly, it turned out, was in the graduate school of English at the university where I was taking my psychiatric internship—what good news! Although the evening was all fun, there was no mistaking her superior character and intelligence and the spark. She kept me at a distance, but she wore no ring and I gathered she was uncommitted, or so I hoped and so I believed. I thought Charles was pretty gone on her too. It was a little awkward, her staying with Josie; I did not feel very free about pursuing her there, and Charles must have felt even less so. Nevertheless, I did pursue and hoped I was not offending Josie; I had always liked Josie so much, and I hoped that she would not resent my obvious rush of Holly. I saw Holly all I could without embarrassment, to her or to Josie or to Charles; and in the three days before returning, I even got her to my home to meet my family, not for their approval but just to meet and chat. I was handling this on my own. Not consciously or deliberately, though. How unconscious we all are! How our lives are lived for us by the forces of our feelings, our dynamics, our childhood emotional patterns! I never decided to do this alone; it was only that this time I felt no doubts or hesitations, no need to ask any other opinions. Time would tell how correct were my feelings about Holly, and she would know if this were to be all-out between us, all-out and also permanent. I simply had to have her and was going after her no matter what, and we would soon see how it all came out. There was nothing to ask anyone.

My father said, "Is she a normal girl with the faults of a normal girl?" I thought this over and replied, "I really don't know. She seems healthy and outdoor. I'm sure she has faults; we all do; I'm sure I have plenty. I don't know yet if she is for me." But my father's words sank in. I would never marry if I sought perfection. It was healthier for a girl to have "the normal faults of a normal girl."

This casually made remark by Father seemed to pass lightly by me with no awareness on my part that it had initiated a revolution in my emotional life. It was a few weeks later before I saw in "a burst of insight" the basic reality: there was no perfect girl, no perfect wife. That relentless longing was for the total love I had enjoyed as a baby; it was a childish longing for mother, and not the mature mating call. I would never get it, but would have to live out my life without it. This was simply a fact of nature to be understood and accepted. What followed was quite natural: a profound, all-pervasive sense of loss, a realization that my deepest longing would never be gratified; therefore I felt an all-encompassing depression. Of course Corey-of-the-strong-ego let no one see this. I went on with my daily work and what social life I had. After two or three weeks I noticed that the depression had vanished and had been replaced by a new inner atmosphere of relief and freedom and of the independence I had sought for so long.

Well, well, I had learned a little about life after all, but only a little. For courting Holly was no unrelieved idyll, mostly because of me. At least she had plenty of chance to see the worst in me and to break it off if she wished. Sometimes she seemed to me to be too definite, not free enough, a little like my mother of the old days; but of course I did not make the connection then, probably because her looks could not have been more different and because the sex attraction overpowered everything else. Whenever I felt Holly was being too definite and determined I rebelled, as I did in childhood, and was stubborn and difficult. Other times I would treat her as only the inferior little sister who made demands and infringed on my privacy. And then I would be haughty and inconsiderate and incredibly selfish. We even had some spats such as I had never had with any other girl. And we were not engaged; I was only seducing her. But the power of the attraction easily sustained everything. Two months showed that we wanted each other and that the differences and frictions were minor and would not prevail. It was sex and personality and also the same kind of intelligence and dynamics, and to some extent family background, with both of us being the oldest child and somewhat preferred, which drew us together. One evening after a movie, as we were walking past some shops, we passed an art store. Featured in the center of the window, under its own fluorescent light on the frame, was a colorful seascape. We stopped to look at it. I exclaimed with feeling, "Gad, that's beautiful!" She looked at me and her face fell. The painting was really the most awful chromo one could imagine, let alone see. I smiled, she realized I was teasing her, and we broke into laughter. Did she think that the great Corey Jones, who had learned art through Nelda, who had been tutored in art appreciation by Jim and Ralph and Ernest, who had spent days in the Louvre, the British National Gallery and some of the other great museums of Europe and America, had no judgment or discrimination about painting? We got to know each other, but we had not yet slept together.

I could hardly contain myself, and I was sure Holly felt as I did. She had been simply and strictly reared, and her bull of a father had threatened to throw her dates down the stairs and out of the house; he could have, and would have, and I think on occasion he had actually done so . . . no sex before marriage. Period. No one really believed they knew the answer in those days, so that "no sex" was the solid rule. Today, some people feel they know the answers, but I wonder. I was devoting myself freely to patients and that was almost all day, every hour of long days. There was little time free, but it made all the difference having Holly, even though I could rarely see her. I couldn't stand it much longer, and was growing up enough now to think of her feelings and wonder if she could stand it. This was not like the time I played tennis with Nelda and thought it wrong to see her breasts. I wanted all of Holly, and felt no inhibition this time from fear that I would hurt her by not marrying her.

Holly and I had been to the Holdens'. I was not looking for any opinion now. Estelle got me alone for a moment and said they would be away for a week; she knew how busy and confined I was at the hospital, but if I cared to look in at their house, to keep an eye on it, even to use it freely in their absence, they would leave the key with me. I have often wondered why they were so kind. Did they understand everything about Holly and me? I thought they were so puritanical. Or did they understand nothing? That was hardly possible. In retrospect, I think it was the remarkable understanding and generosity and love of two remarkable people. If they had wanted the house lived in, surely they need not have chosen us, and they would have been simple and open about saying so. I think it was their anticipatory wedding gift.

For that week I arranged swaps with other interns so that I could be free from Saturday afternoon until the following Friday morning.

Then I waited for an evening off to see Holly. I drove out to the university, took her to dinner and told her of the wonderful opportunity. For weeks I had wanted her so much sexually I could hardly think of anything else unless I were fully concentrated on patients or experiments. I could no longer keep from touching her. That Saturday came at last; I drove out for her and we had a light supper; we went to the Holdens'.

Together in complete privacy at last! This lovely home and not a hotel room. Our music was Brahms' fourth symphony, replaying the first movement with its soaring song. Then it was Bach's great passacaglia and fugue for organ. Then Schumann's unsurpassed piano concerto in A minor with Myra Hess. Then the chorale, the "Ode to Joy," from Beethoven's ninth. I honored Holly from that first second when I saw the character and intelligence in her face. I honored her more as I knew her better; for although several years younger than I, she saw people and situations more quickly and clearly than I did. And I obeyed her, for she had better judgment than I. And the love I felt that first instant has never stopped growing. In those days she was pursued by other men and had been interested in one especially. Of course . . . but that was long since forgotten. I had forgotten that she had a past—or that I had. She was a virgin, and I felt virginal, for in my mind I had already forsaken all others. At last all that health and character, mind and body was in my arms, in bed, with nothing between us. Mutual orgasm. We were one. I still think that when one marries it should be as it was for me, an entirely fresh new life, with all others forsaken even though not forgotten. I never think of those other girls, but I cannot completely erase their memory either, for they gave me so much in my time of need, and so much that has not only enriched my own life but has made me a better husband and father—and physician.

So many members of the animal kingdom mate and rear their young and are faithful for life. This must be so in order for them to care for the young, who are weak and helpless and otherwise would die soon after birth so that particular animal variety would disappear in one generation. Holly and I were mated in that deep biological sense; the ceremony when it came would only be the social sanction. I wondered if the kinds of animals who live in societies also had ceremonies. They certainly have courtship and mating. Sex is not purely a physical drive or reaction; it is part of mating and hence a medium of expression of the deepest feelings, properly an expression of Eros—love. True marriage is of the soul as well as the body.

Even though Holly and I were one before we stood at the altar, even though this step into marriage was what I had sought so earnestly and so passionately for all the years since preadolescence, although Holly wanted it and our families and the church and society all did, yet when the fateful questions were asked—"Do you take this woman . . . (Yes, of course, why else are we here?) to love (Yes, I do love her) . . . and obey (Yes, even that) . . . forsaking all others (Yes, gladly) . . . for better or for worse (Why won't it continue to be wonderful?) . . . for richer or for poorer (Sure, that is up to me, the husband) . . . in sickness and in health (We are healthy and that is a chance we all take)"—only at that next instant, when I heard the words "so long as you both shall live," did the full gravity and permanence of the commitment burst on me emotionally. My knees shook a little. What a terrible responsibility is marriage for us complicated, neurotic humans (for every one of us is neurotic, i.e., has emotional problems stemming from childhood, in some kind and degree). We were forsaking all others—*all* others—we were entrusting ourselves to each other, our needs, our dependence, our desires for companionship, our submissiveness and suggestibility, all to another person *for life, forever.* In that second I could see as in a flash of lightning how little I knew myself, how little I knew Holly, how we were committing each other for all time to whatever unknown springs of feeling and behavior lay within us.

Suddenly fear and awe lent a new solemnity and depth to the idea of marriage; suddenly the brief ceremony was more than a form to be taken lightly—it had become a profound experience. Now that I know a little bit more about the childhood patterns of feeling and behavior that lie latent and unrecognized in each of us, my gratitude is profound that the unconscious patterns in *my* personality led me to Holly, and that hers led her to accept me with all my faults, inadequacies and inferiorities, tangled emotional currents and countercurrents. Many a fine girl harbors within her reactions that only come out in the intimacy of marriage: a generosity that hides demandingness, seeming good humor and maturity that hide childish petulance, and so on. How is the man to know? Or the girl, who has much more at stake— how is she to know what is in the man? Perhaps interviews with a good dynamic psychiatrist might help, but I am not certain. The girl should be sure, though, that her man at least had a good childhood pattern toward his mother. For me, the fears were unfounded; but the more I see of marriages, the more profound are my thanks that my fears were baseless.

The unusual, faulty features in Holly's childhood which I did not know about at the time seemed only to contribute to making her all the more fascinating, remarkable, strong, insightful and very feminine because they were counterbalanced by other constructive emotional forces of parental love and confidence in her and early responsibilities. This was not true for her sisters, who were affected traumatically and suffered as adults. Although it worked out so marvelously for Holly and me, it is safest in marrying to select someone who had all-around good feelings during childhood with parents and other family members. Potentially traumatic interpersonal relations in childhood are a risky prelude to adult relationships, especially one so intimate as marriage. Sooner or later the childhood emotional pattern is certain to come out toward the spouse.

Searching for the causes of the spark of vitality and radiance in Holly's personality, I do not think it was chiefly the result of the conflicts and storms in her home. These played some part in generating it, in that those who successfully weather the storms of life seem to gain certain assets from so doing. As Churchill said of his own lonely rejected childhood, "Lone trees, if they survive, grow strong." Perhaps there is something to an old aphorism I never liked, "Sweet are the uses of adversity." I do not like it because many of the results of adversity are not at all sweet. No, my conclusion is that Holly became such a wonderful person because each of her parents was a wonderful person.

Holly's father—stunningly handsome, built like the statue of an athlete, strong as an ox, with piercing blue eyes—had put himself through medical school, was a beloved horse-and-buggy doctor, and an expert at growing flowers, with the ability to build or repair anything, with a keen mind and unusual insight into people. When we met he seemed my opposite. Yet he and I immediately became close; you might think that there was nothing else he could do but accept me as Holly's choice, but he was not that kind of man—he *had* thrown other of Holly's suitors out of the house bodily. His friendship was genuine, and he really liked me as a son-in-law. Had he not, I would have known instantly. He told Holly that I was "Christlike," but he did not mean that entirely as a compliment. He also said bluntly that he thought I had good genes and that the combination of Holly and me would make wonderful children—and that he did mean as a sincere compliment. And, thank the Lord, his prescience about the children was borne out.

Of course, as I've mentioned, in my seeking a wife the eugenics, healthy minds and bodies for my children, was always a central consideration. If the children were like Holly, I would be well pleased. She was completely feminine, but was strong and sturdy in mind and body. It was many years before it occurred to me that she combined the adult strengths of my mother and the blonde loveliness of my aunt with the freshness and early charm of my "little sister." That is why, I believe, on my part it was "love at first sight" and has continued as a happy marriage. This all occurred before Women's Lib, but Holly asked me my views on having children and agreed that we would have them. My paternal instinct, like the sex urge, was strong, and I would not have married a girl who did not want children.

My father, as I have told you, grew up on a farm, but the only unmistakable residue of it was his love of horses and of riding. Otherwise he was urbanized. But that outdoor yeoman atmosphere still clung to him and even more so to Holly's father. It was, I think, much of the reason that I on my side so loved and accepted her father as my father-in-law, on our first meeting. It has always seemed to me that this yeoman background, close to the soil, is the best there is in all ways in constituting a personality with stability, strength and sense of reality.

Holly's mother, I felt, did very well for a girl who was part of the European aristocracy. She was artistic and discriminating and knew everything and could do everything, including all mechanical matters in the house, and every style of cooking, and anything connected with the garden or with animals. We got on fine; and after Holly's father's death from cancer she came to live with Holly and me for three or four years, helping in every way, not the least of which was her enormous contribution of being a willing built-in babysitter, thus giving Holly and me much needed and relished freedom.

In speaking of what made Holly so great, I have not described in just what ways she *was* so superior; it has been in all ways: intellectual, physical, esthetic and psychological. She has a very high IQ, higher I believe than my own, and, more importantly, a higher degree of intuitive practical understanding and insight. She has occasionally had a fleeting glance at a patient who was arriving or leaving, whom I might have been seeing for months, and made some brief incisive comment that gave me an added insight. She has a fine social sense and excellent taste in people, as well as in art, music and food and in making our home simple, warm and full of inconspicuous good taste. She has been strong and healthy, and a fine companion for me in every way. When I slowed down at age fifty-six from tennis to golf, she joined me. It is one of my great pleasures to see how happy she is after a good round on the golf course, when we come in to shower and have a beer with friends before dinner. She is entirely feminine, with high attractiveness and sex appeal. And she has made me completely secure in marital love. She is so devoted, so securely a one-man woman, that I cannot but respond in the same way with full loyalty to her. Above all, Holly has been a wonderful mother and deserves full credit for our children's turning out well and healthy in minds and bodies, and therefore also as happy individuals in their own marriages and with their own children.

With Holly, it was love at first sight and such passionate, irresistible closeness that we did not drift into marriage but slid into it rapidly, as though it were fated, predestined. It has now long seemed to me that my inability to get married was not entirely my own neurosis, my immaturities, my inhibitions, my egotistical perfectionism, but the fact that among all those beautiful girls, incredible as it may sound, I had not met the right one for me, the one whose dynamics whatever they were, formed by their childhood emotional patterns, meshed with mine. But also, I had slowly become more realistic. I had moved from what was in large part a search for perfection, no doubt for my own egotism, to finding in the words of my father, "a normal girl with the faults of a normal girl." I found her but I did not really find her. Rather, she *happened* to me; more correctly, we happened to each other. We "fit," and now, in my mid-seventies after a youth of struggle and search, I can hardly believe my good fortune. And I am so glad that Frank was right for Joan, and she too has had a happy marriage and life. How I hope Aline and Elaine have been happy!

But why the spark, why the radiance? I cannot help my wanting to know everything; like most strong urges, this one traces to childhood. I think most children ask interminable questions. I don't know if they all want to find out something; but certainly many parents feel their asking is an irritating demand for attention and try to turn it off. Freud wrote that the endless questions are a cover for the real question that a child wants to ask, which is about sex relations between his parents and where babies come from. He thought if the parents were to answer that frankly, the torrent of other questions would cease. I don't know if that is true, or whether it would then be best *not* to tell the child about sex in order to preserve his curiosity. But I do not believe that all curiosity is about sex. I do not think the kitten or puppy or child exploring everything it can is manifesting only sexual curiosity; what I *do* know is that my parents were kindly, tolerant and patient about my ceaseless questioning. My father often remarked to me when I reached adolescence, "What questions! I never heard a child ask so many questions!" But he tried to answer them all with infinite patience. Years later, when I was given a university appointment, he said, "Congratulations! I am not surprised—I thought you would be a professor from all those questions you asked as a child. What questions!"

My parents knew a smattering of French and German. If there were something my mother wanted to say but keep secret from me, she would use one or the other. This I can remember, but I have no memory of asking all my questions. Using the foreign tongues to talk behind my back and prevent my understanding had two effects: it made me feel that grown-ups knew things I did not and intensified my curiosity to find out, and it probably contributed somewhat to my later feelings that I was excessively naive and could never understand people and the world the way grown-ups did. But it also started my interest in French and German and led me to take courses in them when they were available in high school and college.

But why the spark, why the radiance? I can only guess. The key usually lies in the first six years of childhood. My guess is that Joan had had a very stable childhood in a perhaps rather unimaginative bourgeois home, and tended to withdraw from the competition with her younger sister, who became the more vivacious of the two. Holly came from a professional home, a loving one, but one in which all sorts of things were happening. It was too much for Holly's two younger sisters, who became masochistic and never made entirely wholesome, secure, gratifying lives. But Holly somehow, maybe by identifying with her strong attractive father (and her mother, who was strong also), developed the strength to handle it all and came out of it with all this knowledge of people, and with dynamics that made her unusually insightful and independent-minded, very highly intelligent and unusually attractive. Whatever made the spark, Holly had it full and strong, and it ignited whatever it took in me to marry her.

Am I then portraying Holly as perfection, a paragon—or does she have "normal faults"? Of course she does, but in my love, which includes not only sex attraction and the mating instinct but also dependence, gratitude and egotistical identification, her virtues are built up and her faults minimized. In fact, they mean so little to me I would like to ignore them now; but my scientist's temperament requires a certain accuracy and completeness. I do not really know what one would term normal faults, and I should have asked my father what he meant when he asked me if Holly had them. Holly does smoke cigarettes. She started long before anyone thought they were harmful. On Sundays my father used to come in after his morning ride smelling of horse, to which my blessed mother objected loudly but good-humoredly; after dinner he smoked a good cigar, slowly, with great relish; Mother objected to the cigar too. I liked both smells. But when I was grown I was always a little afraid of horses, except on my vacation in the Southwest when I tutored the boy for his exams. Then I became used to horses and understood each individual one. When I tried smoking as a freshman in college I simply could not develop a taste for tobacco in any form: pipe, cigar or cigarettes. For the last I developed an utter loathing. But Holly would not give up her cigarettes. It was not only the stench that bothered me but Holly's manner, which seemed so out of character. Only later did I observe that most cigarette smokers are true addicts, truly unable to give up the so-called habit. Holly denies that she is addicted and points out that she gave up cigarettes completely during the three pregnancies for the sake of the children.

Soon after our marriage I came home to our two-room apartment after a long strenuous day, hungry for her kiss and embrace, and found her hidden behind a newspaper, blowing a huge cloud of the revolting noxious cigarette smoke directly at me. At first in those early days I became enraged by her habit, but Holly stood her ground and became angry back. She was not going to have a lord and master changing her and running her life (as her father had tried to run her mother's life; she told me about this years later). Basically, with my resentment of being overcontrolled and dominated myself, I had to agree. Just then I was reading a story in the *Saturday Evening Post* which made the point that when a marital battle develops one of the solutions is to kiss your wife with affection. I decided that my love would overwhelm all our battles. Even so, they recurred for a while, until one day about a year later as we were boiling into rages at each other, we looked closely at one another and I thought (realizing she was having similar thoughts): "Here we go again!" And with that glance we both burst out laughing; I embraced and kissed her and that was the beginning of the disappearance of our battles. I still think that it takes most couples ten to twenty years to adjust to each other and make a real, truly harmonious marriage. After that battle and laugh we were on our way despite occasional frictions. We had always tried to follow the age-old dictum: "Let the sun not set on your wrath."

Sometimes Holly, with all her strengths, would burst into tears, which often I did not understand. And when I got sick, which fortunately was rare, she never lost her temper but made it clear that she was furious at me and that I should have avoided this inconvenience and disruption. All she wanted was perfection! But this fitted my egotism, and I did not mind trying to oblige her. Love truly conquers all, and she and I both received enough love during our early childhoods to be able to give it to each other and, later, to our children.

One can be completely wrong in speculations about a person's dynamics if lacking the facts necessary to discern them. On the one hand, if I had known earlier of the traumata in Holly's childhood I would have hesitated, intellectually, to marry her. I did not then know enough dynamics and did not look for them. I was guided by my feelings, and it worked out superbly well. But it is risky. It is far safer to fall in love with and marry someone whom you know had a childhood of wholesome, loving, respecting, understanding feelings, especially with Mother, Father and other family members. Marriage is for so long and is so serious, making the greatest happiness and the most dire misery, that the decision requires one's head as well as one's heart. If knowledge of dynamics alone cannot be trusted, neither can feelings alone. For the feelings are apt to arise from one's neurotic motivations; this is especially true when they are of the intensity of infatuation. Joan's lack of spark, for me, might have resulted not from too calm a childhood, but from some form of inhibition, possibly from imperfectly handled rivalry with her attractive younger sister. That Holly made the perfect wife for me may have been less because of her traumatic childhood experiences and her overcoming of them than in spite of them, because of the "fit" between her dynamics and mine. I still think of Joan and that we would have made a fine marriage; after thirty years a mutual friend told me she was as beautiful as ever, although heavier, with three fine children, and was a happy active community leader. Perhaps she only needed marriage to ignite the spark.

Grant, the resident who "felt like a king," because he was at the theater with "such a queenly girl," married a girl who looked very much like Joan. Unhappily, after nearly twenty years of marriage, they were divorced. I was not surprised because I always thought something was wrong with Grant that made him such a stuffed shirt. Although a pedant, he was bright enough to become something of a leader. I hope that he has had a good life in spite of his difficulties with women.

It has been said that much of the art of living consists of drawing correct conclusions from inadequate data. I have been trying to discern what made Holly as she was without prying into her early childhood. After that first instant spark between us, we learned more slowly just how closely we identified. We seemed to feel and think the same on everything; as we saw each other we talked about everything. We felt and thought as one about politics, religion, sex, children, art, drama, poetry, literature and *Weltanschauung*. Happily, over our nearly fifty years of marriage our views have changed with the times, but in unison. We have had wide divergences of opinion, which have only added zest because eventually we have voted for the same candidates and liked the same books and been close to the same friends. For myself, when all goes well for me with women, as it has since marriage to Holly and the arrival and growing up of our three daughters, then my cup runs over and I deeply enjoy all the responsibilities and activities of living.

I still get a great lift from the companionship of beautiful, intelligent, warm, friendly, charming women of all ages, even though sex with them is out. This simplifies the relationship with Holly. I can enjoy that marvelous something, whatever it is, the femininity, without all the inevitable complications that the ultimate physical sexual relations seem invariably to bring. (The vulgar saying is usually true: "The screwing you get is not worth the screwing you get.") Now in my mid-seventies, except for greatly diminished stamina and endurance I feel just about the same as ever, particularly in my feelings toward people, and it amazes and deeply gratifies me that young women still react to me and get pleasure from my company.

My reactions to women are extreme: while I am still so responsive to those who attract me, even at this age, there are others whom I find neuter or revolting. I am extremely sensitive about offering a woman, especially the one in two hundred for whom I feel a warm tenderness and whose response means much to me, anything that she might find distasteful because of my aging. Happily, that day is not yet—may it be long postponed! Older women always repelled me, possibly in my pattern of turning in childhood from my incest-tabooed mother to my fresh, young sister; now I have more identification with older women, can guess how they must feel having lost their feminine attractiveness, and try to be especially considerate of them and give them some attention, although I cannot give them feelings I do not have for them but do have, unchanged, for the younger "one-in-two-hundred."

If some of this sounds boastful, it is probably because some of the inevitable egotism has infiltrated it. Fortunately for me, I have retained a youthful slenderness and clear skin and am still light and agile. A few days ago, chatting with a beautiful young acquaintance at a swimming pool about swimming strokes, I said, "I used to swim the trudgeon for distance, but since becoming old and decrepit, I omit the flutter and only do the scissors, adjusting the overarm to that alone." She snapped, "You are not old!" Of course that is usually flattery, but she replied so fast that she had the ring of sincerity. She cured me of making such self-pitying, flattery-seeking remarks, and restored me to speaking as I actually feel, that is, youthful, although within the limits of my present energies and stamina. But I know we all want to think that we are still young and there is no fool like an old fool, and I am on guard against deceiving myself. The father of one of the small boys playing softball one evening entered the game and went to bat. He made a good hit, but it was well fielded so that he slid into first base, landing on his left elbow, thereby breaking his arm and dislocating his shoulder. It is easy to comment, *post facto,* that a gray-haired man should have known he could not join the kids and should not have tried to prove that he was still one of them. But this is a human tendency, not only to deny aging but to prove one is still young and can continue to attract women and maintain one's own self-esteem, which I include along with vanity, pride, needs for admiration and such, under the general term "egotism" (to avoid the psychoanalytic term "narcissism"). A man I know, on entering his sixties, began to get his friends to feel the size and strength of his biceps; another friend of eighty tries to crush your hand when he shakes it in greeting.

As a person feels weak and inferior, he reacts almost automatically by emphasizing his superior points and even exaggerating them sometimes to the point of delusions. The truth is hard to know because of the limitations of our minds by our feelings, and especially when it touches something in our emotional life as sensitive as our egotism, vanity, pride, self-praise or self-esteem. This attaches even to longevity. I would have felt myself a weakling if I had died before seventy. Now, having escaped that disgrace, I want to continue living as long as it is this enjoyable and as long as I can be of real use to others—to my wife, children and grandchildren, patients and friends. In one way, I am surprised at just how enjoyable life can be in the mid-seventies; in another way, the experience of my parents is apparently so fixed in my mind that, however unrealistically, I expect my life to be unchanged until eighty or even ninety-one. In patients I have seen death wishes because of egotism about longevity. One man unconsciously wished another dead just to feel that he was superior to him because he outlived him. I hope there is no impulse so mean as that in my own unconscious.

College, as I have said, had not been a time for "getting an education." Its chief virtue for me had lain in being part of a great university, which in turn was located in a great city. The education I received was not from the content of the courses but from the opportunity to probe all subjects, have contact with the graduate schools, especially chemistry, physics and engineering, and with the cultural life of the metropolis, as well as have time to try to test all this, while thinking about my career choice. Added to this fascinating and wonderful period, the year in London was sufficient for decision, for launching me on a life in medicine, which combined all the earlier interests in chemistry, biology and physics and in unfolding sociological events of those times. Thus, difficult as it seemed at first, it had taken me only five or six years to find my career.

But finding my true mate had taken well nigh fifteen years for I had really started looking when I was fifteen. At last I had found both career and mate—but how long would it be before I would find myself, and what did "finding oneself" mean? It did not come to mind that by taking responsibilities and by doing the best I could to help my patients and to make my wife and children happy and secure, i.e. by serving others on the two great fronts of profession and home, I was silently on the way to maturity. It was new and soul-satisfying to have the search for a mate at an end, to have an assured sex life, to have a real home with a fine woman, to face life no longer alone, but with a true companion to share its experiences and help with its problems.

23
PSYCHOANALYSIS

Le coeur a ses raisons que la raison ne connait pas.

Pascal

But who will reveal to our waking ken
The forms that swim and the shapes that creep
Under the waters of sleep?

Sidney Lanier,
"The Marshes of Glynn"

Medical school, said Corey Jones, had provided a lot of understanding of people physically, biologically and in relation to the whole microscopic world of our own beautiful cell structure and of the bacteria and viruses among which we live, some friendly and helpful, some inimical and even lethal; naturally it did not supply the wisdom of the good physician, which comes only from experience in observing and living. In the old days, some physicians thought that reading stories, novels and drama helped.* I graduated still feeling naive in the extreme—probably largely because as I met people I continued unconsciously and automatically to try to impress them and win their love, so much so that I did not really observe them. One of my main motives for moving toward psychiatry was no doubt not only genuine object interest in people and psychiatry itself, but also the search for self-understanding, which was an effort to overcome the hurt to my pride caused by the naiveté. It was not until my psychoanalysis that I began to understand the reasons for the naiveté in overprotection and overadulation. Therefore, ironically, I felt weak while wanting to be admired, especially for strength. I felt weak because of wanting too much to be admired, and because I felt weak, I wanted to be admired. The insights into

---

*Aub, J., and Hapgood, R. (1970): *Pioneers in Modern Medicine: David Linn Edsall of Harvard*. Harvard Medical Alumni Association.

myself increased my insights into others and vice versa; the experience of living that the wise medical school had allowed for and, later on, the four years in the Navy and especially the increasing responsibilities started me toward some of the understanding of myself and others and of life in which I felt so deficient.

Dr. Roads with whom I started my analysis, toward the end of his year as visiting professor at the medical center, warned me that when he left to organize a new institute in a distant city he might be too busy to continue with me, and might have to refer me to someone else. And when the business depression decimated my finances, said Corey, he referred me to you. As you know, even though I had been forewarned, when this happened it was a great shock. Dr. Roads was middle-aged, a man of the world, internationally known, and you seemed so young and callow. I did not even know that you were having your own training analysis at the medical center with him. Although you yourself were only a beginner in psychoanalysis, we seemed to like each other, and I respected Dr. Roads' confidence in your potential as a therapist. But whatever the deeper reasons for my ability to develop a transference to you, the single practical factor was this: Dr. Roads had started my analysis by asking only what I thought was important in my background and my development, but you took a detailed history, the essentials of which required two full visits to obtain. It gave me more insight and perspective on myself than the four months of five-days-a-week on the couch with Dr. Roads had yet achieved. But you pointed out that without that experience with him your inquiries into the childhood determinants of my makeup would probably not have been so fruitful.

At any rate, I was soon off to a good start with you. We worked well together steadily for three years and then reduced the meetings to once a week, then—two years after that—I came to see you for a brief retread, and you broached the idea of this book. I, who as yet had had nothing to say and never thought of writing anything but a letter or a postcard, identified with you and began to record observations on patients who interested me. Surprisingly, one was accepted and appeared in a professional journal. Not long after that, I wanted to change from internal medicine to psychoanalysis. Then we had a period of intensive work to try to learn whether this was a neurotic overidentification with you, and I saw Dr. Roads for his opinion. It seemed sufficiently realistic to try—and, feeling strongly about it, I pointed out that if it did not work out, I could always return to internal medicine, the richer for my analytic training and experience. With the decision taken, I plunged into psychoanalysis and have never regretted a moment of it! We started the idea of this book together, and although I found myself able to write more and more, even to the point of being called prolific, we decided to proceed as we had been, staying in touch and with you assembling the material to write this book.

The period of starting practice was a frustrating and strenuous one. I felt strongly that I had to understand every hour with every patient, and of course (as I see now) I couldn't. I turned to everyone I could for help, but in the end had to just stick with it and study every patient of mine for myself. You were right to let me sink or swim this way. It was five years before I even began to feel reasonably secure in understanding each patient's "basic dynamics," as well as what goes on in every hour.

The best part of my analysis, in retrospect, was that you went for the main issues and were not sidetracked by minutiae, useful though they could be; also, you seemed to have basic trust and confidence in me. In fact, I felt inferior, felt that others could run drugstores or gas stations, while I could not do anything that practical and requiring that degree of independence. But you laughed at this, and had full confidence in me, pointing out that I had superior endowment and so, of course, could do any ordinary thing that anyone else could, if I only applied myself.

What dynamics led to my emotional tangles (today called "hang-ups") and to their eventual unsnarling? It is important to examine this closely:

Probably each baby is born with a somewhat different individual temperament and capability; but the major forces in shaping its personality, problems and potentials come from the interactions of these innate factors with its parents or substitutes during its earliest years. Earliest memories, those little fragments of memory before it becomes continuous, remain in our adult minds because they fit something that continues to be emotionally important in our make-ups. My first memory, which I related earlier, is of myself as a baby in the arms of my mother, who is standing by a mantle over a fireplace in a room of our house. She hands me to my father, who takes me; but his face and clothes feel rough and bristly in comparison with the smooth softness of my mother, and I go back to her. I take this to represent my continuing wish to be taken care of, especially by a woman, and indications of this in my lifelong strong attraction to women and of quickly being at ease with women and having them like me. Men like me too, as the memory shows, but I prefer the soft feel of the relationship with women.

The second memory is also of being a baby, nude, prone on the bed, perhaps after a bath. My mother, my Aunt Edie and a nurse we had until I was about one year old were standing beside the bed admiring me, giving me an occasional kiss or pat or cuddle. This I take as expressing my enjoyment of maternal love and its physical demonstration in caresses, which also has continued—my oldest daughter calls it "lech." But their steadfast devotion to me, the pattern of the stable loyalty of my mother and father to each other and other factors also had psychological effects of assuring my being monogamous once I married.

My nurse, much loved by my parents and devoted to me, was found to have pulmonary tuberculosis when I was about one year old, and left for a sanatorium. I think that my mother was very frightened by this contact, and that fear increased her tendency to be over-anxious and overprotective toward me; certainly I grew up feeling more restricted than the other boys on the block. When I was seven or eight, I was attacked by two big boys who stole a small magnifying glass that I treasured and was experimenting with to focus the sunlight and burn a piece of paper. I immediately ran home to Mother. This was the only sensible thing to do, as each of the boys was twice my age and more than twice my size, and it was two against one. But still it seems like an automatic, unconscious running for protection. I think it showed an overly strong dependence and help-seeking attitude that, unrecognized until my analysis, was an entirely unconscious source of much of my inferiority feeling and of the overcompensatory element in the drive to be independent.

The drive to be independent was at first only a gesture to demonstrate that I could be alone. Later, as I saw my tendency to depend upon others, I began to combat it by being sure to do my own thinking before—and after—getting other opinions. My maturing was retarded, I believe, by my reacting to every person as a possible source of love, admiration, protection and help; in other words, instead of making every decision and handling every situation on my own, I put myself in the emotional position of a small child toward its mother and father. Therefore I learned a great deal from others, but still felt childish and hence inferior. This hurt my egotism, which was strengthened by my being the only child for five years. This overly sensitive egotism being always hurt by feelings of inferiority, I was constantly angry and also intensely competitive, but, strangely enough, unaware of this. The reason seemed to lie in the pattern toward my father. At 148 pounds he was slightly under the average size of men, but well-knit and somewhat above average in physical strength and in making his way in the world. I, the little dependent child, could not conceive how he could possibly go out into the world and make a living for all of us, or how he managed to sit a high-strung stallion and control it. Sometimes he would bring home one or more of his managers, a few being towering giants. But Dad always knew his own mind and was unmistakably "the boss." Competition with him seemed to me hopeless. Hence I did not feel that I was also a man, although a small one, but one who would grow and become like my father. This I did not learn until my analysis; instead, I withdrew unconsciously, without even realizing it, or simply remained fixated in the emotional position of child to parent, wanting to be taken care of by his strength and feeling totally unable to be like him or identify with or compete with him.

This desire for independence was made more difficult by the attitudes of my mother. Her love gave me the basic optimism and drive to work things out; but she was not only overprotective, she was slightly dominating. You did as she said because she said so, not because she appealed to your reason. But you knew she loved you— that was all that really mattered; yet it did not prevent an undercurrent of rebellion against her domination. I was not aware of it until early adolescence, for I was trained from birth to obey her, and indeed what she decreed was always for my own good. So it was natural for me to get along by obedience and winning love, without need for independence and accomplishment like my father's. And this pattern in the home continued outside it. But being unable to identify with my father was a terrible hurt to my masculine egotism. It was impossible to be hostile to him out of competition or envy because he seemed to me to be the perfect father, loving me and loved by me; he was always accessible, always reasonable, and I could even go to him with complaints about my mother (e.g., her controlling of me).

I was unable to achieve an identification with my father—at least, it took me fifty years to do so—but it seemed that he could always identify with me. He was totally uncontrolling. His religious training of me in childhood was typical. As he told me, "You will hear all sorts of things about religion; there are more than two hundred kinds of religion in the United States, but all that seems to be important is that there is one God. You will have to decide whether Jesus was a god or a very fine man." (No involved Nicaean theology.)

He also stated: "You should always be honest and straightforward and look every man straight in the eye. I will support your education all I can, but you know that you must carve out your own future and when you marry support our own wife."

The competition with him was entirely repressed, that is, not in my awareness, until in the analysis it emerged repeatedly in dreams, typically of a small animal fighting a large animal. But the envy of his masculine independence and apparent fearlessness and ability to handle and lead men, combined with his good judgment, was quite conscious. Looking back, however, I could see that there actually was some degree of competition with him in relation to my mother. For while she was much in love with my father and recognized that he was pure gold, she could nevertheless comment on his weaknesses and took him more or less for granted, while she conveyed a sense of comparing him and me to my future advantage. While she deeply and steadily loved him, she glowed when she looked at me, as though father was good but I would be great. This was my Oedipus, and in this superficial way I won it, while in my deeper feelings I could not even begin to match my father as a man. And I was sure the girls would all see that I was still only a child and have no interest in me. It was a late and great discovery that by some miracle most girls thought there was something to me after all!

As Freud said (apropos of Goethe), "Boys who win their Oedipus complexes usually become men who are optimistic and this optimism helps them become successful." As George Bernard Shaw said about Franklin D. Roosevelt, "Never worry about a loved first son—the idea of failure will never enter his head."

My mother's apparent preference for me, that glow when she looked at me, her confidence in me, these things were not without effect; I think that may have made me too egotistical, but they were vital forces in sustaining me through all the years of feeling so immature, inadequate, inferior. And these forces were slowly, subtly, unconsciously reinforced by the girls who did accept me in spite of my feelings about myself. Thus, my own feelings about myself were mixed and unreconcilably in conflict until nearly the age of fifty. Partly I felt immature, inadequate and inferior to other adults of both sexes; but also I felt a certain superiority and even a sort of security, and was always optimistic, even through the worst of the struggles to find my way in a career and in my interreactions with men and women and the achievement of marriage.

The turning point analytically occurred many months *after* our systematic meetings had ended. I was in a car as a passenger with some friends and colleagues. I forget what turn the chitchat took, but suddenly I realized my *envy* of you, my analyst. With that, all I had read, all you had interpreted for me so many times, apparently fruitlessly, all my dreams and all I had heard in case conference—all of this seemed to fall into place, and I felt a sudden enormous sense of relief. This was only the beginning of resolution: I had long been well aware of my own feelings of inferiority, my comparison of myself with other men who all seemed bigger and stronger and more capable, and my envy of them for this. Thus it had not been entirely unconscious. Now it struck me with a new impact, because of my being so unconscious of it specifically in the transference to you. I could not see it toward you any more than I could see it toward my father, in whose image I had placed you, despite our closeness in age. I could not realize the hostility from competition and envy toward anyone as friendly as my father or you, my analyst.

I will try to express here what you so aptly call my dynamic diagnosis, my childhood emotional pattern, including the pathodynamics, that is, those dynamics which caused my psychopathology, my emotional problems:

Much love and overprotection + overcontrol by Mother →
overdependence and oversubmissiveness → heightened needs
for love and inability to identify with the independence of

adults, especially Father ⟶ hurt egotism, repression of competition and envy toward Father, fixation in emotional position of a child, getting by on submissiveness and winning love ⟶ further hurt to adult, masculine pride and egotism ⟶ envy and competition + anger ⟶ fight as hostility ⟶ guilt and anxiety and flight as fixation in the receptive, love-seeking, dependence attitudes to Mother and Father.

All this is what made my inner struggles. It includes the love, respect and understanding received from my parents and the identification with them and their strengths, which made the healthy parts of my dynamics, which enabled the rest of me to mature with security, optimism and confidence and through it all to work and to love and be loved, and to play, all with warmth and freedom.

This, then, is the interplay of motivations, conditionings and reactions in which, with or without awareness, my ego has lived for seventy-five years. And in it I went, almost totally unaware, through my formal schooling. Ralph was certainly right: the personal analysis illumined all that came later. And in this way my inner struggles began to diminish; the tension was so relieved that the headaches which began during my analysis and in the overwork and struggles to learn the new field and to start a practice, disappeared and have never recurred; my emotional acceptance of responsibility began to increase, as did my capacity for carrying responsibility. By age fifty, as I have mentioned, I began to see myself as adequate and able; instead of inferiority, envy and competitiveness I could relate to others with a tolerant attitude of "live and let live," with sympathy and identification. At last I was beginning to find myself. I saw my strengths and weaknesses and how I and my work fitted into the present scheme of things, how I could change as times changed. My energies were released from internal struggle and freed for use in living. I could write freely. And with growing serenity, I could face the inevitable death of the body with calm and resignation while still hoping for more decades as enjoyable as those that had passed.

Naturally I have asked myself for what I am most indebted to my parents: the answer is simple and brief, and after decades of private practice seems to me to be one of the basic principles of childrearing. Mother and Father have my deepest gratitude for always treating me as a *person*, with respect for my opinions. They never forced any ideas upon me or pressured me in any way, except for the slight restrictiveness by Mother that I have mentioned. They never acted as though they owned me; they loved me, went their ways and let me go mine; and because of their love and respect for me as a person I loved them back and identified with them . . . and the ways I have found to go have been like theirs, I think—good, loving and productive.

24
WOMEN

Oh woman! in our hours of ease
Uncertain, coy and hard to please . . .
When pain and anguish wring the brow,
A ministering angel thou!

Sir Walter Scott,
"Marmion"

Women have always meant a great deal to me, probably for the reasons I have discussed before, but do I know anything about them? Of course I have read books on the psychology of women. There may even be some truth in the gossipy remark attributed to a relative of Freud: "Siggy is a great psychologist, but he doesn't know much about human nature." Yet no man, let alone a genius, devotes all the hours of a long life to studying people without making some keen everyday observations, in addition to his revolutionary scientific ones. On page 185 of Freud's *New Introductory Lectures*, at the end of the chapter on the psychology of women, he makes an interesting remark: " . . . we have only described women insofar as their natures are determined by their sexual function. The influence of this factor is, of course, very far-reaching but we must remember that an individual woman may be a human being apart from this." (I assume that the "may be" is an unintended tone which slipped in.)

However, as to the far-reaching effects of the woman's sexual function, it does seem that women are more complicated than men endocrinologically. Certainly there is one obvious biological fact about women, and that is the effects of premenstrual tension, which can be great, usually for the week prior to the period. Many a marriage improves greatly when both partners recognize that their more unreasonable spats occur during this week. Therese Benedek has shown that after menstruation when the estrogens predominate in the bloodstream, women dream mostly of erotic relations with men. Then halfway through the cycle after ovulation occurs and the estrogens recede, progesterone is in the ascendancy in the blood, and the dreams are about themselves and their children. But whatever fluctuations in mood are effected by these endocrine crosscurrents, from amorousness to distraction and withdrawal and premenstrual instability, the basic fact is the total personality. This is not always easy for a man to recognize on first meeting a woman when his reaction to her sexual attractiveness is central to his awareness. But if he gets to know her better, it usually becomes evident that the essential is the total personality. This, I think, is the definitive answer. If you have ever gone through a strong attachment to a woman which has for some reason not worked out, so that the erotic feelings are dissipated and you become free and distant enough from her to be objective again, then you will probably see that the reasons for the attachment stemmed largely from her makeup as a *human being.**

It is so hard for a man to evaluate women because they have "beauty," meaning in part at least that it is a man's own male reactions that make women so hard to understand. Women are unpredictable when they have mercurial, unpredictable personalities, just as certain men are.

For the rest, we can say that since man is born of women, it is natural that he should look to a woman for all the love and care he got from his mother or wanted and did not get, with consequent frustration and anger; in fact, we can say generally that a man is conditioned to respond to women with all the emotional patterns he had toward his mother and other females of his earliest years. A man with bad childhood patterns to his own mother is a poor risk for a husband. But woman is also born of woman, and although her sex drive turns her to men, what she is looking for is exactly the same as what the man is looking for: love, care, security, respect. If a man is unpredictable or a "dog" or a "pig" or any other animal, that is not because he is a male but because of his personality as it was shaped in earliest childhood, from conception to the age of about six years—from "0 to 6." The same holds true for women, each of whom is of course different and

---

*"Ben Franklin . . . treated every woman as if she were a person . . . and made her feel more truly one than ever. Because he loved, valued and studied women they were no mystery to him and he had no instinctive fear of them."
Carl Van Doren: *Benjamin Franklin,* Garden City Publ. Co., 1941.

individual. Beyond these elements there are the sociological and economic reasons: if a girl bases her future financial security upon the man she marries, then of course that will affect her attitudes toward men and toward the one she marries, or tries to marry, just as these same circumstances also affect the man's attitudes.

Therefore, I am not certain that there *is* such a thing as a basic psychology of women, but only a psychology of individuals, men or women, with the operation of that tremendous force of attraction between the two sexes.

A man is conditioned to being mothered from birth, and he very soon reaches maturity but repeats this pattern toward his wife, expecting her to "mother" him. But often when she complies, he reacts to her too much as to his mother, with the old incest taboo entering his pattern, and deflecting his sexual interest to exogamic, non-tabooed women, women who are not part of his family, forming a promiscuous trend. Upon this general pattern are superimposed other patterns specific to his relationship to his particular mother: was his mother accepting, rejecting, spoiling, dominating or a combination of these things?

But for women the general pattern of monogamous versus promiscuous trends is less clear. Whereas men are mothered by women and marry women, all in a heterosexual setting, women do not follow the childhood pattern in marrying women. This might be a general source of dissatisfaction in wives: they must do *all* the mothering of children and husbands and feel that they are not sufficiently mothered themselves. Thus many wives might feel like "second-class citizens," giving everything and receiving little.

Holly exhibited some such feelings in our marriage; but I tried to give her enough emotionally, and she tried to be satisfied and not generate resentment from this pattern upon which so many marriages founder.

This mothering pattern seems to be one of the reasons many men turn against their wives but want divorce settlements that give them free relations with their children; and why many of the children sympathize with the father, whom they saw only as a good companion and a Santa Claus while they themselves were trying to escape the restrictions of being socialized by their own mother.

It may be generally the woman's mothering and the man's need of it that gives women so much power over men.

By logic, the whole atmosphere of a person's emotional life must be very different in tone if he is driven by barely controllable urges to embrace a female, to kiss her, fondle and caress her, and penetrate her, from the emotional atmosphere if a person is the female who wants just as strongly to have all these things done to her. As I have said, I could not believe that anyone could want to be the object of this sexual aggression however mixed with tender feelings, until I actually saw, heard and experienced girls who did. The power of this force varies from one person to the next for a number of reasons, e.g., inherited biology and endocrinology, health and vigor and temperament, how the person was treated during childhood and the emotional interrelations with those who reared him or her, and the extent to which sex is used to express or drain tensions from other feelings. All of these factors enter into why some individuals have more or less sex appeal than others. It is seen in the old male saying that "they all look good from far away."

It should be unnecessary to note that this biography is the story of one average man in the Bicentennial Era, from 1900 through 1976. It does not describe a life in other times or other cultures; it is the life of a man and not of a woman. I see as many women as men in my private practice of psychoanalysis and dynamic psychiatry, I have a wife I feel close to, we have raised three daughters, and I have three granddaughters; but I do not think that I could feel my way into the minutiae of the emotional life of a woman as well as I can that of a congenial man. Finding oneself is intimately involved for a man in finding his work. Probably with Women's Lib, the same will hold for working women and those who try, like a man, to be successful in their occupation as well as successful as spouse and parent.

25
MARRIAGE

The reason firm, the temperate will,
Endurance, foresight, strength and skill;
A perfect woman, nobly planned
To warn, to comfort, and command;
And yet a spirit still, and bright
With something of angelic light.

William Wordsworth,
"She Was A Phantom of Delight"

It seems obvious that the life of every relatively normal man and woman falls naturally into two great eras, namely, before marriage and after marriage. And the part before marriage is divided naturally into the years of the establishment of the powerful, significant sexual feelings for the opposite sex and then the time of testing, adventuring, and the premarital peccadilloes. And married life is divided by the periods before and after having children. As I look back over the decades, it seems to me that from adolescence (not later than the age of fifteen) I wanted to be married, and was looking for the perfect wife for me.

I have said that my initial reaction to Holly was "love at first sight," but was it really that simple? In the first place, what is love? And what is "being in love"? I have taken over this simple, apparently offhand definition of love: "an interest in another person for *that person*'s own sake." That is, not for selfish desires, not for something one wants in return. Is such pure, generous, altruistic love a totally unrealistic ideal, or can it be seen to actually exist? I think it can be seen clearly and unmistakably in the form of mother love. And this love of the mother toward her young, especially her physical biological reaction to the newborn baby, is also seen in the father, and is seen throughout the animal kingdom, certainly among the mammals. This parental love very well may be the basis of all love. "A greater love than this has no man, that he gives his life for his friend." But "being in love," while it has or should have this feeling, includes sexual attraction and

261

other elements also. That is why it is so difficult for any girl or fellow to know if he or she really "loves" or "is loved" or is "in love". Is it purely sexual attraction, more or less inhibited, or is it a genuine interest in the other's own welfare? And has it other elements? It has always seemed to me that, under ordinary circumstances, the words "I love you" are empty and all but meaningless. For the person himself, however honest he tries to be, usually does not know himself whether he really does "love" or whether he is "in love," or "is loved in return," "wants love," or is mostly dependent—so little do we really know of what goes on in our minds and hearts. Actually it is the behavior that counts, especially the responsibility for the other's happiness.

Today when I say I fell in love with Holly at first sight, it seems that nearly fifty years of marriage have proved this to be correct. At that time, I was still basically the näive child I had always been, but I had had sex with a number of girls in the setting of more or less close intimate personal relationships with all or almost all of them. I gave them all I could, and they took and enjoyed what they could—although for some that was not enough, for it was not marriage. And I enjoyed what they gave me, more than they did perhaps, because I did not offer marriage. What they gave me was vitally indispensable and memorable. I wonder if I could have continued studying and working effectively and unswervingly without it. I think I have been one of the lucky ones. Happily, as the urge to settle down to monogamy became irresistible, I found at last the girl I wanted to settle down with.

My experiences had gotten a lot of curiosity about women out of my system, and I was all the more impatient to pass into the next great epoch of life: marriage. Despite these sexual affairs I had wanted from childhood to be married, and that concept to me included utter and complete fidelity. This idea probably stemmed, as I have reiterated, from the unquestioned loyalty and devotion of my parents to each other and to myself and my sister. It never entered my mind that marriage was or could be anything else, for I grew up knowing nothing else. I wished somewhat that Holly had been the first girl I had had sex with, but also was satisfied that I had enough experience to forever relinquish the acting-out impulses to promiscuity which lurk in everyone. Mating had now taken over.

At first, Holly and I had verbal fights; I did not have them in my parental home, and they hurt me. Life was full of struggles enough of all kinds, and I thought that the marital home should be a place of harmony and love. Of course I blamed Holly, but she defended herself strongly and blamed me, an idea that was inconceivable to me—I wanted only to give and receive love in the marriage. She never thought much of me, seeing mostly my defects. That hurt too, but worked well because when some virtues appeared, she was so pleased and delighted.

But my personal analysis, which eventually reopened my maturing, at first made me less cocky and certain about myself. Gradually the possibility dawned upon me that I might be treating Holly somewhat after my pattern to my younger sister, expecting from her Judy's adoration of me as the older, superior brother. But Holly was also the oldest, just as I was, and she had her own position of leadership and justified pride. My feelings toward her as only my kid sister naturally hurt her healthy wholesome pride and made her critical and resentful toward me. She was a girl of spirit, one of the reasons I loved her. We, or at least I, did not recognize or understand at that time my unconsciously depreciatory attitude toward her, but only felt the resentments and was unhappy at our vigorous verbal set-to's. There were never blows, and to this day I have never been able to comprehend a man's striking a woman (although I understand through my practice how a man who is mistreated by his mother in early childhood can repress hostility to women and can live out his early pattern as an adult against a woman).

I was the older partner, and the man. Holly liked the idea of having a sophisticated man of the world as a husband and escort. Of course I was far from this, but my years and travel alone had taught me a few things and given me a certain ease if not assurance with people. It was my part to know the restaurants and where to stop for meals or overnight when we took auto trips. But in part I was concentrated on the driving, and in part she had a quicker eye and keener judgment than I in selecting desirable places as we sped along. This was the beginning of her becoming less dependent upon me and of my depending more and more upon her for judgment, until as the years passed I saw her as one of the soundest, most realistic, most intelligent persons I had ever met.

Holly initiated long, leisurely breakfasts on Sunday mornings as a routine. On trips we would arise early, but then, instead of getting on the road, she would insist on a second leisurely cup of coffee, getting us off to a late start, to my irritated impatience. For my own makeup, from my mother's training, was to get along with what had to be done and *then* relax afterward. But I gradually came around to Holly's more deliberate, restful, easier way.

It was the depths of the Great Depression and I still earned only a pittance, but we were comfortable renting a small two-room apartment made by renovating the second floor of a private house. And before many months we acquired a relatively modern, used Plymouth sedan, with nice-looking exterior and interior. One evening we were invited to a dinner party. The host was sidetracked by a fire, for he could not resist following the engines. The hostess served drinks while we waited. We had many drinks. Returning home after midnight with me driving as usual, Holly threw up on the right inside door of the car, and I was very angry; this was not knowing how to drink properly, and at least she should have warned me to stop the car at a curb. I was disgusted and thought next day while I was at work that it was her job to clean it up. I was cruel, and she was embarrassed, but held her dignity. A week later we were again driving home together from a party. Bowling along at a reasonable speed I said, "What are all those silly people doing stopping at that corner?" Of course I had gone through a red light without even seeing it, and this time the joke was on me. And thus we were bound to each other, not in a casual or even only a deep way, but in a free and voluntary way— bound for life; and so by difficult and harsh fights and amusing incidents, by thoughtfulness and thoughtlessness, we became accustomed to each other, adapted to each other, and our relationship deepened in feeling. This is the kind of love that one does not "fall" into—but that is built slowly over the years on that foundation.

Holly was disappointed in me in many ways. And raised with so much affection, I was disappointed that she did not warmly cuddle up to me as some other young wives did to their husbands. But the search was over—for better or worse the die was cast. Holly was beautiful, a definite personality; she was my mate, and in sex we had mutual orgasms.

I do not mean that my sexual interest in other girls or women had suddenly evaporated. It remained as violent as ever to various ones, including one blonde girl, bursting with vitality, whom I saw every morning on the commuting train. I could hardly keep from touching her, from making some sort of pass. But I did nothing. Once I had heard a man say about some party proposed by friends, "I am a married man." This I envied at the time; it seemed right. Now I felt the same. However strongly tempted, I was now "a married man"— not an adventuring youth.

The most overwhelmingly important thing in my life was no longer an intense, satisfying sexual adventure, but the frank, honest, direct look into my eyes of Holly's clear blue, undeceivable ones.

I was still dependent, submissive, easily swayed; still lacking in maturity of outlook and in the ways of the world. But I was a husband, Holly's husband, and what I could offer I did. Medicine was my calling, almost my religion; and to try to increase understanding of the mind, the emotional life and psychodynamics was my occupation, always with me while I was studying patients or observing in life or reading books or seeing plays. I seem to have given Holly most of what she has needed, but she is sturdy and independent. She has fitted into my doctor's life, and by great good fortune I seem to have fitted her needs adequately, if not completely. I have always trusted her implicitly and could not consider so living that she would not completely trust me. We became each other's job. The big thing in marriage, its very core, is an identification with the partner, a sympathetic understanding which makes for considerateness and unremitting efforts to make the other happy. Self-centeredness and selfishness are the enemies of marriage.

I must feel sorry for those men and women who want a stable marriage of trust but who do not have the emotional pattern for it in their own minds, based upon security and mutual loving trust in and between their parents when they were small children. They can float around it, but never settle into a gratifying solid marriage, if the pattern does not exist in their own minds. Yet this is the only sound base upon which to have and rear children, so that the children in turn can grow up with assurance and security instead of neurosis, psychosis and criminality. Natural selection goes astray when a couple marry and have children only because they are brought together by mutual neuroses or even psychoses. Thus it is not only that the childhood emotional patterns mesh, but that there are enough healthy dynamics in them for the individual to achieve a reasonable degree of maturity. Mental health is both maturity and adjustment.

Like so many young couples, we had a dog for two years which we loved and parented; but now we both wanted a child of our own. We felt that our marriage had settled down securely enough to bring a child into it. We omitted contraceptives, sex soon flowered, and we had our daughter. This was a newer and deeper but more anxiety-laden experience. On Holly's initiative we decided to give up the apartment and try to find an inexpensive house. The Depression was dragging on. As usual, Holly was the one who located the house—simple, inexpensive, on the edge of the university campus, with carpeted steps that a child could learn to clamber up and down. From now on our guiding principle in living became, "What is best for the children is best for us."

Years back I had heard a man remark to friends who had just had a child, "Now you know what you live for." That was certainly true in a flash for Holly and me. Suddenly our lives had a new, clear, sharp focus. Thereafter there was only one interruption: the rise of Hitler and our entry into World War II left me no choice but to join the Navy, to at least contribute what medical skills I had to those who risked life, limb and mental stability in action.

Our three girls have remained the focus of our lives forever. Even since they have married and had children of their own, they and the grandchildren have been our greatest pleasure; and to be of help, financial or otherwise, without interfering in their complete independence, became and has remained our deepest joy. Compared with this satisfaction, "peccadilloes" is the correct word for any casual sexual adventure. Such encounters may or may not satisfy a transient tension of the body; but the clear, clean, pure open honesty in Holly's eyes when she looked at me kept me from deceiving her— it satisfied something in my soul. Perhaps not engaging in affairs is only a variation of that craving in the small child for the good, understanding, loving mother, mixed with all the masculine gallantry to protect, sustain and care for her. But whatever it is, it runs deep and pervasive, far more than the momentary ejaculation of sexual juices, pleasurable as orgasms are; it is something deep, something in the soul, something to live for and by.

As I look at the marriages in my practice and among my friends, I think this soul-satisfying relationship is what everyone is struggling toward. That is how Nature uses us to continue the species. Of course, as all couples do, Holly and I have occasionally had our difficulties, even at this time. But I never met a man she might have been happier with, although I always told her that she was free to leave if she did. At rare times, in "mid-channel," I wondered briefly if it were worthwhile to go on. But as always for the scientist, what are the controls, what are the alternatives? For me, none; for her, so far as I could see, also none. If this were not the best that life had to offer, it was very close to it. We were both the oldest children, the primary standard bearers. No doubt in her eyes I could not fill her father's shoes as a big, powerful physique with a strong dominating personality. But when I reached fifty I achieved confidence in my abilities and devoted myself with unswerving confidence and conscientiousness to my study and practice. By then the war was over; Holly and I over the years had become not just marriage partners but close friends, companions and comrades who had shared the storms of life.

With time, Holly and I came to understand each other, our weaknesses and strengths, but above all, our love. The worst times we had we knew we would laugh about together before long. Remarkable as it seems, attractive women seemed to be drawn to me even as the decades passed. Perhaps it was because women and sex, despite my diminishing performance, still have meant so much to me. My reactions to them remained strong and deep, but with no disloyalty to Holly. Of course, some women might be attracted to me because of my being successful in my profession and somewhat well known through my books; but usually I think I detect this reason, and those women do not become part of the group who attract me.

Possibly some of that loving feeling entered into my becoming a physician and being so interested in and devoted to my patients. It seems to trace mostly to identification with my loving mother and also my father. That honest look of Holly's saw me through four years of active duty in the Navy during the war. Perhaps most men will think me a fool to turn down all those sexual opportunities with desirable women. But Holly valued faithfulness highly, I believed, and I valued that look in her eye far above any peccadilloes.

The first girls I met during the war were on the staff of the unit of which I was in charge. That ruled them out; I would not make the same mistake I had made while working at the Children's Hospital, nor would I start an affair myself which was forbidden to my men, nor did I want complications by anyone with anyone in the unit for which I was responsible. One girl was just all sex—her look, her hair, the way she moved—the ultimate in seductiveness anywhere, but especially among all these sexually repressed males of all shapes, sizes, temperaments, dispositions and intentions. Of course I could not know everything that went on, but the women in my unit were off limits. At first there were occasional parties and gatherings. At one of them a young officer introduced me to a pretty Irish girl, Bonnie. I assumed she was with him, but she made it evident that she was not, and she developed a liking for me. As soon as I could without offending or rejecting her I told her I was married. That seemed only fair. She appeared a trifle startled and said, "Then we cannot. . . !" And, like an idiot, I broke in instead of listening and said, "No, but we can go around together to some of these parties and enjoy our company." What an idiot I was not to be quiet and listen! Did she mean that we could not sleep together, or marry, or what? I will never know, for my well-intentioned stupid haste to reassure her shut her off. She was wholesome, pretty, a pleasant companion and a welcome relief and release from the work, which was continuous and arduous, especially for one like myself who had never been trained to this kind of leadership or experienced in it. I was also rather worn out hunting for a house not more than seventy-five miles from the base so that Holly and the children might come there and live while I had duty at this stateside station; for I knew how important it was for the children to have the family intact during their earliest years.

Another officer, Clarence, already had his wife and daughter settled nearby. They both seemed to like me, in a loose but not intimate way. But Clarence liked Bonnie, and at any occasion he danced with her as much as he could. Perhaps all men need a woman, even without full physical sex, to function properly and with complete equilibrium. Perhaps this is mostly true for men like me who were raised by an adoring mother, aunt and nurse, with an adoring sister also. At any rate, although I missed Holly and the children and longed for their arrival, I was in a certain pleasant balance with Bonnie, who lightly made it clear to me that she was happy with me even without sex and did not care for any other involvement.

A week later, however, Clarence came right out with it to me directly; he was cold sober. "I want to switch girls with you," he said. "I'll take Bonnie and you take my wife." He was serious all right. Bonnie was youthful, fresh, healthy, with dark hair and humor in her gray eyes with their long, natural-black lashes. She was attractive all right, and Clarence's wife could not begin to compete with her, for while pleasant, she looked ordinary and careworn. She must have been painfully unhappy under this rejection by her husband, which (although presumably unspoken) she must have felt. Bonnie was one of the one-in-two-hundred who fully attracted me. Clarence's wife was not. Not that I would have yielded to his proposal even had she been good-looking; it was so contrary to my dynamics.

I declined his offer as politely as I could, but he was unhappy and kept trying, ineffectually. I may have been a fool not to go to bed with Bonnie. I had heard all the arguments: it would give us pleasure and would do no harm to anyone else. Fallacy! This meant deception, the sacrifice of the trust I found in Holly's eyes. I was a rotten liar, for my father had trained me to be frank and honest. Bonnie and I liked each other; we provided each other an accustomed, good-humored, pleasant, happy escort over an unnatural, crazy kind of period when it was said that Japan had taken Attu and was threatening to take all the Aleutians and bomb the Pacific Northwest.

One evening, however, Clarence and his wife invited a few people over for the evening; Bonnie and I were included. They managed to isolate Bonnie from me. His wife monopolized me so that I could not get away from her without a direct rejection. After about two hours she left the room for a moment, and Bonnie escaped and spontaneously threw herself into my arms. We needed to talk, but there was no opportunity. Another older, more somber officer caught me and offered me a place to go with Bonnie. Bonnie and I, he implied, should leave as soon as we could politely excuse ourselves and enjoy the night together, which we both deserved. This offer seemed to me genuinely considerate, although perhaps I was being näive. Sex, as I've said, had always meant a great deal to me; it was a deep and very important thing. Would it be that for Bonnie too? This was no one-night stand. We had grown to like each other. Her throwing herself into my arms a few minutes before, as soon as we were free, told the story in one bright flash. It was affection as much as passion. But for the past weeks I had been using my last available calories of energy to locate a house for Holly and the girls, to keep the family close together for as long as possible. A night of Bonnie and myself in each other's arms promised a rare closeness and beauty and a release from the unremitting, fatiguing daily deprivations and struggles. In our psychiatric unit alone, we had to bed down and feed three hundred "boots" pouring in from all over the country with every conceivable variety of sore throat and respiratory infection. Ignorant of administration as I was, by great good luck I had a wonderful, intelligent, considerate staff that was easily organized and got the job not only done but done well. But while a man, at least one like me, deeply needs a mate for change, diversion, recreation and support, how could I go to bed with Bonnie and then five days later with my own wife?

There seemed to be much that I wanted to say to Bonnie, but no opportunity presented itself. There was really nothing to say after all; she had given me a great deal of what I needed, and apparently asked for nothing. I can only hope that she did get a little something of value from me. Certainly I gave her respect, esteem, affection and sexual interest, although inhibited. As nearly as I could see, she was the daughter—the only daughter, the pride and joy—of a poor hill farm family. Perhaps she had some thoughts of socioeconomic improvement, but I hate to think that; she seemed so poised, so nonclimbing, a born good wife and mother deserving the best. But she was not the wife for me. Holly definitely was.

A few days later, Holly and the girls arrived. She liked the house I had located (at the cost of my last energies), and I was back in my real life again. To raise proper children, in love, security and understanding, to become mature, secure, responsible adults of good will—in other words, to form a world of security and good will—requires parents in the home who have those qualities and can do it. The war was necessary to crush the forces of complete evil, sadism and murder; but I would try to prevent its interfering with the proper formation of my home and the raising of my children. How might the world be saved from the immediate present, how might it be built better for the future, and the family still be kept as it should be?

One minor note about Clarence's wife: I introduced the couple to Holly and our girls. Almost immediately after meeting Holly, Clarence's wife mentioned Bonnie in a strange wrong way, as though I had been unfaithful to Holly and then rejected and deserted Bonnie. She seemed set on making trouble one way or another. But some kind of pointed but gentle remark came to my mind, and I said it. She subsided. Maybe she was still smarting under the hurt of the double indignity: her husband offering her to me, and then my rejecting her. I sympathized with her but simply could have no feeling for her.

Then winter shut down; gray, cloudy, bone-penetratingly damp, with ice, sleet and snow. A seventy-five-mile road patched with ice led to home—Holly and the children—and back again. That was it until my plank was floated. Everyone got sick with the flu before March except me; but when I did go down, I went hardest—I barely survived. I lost twenty pounds off my frail frame of 138. I recovered and finished out the war, but at a price; for never again in my life did I regain that pristine, vital energy and stamina. The elastic had been overstretched. That is yet another reason why I feel so grateful for being active and productive and even having sexual feelings in my mid-seventies. The price of it has been taking close care, diet, exercise, ample sleep at night and a nap after lunch every day. The price, though, is negligible for the wellbeing.

I remembered the idea that sex is a surplus. I could see the logic then, but now I can tell you that I have actually experienced it. I took Holly and the children to the train, carrying their luggage through three or four cars in haste. I made it off the train exhausted and walked up to the hospital to turn in sick; there was no choice. I was utterly exhausted, and my previously normal blood pressure was up to about 190 over 114. A pretty nurse whom I knew showed me to a bed on the second floor, which I walked up to with my bag. With my last bit of energy I threw myself on the bed on my back, and that very second the full pressure of the sex drive, which I had been forced to hold under maximal control since the onset of orgasms at age thirteen or fourteen, precipitously dropped off. I was aware of the pretty and friendly nurse, but suddenly there was no sharp, clean, barely controllable drive toward her. What is more, I could perceive that she herself felt its absence in me. I could tell by that certain relaxation, that lack of tension in response to me, that I had never experienced before. I was a lump, with sexual feelings surviving but no longer constantly fighting erections. The electricity was gone. Fortunately, it wasn't gone totally, and not forever. Slowly and after many months, some oozed back. After the war Holly and I had good sex and a perfectly wonderful third daughter, who was worth everything. But the original zip never returned completely. Hence I entered my seventies with some potency but far from full. Yet the warmth and feelings for the women of my choice have continued, as have some of their feelings for me. After all, anything at more than three score and ten years, if one is in good basic health, must be a blessing. It seems to me that the centrally basic thing in life is to "feel good" mentally, emotionally and physically.

The infection was so severe that I was in a coma for a few days, after which I was transferred to a well-equipped, well-staffed hospital in a large medical center. When it was nearly time for me to return to duty after the illness, my weight was still nearly twenty pounds too low, and I did not know if I had the strength or endurance. Another medical officer and his wife—both handsome, intelligent, of good will, charming, in all ways superior—invited me to potluck dinner. Holly had returned home with the children; I was to get orders soon for a naval facility located nearer them. At the dinner was a "young matron" in her thirties. She was alone; her husband was off on some assignment, and her children were ensconced with close relatives. She was pleasant but not striking, not vivid, not beautiful, but rather reserved, every inch the securely married woman. Even her name was the height of propriety: Mary. She was everyday, not outstanding, but nice-looking, pleasant, easy and gracious.

She seemed to be highly moral, proper, inhibited like myself. We greeted politely, cordially, with easy propriety—no sparks, no excitement, just a nice married woman. Two cocktails and a light tasty supper, then one light highball and I had to leave. She offered to drive me and drop me on the way to her home. We had no sooner parked than she leaned over for a kiss goodnight—not romantically but in a friendly way. It was a calm, clear, windless evening with no clouds but with a roseate afterglow. Our lips met in innocence, but a turmoil, a storm, a surging flood was unexpectedly released from within. I had recovered more than I knew. I was taken by total surprise, I was overwhelmed. I said, "I wish we had met before I was sick," which was a truthful but stupid, boastful remark.

At that instant a face appeared in the window—Shore Patrol. Kindly but respectfully, he told us we were off-limits. I asked her if we could make a date for the next evening, and she unhesitatingly agreed.

Again the weather was mild and clear. Mary brought a light supper. We searched for a spot on the not-too-deserted hillside in the rays of the setting sun. Calm as the evening was, the internal climate was tense, stormy, electric. She tended in a most gentle, feminine way to take charge, and I went along with pleasure. We sat and then semireclined together, exchanging a slow expressive kiss. This time no Shore Patrol was near. Mary quietly said, "I cannot make love, much as I want to. For today I got a letter from my husband, Ed, and he trusts me so completely that I simply cannot betray him."

What could I do? I felt sure she was aroused and that I could have overcome this resistance, but I thought all the more of Mary for it. I would have felt the same, did feel the same, toward Holly. Although I must admit to having been tempted, I had no intention of going ahead with any disloyalty to Holly beyond a little necking. Now the letter from Mary's husband fully confirmed my resolve and thoroughly settled the matter. I would still look Holly straight in her honest eyes with my own eyes faithful and honest. That was worth everything. Mary was a fine girl, and I felt all the more for her. I realized that I was not made for casual light affairs that are, as some of the youth declare, "no more than having a cup of coffee together." I had no talent for adultery. We embraced though, despite the barrier's not being down, on that twilight summer hillside in the midst of a world war. Fate was permitting us—two complete strangers who would never meet again, but would never forget the moment—a time of respite, something not disloyal to our mates but still some of the sublime feeling of love, the greater and more eloquent perhaps because we were strangers and always would be. When we parted Mary said, "How can you have so much sex appeal?"

After a lifetime of living with my own lovelife—giving, wanting, receiving, blending, with frustrations and jealousies, sharing it with others and feeling it all with them—I know little about it. I suspect that, at bottom, it is the infant's basic longing for its mother, for both parents, and thus it is not only a physical sexual thing of the body but also a part of what we call the "spirit," the soul. But of course there is also the blatant, glaring sexual part that wants the physical contact, the intercourse, the orgasm. And I think some of these forces harmonize remarkably well in a good marriage but that every man and woman is, however monogamous, also in part promiscuous in inclination. For the sake of the children, if not for the conservation and direction of the energies of the wife and husband, we want stable marriages—monogamous ones. But that means a certain control over the still present promiscuous impulses. And this still leaves questions.

Is the monogamous part of an individual's personality (beyond the biological instinct which man shares with many mammals and birds) in fact largely derived from the mutual faithfulness of mother and baby as well as the child's image of its parents being faithful to each other? If so, do certain squabbles, frustrations, jealousies and infidelities between mother and father, however minor, somehow enter the child's emotional area and concept of fidelity or infidelity, and influence his behavior as an adult? And if the child was deprived of love in its earliest years and left with a sense of unsatisfied longing, or so overindulged that monogamous adult life seems forever inadequate, then is there in his marriage a residue of hunger of the soul? Does a happy, faithful, devoted, loving, securely married, basically monogamous wife or husband occasionally at the dictate of sudden unforeseeable circumstance touch hearts with another, if only for a few hours, with no unfaithfulness but just a warm exchange of love with no guilt, and is it actually beneficial to the marriage of both?

It usually takes about ten to twenty years to make a marriage fully harmonious. Holly and I were fortunate that our childhood patterns meshed so well that although we inevitably had much building of the marriage ahead of us, it went relatively smoothly and rapidly. As I look backward, the reasons seem to be chiefly these:

We learned not to criticize each other, or to do so only with great tact and gentleness; not to try to control each other; not to make demands on each other, for without the demands we each give and get much more, willingly and with love. We do not interfere with each other's freedom, which is possible because we each have complete security in the other's fidelity, loyalty and love.

It is a fine thing to set up rules to be lived by. But life is too complex for that to work, unfortunately, and defeats simple "living by the book." If children are not won over by love, as many, or more, will flout the rules as will obey them. Human nature is so diverse: there are the artists who seek beauty (including beauty in relationships) in love; and there are the scientists whose chosen career is the study of the unknown. But how is it possible effectively to command people to love, or particularly to command parents to love their children properly, with respect and sympathetic understanding? It is the only hope for the world. If love cannot be commanded, should not it and that which opposes it, at least for a start, be clarified and understood and worked toward?

Over the ages folk wisdom and the thoughts of great observers and teachers have provided us with some thoroughly sound basic rules for living. Perhaps the most basic, which appears throughout the world's great religions, is The Golden Rule, paraphrased as follows: "Do unto others as you would have others do unto you."

Christianity: All things whatsoever ye would that men should do to you, do ye even so to them: for this is the Law and the Prophets." (Matthew 7:12)

Judaism: "Thou shalt love thy neighbor as thyself. . . ." (Leviticus 19:18)

Islam: "No one of you is a believer until he desires for his brother that which he desires for himself." (Sunan)

Confucianism: "Is there one maxim which ought to be acted upon throughout one's whole life? Surely it is the maxim of loving-kindness; Do not unto others what you would not have them do onto you." (Analects 15:23)

Taoism: "Regard your neighbor's gain as your own gain, and your neighbor's loss as your own loss." (T'ai-Shang Kan-Ying P'ien)

Brahmanism: "This is the sum of duty: Do naught unto others which would cause you pain if done to you." (Mahabharata 5:1517)

There are of course many other rules, mostly derivatives of the Golden Rule. For example, in the code in which I was reared, as between the sexes, a man does not take advantage of a woman sexually if she is not fully conscious, as when she is ill or inebriated; nor does he do so when she is weakened by emotional deprivation because of stress with her parents or her husband or other misfortune. Unfortunately, people only follow or flout such rules in accordance with their childhood emotional patterns.

26
CHILDREN

As the years passed, said Corey Jones, I became more and more careful about criticizing other persons. But there is one kind of attitude and behavior that strikes me as excessively, even piggishly selfish, and often latently hostile. I suppose as a psychiatrist I should filter out my own feelings and use the more objective but too broad term "immature." At any rate, what I have in mind is the young person (usually the girl, in my experience) who announces that immediately upon marrying she wants to start having babies, and the magic number she usually chooses, for some reason, seems to be six. She then proceeds as best she can to do so. Of course what is wrong with this is that, if the marriage does not work and so many do not, it is always the children who suffer. Also, the sudden responsibilities, demands and expenses of babies often add to the strain of a marriage that might otherwise have worked out, so that the babies have less a unifying than a divisive effect, not sealing the marriage but overstraining it.

I guess I am a supreme egoist, like everybody else, because these remarks seem to imply that Holly and I very maturely discussed having children and decided to wait until we were sure that our marriage was well settled down and ready for them. This is exactly what we did in reality, but was it settled so much by our mature minds as by our instincts?

As I have related, we very definitely did not want children immediately, but we did find ourselves with a dog, a Scotty of course, who rapidly became an integral part of the family, a part of the new identity in which Holly and I lived from the time the ceremony ended. I did well enough as breadwinner for us to move into a more commodious apartment, and we reached the point of being able to laugh at our squabbles, even the infuriating ones. It was then we *felt* rather than reasoned that we wanted a child. Our love life, including sex, remained the same—perfect from my point of view—and with no delay, Holly became pregnant. This led to the next step: she now suggested that for a child it is much better to grow up in a house than an apartment. A girl of sense, practicality and action, she had located a house we could afford in a few weeks, just off the university campus. It was inelegant, second-rate, but possessed the one great virtue of being a house—and it was preeminently livable and convenient to everything. The long flight of carpeted stairs was perfect for the baby to climb up and down, the only safety for a baby being skills achieved through practice. Yet we little expected one day to come upon our firstborn, while she was still in diapers, on top of our highest bureau! How she got there we never figured out.

Recently, Holly and I discussed what each might do if the other died first. Holly is sure she would not remarry, while I thought she should if she could get the right man. Two couples had been lifelong friends of ours; one husband died suddenly at seventy, and not long thereafter the wife of the other couple died. The surviving husband and wife, both of them in their seventies, married and have had a fine life together. But Holly is an unusual girl, at least so she has always seemed to me, and the more so with the passing decades. Her intuition is acute; she told me once that she would never have consented to sex with me before marriage if she had not felt completely certain I would shortly marry her. And her judgment is remarkably accurate; years ago we were friends with a couple, and the wife, so Holly thought, seemed extremely upset. I only noted that the woman was tense, but so are a lot of people. Holly's judgment was proved correct, however, when the woman subsequently committed suicide.

Our love is still growing and deepening. I feel relaxed in the thought that if I die Holly might have an even better life in some ways than we have had together. She does not enjoy housekeeping or food shopping. She does like cooking, and we have worked out an arrangement whereby she only cooks dinner. I have long prepared my own breakfast; oatmeal, toast, occasionally an egg, milk or hot tea—no problem. She is superb at whatever she does, and her meals are simple but imaginatively super-delicious. Having reached my mid-seventies, I am receiving from her a quality of love which feels more pure and deep than ever before, and it shines in the beauty of her face. I always thought she was more dependent on me than she realized, partly because my dependence upon her was so open and on the surface. Now I believe her: she really feels that she could not love another man and, without me, would rather face existence alone—because any marriage for convenience would be unthinkable to her deep sincerity. She is purer metal than I: probably I could not live without a woman. No doubt this reveals the old childhood pattern, but the difficulty is that I cannot imagine living with any other woman I have ever met, except possibly someone who is much younger, yet I could not very well allow a much younger woman to marry me either, for her own good, even if she wanted it. I see no resolution except for both Holly and me to do what we are doing—trying to stay healthy for as long as we can for each other's sake.

The ending of Mark Twain's *Adam and Eve* has always seemed to me beautiful; and I have become able to say to Holly, "Where you are, there is Eden." But why, when Nature no longer needs us for reproduction and parenting, does it still hold us together with an ever-deepening and more gratifying love? Could it possibly be so that we can continue to be parents and grandparents to our children and their families?

From the birth of Julie, and then Ann and then Tressa, I shared in their feedings, diaper changing, bathing and night feedings. Many years later a friend of mine said he never felt that his children were really his until he did those things, and his remark struck a resonance in me. It seemed so true. I did those things naturally because I loved them all so, from the moment of birth or rather from conception; and because I did those things, they became closer to me.

The intensity of the love I felt for my first child, Julie, increased with the passing months and her own development. One afternoon when she was about eighteen months old, I saw her half-walk, half-climb up the front two or three steps of our old house, on those firm sturdy little legs, and I felt that I loved her so much that it must be impossible for me properly to love another child if, as we hoped, we had another. Shortly after that moment I realized that the very intensity of the love for the first and only child can make problems, if this emotional charge which the parents feel is too intense and if there is only one child to absorb it all. Just because of our love for Julie, for her own sake, we should have a second.

I had expected Julie to be a boy and felt some disappointment that she was not. But this was only a perceptible flicker in the joy of a first baby's arrival. I knew, and Holly agreed, that one must be grateful for having a healthy baby with all its fingers and toes, as they say, and not quibble over its sex. Before long I felt just the opposite—I was closer to a girl, and agreed with the old saying, "A son is a son till he takes a wife, but a daughter is a daughter all your life." That is how it has worked out for us; we have lost no daughters but have gained three fine beloved sons and, in time, nine grandchildren.

Why, then, would I have initially preferred a son? Maybe it is part of the old egotism, so colossal and so inescapable in everyone: a desire for something that is closest to a projection of oneself, that will fulfill what one has failed to do or be, but still aspires to. Also, I know from my patients that many or most (statistics are lacking) dream of small children who represent an infantile part of themselves. A baby can be a temptation, for besides the biological instinct to parent the child, the parent also wishes to give the child what the adult still wants for himself such as more tender loving care than this hard, dangerous world can be counted upon to provide. Of course, as with marriage and life and health, all did not proceed idyllically for Holly and me.

Our second child, Ann, had a serious illness in babyhood and we gave her, to save her life, more attention than we would otherwise have done. That was hard on Julie. She was then four, but it seems we failed to make clear to her the reason for our turning so much love and attention away from her to Ann. Perhaps it could not have been done better, perhaps she was too young at four or five to understand, but I think we failed in some degree. This left certain character traits in Julie, not all bad, for she was basically loved. To some extent she became more independent because of surmounting the sibling jealousy intensified by Ann's illness. All this was doubly difficult for the family because I was still in the Navy, and the war was still on.

I felt sure that by the laws of chance our third child would be a boy, but it was also a girl—Tressa. She was the only one born in settled times. The war was over, I was settling into my career of practice, teaching and writing. Remember, I started with an interest in science and scientific research, especially physics, and later neurophysiology, and could think of myself as a researcher; and to some extent, I always have been so, in spirit and outlook if not in discoveries and achievements.

Tressa was over nine pounds at birth, warm, cuddly, happy, and she just "growed." It seemed she required no care or attention, and I can hardly believe that we walked the floor with her almost nightly because of colic, until magically at six months the colic ceased and she became the tranquil, placid self we have known since. We love Julie the best because she was our firstborn and, after she weathered the sibling situation, the most active athletically and intellectually. We love Ann the best because she surmounted what seemed like insuperable difficulties, and in her quiet way she has been an inspiration to all of us. And we love Tressa best because she simply joined the family and grew up so stable and steady, loving us and loved by us. With Tressa we came full cycle, as the expression goes, and began adding dogs to the family again, plus cats. The first dog was a boxer. After she died, we had two dogs, both half-collie and half-German shepherd. There was a series of cats during this time; both dogs died at age twenty of a sort of Hodgkin's disease with greatly enlarged glands. The first cat was Siamese—young and beautiful—who came whining to our kitchen door through the snow on a bitterly cold night in the dead of winter, pregnant. Of course at Eastertime we tried rabbits, but rats entered the scene and beat the rabbits to their food; so they had to go. But then we could afford a series of very inexpensive mongrel horses, on condition that each daughter take the entire responsibility for her own horse—of feeding, grooming, shoveling out its stall, etc. They were a great success and we got out of it with only one broken leg, incurred when Ann was quietly astride her gelding and he was stung by a bee.

For us, the pleasure in the children increased steadily as they matured, and now that they have families of their own, it is still increasing. The grandchildren are a profound pleasure, and it is always great to see them. If geography and our own stamina permitted us to help more with the upbringing of the grandchildren, we would be closer to them. But there are limits to how much the best grandparents in the world can or should help, or even be present, in new families. Holly and I agreed when we were first married that we would raise our own children in our own way, and allow no interference by her parents or mine. Happily, this determination was as unnecessary as it was correct, for both sets of grandparents were completely understanding, never intrusive or interfering and only helpful and loving. We have tried to be the same toward our children and grandchildren. It is not always easy. One little grandson, in all ways a delight, was an irregular eater and we were concerned for his nutrition. I found myself feeling his biceps to get over to him the point that he must eat proper food to be well and strong, not just food he liked but food that was *good* for him—it was terrible! I still feel ashamed and reproach myself. Happily he and I have remained good friends, but it was awful of me to try to influence him instead of just loving him as he was. At least I did catch myself and corrected what I was doing. But this showed me how such a tendency to interfere can creep in. Of course it struck one of my own specific emotional vulnerabilities, my own light weight.

To lecture and moralize to the young is quite apt to reveal the parents' vulnerabilities. Rather than improving the children it gives them something against which to rebel. So I have always tried to say as little as possible to my three daughters, confining this little to pointing out the pertinent realities and risks. When the girls left home for college the gist of my comments to each one privately was:

You have been living at home where your mother and I are always available to you, love you, are on your side no matter what, and where your happiness and satisfaction in life is the main purpose of *our* lives. Now you are going out into the world, which is very different. You will meet very few people who care about your welfare, and few who care about their own. The alcoholics will insist that you drink with them; the insomniacs will insist that you stay up most of the night because they do; the negligent will pressure you to be less conscientious about your work. The boys and some of the girls will try every method of seduction to get you to have sex with them. Listen to all but keep true to your own good sense and judgment. Never let yourself be pressured into anything by threats to your vanity, such as being called "chicken" or "afraid to take a dare." Remember what my friends and I learned on the streets long before we were fifteen: "Only a fool takes a dare."

Careless college athletes are apt to get injuries that trouble or even handicap them for life. You can make mistakes in youth that trouble or even handicap you emotionally for life. Don't let anyone break down or cloud your own good sense. If you have the least question or doubt about anything whatever, phone us collect at any time of the day or night and we will talk it over with you. For now you will not have us physically with you to care for you; you are in charge. We know you can do a good job. And however good a job you do, there will still be plenty of adventures and dangers.

One last word; remember that good health is the basis of everything in life; take the best care of yours.

It has seemed to me that women who were never out in the world and never had to support themselves might never mature fully; what one *does* has so much to do with what one *is*. I was concerned for our girls as they grew to maturity. Tressa married the year before graduating from college. When her husband, quite early in his career, was sent to Europe for two weeks by his company, we assisted Tressa financially so she could accompany him. In one letter she wrote us that she was walking about Paris alone, while her husband was occupied with business. For the first time she felt real independence, walking alone in a foreign city, barely acquainted with the language. Tressa had three children and planned no more. Caring for them has been an enormous job, with two in diapers at the same time, a house to supervise and business worries to share with her husband. It does seem to have matured her, but she confesses to looking forward to that day when the three children are in school and she will have more time to herself, to start her own career in writing. That is Tressa's solution: children first and then career. Ann, our middle daughter, matured in part by overcoming the handicaps of her illness, which occurred at four months and kept her between life and death till the age of seven, preventing her from taking part in all the activities of her peers, physical, mental and emotional, making her an outsider and scapegoat for some years thereafter. Her golden hair turned raven black, but her eyes remained deep blue. She definitely wanted a domestic life and has a good marriage and two children. Before the children arrived she helped out financially by door-to-door selling. I think it was largely because of our unalloyed love that she survived, as well as her determination in the face of delayed development; and all the obstacles the illness caused have been an inspiration to us, for she has surmounted them all.

Our firstborn has been most aware of Women's Lib. Julie once told me, "I wish I had known to plan a career . . . the atmosphere in college was, 'If you do not get married when you graduate, you are a failure.'"

"But," I answered her, "you have your husband and your children and are also working and earning. What would you do differently today?"

She replied, "I am not sure of what I would have done differently, but it would have been *different*." She continued, "I would have planned a career and prepared myself for it, and not felt that I had to marry at graduation." I reflected that Julie was a wonderful person, wife and mother, and had wonderful children, and although she had taken a different route she *had* reached the same point, combining family and career. She could do so in part because of her vitality, which she preserved by the enjoyable activities of tennis and swimming (the combination I myself had for so many years before slowing down to golf).

One need be no psychiatrist, certainly, to see all around him the difficulties people have in handling all aspects of their sex lives and love lives. It seems that the whole reproductive procedure when it goes well affords humans the ultimate in pleasure and satisfaction, but when it goes badly, it causes the ultimate in emotional suffering. I still think that Freud's greatest contribution was the discovery of the dynamic unconscious, of the fact that most of what goes on in the emotional life never reaches conscious awareness. Freud's early emphasis on the importance of sex in human life was not so far off the mark as it first seemed, for he used the term "sex" broadly to include, I believe, what I have just said: *the entire process* of attraction and reproduction.

I think of myself as a sociological unit: the course of my life has been like that of most, I believe. The first thin, wavering, uncertain line of the first awareness of attraction to females, developing very gradually, became the strong firm line of unwavering devotion to Holly and the children. It was clearly repetitive of the original strong, unwavering love and devotion to my parents and sister in response to their love for me. And now I hope that this strong line of love will continue through the lives of our grandchildren.

Somerset Maugham, a writer whose insights into people continue to amaze me, stressed that a story should proceed in one firm line from a beginning through a middle to an end. Aren't there lives that also proceed just like those stories? And is it not our goal as psychiatrists to restore the progress of the line of each patient's life, and also so far as possible, through adding to science and its applications, to give every child that parental love which it needs to make that strong, steady line of its own in sex, love, family life, work and social life?

27

PROFESSION

. . . it will be difficult to escape what is universally known; it will rather be a question of new ways of looking at things and new ways of arranging them than of new discoveries.

Sigmund Freud,
New Introductory Lectures in Psychoanalysis

. . . having lived long, I have experienced many instances of being obliged by better information or fuller consideration to change opinions, even on important subjects, which I once thought right but found to be otherwise. It is therefore that the older I grow the more apt I am to doubt my own judgment and to pay attention to the judgment of others. Most men, indeed, as well as most sects in religion think themselves in possession of all truth. . . .

Carl Van Doren,
Benjamin Franklin

Among the good fortunes of my life was my being trained in psychoanalysis at one of the few institutes that valued openmindedness, originality and freedom of investigation and thought. Also, the faculty and students were, like the playmates of my childhood, of variegated backgrounds. Happily, my own inheritance, religious instruction and first peer group all left me as free from prejudice as I think one can be. But the sense of being a sort of chosen people, which was held by some of those psychoanalysts who had been trained by Freud himself and who felt they were the only true apostles in a hostile world, was antithetical to my nature, both when I was a student and later when I worked with those particular people as a colleague. Some rigidity in thinking must be expected even in the precision sciences, and much more of it in this very new, abstract emotional field of the study of human beings.

American psychoanalysis well into the thirties was a relatively indigenous, exciting new potential science, free from thought control.

Every fact or theory could be exposed to free criticism and evaluation. But with the rise of Hitler, the very lives of the European analysts were in jeopardy, especially as most of them were Jewish, in spite of Freud's efforts to develop a mixed leadership. American analysts all contributed to a fund to bring to this country those European analysts who wished to emigrate. A few who did were grateful, but many of them repeated in intensified form the attitudes of George the Third and the British political leadership, namely, that this was a barbarous country compared with Europe, and they, coming from proximity with Freud himself, were called upon to bring his "light" to the heathen. Although there were many fine men and women among them, a few were arrogant beyond anything I had ever seen except in films of the very oppressors they were fleeing; and like the Nazis, they sought power—in fact, nothing less than the taking over of the whole of official American psychoanalysis.

In part, their motives were pure; they were fervently sincere in their sense of mission. When America entered World War II, most American analysts went into the armed services. During their absence, these European refugees successfully gained control of the American Psychoanalytic Association and of almost all the local institutes. Their influence was prolonged because they did most of the personal analyses, required of every student as the first major step in training. Most students identify so strongly with their analysts that they carry on their analysts' ideas. After the war, some of the Americans returning from service found that they had been ousted from their positions by the refugee analysts, who formed the "education committees" which ran the institutes and which appointed the training analysts. Although I was no political leader, I did try to form a group of scientific-minded analysts within the American Psychoanalytic Association by organizing those I knew to be so inclined; they were mostly leaders in universities. But depleted and exhausted as I was after returning from the Navy, not yet recovered from a severe infection, I began to lose my physical energies; no one else took over, and control of the association remained in the hands of the "orthodox," who had several more votes. Eventually others solved the conflict by splitting off as a new national organization, which I supported as best I could. Hopefully it will soon sponsor its own training facilities with a good scientific outlook and base.

As an example of the atmosphere within the orthodox structure of the association, I am reminded of the attempt to schedule a meeting of prominent leaders of the liberals and the orthodox to try to reach some amicable agreement. One eminent leader from the orthodox group rose at once, poker-straight, and proclaimed, "I will come to the meeting and I will listen, but I will never change my mind, never!" Of course the words "liberal" and "orthodox" were never official, but they were accurate enough descriptively to serve. It was science *versus* religion.

The truly great discoveries by Freud—that most of what goes on in our minds is unconscious; that dreams have meaning which can be interpreted, thereby providing a "royal road" to one's unconscious, to all the interplays of feelings, motivations and reactions—these initiated the new science of psychodynamics. One cannot criticize a scientist for what he does *not* contribute, but can only appreciate what he has done. Perhaps even the rigidity about the purity of psychoanalysis was justified *at that time* for the cohesiveness and survival of a new field.

In striving for scientific freedom I have made many close, loyal, good friends and now they are old comrades, who fought together to keep American psychoanalysis scientific. My patients and students have been an unalloyed pleasure and, with rare exceptions, totally free of the sort of dogmatism and rigidity I have been discussing. This may be so because, in general, it takes a superior person to want an analysis, which means facing himself with total emotional honesty. Being limited in time and energy, I took only those students whom I thought would be future leaders. So difficult is psychoanalysis that many of its students never really master it.

The great virtue of psychoanalysis and also its complication is that it is both a method of psychotherapy and also a research method of investigating the human mental and emotional life. As treatment, it is lengthy and expensive, which makes it a luxury. In suitable patients its efficacy is miraculous—it makes possible those shifts in the personality that provide a whole new emotional atmosphere and freedom and a new life. But not everyone is analyzable. Some are unable to develop a transference of feelings toward the analyst or to work through their resistance. This the analyst should try to determine as quickly as possible. Also, psychoanalysis is fascinating but confusing, for it is partly a science and partly a humanity. Its therapy rests on its understanding of each individual. But the need for therapy is enormous—adults are mostly the frightened, frustrated, selfish, angry children they once were; and I would guess that eighty to ninety percent of our citizens are oppressed with severe and painful emotional problems. To answer this need, dozens if not hundreds of "therapies" have developed, some sincere, some sheer quakery, most of them based upon isolated fragments of psychoanalysis and psychodynamics.

This is 1977, and technology has changed the mechanics of life. In four hours you can cross the country from the Atlantic to the Pacific Ocean in an airplane so steady that a cocktail rests without a quiver on the arm of your seat. But psychologically our times at this Bicentennial strongly resemble Judea of 75 B.C., and in some ways 3000 B.C. For there are hundreds of "therapies," each with its "savior" offering "The Way" and "The Life." The psychoanalytic is mixed with Eastern religions. We have primal scream therapy and groups, transcendental meditation, encounter groups, sensitivity training . . . literally hundreds of such self-help groups exist. The best of them, consciously or unconsciously, take some fragment or facet of psychodynamic reality and try to build a whole system on that fragment. For example, scream therapy uses chiefly the abreaction of anger. Some encounter groups seek to break down difficulties in interrelating with other persons, others to free inhibitions in sexual feelings and relations; one form of sensitivity training concentrates chiefly on the realization of responsibility for anger, another on popular terms for Freud's Id, Superego and Ego, and so on and on. Many of these offerings mushroom in a few weeks into businesses that gross from one to ten million dollars a year. What is significant is not the "system" that is offered but the enormity of the need in our population for help with emotional suffering—a need so great that it often sweeps away all reason and sense of reality even in the highly intelligent. The therapies of today offer instant maturity, instant peace of mind, instant relief from suffering. It is psychological snake oil touted to cure everything. That is why it is reminiscent of 3000 B.C., of Jacob's ladder leading directly up from the hard stones to heaven and to God. Just climb straight up this ladder, brother! for only $170 or $500 or $2,500—you can do it in a few evenings, or a few weekends!

Now I have spent nearly fifty years studying individuals and myself; I believe that in reality instant cure is impossible. The best of these therapies does no more than provide an experience that may be valuable for some persons but is dangerous for others, and in any event deals with no more than a fragment or facet of the personality. The wild enthusiasm of the recent converts is part of the human tendency to proselytize, released in people as a way of abreacting their feelings. It was well recognized in the early days of psychoanalysis and led to the advice given the patient not to talk about his or her analysis, neither for nor against, until it was well advanced. The positiveness of new converts to these "therapies" and their prophets is usually well described as "the dogmatism of ignorance."

The truth—that is, reality in both a physical and psychological sense—is hard to know. Much of psychological reality in oneself and others is too painful for many of us to face. The sense of reality is one of the most precious but also one of the most sensitive and delicate of the human capacities. That is why genius sometimes can be but a step from the mad house. I studied chemistry and physics as an undergraduate and in graduate school before entering medical school. It is esthetically balanced and beautiful and, like any form of art, a gratifying escape from the turmoil, pain and anxiety in the mental and emotional life, about which I still feel we know very little. But in truth a little *is* known; it is this little which is our salvation. It will come (if indeed there is such a salvation in our biological destiny) through understanding the realities of the human mental and emotional life. In the long run, the only rational treatment must rest on science, as "Nut" Beech defined science in high school for me, a lifetime ago: "Exact, systematized, classified knowledge." That is why I am interested in psychodynamics, the study of the interplay of emotional forces in the mind, conscious and unconscious, and that is why I write articles and books on the subject.

The fact that most psychoanalysts, especially the early ones, have had backgrounds in the humanities has influenced the development of the field, and occasioned problems with those like myself who have had some training in the precision sciences.

During the few years of my own professional life, roughly from 1930 to the present (1977), psychoanalysis, in spite of all the elements of orthodoxy, control and cultism, has emerged from a narrow isolation almost limited to Freud's writings and that of a few intimate followers into the second generation of the knowledge of psychodynamics, which has permeated psychiatry, psychology and the social sciences and brought psychoanalysts into contact with all related fields.

My own early clinical writing was of short papers describing observations on patients that seemed to me to be of some interest and possible value in increasing dynamic understanding. As I have emphasized, all during late childhood and young adulthood I felt that I was deficient in understanding people and life. The garageman and the small shopkeeper seemed more independent in life and more understanding of people than I. Much of my life has been devoted to trying to understand better. College chemistry started me on this path to understanding, and the search has been a main theme of my entire orientation, professional and personal: to understand, in the faith that knowledge is power and that eventually the truth will make us free (if *anything* will). Such success as I have had in helping my patients has been with the orientation that the only rational therapy must be based upon *understanding the patient.* This aim led me into psychodynamics, which in my mind and feeling is rather like physics—an interplay of emotional forces instead of electromagnetic or gravitational forces. I still enjoy reading physics, and sometimes get away from it all by reading physics books in the evening instead of short stories, my usual fare.

I wrote some observations while in the Navy in reaction to professional experiences in those duties. Probably that is what a writer is: one who uses writing to express himself, his tensions, his feelings, one who reports his experiences. It becomes a form of self-expression and of abreaction in living, and, surprisingly, I found myself writing in this way. But I have only been able to do it descriptively, having no talent whatever for fictionalizing.

My own psychoanalysis bore fruit in my later being able to feel confident in leadership positions and to write. But it took nearly twenty years for me to feel this way about myself. At age fifty I attended a meeting of the board of a national organization; we were looking for someone to set up and run a large project. Before long the group turned to me, and at first I agreed. Suddenly it struck me: "You really *can* do it," and that feeling altered my image of myself. At last, unexpectedly, I had achieved a conscious identification with my father. I knew it was true, I *could* do it as well as or better than any of the eminent men in that room. From that moment I achieved a new confidence in myself. After thinking it over, I declined the offer to run the project; I did not want to take my time and energy from practice, teaching and writing. The president reassured me: "You are right not to accept. You don't need the publicity and the honor, and your life is already full and productive enough. For you this would be only an added chore." Thus it was not until age fifty that I really began to "find myself." From that moment it progressed quickly, and I began to evaluate more objectively and I think, correctly, myself and my abilities and shortcomings and my place in the world. It was, as usual, part of one's *responsibilities:* I felt an *identity* as a practitioner with a scientific outlook for observation, study, evaluation, formulation, therapy and publication, and an identity in the home as husband and father with the attendant responsibilities of providing love and financial security. I was reaching a degree of maturity and adjustment at last.

It had taken five years to find my career; it had taken over ten years to find my mate; it had taken until age fifty to find myself.

Dynamic psychiatry, the study of the development and interplay of emotional forces in each patient and the use of this for treatment, just fitted my own dynamics with my interests in science and in people. There may be nothing like the chase and the love of women, but marriage to Holly more than satisfied the desire for the chase. I was always a hard worker and fortunately seemed to know the importance of carrying the responsibilities on two fronts, the professional and the domestic. In the early years of learning my profession I worked all day seeing patients and most evenings, reading the pertinent literature; but I also knew the importance of the relation to Holly and the vital importance of being a father and husband for the development of the children. Those Saturdays when we worked all day at the Psychoanalytic Institute, Holly and the other wives would join us at about seven o'clock, and we would all go out for dinner. Some of us formed an "explorers club" to try a new restaurant each time. When I attended out-of-town meetings, we usually made secure arrangements for the children, and Holly accompanied me. In the early years, Holly's mother lived with us, and we could leave the children in her superb care. Sundays were reserved strictly for the family. Saturday afternoons that I did not work, Holly and I spent golfing (which we never took seriously until I gave up tennis for golf at age fifty-six), returning home for dinner with the children. I was home for dinner by 6:00 or 6:30 every night in the week—all this barring emergencies. Although I have said a lot about my development through relationships with women, it is true that the single greatest factor in growth to maturity is responsibility, professional and domestic. Ironically, when I wrote a paper on this subject, pointing out the disregard in the literature of such an essential capacity and its variations as seen clinically, the paper was rejected as not being in the "mainstream of psychoanalysis," which was exactly the point: something so fundamental *had* been neglected. The hour-to-hour, daily responsibility for the mental health of my patients and the overall responsibility for my family in my case constituted the great maturing force.

I would define maturity in this way:

Maturity consists largely of responsibility, and mental health consists of maturity with adjustment. Freud is said to have defined it concisely as "the ability to work and to love." This definition is indeed correct. Maturity requires *responsibility* in loving as well as in working. Recovering mental health is often identical with regaining the ability to work and to love. (And Roazen adds to these the ability to "play.") It is tragic when a person loathes his work and does it only for the money. If a person enjoys his work, it is a punishment if he *cannot* do it. Absence of productive, responsible work is a poor way of life and a poor goal for retirement. Responsible work is a great stabilizer through life's viscissitudes: "keep busy and keep useful." Work is a track on which we can run without being blown off course by every foul wind of life. It includes the very difficult task of a mother in tending her children.

As I took more responsibility, I became more and more interested in my profession, and such interest in something other than oneself is also an important element of maturity. More daily, more pedestrian, less adventurous than relations with women, the interest in my home and patients and responsibility for them both led me gradually ("rung by rung" as the poet said) to such understanding of people and such maturity as I have achieved. In the process it has molded a life style for me so that, despite my more than seventy-five years, and some limitations of health, I still deeply love. This deep love, rather than any single incident, has been my enduring happiness.

Out of my experiences with work and love I have concluded the obvious: that people's cruelty to each other is the central problem of our species; that it is mostly a reaction to mistreatment of children, especially from conception until about the age of six or seven, by which time the basic emotional patterns have been mostly laid down and ingrained in their personalities. Hence crime, war and other violence are surely preventable if we can only get children properly raised with good feelings toward their family members, especially their parents; for those feelings they will carry toward others for life. This conclusion, which I believe has been widely tested and proved true, is my *raison d'être*, and (as I view it) my life will have achieved its purpose in contributing it. It was when Benjamin Franklin perceived the rising hostility of the English and of the colonies that he wrote of the unreasonableness of angry nations and began to give up hope for the growth of America within the British Empire, for which he had labored so sedulously during his eleven years in London.

What greater success, what greater happiness, what greater satisfaction is there than to keep one's health, keep one's wife and children healthy and reasonably happy and satisfied, to see one's children and grandchildren turn out well and to contribute, however infinitesimally, to science, i.e., man's systematic, permanent knowledge and understanding, and especially to an understanding of the greatest cause of man's suffering, namely his own hostile feelings and behavior toward his own kind.

Some authors have plunged into the lowest depths of society for their material, others have prowled the ends of the earth for it, but no sooner did I have an office than I could indeed "stay at home and see the world." Not that I could fully appreciate this at the time, for I was struggling too hard to understand my patients and help them. The work of analytic therapy, based upon understanding the dynamics of each patient, was too demanding and too difficult, and the anxiety about earning enough for Holly and me and finding some security during the Great Depression while reading and studying this new field prevented me from calm observation of the pieces of life that each patient represented. It was some years before such observation was possible for me. But I did achieve it within ten years. So difficult is this field of understanding each person's unconscious that many never master it.

It is easier now to perceive the richness of these samples of human life than it was at the time. I remember my first patients vividly, although not the exact sequence in which they came. A successful businessman was the first patient who paid me the large fee in those days of five dollars a visit, five days a week. He could well afford it, and he was the first patient from whom I felt easy accepting it. While still considering starting, he said to me, "I am Catholic, and I do not want to do anything that will change my religious feelings." I explained, "I will only point out to you the truth of your feelings, whatever they might turn out to be—about anyone and anything—for analytic therapy is simply emotional honesty. The analyst's private thoughts and feelings play no part whatever. I can only interpret a patient's true feelings to himself; I cannot predict what these feelings are." (Today I usually can, and discuss this in the first two or three meetings.)

In his first hour of free associating, this man blasted the Pope and went into a rage at "having to genuflect." This reaction really had nothing to do with the Pope, but repeated his rebellion to a tyrannical father and a tyrannical mother, and was stirred up by his starting therapy because he saw me as an authority figure in that same pattern. I felt so immature, a rank amateur in this new field, that it was inconceivable to me that anyone, let along a middle-aged, experienced, sophisticated, successful businessman, could react to me as an authority! Slowly, as I learned and achieved some proficiency as an analyst, I felt some ascendancy in the office: but it was many more years before I felt independence and authority in life. Active duty in the Navy for the four war years accelerated this independence greatly, although at the price of undermined health, the aftermath of a near fatal infection.

Another early patient was a normally attractive young woman of twenty-four. She had married at eighteen; her husband was an energetic man a few years older. Although both seemed in perfect, vigorous health, she did not become pregnant until her tubes were blown out. At last the great day came. She returned from the hospital with a bouncing baby daughter, both of them pink and healthy. It was the happiest day of her life. But at that point her husband announced that he no longer loved her and had no interest whatever in "the kid." I asked them both to come in, and to the wife's surprise the husband, who had withdrawn totally, came with her. He claimed that it had been years since he had felt any love for his wife, but he had lacked the courage to tell her until now. Why now? He admitted that he had another woman. He did not like being married and was leaving. The selfishness was almost unbelievable. To marry a girl, have a baby with her and then, in cold blood, abandon both was heinous. As an analyst, however, I could not permit myself moral outrage. My job was to perceive the truth, to find the reasons for this. The husband was willing to come to see me for one visit by himself, and the visit was revealing: by use of free association, dream interpretation and first memories in ways that I felt sure he could not malinger, it turned out that he had never been close to anyone in his life, going all the way back to earliest childhood, not even to his mother. My moral outrage turned to the clinical realization of how very sick this man was. His wife came to see me alone also. I told her I thought her husband was withdrawn, but that from one visit I could not be sure; yet she was in love with him in spite of everything and wanted to do what was possible to save the marriage. She would come to see me further, but he was adamant against any more visits for himself. Using the same analytic techniques I had employed with the husband, I found that the wife seemed to have had normally warm, good relationships with her family and others since birth. We decided on a policy of watchful waiting. She phoned me a week later to say that her husband seemed better for the weekend. But ten days later he swore at her with obscenities, and when she pointed out that their daughter would need a male figure in her life, he callously said, "Oh, let the kid be a lesbian."

After this ghastly evening the wife decided she no longer had a choice and was best out of the marriage to such a man. Now all the support she had internalized from being a loved child sustained her, and her depression in reaction to the husband's semipsychotic behavior was transformed into fighting spirit. As usual, the complication was her child. The wife had the spunk to go out and find a job and make her own way, but she knew how important it was for the baby's development to have its mother close for the first three months, and even the first six years. She did not want to place her daughter in a day-care center even if she could find a suitable one. I saw that, for the conscientious analyst, practice would not be easy; I glimpsed something of man's hostility to man; and I began to understand the difficulties of marriage. About then I read Freud's remark: "People try to love each other, but cannot."

In any case, this patient would still need emotional support and guidance but, so far as I could see, not systematic psychoanalysis, at this point. So I referred her to an excellent, experienced social worker with whom I would be in close communication and whom she could see regularly. The social worker in turn would refer her to a lawyer if need be to learn her legal rights and position. This wife would have a hard road, but she was a loved child and would come through, I felt certain, probably making a good marriage the next time, although it was too soon for her even to think of that. I only hoped the baby's emotional needs could be satisfactorily met in the meantime.

This experience taught me early that I must be realistic and flexible and that not everyone who came for help was to be persuaded to lie on the couch five days a week and be analyzed. Also, it was only the first example of a long series of husbands who reacted violently to the birth of their first child. Before long, I had seen many who reacted by becoming alcoholics, or by escaping into the armed forces, and many who ran from wife and child into the arms of another woman. Life is indeed full of dependent hostile men.

I saw many seniors in college who went into states of withdrawal when faced with graduation and making their way in the "big, bad world." From them I learned that I was not the only young man who found the mastery of a profession and the achievement of security, emotional and financial, a strenuous struggle. I was a loved child and had the confidence and optimism and fighting spirit for it.

Like myself, every analyst continues to learn from his patients so long as he practices. Neither the analyst nor anybody else is ever "completely" analyzed. One is fortunate if his analysis reveals the *main* dynamics, the main forces in his childhood emotional pattern, so that he can continue to learn about himself and thereby continue to mature by dealing with some of his emotional problems consciously.

I would like to give an example of my routine in the course of a typical week. In those days, I worked from 8:30 A.M. until 5:30 P.M., with twenty minutes between appointments to write notes on each session. This routine was interrupted a few times a week by research and teaching seminars, in which I heard the patients of other analysts discussed by the senior staff. It was intensified learning, in fact, too much to describe at length here. We just lived in the unconscious, our own in our personal training analyses, and the unconscious of the patients we treated or heard discussed. Each one was dramatic; I have always regretted my inability to turn them into short stories. But it is no small satisfaction to be able to write about them professionally and scientifically. I do not really desire to write fiction, which always seems to me to express feelings and conflicts of the author. His characters, whatever they are to start with, soon become projections of the author's own strong feelings, mostly unconscious. My wish is to report with scientific accuracy, clarity and simplicity. It is only the sense of drama which I feel for almost every patient that I cannot convey with the impact I feel. Perhaps drama and science are incompatible, and that is why we are more apt to be inspired to weep or be otherwise moved emotionally by fiction than by reality.

At any rate, I am grateful to the analysis with you, said Corey, for helping me to so freely write professional articles and books. It comes in part from my identifying with you and your constant stream of writings.

28
THE DYNAMICS OF ·HAPPINESS

We look before and after,
And pine for what is not;
Our sincerest laughter
With some pain is fraught;
Our sweetest songs are those that tell of saddest thought.

Percy Bysshe Shelley,
"To a Skylark"

I think, said Corey Jones, that so far my life has been happier than most, but how can one know about anything so subjective?

The negative side of happiness must be freedom from psychic and physical pain. But is there positive happiness beyond freedom from suffering? Yes, I think so. It is probably different for each of us, depending on our desires. I asked a close friend for his idea of happiness and he replied almost unhesitatingly, "Freedom from responsibility." He was sincere and to an extent he was correct, for some people at some times. I immediately thought of Holly when we were on vacations. One of my happiest memories (I'm sure it was also one of the happiest for Holly) was of our playing golf together. I have always tried to keep the two-month academic vacations of my school years, and eventually came to vacation at a simple, inexpensive place in mountain foothills. We did not mind the rather crude accommodations, much preferring to spend our money on long vacations. We always recoiled from plush surroundings and tipping anyway. After a morning of golf together with friends, usually another couple, I would go directly into the cold pool and emerge in a glow. And there on the porch would be Holly, usually having a beer with friends before showering and changing for lunch, with a glowing smile, which satisfied my soul.

Part of this light of happiness that Holly had was derived from the freedom she felt from responsibility—not having to plan, cook and serve meals; knowing that we would go in and eat fresh farm food country-style and that she could relax over her coffee and cigarette for as long as she desired, and go right back up on the hill if she wished under a gold and azure mountain sky, with no concern or responsibility for dinner; and this was all with congenial friends of many years, who felt the same way. It was a sort of heaven for her. And for me, too—for a while.

I cannot stand prolonged idleness with only golf, swimming, sunbathing and chatting. After a while, like my father before me, I do not know what to do with myself and find myself starting some kind of work, usually writing, during that rather blank period before lunch or before or right after dinner. True, I would like a somewhat lighter schedule than I have carried all my life, but my need is for balance—not too much work, but also not too much leisure. A light routine, as I get older, seems the ideal. Also, I like to do that work which I feel like doing, free of compulsion. It is a pleasure to write in the evenings when the day's work is done and all correspondence or phone calls are taken care of. Thus my desires may differ from those of my friends, and what each of us might want for happiness in life would also differ. But it seems to me that there are many different kinds and levels of happiness. What would you say if someone asked you, "What were the happiest moments in your life?"

The happiest moment in my life is surprising: my oldest daughter, then still in college and unmarried, was with us at the shore. She and I were in the surf, which we both love as only those do who have a deep primitive love for the sea. We were just beyond most of the breakers. We rode the swells, but every few minutes a huge wave would break just where we were or a little bit farther out, and we had to dive under it. I would yell to her, "Watch out, here comes one!" Or she would yell to me. And we would be lifted skyward on the mighty swell, or with a "Here we go!" we would dive into the hollow curve of the comber or under the boiling foam of white water if it surprised us by breaking out farther than the rest. What I remember most vividly are these moments with both of us together, so alive, so happy.

I think of Byron's "Apostrophe to the Ocean":

> And I have loved thee, Ocean! and my joy
> of youthful sports was on thy breast to be
> Borne, like thy bubbles, onward: from a boy
> I wanton'd with thy breakers—they to me

Were a delight; and if the freshening sea
Made them a terror—'twas a pleasing fear,
For I was as it were a child of thee,
And trusted to thy billows far and near,
And laid my hand upon thy mane—as I do here.

Does it seem strange that a peak of happiness can be with a tiny baby? When Ann, our second daughter, had been back from the hospital after birth for only a few weeks, I went in to see her as usual after work one day. She was lying on her back in the crib. As I bent over to look down at her, she stared back at me with those serious deep blue eyes, and it was like love at first sight, as though in that mutual look we were linked forever . . . as in fact we were linked through all her childhood difficulties and as we still are these decades later, with Ann married and the mother of two children, and still the possessor of those calm, innocent, serious, deep-blue eyes.

Tressa, too, provided a peak of happiness and lifelong satisfaction. She was about five years old, and it was just after dinner. Tressa had left the table, because Holly knew the limited attention span of children and was quick to suggest that the children leave the table when they wished. I can still hear with deep pleasure their musical children's voices asking, "May we be excused until dessert is served?" This particular evening when the meal was finished, while Holly and I were still at table, Tressa returned and, looking me straight in the eye, exclaimed, "I hate you! I wish you were dead!" She and I had never had a harsh word between us. I had no idea what this could possibly be about. Simultaneously it flashed through my mind that the little thing was secure enough in my love to launch such an attack and that this was good, very good. It was difficult to control an impulse to burst out laughing, but I did not want to offend or demean her. So I took it seriously but lightly and suggested in a casual friendly way that this was the sort of thing that we should talk over, thus treating Tressa as an adult. She reacted by quickly controlling her momentary rage and trying to explain. Today I cannot even remember what the dire problem was, but together in after-years we have shared many a chuckle over the great outburst: "I hate you! I wish you were dead!"

Perhaps I have found my happiness in highlights rather less often than most people do; my happiness has come more from other quieter, much deeper satisfactions. As I think about my life, I can recall other moments such as the day in the surf with Julie, but none quite so thrilling. Happy as the lovemaking with girls before marriage was, it consisted more of happy *experiences* than peaks of happiness.

Another remembered high-point of happiness also seems strange: I entered a restaurant shortly after meeting Holly and before we were married, to wait for her to have dinner with me. She had not arrived, and a young male acquaintance who happened to be there joined me. It was a cold evening. I looked up and coming down the stairs from the street was Holly, cheeks pink from the cold, eyes alert, scanning the crowd for me. My acquaintance commented, "You sure can pick 'em!" Truly Holly was beautiful, and I have always remembered that brief moment. She was thrilling, and she was mine and I hers.

On our honeymoon we drove far north, trying to find a cabin in the woods to rent, but all we could find was a tiny cabin on a remote island in a large lake, sixty miles from the nearest small town. The island was idyllic. We had unforgettable lovemaking and many small adventures—which leads to the thought that perhaps some people have many more of these happy memories than others. I have mentioned only a few that come to mind, but as I glance back, an endless number of them appear to bring me much pleasure in recall. They have not entirely vanished but are available to provide stores of happiness; in-dwelling though they are, they can be readily summoned to my consciousness.

There was the first time Holly and I were together in the Holdens' house. And there was a time soon after Holly and I were married—or was it later, perhaps after our first child was born—when we were going out to some sort of formal dinner. We were showered and were dressing. Holly looked just purely beautiful, just perfection, with an added glow from the shower and the anticipation of the evening out. I felt irresistibly impelled to lovemaking, and it was enormously satisfying. But why in all the lovemaking during decades of a compatible and happy marriage, with mutual orgasms, should there be anything noteworthy about this particular time? These memories form and shift unconsciously over the years, some settling like villages in a valley, rarely recalled, standing out in retrospect like golden sunshine on mountain peaks. Freud and many others are, I think, correct in discerning two streams in a man's love of a woman, which is for the normal man probably the greatest enduring experience of life. There is the tender, loving feeling and the somewhat sadistic, purely sensual one that requires only a female body. Sex for me had always been a wild thing. In practice, it varied greatly from the animalistic attack to the expression of the tenderest regard and affection; it was always with much loving concern and affection on the surface, no matter how wild and even sadistic at times the underlying impulses. Some of the wildness was probably from breaking the inhibitions of the incest taboo and of my identification with Dad's high moral standards, and of my training in the Protestant ethic.

Holly once said she liked me to be physically cruel but mentally kind. She did not mean literally or actually cruel, but only animalistically unrestrained. This probably represented the tender and loving versus the sensual currents in her. Between us these two currents in both her and me met in varying proportions at different times, but always in the setting of love; all the varieties of the experience emerged over the years. This was a fortunate outcome because one current so often inhibits the other. A man is not always fully potent with a woman he respects and loves, and is apt to feel no love for a woman he is fully potent with because he sees her too much as a yielding body. My guess is that the particular memory of lovemaking before the party with Holly leaps so quickly and vividly to mind because it represented a full fusion of both our currents, an acme of love and admiration and respect combined with the free, wild sexual attack. The tender and the sensual fused. Precipitous falling in love, what happened to me from my first glimpse of Holly, is still only a beginning. True love must mature from that first experience. It is a matter of the soul, of the coming together into closeness of two personalities, and also of the achievement of this union of the love and the sensual, of love sacred and profane.

Last Thanksgiving Holly and I went for the traditional dinner to the home of Julie and her children. The two oldest grandchildren wanted to return with us for the weekend. We were thrilled as always by their wish to be with us and agreed with alacrity. The weekend was better than our most optimistic expectations; the boy (eleven) and his sister (nine) got on with not a harsh word. Everything delighted them. They helped us with the cooking and kitchen cleanup and made the beds, unrequested. It was all relaxation, good spirits and love of each to each. Here was a highlight of life in my seventies. I think of something Jim used to quote from George Bernard Shaw, who had translated it from the Greek: "He who can know, as the long days go, that to live is happy, has found his heaven."

Yet it seems to me that the main happiness does not really lie in just these certain joyous moments; it is not in these brief sunlit peaks but in the quieter deeper satisfactions of life. Marriage is largely discovering each other's faults, each other's worst faults, and then coming to terms with them, loving and drawing closer in spite of them or because of them—for they are mostly residues of childhood, traits of immaturity, which can be endearing, and the process of coming together in one's deepest feelings is what love really consists of, not just a physical relationship such as predominated in youth. This emotional or "spiritual" closeness constitutes true love. After the first violent impact of "falling in love," it grows deeper and broader as it requires patience and tolerance, and gradually the marriage is consolidated. Paradoxical as it may seem, it was only when our marriage felt fully consolidated, when the storms of life had drawn us truly together, that I ever thought of any previous girl. In the same way I was well established in medicine before I went back to reading physics and chemistry for pleasure, to follow developments that were so excitingly begun in the early studies of the atom. I wanted to see how chemistry came to be based so thoroughly on the understanding of atoms, how Einstein's relativity equations were found to hold for newly discovered phenomena, like "black holes" in space, and to review the rise of quantum mechanics and particle physics.

Parties, temperate drinking, sex, athletics (like tennis, swimming, skiing, ice-dancing, bowling and golf) are transient but intense and exhilarating pleasures; but they are the garnishing of the deeper happiness that, rather than in isolated personally happy moments, seems to lie more in the ongoing, profound satisfactions—in the evolution of a true marriage, in the well-being of children and grandchildren, in hard-earned successes with patients over the years, in friends old and new, in having put down in books some of what I've learned for whatever use to others it may prove to be. These quiet satisfactions are why it seems to have been a good life, a satisfying and a happy one, and why I hope that nothing changes, saying with Goethe's Faust to the passing moment, "Stay, thou art so fair."

Throughout my life I have exerted the best judgment I could, but I think it was the good fortune of having such good parents that made my dynamics basically healthy and free from too much psychopathology, that made me gravitate toward a wife who was also basically healthy and who had strengths which I lacked, and developed only later. This is what made our mature love so strong, harmonious and gratifying—we complemented and learned emotionally from each other.

No one can remain a part of his mother, or can retain such closeness to and dependence on another human being as a baby has with its mother if the mother is loving. But if one matures, however difficult the road, then he or she is secure enough in independence of personality to indulge the closeness without involving all sorts of residual emotional problems from childhood. I fear that only those whose closeness to mother and father in earliest childhood was basically loving and whose maturing has reached adequate thoroughness can build the ultimate marital closeness free from childhood conflicts and discords—a conjugal harmony that is the crowning blessing of life, a more than adequate repayment for all the conflicts, struggles and difficulties of adapting to another, slowly building the ultimate deep and mature love from the initial attraction. Each individual becomes somehow both closer to the marriage partner and yet more fully an independent person.

In a heart attack when the muscle dies quickly, the pain may be neither too severe nor prolonged. Mine was mostly an ischemia, that is, a lack of blood coming to the heart muscle. It struck at three in the morning when we were vacationing in the mountains. I did not want to awaken Holly, but the pain grew so unbearable I had to, asking her to try to locate a doctor. Meanwhile, I took nitroglycerin tablets under my tongue, one or two at a time, with no effect.

A wonderful nurse was in charge of the intensive care unit at the hospital about fifty miles away, and this friendship eased the unpleasantness of the incarceration. Later came three months' recovery in the great hospital near home. One night I had agonizing angina every hour. It felt as though a small boa constrictor were curled inside my chest cage, down about at the diaphragm, and that each hour it constricted; I felt as though I was being wrung out like a wet towel. Nitroglycerin was of no help whatever. The nurse, a dedicated girl, called the resident each time. Finally about four o'clock he said, "There is nothing I can do except come and sit here with you."

I did not want to say that this would help very much because I did not want him to feel obligated to come. His sleep was already ruined for that night. The dull constricting pain, the terrible cramp, lasted about thirty minutes each time, and then I hoped to fall asleep. But a half hour later, just as I was dozing off, those ghostly hands began to wring me out again. At 4:30 A.M. I asked for some more seconal to help me sleep, and it broke the chain of pain. That was the low point.

After three lost months I was home. The time was not totally lost, because I read some books from the hospital library that I would not otherwise have seen. A year later I was walking about 150 yards. After three years I was walking a mile before lunch and again before dinner; I was playing some golf and swimming in a cold pool. Now, nearing seventy-six, I no longer risk golf or swimming, but still walk the preprandial mile twice a day.

It is not great fun to start and end the day giving myself an injection of heparin in my small abdomen almost devoid of fat, which has become a mass of beads—nodules of little hardened blood clots under the skin. But I think of an eight-year-old girl I once saw with diabetes, who was learning to inject herself with insulin, and I think of what my middle daughter went through without complaint during early childhood until the age of seven, and I reflect on my seventy years of vigorous carefree health—and I see this as only a minor nuisance. And the same with my no-fat, no-sugar diet, and constantly caring for myself, bound to naps after lunch every day, no longer being free to come and go and do as I wish, always early to bed and still suffering angina attacks, but happily not so severely as before.

The point is that none of these nuisances and restrictions and warnings of illness or death amount to much, and they have not impaired my enjoyment of life. This is why I conclude that happiness lies so much in how one reacts to things—I feel that I still enjoy life to the full. The only difficult part is in how it all restricts Holly; I can no longer take her out evenings or on long trips. I hate to see her restricted because of me, but I can only follow the orders of my cardiologist, whom I trust, and hope that collateral circulation will develop with my increasing exercise until the angina diminishes. The chances of this are slim, of course; but improvement is possible and worth working toward, for healing takes place at all ages. I can hope that the process of healing will go faster than that of aging, and that medicine will develop some nonsurgical treatment of angina in time to return me to good health as a husband. Now at least the heparin is discontinued.

But there is good in it all, for my heart attack has left a profound appreciation of so much that we take for granted: the freedom from pain and from restrictions, and the freedom for just thoughtlessly living as one wishes. (A friend told me that happiness was "doing what you want, when you want." Needless to say, he felt his life was overly burdened and constricted.) Now I am so grateful for being free of pain and being able to practice that I enjoy the more intensely seeing my patients and losing myself professionally in efforts to understand and help them. I am grateful for being able to walk, eat, sleep and read, and write papers and books. I enjoy all the more my friends and their sociability, just because I must arrange the infrequent evenings so as to get to bed early. I appreciate the outdoors and being able to walk in fields and woods during the changing seasons, and seeing the sky and the sunsets. My feeling is that I appreciate it all much more than before the heart attack and angina, and am as happy as I have ever been. Because my dreams are mostly happy, this is probably not a superficial defensive euphoria, but a genuine feeling.

At the peak of my activities, some of my friends told me that I did about four times as much as the average man my age: full private practice, teaching at the medical school and psychoanalytic institute, running a group research project, consulting for a college and a large social agency, turning out books and articles in professional journals, as well as book reviews and occasional lectures, and maintaining a considerable correspondence. Like so many others, I did not realize this until my heart attack stopped all activity. And then, while in the hospital, I took out the clipboard and pad that are always with me and wrote a list of all my activities, checking those which could be eliminated.

What I have learned is how difficult it is to change one's own psycho-dynamics, even when one knows them as well as I do mine. As my recovery progressed, I tried, by a careful regimen, to regain sufficient health to have again a sense of well-being. But as I slowly improved, my dynamics led me into the old patterns. I could by my willpower limit my activities; but it seemed folly to deny myself seeing patients, which I enjoy more now than ever, as my experience helps me understand them better and helps them recover less slowly and more effectively; and as ideas and insights come to mind, it is an outlet and a pleasure to write them down. Hence I travel about much less and undertake nothing that is demanding for hours at a time, because of the angina. But I am back in my old pattern, minus all the teaching and consulting. I have learned that people are not productive primarily because they sleep little, as Napoleon and Edison are reputed to have done, but because they think and write freely, without inhibitions. I have always required a full ten hours of sleep a night, and in recent years must nap, often sleeping soundly, for an hour or more after lunch. I find that this time out for sleeping has a negligible effect on my productivity, which depends chiefly upon my being thoroughly rested so as to function alertly, smoothly and rapidly. Incidentally, in Carl van Doren's biography of Benjamin Franklin, it is noted that Franklin even as a young man arose at five but was always in bed by ten.

After all the years of struggle, first in the choice of career and then in the choice of mate, both decisions were made—made probably by my dynamics almost in spite of my conscious struggles. With the arrival of our first daughter I was thoroughly settled at last and knew what I was living for. I could begin to lose myself in devotion to wife, children, patients, friends, and in writing some of what I had learned in the hope that it might prove of some value to suffering humanity, in spite of being told now and then to "stop saving the world." I had become an instrument to serve, in my own way, and with reasonable recompense—and I had also found myself.

As I reflect on my life, the deep happiness that is the essence of our being seems to be revealed as that *fit and mesh between reality and our basic dynamics.* I experienced it three times: the first was when I stepped down off the curb into the sunshine to cross a London street and in that split second knew that my career should be medicine; thereafter I had not the faintest doubt. Medicine fitted my childhood emotional pattern.

The second time was my split-second glimpse of Holly over Josie's shoulder, when I suddenly knew Holly was for me and never doubted again whom I would marry. Her childhood emotional pattern meshed with mine.

The third time was when the leaders of a national organization which I had served as president some years previously offered me a prestigious job. That made me suddenly realize that I could indeed do it, and probably better than anyone else they might find at that moment. I was not just an inadequate child, but now I could actually be a man among men, out in the big world, carrying weighty responsibilities. Thereafter I never again doubted my essential self. The instrument was sound, and I could use it effectively and realistically. I was less able than some, more able than others, but I could accept myself as I was and use my talents to the best advantage; whenever I failed, it was acceptable, for I had only to do my best in what I chose and no one was perfect. I have enough strengths and good points to accept my weaknesses and bad points. I still try to correct the weaknesses and that is satisfying, because I feel that I am still young enough to grow and improve. Such acceptance of self yields an equanimity and inner peace of mind that is one of the ultimate satisfactions and is the greatest benefit I have derived from my psychoanalysis. It did not come during the analysis, but my analysis opened the way to it, making it possible fifteen years later. This happiness is present every moment of the day, waking or sleeping, because it is the whole emotional climate in which I live. My childhood emotional pattern at last meshed with my life.

It has been said that in a relationship, one always kisses and the other turns the check. In our marriage, it is I who kiss while Holly turns the cheek. This is no hurt to my vanity. If she likes it that way, that is all I care about. Our marriage works. My profession is gratifying for I enjoy every minute of it. My writing works for I enjoy that, the ability to put my thoughts in order and express them, and the feeling that they contribute, however slightly, to human knowledge. The contribution is the important thing, although every author wants his books to sell well also. My professional articles yield nothing financial, but I would like to think they exert some influence on the thought of others in this field. That I am not a stylist or rhetorician I know; I must hope that simplicity and clarity of language will make readability without the unusual word or phrase, and without colorfulness or grace. I must settle for writing as one trained in science, not in belle lettres, just putting down what I sincerely see and think.

Fitting my dynamics to career, mate and self has meant that for me "life began at fifty." That is in part because at age fifty we have become, to the succeeding generation, "top dogs"; but mostly it has been because of seeing external and internal reality more clearly, accepting it and living in it. So my happiest decades have been since the age of fifty, in spite of limitations of energies, especially since my heart attack. Omar Khayyam wrote:

> With Earth's first Clay, They did the Last Man knead,
> And there of the Last Harvest sow'd the Seed:
> And the first Morning of Creation wrote
> What the Last Dawn of Reckoning shall read.

This may or may not apply to all humanity; I think it does apply to the individual life. From birth, how the newborn babe is treated shapes his particular psychodynamics; and what is shaped in those first days, weeks, months and years to about age six (0 to 6) determines the emotional climate of his whole life, including what he will be like and how he will feel during his old age until death, his last Dawn of Reckoning.

Insofar as his dynamics fit with each other and his *internal* health or illness, and with the *external* circumstances of his life, to that extent will he have inner peace and happiness.

Happiness, I conclude, consists of feelings of satisfaction from the meshing or fit of the emotional forces that constitute a person's childhood emotional pattern or "dynamics" with each other internally and with all aspects of the person's life, for example, in relation to one's spouse, children, career, friends, recreation and other persons and activities. This meshing or fit within oneself and in all one's relationships provides the components of the sense of satisfaction that constitutes happiness. When I asked Holly what she thought happiness was, her response was immediate: "Being satisfied with the status quo of one's own life." This is essentially my own conclusion, very succinctly stated.

How this works with my dynamics can be illustrated briefly by describing the main elements without every detail:

The meshing of the emotional forces of my childhood emotional pattern with each other developed as follows: I became aware of the fact that toward everyone I met I was taking too much a child's attitude toward his mother, that is, the attitude of trying to win love and approval, trying to be protected and dependent and submissive, and I recognized that this caused inferiority feelings. I reacted strongly against this and consciously adopted Shakespeare's phrase from Hamlet, "To thine own self be true." This supplemented Matthew 10:39, "He who loses his life for my sake shall find it." To this I added, "Abandon your narcissism," in order to reduce in all my relationships those wishes for love and approval and attitudes of submissiveness. This in turn resulted in a diminution of ambition, but an increase in productivity and effectiveness. It freed an enormous amount of energy. It enhanced the capacity to be interested in people, things and ideas outside myself (object interest). It opened the way to identifying with my father and mother and other adults. The hurt to my self-esteem diminished and with it the feelings of inferiority, the envy and competition, the impotent rage and the consequent guilt and anxiety. These were replaced by a live-and-let-live attitude and a sense of equality with others, and then gradually an identification with parent-figures and confidence in my independence, abilities and judgment.

The mesh with Holly and my children I have already described. While I was still so immature, not having resolved or outgrown my pathodynamics sufficiently, Holly had the strength to satisfy my feelings toward Mother, the beauty to fit those feelings toward my Aunt Edie, and the youth and freshness to fit my feelings toward Judy, my sister. In addition, Holly's dynamics were enough like mine, with both of us being firstborn children in our families, for us to identify with each other. Our daughters represented the childhood parts of me, and I helped Holly raise them as I wished I had been raised. I could identify with their dependent love needs, and, having been given much love myself, I could give much to them. I could give it without overcontrol and overprotection because I resisted those things in myself and identified more with Father's attitudes of support, love and understanding, without interference. The increasing responsibilities for Holly and the children in our personal relations as well as our financial relations helped in my maturing.

An example of the importance of emotional forces intermeshing in making happiness is so evident in one like myself, who was a loved child: when my love life is smooth, stable and happy as it is now in my marriage, then I work swiftly and effectively. Although I have a strong-enough ego to analyze therapeutically, to write and think clearly and hammer out puzzling points effectively, it is at less than peak efficiency if there is any appreciable frustration or anger in my love life. It is one of the greatest good fortunes of my entire life that Holly is so understanding and that whatever frictions we have are rare and transient. I know that basically she loves me and our children and grandchildren, and that above all she wants the best for us.

Conversely, work is the great stabilizer. Whatever problems or difficulties or ills in personal life one must sustain, if an individual gets up in the morning to face the day's work, persons to be helped and formulations to be made or hammered out, or to be written down evenings while they are clearly in mind—if one is committed to a life thus busy and useful in serving others, it keeps him or her stable and provides protection from the slings and arrows of daily living.

Much of these dynamics fitted perfectly my career in medicine in the subspeciality of analytic psychotherapy. In coming to understand my own childhood emotional pattern, I could more readily identify with my patients and understand their patterns. I had enough love, through identification with my parents, sublimated into therapeutic sympathy and effort, to sustain the huge energy needed to understand the pathological dynamics of my patients and help them resolve and outgrow those dynamics. The residue of this energy has gone into writing, which, as I've said, includes some exhibitionism and needs for security, in addition to the mature motivations of self-expression by contributing.

The way these major areas mesh extends into looser relationships with friends, societies and groups. Having been loved in early childhood (0 to 6), I expect love from others and have plenty to give them. If they do not give it and I meet rejection combined with anger or hate, I have learned to take an understanding attitude and not be thrown by it. I like to expect the best and live in an atmosphere of loving and being loved and then accept slings and arrows when they come—as they must—rather than live constantly defended.

When all the forces in one's dynamics mesh with each other and with the relationships one has with others in life, then they work like a smoothly operating machine, and we feel good and are happy. If some of the motivations and reactions conflict and clash, internally or in relations with others, we feel unhappiness and pain. If some are blocked, we are apt to feel bored; but I don't think anyone is bored whose dynamics are actively running and meshing smoothly.

Of course after this description of the dynamics of happiness I will perhaps be labeled, if not attacked, as a "mechanist," but how it all fits into a larger picture remains to be seen. I can only think with Kipling* that

Each for the joy of working, and each, in his separate star,
Shall draw the Thing as he sees It for the God of Things as They are!

*Rudyard Kipling, "L'Envoi."

29

HUMAN LIFE

It gives the impression of a pursuing fate, a daemonic trait, and psychoanalysis has . . . regarded such a life history as in large measure self-imposed and determined by infantile influences . . . -Thus one knows people with whom every human relationship ends in the same way . . .

Sigmund Freud,
"Beyond The Pleasure Principle"

[A person who is unaware of his childhood emotional pattern is compelled to act it out unconsciously and repeatedly.]

What can we say, then, said Corey Jones, about the whole panorama of life? Is it just chaos? All serious students of human life, whether writers, philosophers, or scientists, agree that all their knowledge yields no trace or clue as to a purpose in life. The Bible tells us that God created the heavens and the earth and all living creatures, and man in His own image. But it does not tell us *why* or for what purpose, if any. To one trained in the scientific approach, life is not chaotic nor is it unintelligible. The human scene is only very complex, just like the brain and the mind, and the atoms and cells that constitute us. We can at least discern in life some process, cause and effect. Freud's great discovery was, as we have emphasized, the complex interplay of powerful emotional forces that goes on in our minds, most of which never reaches conscious awareness, but much of which nevertheless can be made conscious by the use of certain techniques, such as free association and the interpretation of dreams. Thus, even the unconscious and the irrational forces can be studied and understood. Mostly what is unconscious turns out to be part of the emotional patterns of childhood. Therefore the *sense of reality* is one of the most essential and precious capacities of the human mind; its child— science—is its greatest, most characteristically human achievement.

When the sense of reality is disordered we see psychosis, insanity, craziness and irrational, hostile acting-out.

The immediate purpose of human life is to fulfill the life cycle: survive, mature, mate, rear young properly and go inevitably into decline and death. For animals in the wild this is a clear-cut simple process, however difficult and imminently threatened with violent death. But humans must not only guard against external dangers, especially from other humans, and internal dangers such as disease— they must live out their cycle in a society, a culture, which subjects them to all kinds of repressions, laws and rules for behavior and to manifold, often very complex, forms of work by which to survive. That is why most of us need insights and guidance in living.

Even some very good analysts and dynamic psychiatrists seem to "give up" on understanding the complexities of the world and of the individual mind. Scientifically, "understanding" means perceiving cause, process and effect, analyzing the components of what is going on. Ideally this understanding becomes so accurate and detailed as to be expressible in mathematical formulae. It has been achieved with the forces of gravity and operates in astronomy with such precision that we have put men on the moon and returned them to earth within an accuracy of a few miles and a few minutes. What I refer to here specifically as the "giving up" are the few articles which question the existence of cause and effect in the mind. This attitude is intelligible emotionally, for we do not like the idea of psychic determinism, of not knowing the emotional forces in our minds that so extensively determine our decisions, choices and lives.

Neither the human mind nor the world of human interaction is chaos. It is only inordinately complex and requires correspondingly enormous scientific effort to understand it. Einstein said, "The most incomprehensible thing about the universe is that it is comprehensible."

Is there then anything that can be said with reasonable certainty about the material and psychological universe of man? Is there anything we can tell our children to help them place themselves in the universe and by which they may guide their lives?

We can start with the instrument of observation, the human mind itself. We know that it is not completely reliable for objective observation because the strongest emotional forces, many of which the person may not even recognize, can influence its perception and reasoning. In the observer, a gay mood or even pathologically euphoric feelings may cause him to see the world through pink glasses; if he is depressed, the lenses may be dark. If he is somewhat paranoid in his dynamics, he may exaggerate dangers and threats, and so on. This source of error can be counteracted to some extent by the consensus of a large number of observers if they are reasonably normal mentally and have a general agreement about the degree to which one's observation is influenced by mood and allow for this in evaluating his reports. It is counteracted in the physical sciences to some extent by the use of precise measurements and the expression of results in mathematical terms that can be tested intellectually for their quantitative accuracy. But probably ultimately scientists must have faith in their own sanity and the evidence of their own senses, and in cross-checking their results and conclusions.

Scientific observation involves recognition of the limitations of the human senses and the human mind. Our eyes can see only a very narrow band of wave lengths; in other words, only a little of the whole spectrum of light. We see the solar spectrum, in increasing wave lengths, as violet, idigo blue, green, yellow, orange and red. We cannot see ultraviolet or infrared and longer waves.

Our ears hear only certain frequencies of the vibrations that we detect as sound, roughly from about 20 to 18,000 vibrations per second. The dog can hear higher pitches, and so we can purchase a whistle that our dog can hear but we and our neighbors cannot. It is as though we were only able to see and hear the middle octave of an 88-note piano. Science can compensate for these deficiencies of our senses by devising instruments that can do what our senses cannot: the telescope increases our distant vision so that we can see far into space; the optical microscope magnifies to make visible what the naked eye cannot see; the electron microscope goes much further, and so on.

But perhaps the human capacity to imagine, the visualizing, the comprehension, is also limited. It seems probable that our earliest thinking in life is in the form of pictures, of images; and dreams may signify the continuation of this form of thinking while our consciousness is mostly suspended during sleep. After a child learns language, its conscious thinking is predominantly in words. Words are the fundamental entities for thinking and communicating, but we mostly abandon them in sleep and dream predominantly in pictures. Einstein wrote that in developing his Relativity Theory he thought primarily in images. At age seventeen he already had the idea of this valuable theory, the equations of which fit so many physical phenomena not discovered until long after its formulation. For Einstein was just seventeen when he began to work out what a light wave would look like to an observer who was himself traveling at the speed of light.

Through visual and verbal thinking, man has come far beyond the animals in intelligence and understanding of himself and his world. We are aware of the limitations of other mammals, even of the higher apes, in thinking and comprehending. Do we ourselves not have our own limitations? We are certainly well aware of the variations of intelligence from person to person, from imbecile, idiot, moron up through the average range to geniuses of all kinds. We also find that human intelligence is a very specific capacity. The person who is brilliant in one area may be stupid in another. There are children who make top scores on a national test in mathematics but do poorly in the verbal part, and vice versa. Must there not be a certain limit to intelligence of all kinds? As this question is studied, we can expect to learn what limitations there are, and perhaps we will find means of circumventing or overcoming them. But perhaps there are phenomena in the universe that the greatest of human minds cannot comprehend because of its own limitations.

Yet we can be sure that our intelligence is more than sufficient to make a better life for humanity than it has had; for its sufferings are mostly manmade by the human's terrible behavior to his own species— this is something that is observable, is susceptible of scientific study, and can be dealt with.

Needless to say, this discussion is proceeding from a strictly scientific, realistic approach and does not consider the supernatural. I share the scientists' faith that a reality exists and that, up to whatever point our own limitations permit, this reality is knowable.

It is logical to start with our setting. Humanity dwells and loves, but mostly hates, on the planet Earth, which is only one small planet in our solar system; the sun is the center around which all our planets revolve. There are probably ten million other such solar systems in as much of the universe as we now know. Thus, the planet Earth is little more than a speck of dust in the universe.

This brings us to two psychological facts:

The first is what may or may not be a limitation of our intellect, namely, our inability to grasp the concept of infinity. We do not know whether infinity exists, but if it does we cannot imagine it. What is beyond the known universe with all its galactic systems, stretching out beyond what can be perceived by present-day instruments? Beyond all this is there empty space, and if so, how far does that go? Forever? Without end? We cannot imagine it. Is that the reality, is there such a thing as infinite distance and space? Or are our minds so accustomed to finite, limited distances and times that we cannot even imagine anything else? Einstein, whose mind was certainly one of the most daring in the history of science, once referred to the beginning of the universe with the qualification, "If there was a beginning." I think he meant that we ourselves have a beginning and an end, and so does everything in our experience, and therefore we think that everything else must have a beginning and end also. Certainly some vast astronomical bodies, such as stars (i.e., suns) do explode or collapse and eventually "die." There are endings in astronomical space, and our earth seems to have had a beginning and a predestined end. It was thought that our sun would cool and therefore our earth would become too cold to sustain life. But now it seems more likely that as radiation leaves the sun it will leave mostly atomic nuclei behind, the nucleus being the greater, heavier part of the atom. This increase in nuclei will therefore mean an increase in the sun's density and further atomic explosions, which will make its radiation so intense that the earth will become too hot for living things.

The second psychological fact is human egotism. This egotism is one of the most powerful forces in the mind and as yet not very much is known about it. It is certainly offended in most people by the astronomers' picture of man's place in the universe—a mere dab of life in the form of a fragile watery colloidal suspension on a bit of cosmic dust called "Earth." Perhaps in these ten million other solar systems there are other bits of life. But there is no sign that these earths, or the forms of life upon them, are of any special consequence. As our friend, the tentmaker, wrote:

> And that inverted Bowl they call the Sky,
> Whereunder crawling coop'd we live and die,
> Lift not your Hands to It for help—for It
> As impotently moves as you or I.

As Holly said, "If there is life, it would not be in the form of human beings because God would not make the same mistake twice."

I read of a man (could he have been a scientist?) who said that if he could get the answer to one single question he would ask the universe if it were friendly. All the evidence seems to me to indicate that it is neither friendly nor hostile, but utterly indifferent; it does indeed move impotently, in accordance with the most precise physical laws—laws that we can express so accurately in mathematical formulae as to send spaceships to distant planets and have them analyze the soil and send back photographs and messages. The Relativity Theory was proved when an eclipse made it possible to measure the deflection of light from a distant star by the gravitational pull of our sun, and it was deflected, within permissible margins of error, to almost precisely the degree predicted by Einstein's equations, which also showed how much of our observations were relative to the position and movement of the observer.

Scientific or provable facts about the physical world can stimulate strong emotional reactions in us. They can offend our egotism and threaten our sense of security and stimulate our drives to mastery.

As we bring down our focus from the vastness of space and the gigantic hurtlings and explosions of the astronomical bodies and gases, any one of which could totally destroy our earth, let us view what the phenomenon of life on our planet is like. All living things are fragile in the extreme compared to the inorganic formations of our earth— the seas, the mountains, the plains, the ice caps. For life consists primarily of molecules and clusters of molecules, mostly salts and proteins, suspended in water. All the evidence indicates that life began in water and gradually evolved into forms that could breathe oxygen from the air instead of from the water, whereupon these forms evolved upon land. It seems to me that the most striking fact about these myriad forms of life is the widespread carnivorism, that is, of forms which survive by devouring other forms. This is more and worse than the indifference of the earth and the universe. The hyenas pursue the zebra or the wildebeest, tearing the animal's rump as it tries to run away and then, once it is downed, rending and eating it without first killing it. And the cat, once it catches the mouse, plays cruelly with it before eating it. The nitrogen cycle is a peaceable kingdom. The vegetarian animal, the horse or cow, eats the grass and then its excreta return the nitrogen to the soil, the animal and the vegetable thus nourishing each other. But the carnivores kill cruelly and indifferently. And men are carnivores. So are the pathogenic bacteria and viruses; if they can break through the body's immunological defenses, they devour our tissues, indifferent to whether we die. Nor is the vegetable kingdom kinder: any patch of woods will demonstrate struggles to the death, such as vines strangling trees.

We live, then, on a tiny sphere (oblate spheroid) moving precisely and helplessly in space, vulnerable to destruction by other astronomical bodies and processes, ourselves immersed in other forms of life upon which we must live, and insects and microscopic and submicroscopic forms which live by feeding upon us and other species. One would think that with all this constriction and danger human beings would feel the need for close cooperation to further their security and enjoyment of the brief years of their existence. But amazingly we see that the greatest cruelty and destruction visited upon man comes from man himself. This is unique in the animal kingdom.

Hyenas snap at each other but, apparently just because their teeth are so sharp, by instinct they do not seriously injure or kill each other. A Norway rat or a polar bear, if starving, will eat another of the same species. Men do the same thing when starving. But animals are not criminals to their own kind, nor do they wage war against them. Red ants war against black ants but not against other red ants. Recently a sex-murder ring was exposed in Texas, and the bodies of about twenty boys were found. Such brutality is characteristic of humans and not of "brutes," who usually are peaceable, and do not attack unless they are attacked; although they fight their own kind for dominance or mates, they do not seriously injure or kill as man does. Why this hostility, this cruelty and destructiveness of man to man? I think it is mostly irrational. Killing the boys in Texas yielded no money or fame, but—like the Manson murders in California, however it might have been rationalized to make it seem excusable if not noble—it must have been for the sake of the satisfaction or pleasure in cruelty and destruction that it afforded.

But how can cruelty and killing one's own kind give satisfaction? Most irrational action becomes intelligible in terms of childhood emotional patterns. If a child is badly enough treated by its parents and others close to it, it is understandable that the child should grow up filled with hate for them. This hate is often repressed so that the child is not fully aware of it. Then it has two characteristics: the hate is readily displaced or redirected to a different object, such as a defenseless animal or child; secondly, the pattern once formed usually lasts for life. If human beings have been cruel to the child, physically and psychologically, then the child grows up filled with hate and cruelty in retaliation. The child's anger against its parents "spreads" or "deflects" or is "redirected" to other human beings, and becomes an intrinsic part of its personality for life. This is how perverts and sadists are made, individuals who are just the opposite of, and enemies of, persons of good will—persons who grew up as constructive, loving, responsible spouses, parents and citizens because they were loved and respected in childhood.

What, then, can I tell my children? In part, this:

If you notice anything about yourself that makes a problem, a tendency to excessive anxiety, anger, hate or cruelty, or anything not normal and healthy, that could be a symptom of emotional tension, then talk with us—your parents—or if you prefer, with a good psychiatrist or with some professional well-trained in psychodynamics and its therapeutic use. (As this knowledge is disseminated there will be more helpful, effective people in many fields: analysts, psychiatrists, psychologists, clergy, social workers.) The same rule applies with any questions you may have about sex or other matters, whether feelings, ideas or behavior. I think we, your parents, can handle that, but you are still welcome to talk to a *good* psychiatrist or other psychodynamically trained professional. In your contacts with others, stay completely out of the awareness of anyone who seems to you to be hostile or dangerous. When you are mature and experienced, you may do it differently, but until then, stay away from trouble. There are so many hostile people in the world and they spell only trouble and danger, of which life is too full at best. Treat everyone with friendliness, love, understanding and respect and never offend their egotism (colossal in everyone!) and self-image. For love breeds love, and hate breeds hate. In general, it is true that "a thousand friends are not too many but a single enemy is." Life is mostly human relations. You want these to be with people who will bring you health, help and pleasure and not hindrance, pain and opposition in your main task in life, which is the living out of your life cycle. You should understand something of this life cycle while you are young, and you should try to flow along with it, for it is your inescapable biological destiny. You have been born and survived, thus far, against various difficulties; at the end, you must die. But that should be so long hence that you need not think about it now. What you *will* need to think about are the main features of your living until you reach old age. What, then, *are* the main features of the life cycle?

One feature is that the cycle is lived throughout in close, emotionally charged interrelations with other persons—"interpersonal relationships." All of our feelings and passions are primarily toward other persons. Therefore, anything having to do with your feelings toward yourself and others is fundamental. The most obvious of these feelings is dependence, for we are all born totally dependent upon our mothers or substitutes for them, and we would not survive for even a few days without those things that must be provided for us while we are too helpless to get them for ourselves—essentials such as food, shelter, warmth, etc. Closely interrelated with this dependence are the needs for love and affection, which the normal good mother naturally provides from her own impulses toward her child—feelings of love and affection that are obvious not only in humans but in the mother cat or dog or any mammal or bird. A person whose childhood experiences have made him *too* dependent or needy of love, or have deprived him of it, or whose experiences have made him repress and deny those needs, will have problems as he grows up in his interrelations with others.

Recognize your dependence and needs for love, and watch for their being too strong, and watch for feelings of their being deprived or frustrated. But remember that it takes many years to diminish them, and that they can endure for life and perhaps even increase again in age, when one's strength wanes. The life cycle includes outgrowing the complete dependency and love needs of infancy and moving through the transitional period of adolescence to adulthood, in which we must each learn to satisfy those needs for food, shelter and leisure for ourselves, with no all-giving, all-loving parents to provide us with everything. In fact, we must learn to provide not only for ourselves, but also for others, and on two fronts: domestically for our spouses and children, for what we got from our parents we must now give to our family; and occupationally, to keep society functioning, for that is how the necessities of life are produced and distributed in this stage of the industrial revolution. If we are not thieves, then we live in society by giving a value for a value. Today we cannot each grow our own food or make our own clothes or build our own houses. We live in an age of specialization, which necessitates cooperation.

Part of the problem of going through the life cycle lies in choosing a career in this great expanding, rapidly changing, industrial society. Only recently have there been careers in computers and in mass communication. New careers appear and old ones contract and disappear.

In which one would a person be happy fulfilling his life cycle, giving what value he has for the values he wants and needs in return? How can one get external reality to fit his dynamics, and how much must he change his dynamics to fit external reality?

We no longer use barter in our sophisticated society. Our medium of exchange is money. We must give something of sufficient value for people to pay money for it. And the money we receive we use, of course, for survival, self-expression and enjoyment. For me, the value given is helping people with their emotional problems, i.e., with fulfilling their own life cycles. I help them with their lives, and in return they help me with my living. What help I give is accomplished largely through insight, through that understanding in which I felt so deficient and therefore so inferior in my youth. It is an essential part of the understanding of the big world, the broad reality of human interaction—national and worldwide. For every group, society and nation consists of individuals, each with his or her particular psycho-dynamics interacting with all the rest. And there is ample opportunity for the research attitude. Since our mental and emotional lives are part of our bodies, the physiological and the biochemical remain active interests for me, alive in my everyday work; and since I am a physician and psychiatrist as well as an analyst, dealing constantly with human problems, I have ample material of human interest to write about, fulfilling the scientist's cycle of investigation, formulation and publication of findings. To have a career in which one is not focused on making money but is assured a reasonable return if he concentrates completely upon understanding and helping others is so gratifying that I cannot imagine myself in any other occupation. A friend of mine recently said, "I came across a book by Axel Munthe and it said, 'Axel Munthe: Physician, Psychiatrist, Author.' I thought of you as just that!" Needless to say, I took this as a generous, loving compliment.

What I do for others is deeply gratifying. It fits my dynamics as I have related before. It is giving in different form to my patients some of what I enjoyed so deeply from my parents—the love, respect and understanding—and the *way* I do it is through insight, which is a form of teaching (as my mother taught me reading and my father taught me sports), and moral support and confidence in their strengths (as my parents gave these to me during my own emotional struggles).

What is egotism? Like the needs for dependence and love and the mature necessity of responding to those needs in others, egotism is one of the fundamental emotional forces in the mind. Are there, as with most emotional forces, a healthy form and a pathological form? Or is it all quantitative? Why is it so often a bad thing?

In part, egotism seems readily to become exaggerated into selfishness, self-centeredness and, in part, self-overevaluation and also exhibitionism, our trying to show others how superior we are, praising ourselves and, in part, seeking praises and attention from others; this brings to mind a saying from what source I don't recall: "Self praise stinks." When Churchill was visiting Stalin during World War II and went to see the Russian front, he remarked to Stalin, "Not bad for seventy years old," and Stalin replied, "Don't boast. I am only four years younger than you." At any rate, I often have occasion to tell my patients, "Abandon your egotism." No one can do this completely, but my patients understand that I mean "reduce," for egotism does usually make trouble. For one thing, it makes a person vulnerable to competition and envy, so that he is apt to do all sorts of things to demonstrate his superiority, things that waste his time, antagonize others and cause guilt and other effects which are not right for him. Just empirically I have observed that when egotism enters, complications come with it. It is safer to base one's life, not on egotism, but on that which one enjoys and at which he is effective. As in most aphorisms, there is much truth in the saying "Pride goeth before a fall."

One has his own spouse, children, career, life style—let the next person have his without measuring oneself egotistically against him, in competition and envy; "live and let live." And in personal relations it is well to remember that even if you meet someone who is somewhat retarded and does not know one tenth of what you know, what knowledge he *does* have is different from yours, for he has different dynamics and experiences, and you can learn from him and must respect him. Each individual's dynamics were formed in childhood, just as yours were, by the accidents of genes—interacting with the accident of family environment—and no one is more responsible for his dynamics than you are for yours.

Perhaps egotism usually brings trouble because it is a childish attitude and because it is closely associated with hostility. If we try to make ourselves superior, it is usually at the expense of others, and hostility is a component of envy. Everyone needs self-respect and needs to feel valued in his own eyes and in the eyes of others. This feeling is healthy and not the egotism of vanity and envy, which is destructive. Fame and prestige are not directly achieved by demanding them, but by giving good values. They are by-products of accomplishment and can rarely be achieved by pursuing them directly.

There is another combination of emotional forces in oneself and others that is of great practical importance, namely, the fight-flight reaction. This I believe is a biological mechanism of adaptation seen in all forms of life, a way of self-preservation in the face of danger. The body, when threatened, arouses itself physiologically for action, to remove the danger by destroying it or by running away from it. For example, if a hornet comes at you, you may try to kill it, or you may turn up your collar and run. You feel the physiological arousal in the increased rate and force of your heart beat, and in other ways. But the choice of destroying the danger by fighting it or escaping it by fleeing—that is, how the physical effort is directed—is a psychological decision, even though it may be made more or less reflexly, automatically; in fact, in most situations of unexpected danger you simply do not know in advance what you will do.

Another infinitely more effective biological mechanism of adaptation is *social cooperation*, which is also seen throughout the animal kingdom and which is so highly developed in man as to make possible our complex highly specialized industrial society. If this were the only mechanism used, if all humans got together with good will and used their intellects to solve our problems, then there would be no problems that could not be solved with little difficulty. But the fight-flight reaction interferes. It is kept aroused so strongly and in so many people throughout the world—either rationally because they are threatened in reality, or irrationally, which is overwhelmingly more common, because they are filled with fear, hate and hostility toward other humans because the first human beings in their lives, their own parents, treated them badly as children and their hostility became a fixed part of their childhood emotional patterns for life. Those badly treated children therefore grow up to become people of hostility and violence rather than people of love and good will. This is most obviously true if there was open violence within their families. There are two points here:

First, children who are badly treated react with hostility, the fight part of the fight-flight reaction, and continue this reaction in their dynamics because, unconsciously if not consciously, they never forget the images and memories of this bad treatment. They react to hostility with hostility. Also, they identify with parents who are hostile. But in addition, it seems that their emotional development is warped, because no child can mature properly emotionally who has not been reared with love, respect and understanding. His dynamics, if pathological enough, tend to remain so for life. That is why rehabilitation of the violence-prone individual so rarely succeeds.

Then the warpings in the emotional development and the failures to mature adequately create further frustrations, which are also reacted to with fight or flight. Hence the world is so filled with neuroses and psychoses and warped personalities full of hate and violence that humanity's central problem becomes *pathological hostile acting-out*, even though this is not yet an established diagnosis in the official psychiatric nomenclature. It may be a bitter truth to face that most people in the course of their lives, in spite of eulogies after their deaths, do more harm than good, are more useless or even harmful to others than they are useful.

But is not Nature supremely wise? Surely Nature, which has created this marvel called "man" and the master tissue of the universe, man's brain, will not let man destroy himself as a species and vanish like the dinosaur? We cannot be reassured, however—first, because we know nothing of Nature's purposes or even if there *are* any; and second, because Nature which is so wise in many ways is imperfect in others—yes, even blind in many ways. Many children are born with birth defects and with hereditary diseases. (This recalls the Children's Hospital and some of the more harrowing experiences, such as the ten-year-old child gradually going blind and deaf and losing all coordination because of an incurable hereditary disease of the nervous system.) And Nature, through the sex drive, assures humanity of continuation of its species, but it does not make the parental instincts in *homo sapiens* of such strength and maturity that they assure every newborn baby the proper treatment during its formative years. In fact, man's superior intelligence may work against this as parents prefer other interests to the proper rearing of their young. Therefore, we see individual children mistreated and growing into warped adults, who in turn warp their children (even by "battering" and torture, sometimes causing death), and warp the process of social cooperation, so that we have warpings in society that in turn affect the rearing of children, probably continuing in ever-widening vicious circles.

I see only one hope in Nature: that is man's intelligence. A happier age can dawn for humanity if we all—church, state, education and communications media—join in one enormous but magnificent effort to assure every child an upbringing from conception that is adequate in love, respect and understanding, assuring the birthright of a good healthy childhood emotional pattern. That is why I write articles and books. If I am only a sociological unit like millions of others, as I have always thought, then if we agree on the goal we will find means—but is this my optimism more than hard reality?

Two such keen and radically different observers as Freud, the humanitarian student, and Benjamin Franklin, the genial many-sided leader, scientist and man of affairs, came to a similar mutual conclusion about man. Freud wrote, "I have found little that is good about human beings on the whole. In my experience most of them are trash, no matter whether they publicly subscribe to this or that ethical doctrine or none at all."*

Benjamin Franklin a century earlier concluded: "Men I find to be a sort of beings very badly constructed, as they are more provoked to do mischief to each other then to make reparation . . . and having . . . pride and even pleasure in killing . . . for they assemble great armies to destroy and when they have killed as many as they can they exaggerate the number to augment the fancied glory . . . a vicious [action] the killing of them, if the species is really worth producing or persevering; but of this I begin to doubt."**

And yet, if every child were a wanted child raised with love, understanding and respect for his or her individuality, "man to man the world o'er would brothers be."

*Meng, H. and Freud, E. (1963): *Psychoanalysis and Faith: The Letters of Sigmund Freud and Oskar Pfister*. N.Y.: Basic Books, pp. 61–62.
**Van Doren, Carl (1941): *Benjamin Franklin.* Garden City, New York: Garden City Publ. Co.

30
LAST MILES

And fear not lest Existence closing your
Account and mine, should know the like no more;
The Eternal Saki from that Bowl has pour'd
Millions of Bubbles like us, and will pour.

Omar Khayyam,
"The Rubaiyat"

From age fifty to seventy, said Corey Jones, life was a most pleasant routine, with my working somewhat too hard, not at the dictates of cruel necessity so much as those of my internal dynamics. I was aware that the wellbeing of Holly and our three daughters rested financially entirely upon me. So far so good. Perhaps I took on too much, but it was for deeper reasons than money: I felt a continuing identification with scientists such as the Curies, Einstein, Bohr, Lorentz, Planck—none of them rewarded financially in proportion to their great contributions. Without realizing it, and with my goal that of understanding humanity's greatest problem, man's hostility to man, I became so deeply involved that even on summer vacations I felt an obligation to write of what I knew; and I did so in the quiet times before lunch and after dinner, as a form of recreation.

Then the heart attack . . . and that three-month recovery in the hospital gave me ample time to realize that I was overly committed to activities seemingly indispensible to others and myself. That is when I made a list and then carefully considered which responsibilities of consulting and teaching could be relinquished to others. I only knew that I could not bear to give up my private practice, and age seventy meant compulsory retirement from most positions anyway. And so I followed the excellent Quaker principle: "Proceed as the way opens."

Of course I resent the restrictions the angina imposes, being no longer free to have dinner and evenings with friends. Jim and I have again established communication, but I am not up to traveling to meet with him. He is well and eventually will, I hope, be able to come here to visit me; I must be in good enough shape for that to go well. I have dreams of golfing but being unable to swing as I wish; and there are dreams of beautiful water, usually the ocean, and I am about to swim but rarely actually do. I go fast and freely, though, in the dreams of ice-skating, usually alone and not ice-dancing with a partner as I actually used to. So the frustrated wishes for physical activity seem to be taken care of in the dreams, for these are still pleasant dreams. Perhaps seeing the inviting water, often in color, glistening in the sun, also symbolizes sex, which, though the drive continues, is inhibited by the angina. But in all these dreams I enjoy the beauty of the sea, or of a particular landscape or activity, and then am distracted by something, so that there is no sensation of the frustration which exists only mildly now in waking life.

Dreams are in some ways the most amazing and impressive of our psychic productions. Many of them portray how a person's life looks to him unconsciously, depicting it more clearly than he sees it or could describe it consciously. Thus, in these dreams of the glistening water I am taken back some sixty years to the feeling, once again, of being only on the shore of the sea of life, with all its sexual and other activities, and not swimming in the midst of it as I still so long to do fully and freely. Now I am prevented, not by immaturity and inexperience as I was then, but by illness. I still hope to recover sufficiently to do some more such "swimming" before the end; but I have no complaints because I feel well, eat well and sleep well, and my professional activities are but little diminished. I still work twelve hours a day except for the walking and a nap of an hour or more after lunch. In some of my dreams of the beautiful wide water it turns out to be a river and not a lake or an ocean, which I have always loved; possibly because basically, like a river, one must flow along with Nature through birth to maturity, decline and death. That is the life cycle, our destiny, the basic story of our lives.

My childhood emotional pattern meshes smoothly internally and with all external relations so that I still love my life as it is. I see nothing to do but try to maintain it, lasting out and possibly even gaining back a little more strength. In Holly's words, I am well pleased with my status quo, which involves working to improve the lives of others, my patients and the world. I can appreciate Robert Frost's famous lines: "The woods are lovely, dark and deep, but I have promises to keep, and miles to go before I sleep." But the woods do not tempt me, not yet. I want to recover and swim in the glistening waters and rolling swells of the ocean again.

I have said almost nothing about money except that, as I work as a dedicated physician, simply doing what I want to, namely, helping my patients, enough money for our needs comes in. I have no wish to accumulate money but only want it, as Robert Burns* said:

> Nor for to hide it in a hedge,
> Nor for a train-attendant;
> But for the glorious privilege
> Of being independent.

Holly is superbly efficient in handling our accounts. Although past seventy-five, I cannot afford financially to retire; I must continue to work and earn. Yet if we had a million dollars, it is doubtful that I would live or behave differently from the way I now do and love doing—practicing and writing and teaching a little. But it might be pleasant to feel relieved of the necessity to work and to be able to carry a somewhat lighter, more flexible schedule.

A few years ago I was attending a seminar at my old university and found Nelda's married name in the phone book. I happened to reach a relative of hers and learned the following:

Her husband, Tad, deserted Nelda after three years. She and the two children lived with Nelda's parents. Something in this was extremely traumatic for the children, who became hostile and aggressive in spite of all Nelda's understanding and gentleness. Then she remarried; this time she was happy. This second husband completely adored her. Nothing was too good for her in his eyes. For her, he would drop anything he was doing at any time. This was all I could find out. Whether Nelda was excessively dependent or demanding I do not know, but I doubt that she was. Clearly, however, her husband was entirely attentive to her; she was his first interest in life, and she knew it and responded to it. This was more than I, as a physician, could ever have given her. At any rate, you can imagine how deeply gratified I was to hear that Nelda had these happy years. But they must not have been unalloyed for her, while the children were young, and must have been vitiated when the children passed adolescence and were so hostile and

---

*In "Letter to a Young Friend."

demanding that Nelda had to protect herself against them. Apparently the usual, painful vicious circle developed: the more defensive she became, the more rejected they felt, and the more demanding and hostile they became, until Nelda and the children were all but estranged from each other. What psychic pain this must have caused that sensitive soul; how awful for the children. For me, Nelda was a beautiful spirit and not common clay.

I hated to hear of Nelda caught in this unjust tragedy of life. Something goes wrong in a marriage, and the husband deserts; the children are hurt in some way and react with anxiety and demands; hostility and bad behavior reach such an extent that the mother cannot handle it. She suffers poignantly, and the children's lives may be ruined. In the end, it is indeed always the children who suffer most. But thank goodness Nelda's second husband was so devoted. Also, I found out that Nelda's mother died at a very advanced age and Nelda came into a sizable inheritance; it gave her a kind of freedom, and she could enjoy travel with her husband and studying the art treasures of Europe. Nelda always kept the very modest old studio of her own, almost an exact replica of the one we shared. I learned from her relative that Nelda died in her studio of cancer at the age of only fifty-six. It is hard to believe that this lithe and perfect being is returned to dust; it is harder *not* to believe that this beautiful soul, released from the struggles of common living, is no longer earthbound, but free in some airy realm of light.

I had often blamed myself for losing touch with Jim. It was natural, of course, that we should have drifted apart, for we were separated geographically and were absorbed in our marriages and in starting careers, which were demanding and difficult. But now in the later years when one looks back, I reproach myself for losing touch with him. Therefore, I searched for his name and found it listed in a scientific roster. I wrote to him, received a reply, and phoned for a chat. We found that we still had interests in common, and arranged to meet. Jim told me his story:

For Pam, the cleancut, all-American girl, it was unmitigated tragedy. The best available psychiatry and psychoanalysis of the time failed to halt her deterioration into psychosis. (Perhaps it was an organic disorder of the brain.) Eventually she had to be committed. Jim visited her periodically. But then, as so often occurs, the visits became too upsetting for Pam, and she and her doctors decided they should be discontinued. What anguish she and Jim must have endured! Five years passed and the doctors very firmly told Jim that it was hopeless, he should get a divorce and rebuild his own domestic life. Pam is still alive and still in the hospital—old without having lived. I can hardly bear to think of her and recall her only as the lovely girl I once knew. I still keep a plaque on my desk that she gave me, the Sanskrit "Salutation of the Dawn."

Ralph Ackley, who married the young widow who bore him twins, discovered from his doctors that he had leukemia and a life expectancy of not more than two years. As a physician, Ralph understood well, and as a superior human being he faced the fact directly and thought of others. How highly he regarded Jim became apparent when Ralph asked Jim, then living in the same city, to do what he could to take care of Ralph's widow and children. Eventually, some years after his divorce from Pam, Jim remarried—and his choice was Ralph's young widow, Eunice. My initial impression of Eunice was borne out. Small wonder, since Ralph could never have married anyone but a superior person. Fortunately, she and Jim have had a happy marriage and have seen the children grow up to be admirable, happy, successful adults, and are now enjoying their grandchildren.

Thus Eunice has been married to two of the best friends of my youth, who were so important in guiding me toward finding my way in the world. She is basically healthy still, but handicapped by arthritis that keeps her from traveling. Jim has enjoyed an eminent career, and has been decorated for his contributions during the war. He developed a device of critical effectiveness in the defense of England and was given the Order of the British Empire. But it is not his technical and professional achievements but his personal qualities that make me still admire and feel devotion for him. A fragment of conversation occurred when we talked. He said, "I am surprised that you are only one year younger than I. I thought I was a lot older than you!"

I replied, "That is because you were so much more mature than I was," to which Jim responded with a laugh, "Well, I guess I'm not any more!"

What was it in my dynamics that led to such friends as Jim and Ralph, and through them to Pam and Eunice? Eunice I saw too rarely to know well; and you might say that Pam could not have been so much as a person if she could break down mentally—but that is not true. In psychoanalytic jargon, Pam had a superior ego, i.e., her character, standards and intelligence. No one knows the cause of schizophrenia. It may be physical, organic, some chemical disorder of the brain. Insofar as it is an emotional disorder, I take it as a rough unproven guide that neuroses result from disorders in the emotional relationships and therefore in the childhood emotional patterns before the age of six or seven. Psychoses result in such disorders (reactions to faults of commission or omission that disturb the child's relations with those responsible for him and close to him) before the age of three, and even two. In Pam the symptoms seemed to be those of some biochemical disorder of the brain. But whatever faults lay beneath Pam's usual, conscious self, this usual self was unmistakably superior. As in a geological fault in the earth, something cracked and caused an eruption that shattered a lovely landscape.

My own dynamics in finding these friends derived largely from my father. I felt that he understood me, identified with me, supported me, even against my mother when I felt she was exercising too much control. Father took me swimming and skating, cultivating a taste for sports and physical fitness, which have yielded health and pleasure throughout life. He came from a farm, and while successful in the basic ways that really matter—in character, family, health and enjoyment of living—he worked hard and steadily, could not guide me in the cultural sophistications of metropolitan life. He assumed I would inherit the business he had built from nothing, and I never hinted at the struggles I was having over choice of career. When I chose medicine, he reacted typically despite his disappointment that I would not be with him. He offered to support me until I was able to stand on my own feet and "carve out my own future." He gave me sound basic principles by his example. I profited from the privileges my father's devotion and hard work had provided; he knew the real world of business far better than I, with my temperament, ever could. But for the last steps in reaching contact with the life of the mind and becoming educated in it, I turned unconsciously to those like Jim and Ralph whose dynamics were similar to my own, who knew those areas of life and who could guide me. And that world of the mind became my life, my career; but I am grateful only to approach and not even reach my father's level in the basic masculine virtues.

31
EPILOGUE

. . . who says what he knows, who gives what he has, who does what he can, is not called upon to do more.

Alfred de Musset,
"Mimi Pinson"

"Work as to live forever, live as to die tomorrow." This is a poetic admonition with much food for thought. I picked it up in youth from so great a person as Harvey Cushing himself (the father of brain surgery). But it is not for me—my dynamics make me work as to live forever, but also *live* as to live forever. Of course I know full well that after age seventy-five one can become fatally ill, and that there is no protection against sudden death. Yet I find myself planning and living as I did in youth, as though another twenty years await me to live, love, work and enjoy.

If you have been loved as a child and if your parents gave your body the best of care during babyhood, you naturally take over this attitude; you care for your body, keep it clean and healthy as possible. For that reason alone, the concept of it as dead and decaying is against your whole self-image, against all you have lived and worked for. Maybe there is a deeper instinctive tendency to shun death and decay, part of the instinct of self-preservation. I should think that everyone would be well defended psychologically against thinking of death. I can only imagine death in the way I always have, as a state of feeling similar to that before one was conceived—all those millenia and all the eons of history and pre-history when I simply did not exist. So there will be coming eons during which again I will not exist. I simply will not *be*, just as previously I *was not*. And I will not perceive anything because both film and camera will no longer exist.

I used to think of death more as rest, as sleep. But once, just after my heart attack, I collapsed. I found myself lying on the floor and recalled having started to arise from a nearby chair. My cheek was bleeding slightly. I was only unconscious for two or three minutes, but it was nothing like sleep, nor like being under an anesthetic. It was total oblivion. I remembered starting to stand up, and then here I was, on the floor, coming to. I have always enjoyed sleep; and after I was married to Holly, my anxiety dreams ceased, so that I have been blessed with pleasant dreams, some deeply enjoyable. But this moment of oblivion was definitely not pleasant. As I came to I thought, "If this is what death feels like, I don't like it." But since then I have recovered and have forgotten most of it. I do not think of death, and can only imagine it as the total state of not being.

But we can come to terms with the idea of death. These terms are probably partly dictated, like almost everything else, by one's early experiences with one's parents and the childhood emotional pattern that developed from them. If they were kindly and loving, then one's expectations toward the unknown probably will be colored with anticipations of kindness and love: "Though I walk through the valley of the shadow of death, I fear no evil, for thou art with me. . . ."

But the way dying will occur is unknown in normal circumstances. We all hope that it will be swift and painless. For a while, after my heart attack, I felt exhausted. It seemed that my heart might just stop beating. I felt no fear; death then seemed like simply going into a sleep which was not unwelcome. But I still felt very much needed and therefore I wanted to recover; I did everything I could to recuperate. And this recovery has brought a new appreciation of how wonderful it is just to feel well. No longer can I take feeling good for granted. Now I know how it is to be relished and appreciated.

I find it easier to face the end because I think that in spite of my early struggles, I have succeeded in being a good husband, father, grandfather and physician, and a reasonably good friend. I have said my "say" professionally so that all who are interested can read what I have learned. I have accomplished what has seemed important, contributed all I could, been—I believe—basically helpful and not hurtful, and given more than I have taken. I think my life has been successful and might even be called "well-lived." As at the end of a day's work and accomplishment, I can feel ready to rest. Maybe this is all egotism and vanity, but I think some satisfaction in accomplishment is justified. All the good in my life for others and for myself is the result of the good childhood emotional pattern formed in me by those close to me and responsible for me from conception to age six and beyond: my mother, father, Aunt Edie and "little sister" Judy.

I hope for a long pleasant epilogue to my life; perhaps in these after-years I can continue to contribute something. I feel that the basic job is done; but I know life never ceases to present new unexpected challenges, and that so long as one is active people make demands upon him. I think of the popular song: "I do not know what fate awaits me, I only know I must be brave." And then, putting thoughts of fate aside, I must work and live as though to live forever and trust that the firm line of my life's story will come to a proper end.

L'ENVOI

"Corey," I said, "knowing you has enriched my life. I am glad that we were born so near the same time and have lived as contemporaries. When I began writing your biography, it seemed like adding one more weighty obligation to my already heavy, overloaded responsibilities. But it has turned out to be a pleasure to write and a valuable analytic experience for me."

"I too have gotten a great deal from our relationship, as you well know," Corey replied. "First professionally, and then as trusted friends. I admit that there were times when I thought you would never get to writing all this down, and I am relieved that we have both survived long enough to finish it. The delays, though, have made it possible to better round out my story. I feel that the tale is told, and whatever follows will be epilogue. Let's stay in touch and follow your suggestion of catching up at least once a year."

We shook hands and I felt his forthright, firm grip as we said our goodbyes. I thanked him profoundly for articulating the highlights of his life, and we parted with the hope that our labor was not in vain, that others would learn at least a small fraction as much from this record as we both did. I watched his upright, slender, active and still productive figure as he moved down the walk, and felt again the privilege of having known him and reflected that this serenity of his had only been achieved by his long struggles to resolve the conflicts caused by his childhood emotional pattern. I hoped we both might have ten or more years of this good life. If a loved and respected child such as Corey Jones went through such inner struggles to achieve serenity, perhaps Thoreau was accurately describing man's condition when he said, "The mass of men live lives of quiet desperation."

As I saw Corey off to his responsibilities and activities, and turned back to my own, lines from Lamartine's "Le Lac" that I picked up from my mother a lifetime ago flowed through my mind.

Ainsi, toujours poussés vers de nouveaux rivages,
Dans la nuit éternelle emportés sans retour
Ne pourrons-nous jamais sur l'ocean des âges
Jeter l'ancre un seul jour?

[Thus ceaselessly urged onward toward new shores,
In the eternal night carried on without return;
Can we never on the ocean of the ages
Drop anchor for one single day?]